HISTORY OF THE WALKER ART GALLERY, LIVERPOOL
1873-2000

About the authors

Edward Morris studied history at Cambridge University and art history at the Courtauld Institute of Art. He joined the curatorial staff of the Walker Art Gallery in 1966 and remained there for his entire working life, retiring as Curator of Fine Art. He has published numerous detailed catalogues of its collections, as well as many scholarly exhibition catalogues, books and articles.

Timothy Stevens studied at Oxford University and at the Courtauld Institute of Art. He became a curator at the Walker Art Gallery in 1964 and Director in 1971. He left the Gallery in 1987 becoming Keeper of Art at the National Museum of Wales and then Assistant Director at the Victoria and Albert Museum.

HISTORY OF THE WALKER ART GALLERY, LIVERPOOL 1873-2000

Edward Morris & Timothy Stevens

Sansom & Company

First published in 2013 by Sansom & Co., 81g Pembroke Road,
Bristol BS8 3EA
www.sansomandcompany.co.uk

© Edward Morris & Timothy Stevens; cover photograph Stephen Morris

ISBN 978-1-906593-71-1

British Library Cataloguing in Publication Data
A catalogue record for this book is available from the British Library

All rights reserved. Other than for review no part of this publication may be reproduced, stored in a retrieval system, or transmitted in any form without the written consent of the publishers.

Warnock 10/10
Cover photography, design and typesetting: www.stephen-morris.co.uk
Printed by Hobbs the Printers, Totton

Contents

Acknowledgements and picture credits 6

Introduction 7

1 The Building of the Gallery and the Liverpool Autumn Exhibitions 9

2 The Growth of the Collections 1871-1930 37

3 The Making of the Modern Walker Art Gallery 65

4 The Struggle for State Aid, 1860-1986 87

5 The Years of Growth 105

6 The County Council and the Lady Lever Art Gallery 130

7 Nationalisation and the Great Liverpool Art Boom 152

8 The John Moores and the Peter Moores Exhibitions 171

9 Loan Exhibitions 196

10 Conservation 224

11 Education 246

Abbreviations 256

Bibliography 257

Notes 276

Index 289

Acknowledgements and
Picture Credits

The authors are most grateful for the assistance of many of their former colleagues at the Walker Art Gallery and at National Museums Liverpool, and of other curators and historians employed elsewhere. These include Mary Bennett, Xanthe Brooke, Ann Bukantas, John Clark, Michael Compton, David Crombie, Gigi Crompton, John Edmondson, Mark Evans, Jim France, Lady Graham (née Halina Grubert), Francis Greenacre, Andrew Greg, Malcolm Harrison, Martin Hopkinson, Amy de Joia, Michael Kauffmann, Alex Kidson, Peter Kidson, Reyahn King, John Larson, John Last, Adrian Lewis, Arthur MacGregor, John Millard, Frank Milner, Sandra Penketh, Jacqueline Ridge, Jane Sellars, Colin Simpson, Michael Stammers, Julian Treuherz, Lucy Wood, Sally Ann Yates and Sir David Wilson. We are greatly indebted to all of them. Amy Woodson-Boulton kindly sent to us a section from her very useful unpublished Ph.D. thesis of 2003, *Temples of Art in Cities of Industry: Municipal Art Museums in Birmingham, Liverpool and Manchester, 1870-1914*. Suzanne MacLeod and Giles Waterfield kindly provided draft copies of their forthcoming books, *Museum Architecture: A New Biography* and *The People's Galleries: Art Museums in Britain, 1800-1914*. Both made helpful comments on a draft text for this volume. The Walker Art Gallery and National Museums Liverpool generously provided extensive access to documents and images. The staff of the Liverpool City Libraries and of the Liverpool Record Office were also most helpful. The authors and publisher are most grateful to the Paul Mellon Centre for Studies in British Art which provided a generous subsidy towards the costs of production. All the illustrations in the book are reproduced by courtesy of National Museums Liverpool except for William Scott's *Liverpool Still Life*, which was provided by the William Scott Foundation (© William Scott Foundation 2011), for David Hockney's *Peter getting out of Nick's Pool*, which was supplied by the artist (©David Hockney), and for Frederic Leighton's *Captive Andromache*, which came from Manchester City Galleries.

Introduction

The Walker Art Gallery was built by Andrew Barclay Walker, a local brewer, between 1873 and 1877 as a municipal gallery to display an annual exhibition of contemporary paintings for sale to its visitors and as a home for a permanent collection yet to be formed. At its re-opening in 1951 after the Second World War the Lord Mayor, Vere Cotton, who had over the past twenty years done much to reform it, described it as a gallery 'which in the past has been a provincial gallery, [but which] has now reached, or is quickly reaching, the status of a great national institution'. In 1986 it did indeed become a national gallery.

This book, written by two former members of its staff, attempts to describe this evolution. It is not an official history and strives to be a simple factual account. It combines a chronological and a thematic approach since so many issues recurred throughout the Gallery's history and demand separate and specialized discussion. The Gallery's major difficulty before nationalisation in 1986 was simply a lack of reasonable financial support. A chapter on Liverpool's municipal finance might have explored the reasons for this and provided an explanation.

British museums and galleries have an unusual and distinctive structure. First there are the great national institutions mostly situated in London but with important collections in Edinburgh, Cardiff and more recently in Liverpool. Then there are the University galleries again largely based in south-east England at Cambridge, Oxford and London, although there are also notable but more modest collections in Birmingham, Manchester and Glasgow. Lastly there are the museums and galleries run by local authorities. They are spread more evenly across the country but their distribution is still capricious. York has a splendid collection while Peterborough has virtually nothing, although the two cathedral cities are of approximately the same size. This tripartite arrangement, not found outside Britain, is significant. The national galleries in the first division are well funded from national taxation and their staff are effectively civil servants. The university galleries in the second division are run by respected academics and are reasonably well maintained again from national taxation but passed down to them by their universities. The municipal and county galleries in the third division are staffed by local government officers, generally graded at rather low levels within town hall hierarchies, and they are usually poorly supported from local taxation, although this situation is now at last changing with substantial government funding from the Arts Council. In the late nineteenth century British local authorities enjoyed international esteem for their honest, efficient and democratic administration and for their progressive and independent policies. A century later they had largely lost control of utilities, health, tertiary education and some aspects of social welfare, while in their remaining functions they had generally become merely the tools of central government. The civil service and the universities receive a considerable if often rather reluctant respect, but even that modest level of approval is widely withheld from local government.

Although the larger local authority galleries are often called regional collections, they are in fact the responsibility of city councils and more rarely of county or borough councils. British counties are not regions, and any that grow too large are sub-divided into smaller areas as in Yorkshire, Sussex and Cheshire. London is an exception but there are very few local authority galleries there. There was a brief experiment with 'regional' government in England between 1974 and 1986, but the 'regions' were small and the powers of their councils limited. One of these regions or counties was Merseyside and its Council briefly took over the Walker Art Gallery from Liverpool City Council.

The Gallery had various advantages. It had a collection distinctly superior to those possessed by the other English local authority galleries, and it had much more space. It was not encumbered with decorative art, and, unlike many of the other large municipal galleries, it was not responsible for any country houses which always present intractable problems of display, security, maintenance, environmental control and public access. It did control Sudley but that was a modest suburban villa and was treated as an art gallery. There was no serious competition from other nearby municipal galleries or the local university art gallery. Merseyside's appalling levels of social deprivation qualified the Gallery for generous grants from London and Brussels covering the arts as well as other fields. The county also had within its boundaries perhaps the most important independent British art gallery, the Lady Lever Art Gallery in Port Sunlight. Lastly the Walker Art Galley staff and their governing committees were more ambitious, although not necessarily more competent, than those in other local authority galleries. They wanted a gallery of the highest quality. This situation presented opportunities which resulted in amalgamation with the Lady Lever Art Gallery in 1978 and in national status for both Galleries with much enhanced funding in 1986.

Chapter 1

The Building of the Gallery and the Liverpool Autumn Exhibitions

In April 1850 the Liverpool Town Council formed a Library Committee, later to become the Libraries, Museums and Arts Committee, with James Picton (1805-1889) as chairman in order to provide the town with a public library.[1] Although apparently confined to libraries, it immediately tried to take over the Liverpool Royal Institution's purpose-built art gallery together with its collections of old master paintings and drawings which included William Roscoe's famous collection of early Italian and Netherlandish art. Mistrust between the Institution's trustees and Picton's new Committee resulted in failure, but Picton had established the principle that an art gallery and museum, as well as a library, were needed and the Liverpool Library and Museum Act of 1852 authorized the construction of a 'Public Library, Museum and Gallery of Arts'.[2] The museum, rather than the art gallery, received priority in order to house the 20,000 natural history specimens bequeathed to the Town Council by the thirteenth Earl of Derby in 1851. The William Brown Library and Museum, built at the expense of the Liverpool merchant Sir William Brown (1784-1864), opened in 1860.[3] It had cost Brown, who was very prominent in the American cotton trade and the founder of the bank Brown, Shipley & Co, some £40,000 and was then by far the largest and grandest municipal museum in England.[4] Its fame and status were yet further enhanced by Joseph Mayer's magnificent collection of antiquities, which he gave to the new museum in 1867.

Until the 1930s committee chairmen not directors or curators ran the Walker Art Gallery and Picton was certainly the most distinguished. He was the son of an unsuccessful timber merchant, left school at the age of thirteen and later worked as an architect and surveyor. He designed some important Liverpool office buildings including several for Brown rather in the style of Italian Renaissance palaces. Through self-education he became one of the most erudite historians and linguists of Victorian Liverpool. He had a good knowledge of classical literature but could also read many modern languages as well as Hebrew and Sanskrit. He published extensively and his *Memorials of Liverpool, Historical and Topographical* of 1873-5 together with his volumes publishing municipal records have never been replaced as standard sources of local history. He strongly supported Liverpool's cultural institutions and his artistic prestige in late-nineteenth-century Liverpool rivalled that of William Roscoe earlier in the century. He met and corresponded with Ruskin who did not share his enthusiasm for Liverpool. Politically he was a Liberal but he often voted with the Conservatives, the dominant party in

Liverpool between 1842 and 1955. Having the confidence of both parties allowed him to pursue a bi-partisan policy in support of the arts in Liverpool and to remain as chairman of the Council's Libraries Museums and Arts Committee for thirty-nine years until his death in 1889.[5]

On that Committee art was the special responsibility of Philip Rathbone (1828-1895) and Edward Samuelson (1823-1896). Rathbone was, like Picton, a Liberal with Conservative leanings.[6] At the municipal elections of 1885 the more Radical Liberals in his Rodney Street ward nominated a former Chartist as a rival left-wing Liberal Candidate, and Rathbone only narrowly survived with some Conservative support.[7] He was a younger son in one of Liverpool's most prosperous Liberal and Unitarian merchant families. After a successful business career mainly in insurance he joined the Town Council in 1867 and soon became the most important member of its Arts and Exhibitions Sub-Committee. 'Few could or would recognize in the connoisseur of art the underwriter or the Radical', commented his obituarist.[8] His dominant idea, repeated in his many speeches, pamphlets and articles, was that art was an essential ingredient in the political, social and moral life of the city. 'Art is the permanent expression of a nation's thought...what literature is to the individual mind art is to the common mind of the community.'[9] His cousin, the great feminist and social reformer Eleanor Rathbone, explained: 'he believed in strengthening corporate life and in quickening civic patriotism by appealing to men through their senses and making the visible city a place to be proud of.'[10] He secured the completion of Thomas Stirling Lee's powerfully symbolist reliefs, *The Progress of Justice*, on St George's Hall, although he failed to persuade the Council in 1875 to commission William Blake Richmond's *Triumph of Commerce over the Elements of Barbarism* in the Council Chamber.[11] He used to counter the traditional Liberal emphasis on municipal retrenchment with only three words: 'Damn the Ratepayers.'[12] He was an important collector of both early Italian paintings and of nineteenth century art.[13] On his death the Library, Museums and Arts Committee recorded of his work for the Walker Art Gallery: 'His wide and catholic art-culture and taste, and his strong individuality, were so woven into the history, daily work and life of the institution that it seemed as if the ruling spirit of inspiration and guidance had gone for ever.'[14]

Edward Samuelson became deputy chairman of the Committee in 1866. Between 1871 and 1895 he and Rathbone alternated as chairman of the Arts and Exhibitions Sub-Committee which actually ran the Gallery. These were the two men who under Picton's general guidance were to control the Walker Art Gallery during its first twenty-five years. Samuelson himself was the only Tory in a large and distinguished family dominated by Radical Liberals. He nearly became a professional violinist but in fact emerged as a successful tobacco merchant in 1845. He was a significant collector concentrating on landscapes and genre paintings by contemporary local artists. Over 200 works from his collection were exhibited at the Gallery in 1886.[15] He supported populist, unsophisticated art. 'One of the great efforts of his life was to make art and culture popular and easy of acquisition and to raise the tone and excite the interest of the people generally...He admired pictures which told at a glance some simple pathetic story of every-day life.'[16] However Rathbone, with very different tastes in art, was always the dominant figure, and Samuelson retired to North Wales in 1887.[17] Picton's and Rathbone's Liberal principles, tempered by Tory inclinations, together with Samuelson's more committed Conservatism enabled the three men to appear as a cultural triumvirate above the mundane struggles of party politics.

They were succeeded in 1895 by John Lea (1850-1927), another Liberal with Conservative instincts, which permitted his election by the Conservatives as Lord Mayor in 1904-5. He remained as chairman of the Arts and Exhibitions Sub-Committee for thirty-two years until 1927. He inherited coal mines both from his father and father-in-law. He was a fervent Presbyterian and 'an able advocate of the temperance and social purity movements'.[18] He joined the City Council in 1890 expressly to oppose the Sunday opening of the Museum and Art Gallery, the great museological issue of the period. In the same year at the age of forty he visited Italy where he apparently acquired some modest interest in art.[19] Twenty-three years later the *Porcupine* noted: 'It has been urged with some astuteness that Alderman John Lea's admittedly superficial knowledge of painting is the best sort of equipment for an Arts Committee chairman. Philip Rathbones are not born every day.'[20] In his eulogy of Lea, Frank Elias, his nephew, praised Lea's taste in art but added that Lea understood 'the technique of the Victorians but he had less sympathy with modern art'. Lea 'had certain spiritual and intellectual limitations' and he made friends among artists 'as a missionary does among savages, by a friendly smile and a language of signs'.[21] Lea was particularly concerned with the Autumn Exhibitions as 'one of his hobbies', although he never ignored the permanent collection.[22] Edward Rimbault Dibdin (1853-1941), curator of the Gallery under Lea between 1904 and 1918, commented in 1931 that Lea's 'reign has been characterised...as a long and disastrous dictatorship' and as the cause of the decay of public confidence in recent years. Dibdin added: 'It may be admitted that Mr Lea lacked the knowledge and skill of his predecessors. The effect of this was intensified by the fact that, being a man of ample leisure and plenty of energy, he was constantly active in the work of the Gallery.'[23] Lea was succeeded by Frederick Bowring (1857-1936), another Liberal and an important figure in banking, insurance and shipping but with limited and very conservative artistic interests. Although Committee chairmen were supposed to be elected by the Committee itself, they were generally imposed by the ruling party leaders, and it is difficult to see why the vigorous Conservative City Council dominated by Archibald Salvidge (1863-1928) should have tolerated Lea for so long. Their interest in working-class Conservatism probably encouraged them to see art as a matter of small importance, appealing only to the middle classes and appropriately relegated to the care of an ineffectual but influential Liberal alderman.

The chairmen of the parent Committee, the Libraries, Museums and Arts Committee, were, unlike Picton, not generally significant figures in civic culture during this period.[24] An exception was Henry Cole (1862/3-1939), the Conservative chairman between 1921 and 1939. In 1884 he had studied art under John Finnie (1829-1907) at the Liverpool School of Art and he later exhibited watercolours at the Autumn Exhibitions. His company manufactured belting for cotton factory machinery but by 1921 he was close to retirement at nearly sixty and he was able to work full-time on Committee affairs. His business experience enabled him to play the leading role in the construction of the Gallery's great extension between 1931 and 1933.[25] Prominent local business men remained active in Liverpool City Council well into the twentieth century while in other cities they tended to move away into distant suburbs or seaside towns.[26] Cole however was the last man of very considerable wealth to be active in the management of the Gallery. It was perhaps the availability of men like Lea and Cole that delayed the professionalization of the Gallery's management until the 1930s.

With both Rathbone and Samuelson on the Libraries, Museums and Arts Committee by 1867, pressure for the construction of an art gallery as well as a museum became much stronger. In 1868 the borough surveyor reported that about £18,000 would be needed to start work on the gallery. He was asked to prepare plans and these were approved.[27] Liverpool ratepayers, who had gained a great library and museum at no cost to themselves, were always reluctant to pay for culture, and nothing was done until 1873.[28] In July of that year the Committee recommended the construction of an art gallery on the vacant site east of Brown's Library and Museum at a cost to the Council of about £18,000 without fittings. It was a good time to press for the gallery as Samuelson was now Mayor. There were however immediate protests in the Liverpool press, and a public meeting of ratepayers was convened to oppose this proposal on the grounds that an art gallery was a luxury that the Council could not afford and that the expenditure would inhibit the growth of the libraries. At the meeting Picton stated that he supported the building of the gallery in principle but not at that particular moment. The proposal had appeared without his approval while he was away on the continent. Opposition to the gallery was general and the *Liberal Review* was especially hostile.[29] The *Porcupine*, another Liberal weekly journal, did support the project, reflecting the sharp conflict in the Liberal party between those who favoured cultural spending and those who preferred municipal economy, but it was the only Liverpool newspaper or magazine to do so.[30] In 1856 Glasgow City Council had bought Archibald McLellan's private gallery and his collection of paintings for £44,500 to form a new public art gallery.[31] It seems that some leading Council members had a financial interest in McLellan's estate and the British economy was generally more prosperous in the 1850s than in the 1870s, but Glasgow City Council's enthusiasm for art would have been inconceivable in Liverpool at any time in the nineteenth or twentieth centuries.

At the next Liverpool council meeting Rathbone still pleaded for the art gallery claiming that it would encourage tourism and have great educational value. He could not easily use the most familiar mid-nineteenth-century argument in favour of art galleries – that they would improve craftsmanship and industrial design – because Liverpool was not a manufacturing centre. He did however argue that Liverpool with more art-conscious workmen might eventually become a centre of industry. However without Picton's support his report had to be withdrawn.[32] The gallery's supporters now tried to raise the money in small instalments of about £1,000 each. Picton himself and the great Liverpool collector and industrial chemist, A.G. Kurtz, both offered £1,000 but by October only about £7,000 had been pledged and the project was pronounced dead.[33] In November however Andrew Barclay Walker (1824-1893), a brewer and probably the richest man in Liverpool, was elected Mayor and in his acceptance speech he announced that he would erect the gallery 'at my sole expense' after discussions with 'my architect', Cornelius Sherlock, at a cost of about £20,000.[34] A rumour circulated that Walker would never have been elected mayor without his private advance assurance that he would pay for the gallery. This was generally and probably rightly denied but 'many commentators clearly saw a close connection between the Conservatives' decision to elect him as mayor and his offer to construct a £20,000 gallery for the town.'[35] Walker himself, who had only a very modest interest in art, was widely regarded as a 'very wealthy, respectable and unpretending man, and a staunch Conservative' in the words of Viscount Sandon.[36] Brewers could profit from lax supervision of their public houses from the police who were controlled by the Town Council. William Sproston Caine (1842-1903), a prominent Liverpool Liberal politician with a considerable interest in art, noted in 1877 'that a policeman whose wages are at the rate of 24 shillings a week may be very largely influenced by the fact that the chief magistrate of Liverpool [that is the mayor], at present, is the owner of 78 public houses.'[37] There was considerable hostility from the more extreme members of the temperance movement, who were shocked that a brewer with apparently little interest in civic affairs could become mayor of Liverpool, and from those councillors dedicated to municipal economy and retrenchment, who argued that the Council still had to provide the land and run the Gallery.[38] Both these two groups were Liberals and thus Rathbone was attacked less by the Tories but more by his own party, generally seen as the party of progress and enlightenment in its social and educational policies. With Tory support this opposition could be easily ignored. However at a time when one of the principal arguments in favour of public art galleries was the hope that they would to some extent displace public houses as the principal centre of working-class leisure, the offer of a brewer to erect a gallery was sure to prove a sensitive issue. A cartoon parodying the Gallery as built on alcohol was widely circulated and some Liberal families distanced themselves from the project.[39] But Walker had been careful not to intervene with his money until Picton, Rathbone and the great high-minded Liberal merchants had tried to raise the required funds and had failed. In 1888 the curator of the new Birmingham Public Museum and Art Gallery gave a lecture in Liverpool about his building which had opened in 1885. It had cost his Council nearly £50,000 and by 1888 £27,000 had been raised towards making acquisitions, while works of art to the value of about £45,000 had been donated.[40] Sums of this size were certainly not available in Liverpool.

The plans of Sherlock and his partner Vale for this project were approved by the Council in April 1874.[41] The building was now likely to cost Walker about £25,000. The foundation stone was laid by the Duke of Edinburgh on 28 September 1874 and the Gallery was opened on 6 September 1877 by the Earl of Derby after the Prince of Wales had declined the privilege.[42] Both events were witnessed by huge crowds. For the opening the Conservatives on the Council had elected Walker as mayor for a second term, a very unusual honour. This was too much for the *Liberal Review*: 'the honour has been knocked down to him as the highest bidder and his philanthropic gift of an art gallery has thereby become tarnished.'[43] By then the cost of the Gallery had apparently risen to about £35,000 largely due to Walker's decision in October 1875 to commission sculpture on a large scale for the exterior of the building from John Warrington Wood (1839-1886), the local sculptor, then working in Rome, who had supplied a statue of Eve in 1871 for Walker's country house, Bewsey Hall, near Warrington. Relief panels of royal events from Liverpool's history, the granting of the charter by King John in 1207, the embarkation of William III from Hoylake for Ireland in 1690, Queen Victoria's visit to Liverpool in 1851 and the laying of the Gallery's foundation stone by Queen Victoria's son, the Duke of Edinburgh, appeared on the facades. A colossal marble statue of Liverpool, originally intended to be the 'Genius of Art', was placed on top of the Gallery, and huge marble statues of Raphael and Michelangelo representing painting and sculpture were located at either side of the steps up to the Gallery.[44] The Libraries, Museums and Arts Committee explained that these two statues would 'render the exterior of the building a fit index to the artistical purposes for which it is designed.'[45] As architecture it is a fine but not exceptional classical building well adapted to its location and purpose. C.H. Reilly, a perceptive critic of this style, rated it as inferior to the Picton Reading Room (also by Sherlock) but superior to the other three classical buildings alongside it on William Brown Street.[46]

Sherlock may not have designed as elegant an art gallery as Charles Barry's not dissimilar Manchester City Art Gallery (1824-35) which, like the Walker Art Gallery, had to serve for both temporary exhibitions and the display of a permanent collection, but he produced a building remarkably suited to its purpose. Like Manchester it had two storeys of public display galleries, leaving the lower galleries without the top lighting generally regarded as essential for oil paintings. Sherlock took care to maximise the amount of public gallery space that could be fitted on to an irregular site by varying the sizes of the galleries at the northeast corner. Most remarkable is his enormous internal loading yard (part of the 1884 extension) which enabled pictures and sculpture to be unloaded from vans in a dry and secure space. A basement ran under the front of the building for the temporary storage of exhibition exhibits. Facilities for all staff were modest but quite rightly the architect had focused on visitor requirements. An office for the curator was eventually inserted into a redundant corner making clear his status. Naturally the new Gallery was larger than its Manchester counterpart. Internally the picture galleries were functional and utilitarian in character with pitch pine floors and canvas painted walls. *The Builder* particularly commended the lighting in the upper galleries and noted that the design permitted future extension.[47] Decoration was limited to the entrance hall with its colourful Minton tile floor and staircase modelled on that at the recently completed Royal Academy at Burlington House, which was swept away in the 1931-3 remodelling. The stairs were to have had murals. The resulting enormous display space, especially apparent after the extensions of 1884 and 1931-3, permitted exhibitions on a scale impossible elsewhere outside London. Walker's Gallery set the pattern of a substantial art gallery separate from the local museum which was followed throughout most of provincial England. Over the next thirty years his generosity encouraged other local benefactors to establish art galleries in their own towns often named after them, J.N. Mappin in Sheffield, Sir Joseph Whitworth in Manchester, Alexander Laing in Newcastle, S.C. Lister in Bradford, Sir William Wills in Bristol, Merton Russell-Cotes in Bournemouth and many others. Both Laing and Mappin were, like him, brewers. Russell-Cotes knew the Walker Art Gallery well. He lent part of his large collection to the Gallery in 1884 and frequently bought paintings at its exhibitions.[48]

The Gallery was not built to house an existing permanent collection but in anticipation that one would be gradually developed. Before 1873 the Town Council owned a very miscellaneous group of about thirty-five works of art including Daguerre's *Ruins of Holyrood Chapel* (fig. 11) presented in 1864,[49] together with about thirty portraits of kings, queens, statesmen and mayors hung in the Town Hall. These paintings and sculptures could not have justified the construction of an art gallery in the way that the gifts of the thirteenth Earl of Derby's zoological and of Joseph Mayer's archaeological collections necessitated the building of the William Brown Library and Museum. Initially the Gallery was used primarily to house the Liverpool Autumn Exhibitions, which gradually generated the necessary funds for the acquisition of a permanent collection. These exhibitions, which began in 1871 in the William Brown Library and Museum, were almost certainly the first series of exhibitions of new art for sale in Britain to be promoted and controlled by a public authority.[50] They were originated primarily by Samuelson and Henry Benjamin Roberts (1831-1915), a Liverpool artist who had moved to London in about 1861, and they were managed by the Council's Arts and Exhibitions Sub-Committee first established in December 1870. The Sub-Committee at first relied heavily on advice from three local artists who all taught in leading local institutions, Finnie, headmaster of the Liverpool School of Art, William James Bishop (1805-1888), drawing master at the Liverpool Collegiate Institution, and William Lewis Kerry (1818-1893), headmaster of the School of Art at the Royal Institution.[51] Samuelson was the first chairman although Rathbone soon replaced him. In April 1871 Rathbone and Samuelson 'personally called upon' between fifty and sixty leading London artists and they all promised their 'hearty support'.[52]

Exhibitions of this type, organised by private societies of artists or patrons, had been held in some of the largest British towns and cities outside London since the late eighteenth century. The first was held in Liverpool in 1774, and between 1810 and 1867 the Liverpool Academy and its local competitors arranged the most successful of them. The popular Liverpool Academy exhibitions ended due to feuding among the artists and patrons over Pre-Raphaelitism and to disagreements between the same groups over control of the exhibitions, a very common source of conflict in the organization of exhibitions in that period.[53] Finnie, Kerry and Bishop had been closely associated with these earlier exhibitions and unlike most of the other local artists had remained in Liverpool after they collapsed. They could therefore offer valuable advice to Samuelson and Rathbone.

The Liverpool Autumn Exhibitions, intended to replace the Liverpool Academy exhibitions, had four new advantages over their competitors in Liverpool and elsewhere. First they were organized by the Town (later the City) Council in its own buildings. This gave them an official status, a financial stability and a guarantee of efficient and impartial management, none of which could be offered by the exhibitions of the private societies run by artists and patrons in Edinburgh, Dublin, Glasgow, Birmingham, Manchester and Bristol. Local councils had been gradually extending their influence over many aspects of their citizens' lives from policing, trading, sanitation, health and planning to housing, markets and the supply of water and gas; it was argued that art, which promotes civic culture and refinement, should also be included. Just as municipal authorities could provide gas and water more efficiently than commercial undertakings so they could supply art exhibitions more effectively than private societies. Secondly the exhibitions would encourage both large-scale history painting and work by young and unknown artists to an extent impossible in the exhibitions of dealers and societies.[54] Thirdly regular acquisitions for the Gallery's permanent collection were made from them thus providing a market for the exhibited paintings, enhancing the reputations of the selected artists and encouraging all artists to send their paintings to the exhibitions. The local public could easily compare on the Gallery walls the pictures bought for the Gallery with those thought unworthy of this honour, and they could thus form their own judgement on the Sub-Committee's competence as selectors. Lastly the Autumn Exhibitions went far beyond the Liverpool Academy and other earlier provincial exhibitions in attracting artists from all parts of Britain. They were from the start national exhibitions with ever increasing numbers of paintings coming to them from the Royal Academy and from the other London summer exhibitions. By 1871 the earlier provincial art centres in Norwich, Bristol, Liverpool and Edinburgh had greatly declined, and nearly all significant British artists worked in London. Success therefore for regional exhibitions depended on persuading the London artists to exhibit.

The Liverpool Academy, with financial subsidy from the Town Council in its later years, had attracted some of the leading London artists by awarding a prize of £50 for the best painting at the exhibition, by exempting their paintings from the scrutiny of the exhibition jury and by subsidising the transport of their paintings between London and Liverpool. The Academy exhibitions opened in the autumn, enabling London artists to send their paintings directly from the summer London exhibitions to Liverpool. The leading artists of the period, Turner, Lawrence, Mulready, Etty, Constable, Eastlake, Stanfield, Landseer, Maclise, Redgrave, Cope, Dyce, Elmore, Millais, Holman Hunt, Madox Brown, Hook, Goodall, Horsley and others did exhibit in Liverpool between 1810 and 1865, but rarely, apart from the Pre-Raphaelites, on a large scale.[55] The animal painter T.S. Cooper observed in 1890: 'those pictures that were left on my hands after the close of the [Royal] Academy Exhibitions I generally sent to one of the exhibitions in the North of England – Liverpool, Manchester, etc – where they found a ready sale.'[56] There were however complaints by 1854 that the major London artists were not sending paintings to Liverpool.[57]

The organisers of the Autumn Exhibitions followed the same methods as the Liverpool Academy but avoided the prize, which had caused much strife within the Liverpool artistic community and had been partly responsible for the ending of the Academy exhibitions. By 1871 they could rely on new faster, cheaper and more efficient railway services between London and Liverpool for the transport of the paintings, but above all they acted with great determination and worked out a detailed administrative system which remained substantially unchanged between 1871 and 1938. Around March a group, generally including the chairmen of the Sub-Committee and of its parent Committee, the Libraries, Museums and Arts Committee, together with one or two other councillors on the Sub-Committee and the Gallery curator, travelled to London and visited over one hundred and sometimes nearly two hundred artists in their studios, which were then concentrated in Kensington, Chelsea, Holland Park and St John's Wood. At that time these painters would be finishing their works for the major London exhibitions, above all the Royal Academy, but including also at different periods the Grosvenor Gallery, the Royal Society of British Artists, the Dudley Gallery, the New English Art Club, the New Gallery, the International Society of Sculptors, Painters and Gravers, the Society of Oil Painters, the Society of Miniature Painters, the Pastel Society, the Royal Society of Painter-Etchers and Engravers, the Royal Institute and the Royal Society of Painters in Watercolours, as well as many other public and commercial galleries. The Liverpool delegation would inspect the work of each artist and invite him or her to send the best of them to the Liverpool Autumn Exhibition, guaranteeing acceptance by the jury in advance and offering to pay for transport, thus making these paintings effectively 'hors concours'. Once the many London exhibitions were open in May or June a smaller deputation from Liverpool would visit them and invite with the same conditions more paintings and sculptures, especially those which they had been unable to see earlier during their tours of the studios.[58] Many artists would agree to send their paintings to Liverpool under these favourable terms. The Liverpool showing would give them a second chance to sell their paintings within the same year. Of course some of the invited paintings would have been sold in London, and in these cases the Liverpool organizers would have to rely on the artist and on the new owner permitting the display of the painting in Liverpool. Leighton, always very well-disposed towards Liverpool, sold his *Clytemnestra on the Battlements of Argos* (Leighton House, London) in London in 1874 subject to the condition that the new owner must agree to its display at the Liverpool Autumn Exhibition of that year.[59] Some artists might be unable to finish their paintings for the London exhibitions or might paint new pictures in the summer months. These too could be allocated to Liverpool during the earlier discussions in the artists' studios and would have novelty value at the Autumn Exhibitions.

By the 1880s the small Liverpool team were also looking at studios and exhibitions in Paris for paintings and sculpture for the Autumn Exhibitions.[60] Later they included Edinburgh in their itinerary as Scottish art became popular throughout Europe. They had some success with French artists, largely excluded from the Royal Academy exhibitions, although in the nineteenth century only those foreign artists living in, or closely associated with, England exhibited major works in Liverpool with any frequency. Henriette Browne's *Alsace, 1870*, priced at £1,000 in 1875, was perhaps an exception, but she did have a modest English following and the subject was topical. Between 1901 and 1913 a 'continental room' was a feature of the Autumn Exhibitions, and by 1909 it included over seventy works. There were twenty Swedish paintings in 1911. In 1913 there were sixty-one modern French and Dutch paintings lent by the London collector Denys Hague. Plans were made for a display of German art in 1914 which would have been of exceptional importance for Britain where modern German art was largely unknown. The curator and the chairman of the Sub-Committee visited six major German galleries in 1913 and the curator returned to Germany in late July 1914 to complete the arrangements. On the outbreak of war he only just escaped internment after a railway journey of over thirty hours between Hamburg and Denmark.[61] A 'continental room' was not possible during the First World War, although, as at many other British art galleries, there was an important display of contemporary Belgian art in 1915 reflecting British solidarity with her defeated ally. Foreign art re-appeared in 1923 and especially in 1924 during the brief period of post-war prosperity for the Autumn Exhibitions. In 1924 Lea and Arthur Quigley (1867-1945), the curator of the Gallery, went to Paris in May to visit the Salon and many artists' studios in search of paintings for the exhibition.[62] Most of the artists were not well known but Gervex, Le Sidaner, Aman-Jean, Henri Martin, Besnard, Lucien Simon, Charles Cottet, Lhermitte and J.E. Blanche all sent paintings. The 1927 Autumn Exhibition included an even more ambitious continental section with a room devoted to impressionist and post-impressionist paintings including works by Monet, Degas, Renoir, Cézanne, Van Gogh and even Matisse.[63]

As the London exhibitions closed in the late summer all the paintings from each gallery destined for Liverpool could be dispatched there in a single consignment from the exhibition. About one third of the Autumn Exhibitions were pre-selected by the organizing Committee. By 1912 there were about 600 invited pictures. By 1923 500 invitations were issued although only 350 of these paintings were actually expected to reach Liverpool. In 1935 there were about 300 invited pictures.[64] In theory at least the Liverpool public could enjoy a careful selection of the most important pictures from all the London exhibitions. The remaining space would be occupied by artists submitting their works to the exhibition jury which would select the best of them for display. The jury was usually composed from the same group of councillors who visited the artists' studios assisted by two or three professional artists and of course by the Gallery curator. The presence of the councillors and of the curator on the jury was intended to reduce the favouritism often displayed by artist members of juries. The artists on the jury, who had played no part in the selection of the invited paintings, might still attempt to exclude some of these works pleading absence of space.[65]

At first these artists were chosen from the three local men, Bishop, Finnie and Kerry, who had helped to set up the exhibitions in 1871, assisted by H.B. Roberts and A.D. Fripp. Roberts, originally from Liverpool, knew the London artistic scene well. Fripp, as Secretary of the Royal Society of Painters in Water Colours, could encourage the London watercolour painters to exhibit in Liverpool, and their contributions were always a very important part of the Autumn Exhibitions. In 1878 Rathbone, fearing that local artists wished to dominate the exhibitions, established a new method for selecting the artists on the jury. Now there were to be two artists from London and one from Liverpool, who all served for only one year. Normally each year one of the London artists would be informally selected by the Royal Academy and the Liverpool juror by the Liverpool Academy. The other London juror was seen as an 'independent' or 'outsider' voice in the selection and hanging of the exhibition.[66] The arrangement was described in 1909 by Henry Carr, a Liverpool portrait painter and member of the progressive Sandon Studios Society, from a rather prejudiced modernist perspective: 'as to the hanging committee; first and foremost a Member or Associate of the Royal Academy is invited from London to choose places for himself and his friends. He is generally assisted by an aspirant to academic honours who is slightly inferior in position and who is always mentioned second in the speeches. Thirdly it is garnished by a local artist, who really does not matter much and who stands in the position of the parsley to the sole'.[67] In effect the Royal Academy took over the dominant role on the exhibition juries from the local artists, although as long as Rathbone remained alive more independent artists were not excluded. Above all Rathbone's reforms reflected his determination that the Walker Art Gallery, although physically situated in Liverpool, should be a national institution, not a provincial or even a regional gallery. In the twentieth century with its insistence on categories and definitions Rathbone's concept proved hard to accept.

The exhibition jury also controlled the arrangement of the exhibited paintings, a contentious and difficult task as works were often hung in all the available space from floor to ceiling, and a poor location greatly reduced the reputation of the artist and the chances of a sale for the disadvantaged picture. In emancipating the exhibitions from local artists and asserting their national status Rathbone had been assisted by a scandal in 1877 over allegations that the local artists, while acting as jurors, had been involved in accepting bribes from certain painters in return for allocating prominent positions to them in the exhibition. Caine, one of the local Liberal parliamentary candidates, apparently supported the accusation. Both he and Samuelson were enthusiastic patrons of local artists and Samuelson seems to have been implicated.[68] The quarrel between Rathbone and Samuelson apparently also extended to the morality of Alma-Tadema's *Sculptor's Model* exhibited in 1878 and to an alleged manipulation of the Autumn Exhibition accounts.[69] Rathbone replaced him as chairman of the Sub-Committee.[70] In the long nineteenth-century battle between artists and 'gentlemen' for control over provincial art exhibitions Rathbone was determined that at the Autumn Exhibitions the 'gentlemen' should win. By 1912 however the Gallery's curator, although traditionally regarded as responsible for the permanent collection rather than for the Autumn Exhibitions, was asking for less intervention from the councillors over the selection process in Liverpool and over the hanging of the paintings which, in his view, should be left to him and to the professional artists on the jury.[71]

The Autumn Exhibitions rapidly became highly successful. In 1871 about 900 paintings and sculptures, of which over a quarter were sold during the exhibition, were exhibited in four rooms of the Museum. The exhibition opened on 2 September, the earliest possible date after the closure of the Royal Academy, and closed on 18 November. There were about 30,000 visitors and the total income was £1,523. There were some complaints about the effective exclusion of 'artisans' by high admission charges and limited opening hours, but by 1873 this problem had been largely resolved by concessionary rates during evening openings.[72] In 1872 so many paintings were submitted that 100 were 'stopped on their way from London' and a further 201 oil paintings and 120 watercolours were rejected by the jury.[73] Like the Liverpool Academy the Autumn Exhibitions always had to place excessive reliance on the modest landscapes, genre paintings and unpretentious watercolours necessary to generate sales, but the first exhibition did include Leighton's uncompromisingly grand and violent *Hercules wrestling with Death for the Body of Alcestis* (Wadsworth Atheneum, Hartford, Connecticut). It was priced at £1,312 and bought at the exhibition by Sir Bernhard Samuelson (1829-1905), the great pioneer in technical education and a brother of Edward Samuelson. The Sub-Committee observed that at each exhibition there should be 'a large and striking gallery picture telling some tale of human action and passion with simple and effective power...Such a picture as Mr Leighton's *Alcestis* in the first exhibition, although the subject was one far enough removed from their daily life, spoke directly to the heart of the masses.'[74] The *Porcupine* reviewer, already pleased to find so many paintings by London artists at the exhibition, found Leighton's painting 'rather above the ordinary level of public taste' with 'classic simplicity and vigour of idea'. The other painting at the exhibition which he praised for 'elevation of aim' was Albert Moore's *A Venus* (York City Art Gallery) even with its 'excessively low-toned flesh colour – if it can be called flesh colour'. It had apparently been lent by the local shipping magnate and great art patron, Frederick Richard Leyland (1831-1892). At a less exalted level the same critic liked Pettie's *Love Song*, a characteristic medieval troubadour picture, and Orchardson's *St Mark's Venice*, one of the first of the Venetian genre paintings which became immensely popular ten years later and already expensive at £800.[75]

In the following year the same critic was most impressed by Millais's *Flowing to the River*, one of the artist's first pure landscapes and evidently already sold in London to Samuel Lewis. For the critic the financial success of the exhibitions was less important than their value for the 'education of the people in a love for pictures'.[76] In that year and in 1873 Leighton exhibited first his *Weaving the Wreath* (Sudley, National Museums Liverpool) and then his *Antique Juggling Girl*, both distinctly more charming and less demanding subjects than the *Alcestis*. On both occasions he sent the paintings for exhibition in Liverpool not in London, and he was immediately rewarded by George Holt (1825-1896), one of Liverpool's great collectors, who bought *Weaving the Wreath* for £250 while it was on display at the Autumn Exhibition. In 1872 Legros exhibited one of his most moving realist scenes of popular piety, *The Pilgrimage*, which Rathbone bought for the Gallery. *Leonora di Mantua* by Val Prinsep, a close friend of Leighton, was another picture shown first in Liverpool at the 1873 exhibition straight from the artist's easel, and it was promptly bought jointly by Holt and Rathbone for the Gallery. Sadly neither man bought from the 1872 exhibition *Arrangement in Grey and Black: Portrait of the Artist's Mother* (Musée d'Orsay, Paris) by Whistler, who was frequently in Liverpool in the early 1870s visiting Leyland and his other notable early patron, Alfred Chapman (1839-1917), a local engineer and industrialist. Fantin-Latour, another member – with Moore and Legros – of Whistler's circle, showed his great *Portrait of Mr and Mrs Edwin Edwards* (Tate Gallery, London) in 1877 and many flower paintings at later exhibitions. Leighton continued to exhibit important paintings with his *Clytemnestra* (Leighton House, London) in 1874, his *Eastern Slinger Scaring Birds* in 1875 and, in 1879, his *Elijah in the Wilderness*, which his most important Liverpool patron, Andrew Kurtz, had commissioned two and a half years earlier for presentation to the Gallery.[77]

Leighton had been one of the few important artists to contribute major history paintings to the Liverpool exhibitions of the 1850s and 1860s and he was greatly interested in the new British provincial galleries as a source both of patronage and of cultural advancement.[78] G.F. Watts, another close friend of Leighton, sent his *Prodigal Son* to the 1874 Autumn Exhibition. However it was 'that soul-stirring picture' Luke Fildes's social realist *Applicants for Admission to a Casual Ward* (Royal Holloway College, London) which was the sensation of that exhibition as it had been of the Royal Academy exhibition earlier in the year. This was 'art of the highest order striking home to our feelings' observed the enthusiastic *Porcupine* as it described the unhappy condition of the individual figures in the painting.[79] Two years later in 1876 Fildes' *The Widower* (National Gallery of New South Wales, Sydney) received great praise even from the sceptical *Liberal Review*, which was now complaining that there were too many portraits.[80] In 1878 it was deploring the absence of 'grand works suitable to the gallery'.[81] Edward Armitage, a pedantic and reactionary exponent of early nineteenth-century neoclassicism, did exhibit in 1875 and 1877 two such 'grand works', his *Serf Emancipation* and his *Julian the Apostate Presiding at a Conference of Sectaries*, earlier condemned by Ruskin as irreligious and by the critics as tedious. At £1,575 and £1,500 they were the most expensive paintings at the exhibitions, but Alderman William Bennett, a local iron merchant, bought them both and promptly presented them to the Gallery. The great sensation of the 1878 Autumn Exhibition was in fact Alma-Tadema's *Sculptor's Model*. The nude life-size female model stands on a table with the sculptor about half a metre behind her looking up at her. He is simply enjoying the view rather than working on his clay model, which is concealed by a large plant. Alma-Tadema covered his tracks by using a classical pose, by painting the sculptor on a relatively small scale suggesting that he is further from the model than he actually is, and by later repainting the sculptor's toga as an artist's smock in order to emphasize the studio setting which justified the model's nudity. The full frontal female nude had become familiar in British exhibitions by 1878 but only in the context of the bland, idealized settings and paintwork of the classicists. Alma-Tadema's descriptive naturalism and sensitivity to surface colour and texture, together with his setting, transformed a remote vision into a very real and highly desirable event. The reviewers at the 1878 Royal Academy Exhibition expressed some disapproval. One was rather unhappy over suggestions in the painting 'of the personal relations of the model to the artist.'[82] The less sophisticated Liverpool critics and public, including Samuelson, were outraged with many letters to the local newspapers from angry parents concerned for their children's morals. Rathbone was unrepentant and taunted them by explaining that the painting had come to Liverpool at his request without the active participation of the owner or artist.[83] He then left for Cheltenham where in a speech at the Social Science Congress in November, published that month as a pamphlet in Liverpool, he denounced opposition to the nude as Asiatic barbarism. He was the winner. Attendances at the exhibition rose by about 20% over earlier years and were not surpassed until 1884. The profit on the exhibition, about £2,300, was the largest ever made at any Autumn Exhibition.[84]

    Despite this patronage from Bennett, Rathbone, Holt and others the Autumn Exhibitions struggled to attract the major London artists and academicians in the 1870s and it was not until the later 1880s and 1890s that they became 'the most important annual collections of modern art in the country, with the possible exception of the Royal Academy' as the preface to the 1913 exhibition catalogue put it. The Pre-Raphaelites, the great supporters of the Liverpool Academy in the 1850s, were less interested in the Autumn Exhibitions. Rossetti, who greatly disliked exhibiting his work anywhere, could only be persuaded to show his *Dante's Dream* at the 1881 exhibition on the understanding that the Gallery would buy it from him. Millais exhibited a very small proportion of his prodigious output in Liverpool. Ford Madox Brown, who liked provincial exhibitions and knew the Rathbone family, displayed some sixteen works in Liverpool. Whistler, another artist hostile to the Royal Academy, was one of the artists on the jury of the 1891 Autumn Exhibition, where he was allowed to hang one small room entirely by himself. Its principal feature was his own *The Fur Jacket* (Worcester Art Museum, Massachusetts), very conspicuous in a room of fewer than 30 paintings. There was a suspended curtain controlling the fall of light onto the paintings, and the walls, carpet and doors formed 'a harmony of golden brown and green'.[85] He organized the arrangement of the Royal Academy paintings in one of the larger rooms so that, as he told his wife, 'the work of these absurd impostors in all its revolting details of ignorance, pretension and incapacity may be leisurely experienced with the utmost ease'.[86]

Generally the principal contributors to the Autumn Exhibitions were firstly the classicists, Leighton, Watts, Poynter, Moore, Waterhouse, Walter Crane, secondly the Newlyn School and the British followers of Bastien-Lepage, Stanhope Forbes, O'Meara, Langley, Gotch, Clausen, La Thangue, Edward and William Stott, thirdly the Glasgow school, especially Lavery and Hornel, and lastly the landscape artists, most notably David Murray, Waterlow, Joseph Farquharson, Adrian Stokes and East.[87] O'Meara was exhibiting in Liverpool by 1883 and William Stott by 1878, probably earlier than anywhere else in Britain.[88] In the twentieth century those artists closely associated with the Royal Academy such as Brangwyn, David Cameron, Augustus John, Laura Knight, Orpen, Munnings, Charles Shannon, Charles Sims and Sargent were prominent as exhibitors. More independent artists including Paul and John Nash, Hitchens, Matthew Smith, Tonks, Gertler, Duncan Grant, Stanley Spencer together with the Camden Town and London Groups did exhibit but much more rarely. Sickert however sent more paintings to the Autumn Exhibitions than to the Royal Academy, including two in 1892 and 1893. P.W. Steer, who had been born in Birkenhead, very rarely showed his paintings at the Royal Academy but contributed extensively to the Liverpool Autumn Exhibitions, and Roger Fry, who never exhibited at the Academy, sent five paintings. Fry's *Portrait of Edward Carpenter* (National Portrait Gallery) was an invited work at the 1894 exhibition, greatly encouraging the young artist.[89] Epstein sent eight sculptures to Liverpool although at the Royal Academy he only exhibited two works, both Chantrey Bequest pieces shown there as a matter of routine. However before 1938 Epstein represented the limit of acceptability at the Autumn Exhibitions. In his speech at the 1926 Autumn Exhibition Lord Wavertree (1856-1933), deputy chairman of the Arts and Exhibitions Sub-Committee and a son of the Gallery's founder, attacked the works shown by the sculptor, who was already notorious among conservative critics and artists: 'poor fellow I have no doubt that he has done his best. But after all many other very poor artists could have done much better if they had done their worst (laughter).' Epstein threatened to withdraw his sculptures until Lea, who had invited Epstein to exhibit, apologized to him.[90]

In the 1880s separate rooms were occasionally allocated to paintings from some of the leading London exhibitions. In 1886 many of the paintings shown during the summer at the first exhibition of the New English Art Club were moved up to the Liverpool Autumn Exhibition where Clausen arranged them in their own room. The *Liverpool Mercury* described them as the 'leading feature' of the exhibition.[91] The initiative and the paintings were praised by the *Art Journal:*

> Prominent on the walls are many of the principal works of the current year recently seen at the Royal Academy and other London exhibitions, while in a separate gallery the disciples of the New English movement boldly challenge orthodoxy in the display of pictures which were seen at the Marlborough Gallery in London during the summer. The Committee have shown considerable judgement in thus affording the public an opportunity of comparing the merits of different styles of art – the art which is the outcome of Royal Academy training and influence and the recent development of the advanced school, who see nature in a different way and interpret her aspects and moods with a more vigorous breadth and soberer tints than we have been accustomed to in the methods hitherto employed.[92]

Rathbone himself had written in 1883 a pamphlet entitled *The English School of Impressionists as illustrated in the Liverpool Autumn Exhibition* describing principally a group of artists influenced by Jules Bastien-Lepage. It was notable for its very early use of the term 'English Impressionists'.[93] Now in 1886 he analyzed their identity: 'Sometimes they have been called the English-Impressionist school, but this is a misleading name as many of them are not Impressionists; sometimes the Broken-English school or Anglo-French school, partly under the idea they have received their artistic education in Paris, which is only true of some of them.' He went on to describe their tonalism, their 'tipped-up' compositions and their high horizons 'scarcely convenient when the picture comes to be hung over a sideboard'.[94] In 1893 Monet exhibited one of his haystack series at the Autumn Exhibition and it was the second painting which Rathbone discussed in his review of the exhibition: 'It is one of a series representing a haystack at different times of the day, illustrating the play of light under different conditions…It is a study of sunlight pure and simple'.[95] In 1895 there was a 'Whistler Room' containing paintings seen by Rathbone, sometimes with little justification, as reflecting Whistler's style.[96] The 'Grosvenor Room' and the 'Marlborough Room' – Marlborough from the name of the gallery where the New English Art Club held their first exhibition – became standard features of later Autumn Exhibitions, although the names of the rooms only reflected very loosely the style of the paintings inside them. In 1892 there was a special display of paintings by the new Glasgow School who had already exhibited successfully at the New English Art Club, the Grosvenor Gallery and as a group at the Munich Glaspalast. James Paterson, who had Liverpool connections, was the intermediary between Rathbone and the other Glasgow artists, although it is not clear whether he or Rathbone made the first move.[97] The Glasgow paintings were not all hung together but their impact was considerable. The *Liverpool Echo* commented: 'The battle is likely to centre this year chiefly around the remarkable productions of the Glasgow School, a knot of young painters whose work...is marked by an eccentricity of treatment which many...will find very difficult of acceptation.'[98]

In 1877 the Autumn Exhibitions had been able to move to the newly built Walker Art Gallery where they occupied the entire upper floor, a total of six rooms, leaving the four rooms of the lower storey for the embryo permanent collection.[99] The new extension of 1882-4, which cost Walker about £11,500, was intended primarily to enable more of the growing permanent collection to remain on display during the Autumn Exhibitions, but it did permit some growth in the size of the exhibitions, 1,062 works in 1878, 1,315 works in 1890. The total income generated by the exhibitions rose to a record of £4,790 in 1884 when paintings worth £12,313 were sold at the exhibition and there were more than 100,000 visitors. After 1898 however income began to fall each year at first slowly and then more rapidly, until in 1913 it was only about £2,000.[100] The Autumn Exhibitions held during 1915 and 1916 understandably lost money, repaid to the Gallery by sponsors. They were suspended in 1917 and 1918 partly for this reason and partly because much of the Gallery was occupied by the civil servants controlling the rationing of food and fuel. There was a short-lived revival in the exhibitions' fortunes during the period of post-war prosperity, and in 1922 there were about 62,000 paying visitors and a total income of £3,873, nearly double the corresponding figures for 1913. But by 1929 attendances were down to around 26,000 and income was only £1,776 falling to £1,600 in 1930, as the great economic depression set in.[101] The building of the second extension to the Gallery between 1931 and 1933 permitted only a small and inexpensive autumn exhibition of Lancashire and Cheshire artists in 1932, but even this only made a profit of about £15. The newly appointed director Frank Lambert observed morosely to his Sub-Committee: 'The public taste in art is so low that a good exhibition of pictures is very unlikely to prove successful financially'[102] This gradual decline had been most severe between about 1908 and 1914 and Dibdin attributed it to 'numerous picture palaces and the taste for motoring.'[103] In that period some 40 cinemas were opened in Liverpool reflecting a revolution in popular culture. They had admission charges very similar to those of the Autumn Exhibitions and some causal connection seems likely.[104]

Various measures were taken to enhance the dwindling popularity of the Autumn Exhibitions in the early years of the twentieth century. The number of works displayed rose to over 2,000. After the termination of the Gallery's Spring Exhibitions in 1898 the prints and decorative art exhibited there moved to the Autumn Exhibitions providing cheap alternatives for a less affluent buying public, who could not afford oil paintings or even watercolours. In the spirit of the Arts and Crafts Movement there was more sculpture often merging into applied art. After 1902 jewellery and ceramics, especially art pottery, became common. In the 1920s and 1930s this section was expanded to include glass, metalwork, leather, embroideries and fabrics under the general heading of 'handicrafts' There were still many watercolours, which were now joined by numerous miniatures and pastels. A few etchings had been included in the exhibitions even in the early 1870s and large numbers of prints appeared in 1906. By 1911 over 400 were exhibited with a special display from the newly fashionable Society of Graver-Printers in Colour. The number of prints only began to decline in the 1920s and 1930s. These trends reflected a new national preference for ancillary types of art over traditional oil paintings, which had been discredited by the revolutions in taste over this period.

An Art Union, a legalised lottery with the paintings as prizes, was begun in 1911. Another new initiative was the inclusion of a group of paintings by one or more well-known artists lent to the Autumn Exhibitions to form a special feature within the display. The annual exhibitions of the Royal Manchester Institution in the 1870s had included a few important paintings loaned by the city's major collectors in order to raise the standards set by the large quantity of works for sale. The first example of this new initiative in Liverpool – apart from the display of the Glasgow School paintings in 1892 – seems to have been the inclusion of twenty-one works by the Liverpool-born Tom Mostyn (1864-1930) in the 1911 exhibition. Lavery was honoured in the same way in 1912, Lawrence Alma-Tadema in 1913 and Laura Knight in 1916. More modest displays appeared within subsequent Autumn Exhibitions. The 1922 exhibition included about fifty historic British paintings borrowed from a group of public and private collections. This category became more prominent in the later Autumn Exhibitions reflecting a general loss of public interest in the contemporary art that the exhibitions were offering. In 1925 George Audley (1864-1932) lent some forty paintings 'illustrative of the Victorian period' which he later gave to the Gallery. Some works by dead artists were borrowed and some seem to have been submitted by dealers or by the artist's heirs for sale. In the early Autumn Exhibitions all paintings submitted had to be the property of their artists to prevent dealers selling their stock at the exhibitions – a practice alleged to have been frequent at the old Liverpool Academy exhibitions. This regulation was gradually relaxed in the interests of diversity and popularity.

The re-opening of the Gallery in 1933 with its new extension provided the opportunity for an exceptionally ambitious Autumn Exhibition with a large group of about 200 historic British paintings. Continental art was represented by a room of French impressionist and post-impressionist works, which also contained paintings by Braque, Derain, Picasso and Matisse. It demonstrated clearly the strength of the British provincial cult of impressionism, which persisted throughout the century and beyond. The British historic section began with Hogarth and finished with Augustus John and Paul Nash. There were ten paintings by Sickert and sixteen by Steer. This section covered very much the area in which the Gallery was about to collect. Hogarth's *David Garrick as Richard III* (fig. 6), bought in 1956, and Raeburn's *Mrs Anne Graham*, bought in 1933, were both shown in it. The Camden Town artists were strongly represented. There were also the usual Autumn Exhibition pictures straight from the artists' easels. Most of these were the familiar conservative and academic works but there were exceptions. Ben Nicholson and Barbara Hepworth, whose *Mother and Child* was priced at £150, both exhibited. Epstein sent four sculptures including his *Madonna and Child* costing £2,000. It was the only exhibition ever to occupy the entire first floor of the Gallery and was probably the largest and most comprehensive art exhibition held in England outside London in the twentieth century. There were over a hundred lenders. Costs however were inevitably high and there were only some 31,000 visitors despite a royal opening by Prince George (later Duke of Kent) of the refurbished and extended building. The loss was about £330.[105] Lambert must have been deeply disappointed but the message at least for the rest of the century was clear. Firstly the Autumn Exhibitions could not be revived even by generous reinforcements from the art of the past. Secondly large and ambitious art exhibitions in the provinces would not pay and would enjoy only modest popularity. The usual and much simpler exhibition of the following year lost £150. Lambert recommended that the exhibitions should be reduced in size, especially by taking two rather than three paintings from the invited artists. He also suggested that admission charges should be reduced from one shilling (about £2 today) to sixpence (about £1 today) and that there should be fewer evening openings. By 1935 there were only 1,109 exhibits while a few years earlier there had been over 2,000. Lambert, like his predecessors, saw the causes of the problem in the growth of the cinema, in the decline of the exhibitions as social events and in the growth of rival attractions made possible by the motor car. Concerts were held in the exhibition and the Art Union was revived, but neither remedy was effective. In 1937 there was a loss of £150 on the exhibition and only £543 was spent by visitors on buying works of art at the exhibitions. In 1881 they had spent over £12,000 and even in 1920 over £8,000.[106]

In March 1936 the exhibition 'Abstract and Concrete' with works by Hélion, Kandinsky, Miró, Moholy-Nagy, Gabo, Hepworth, Piper and others came to the Liverpool University School of Architecture. This was probably its only showing outside Oxford, London and Cambridge, although it may have been displayed in Newcastle. It was organized by Nicolete Gray, a well-connected young patron of progressive art, in association with *Axis*, the leading 'review of contemporary abstract painting and sculpture'. For the *Daily Mail* 'it was a jolly leg pull', but for Piper it was 'by far the best [exhibition] there has been in England in this century'. In Liverpool the *Liverpool Daily Post* gave it a considered and dispassionate review.[107] It was also the first important exhibition in which advanced contemporary British and continental artists exhibited together.[108] In 1932, a year before his retirement, the School of Architecture's charismatic director, Charles Reilly had appointed Gordon Stephenson, who had just returned to England after eight months work in Le Corbusier's office, to a lectureship, having decided in Stephenson's own words that 'the School should go modern'.[109] Stephenson's close friend and partner, William Holford, joined the School as a Senior Lecturer in 1933, and, at the age of only 28, became Professor of Civic Design early in 1936. Holford was a less convinced modernist than Stephenson, and in fact the School only gradually relinquished its classicist roots in favour of the new International Style, but with these two men on its staff the School could welcome an exhibition of continental and British surrealist and abstract art.[110] Lambert would have met these and other modernists at the School while giving his course of lectures at the University on art history.

His opportunity for an exhibition of continental progressive art at the Gallery came in 1938 when the special feature planned for the Autumn Exhibition, a display of the paintings of Augustus John, failed because neither the artist nor his agent replied to Lambert's letters about the arrangements. With very little time available Lambert reported to the Sub-Committee that the best alternative would be the 'Realism and Surrealism' exhibition. This exhibition had first been shown at Gloucester in June, despite some strong local opposition, had then travelled to Toronto, with fewer realist but more surrealist paintings, for display at the Canadian National Exhibition. By September it was returning through Liverpool to London.[111] The International Surrealist Exhibition held in the New Burlington Galleries in London in 1936 had proved very successful because the British public greatly preferred the flamboyant surrealists to their more austere modernist rivals, the abstract artists. The British Surrealist Group and the London Gallery in Cork Street immediately began to promote surrealist exhibitions throughout Britain and beyond. The Gloucester exhibition, the largest surrealist display so far held in Britain outside London, was organized by E.E. Pullé, the young principal of Gloucester's School of Art and Crafts, by Hugh Willoughby, an early collector of works by Picasso originally based in Cheltenham, and by Alfred Thornton, an artist originally associated with the New English Art Club but by 1938 sympathetic to surrealism.[112] The prefaces to the 1935 and 1936 Autumn Exhibitions had explained that these exhibitions were 'intended to offer a survey of "academic" art in the broad sense of the word. Abstract and surrealist paintings are not included for these movements depart so widely from tradition that they seem to demand separate treatment'. Here was an opportunity for this 'special treatment'. British modernism had already arrived at the Gallery with a Unit One travelling exhibition in 1934 but this was the Autumn Exhibition, the central cultural event of the year in Liverpool.[113] Three members of the Sub-Committee voted against the surrealist display, probably reflecting the close association between surrealism and certain left-wing political movements which were not popular on Liverpool's Tory City Council. There were some sixty paintings with works by Ernst, Miró, de Chirico, Magritte, Picasso, Klee and many British surrealists. Two paintings were lent by Edward James and nine paintings by Roland Penrose, the two leading British collectors of surrealist art. There was an explanatory introduction in the catalogue by Herbert Read. A few works by Picasso, Miró, Giacometti, de Chirico and Klee shown at Toronto were not on display in Liverpool, but Lambert could reasonably claim in his Annual Report that this was the first significant British provincial surrealist exhibition.[114] The critic of the *Liverpool Daily Post* saw the exhibition as an improvement on its predecessors as 'modern theories of art are, for the first time, given a definite place in it'. He found the surrealist paintings 'lively and intelligent' and particularly commended the work of Picasso, Klee and Miró.[115] Albert Richards (1919-1945), later a distinguished war artist, and George Jardine (1920-2002), a well known post-war Liverpool artist, were then both students at Wallasey Art College, and both in part derived their surrealist tendencies from the exhibition. Jardine remarked later: 'I was simply bowled over by it.' [116] The prices of the foreign surrealist works available for sale were between about £75 and £120. None were bought by the Sub-Committee who preferred McIntosh Patrick's *Springtime in Eskdale* at £225, a work much loved by the public.

The organisers of the Autumn Exhibitions had always faced certain difficulties. First many artists simply refused to send their paintings to Liverpool because they believed it would neither enhance their reputations nor increase their sales. Although they knew that after the industrial revolution many of their patrons lived in the north they were also confident that these patrons would prefer to select their pictures in May each year from the London exhibitions, where they had the first choice of the year's art, rather than wait for these pictures to reach Liverpool or other provincial galleries in September, when the best paintings might have been already sold. By the 1880s wealthy Liverpool residents were being accused of buying their luxury goods in London, and art was not exempt from this tendency.[117] Many artists of 'first class works of art, especially those amongst them who cannot afford to wait and hope,' were 'not too eager to send their pictures into the country upon mere speculation,' asserted the *Porcupine*.[118] Works of art valued at a total of £374,823 were sold from the 57 Autumn Exhibitions between 1871 and 1929, an average of £6,576 for each exhibition.[119] More may have been sold privately without the involvement of the Gallery, but this total is not a large figure in a period when fashionable artists could command enormous prices. Even in 1869 nearly £15,000 was spent on paintings at the Royal Academy and that exhibition made a profit of the same amount.[120]

Secondly the success of the Autumn Exhibitions created imitators and competing exhibitions as other provincial towns and cities copied their methods. London artists were induced to send their work by rival provincial deputations not only to Liverpool but also to other cities holding autumn exhibitions, a group which by 1902 included Manchester, Birmingham, Aberdeen, Hull and Belfast.[121] In 1891 Rathbone complained that he also faced competition from foreign, especially German, galleries who were seeking British paintings for their exhibitions.[122] In 1902 the Gallery's curator, Charles Dyall, estimated that of the forty-three British provincial art galleries that had opened since 1877 eighteen held annual autumn or spring exhibitions of new works for sale with rules similar to those operating in Liverpool.[123] Manchester was of course the most serious rival. The Royal Manchester Institution had been holding annual exhibitions since 1827 competing first with the Liverpool Academy and then with the Autumn Exhibitions. In 1877 a Liverpool critic reluctantly conceded that the Manchester exhibition, although smaller than the Liverpool Autumn Exhibition, was generally better with more subject paintings and more works by the most celebrated London and foreign artists.[124] In 1882 Manchester City Council took over the Royal Manchester Institution to form a new City Art Gallery, continuing the Institution's annual exhibitions as its own autumn exhibitions. One of the reasons for this change was the Institution's conviction that, despite the views of the Liverpool critic in 1877, the Liverpool Autumn Exhibitions were now superior to its own displays, reflecting both the public status of the Liverpool exhibitions and the encouragement offered to artists to exhibit there by the hope that their paintings would be bought by the Walker Art Gallery.[125] In 1880 a prominent group of Manchester reformers wrote to the Institution that the Walker Art Gallery 'seem[ed] to derive its chief strength from its association with its rich and powerful Corporation [that is the Town Council]' and that it was attracting 'through its power of purchase more attractive and prominent works' and more visitors; it was 'the property of the People who recognize that it is maintained for their advantage and enjoyment'.[126] Manchester should therefore imitate Liverpool. Manchester's managing committee, of whom a third were outsiders appointed by the Institution, was probably more expert than Liverpool's Arts and Exhibitions Sub-Committee. The outsiders included C.P. Scott, the celebrated editor of the *Manchester Guardian*, and Thomas Worthington, Manchester's most distinguished architect who played a large part in the take-over of the Royal Manchester Institution by the City Council. Competition between Manchester's and Liverpool's exhibitions was however brief, because even by 1884 Manchester had less than half Liverpool's space for its exhibitions. As part of the take-over agreement Manchester City Council provided £2,000 annually for increasing the new Art Gallery's permanent collection, which rapidly expanded and drastically reduced the modest space available for the Autumn Exhibitions.[127] Thus acquisitions were not dependent – as in Liverpool – on profits from the exhibitions, which were allowed to decline dramatically in size from about 1,000 works in 1886 to about 250 works in 1899. Admissions in Manchester peaked at about 117,000 around 1885 yielding a profit of £770 but falling to only 12,981 in 1899 producing a loss of £143. Even by 1891 only three galleries and some passages were provided for the exhibition 'owing to the exigencies of space occasioned by the permanent collection being housed in what should be the exhibition galleries,' and the exhibitions ceased in 1908.[128] Similarly the artists' exhibitions in Leeds and elsewhere declined sharply in popularity in the early twentieth century.[129] Even by 1884, the date of the completion of the Walker Art Gallery's extension, Liverpool's superiority not only over Manchester but over all British exhibitions was asserted by the *Art Journal*: 'The Arts Committee of the Liverpool Corporation who have for years been the pioneers in the progress of art in the provinces have inaugurated their additional galleries recently erected with a collection of contemporary art which for extent, variety and excellence has, we believe, never been equalled in or out of London'.[130] In 1879 the Newcastle Arts Association was encouraged by its local newspaper to emulate 'the great success of Liverpool' in art exhibitions.[131] Even George Moore, with very different ideas about art, conceded in 1892 that 'the Liverpool exhibition has reached an extraordinarily high level of excellence and I have no hesitation in saying that the present show is finer than anything we have seen in London during the present year.'[132]

Leeds and Bradford held spring rather than autumn exhibitions which did not compete directly with Liverpool's Autumn Exhibitions. Spring exhibitions, usually held by smaller towns, took paintings still unsold after the summer exhibitions in London and after the autumn exhibitions in the larger towns and cities. In north-west England the best of the spring exhibitions took place at Oldham and Southport. Oldham's spring exhibitions began in 1888 and ended in 1935, a victim of the great depression. However exhibitions at Southport, a wealthy residential town, began in 1879 and did not cease until 1966. Birkenhead experimented with a spring exhibition in 1913 but abandoned it after 1914. The town was probably too close to Liverpool, and the First World War depressed interest in art.[133] Paintings filtered down from metropolis to city and from city to town, often attracting a buyer at one of these stages. The public could expect to see a new sample of contemporary British art each year even in the smaller art galleries. Gallery curators and chairmen could select new acquisitions from the exhibitions. In those towns and cities where the new art galleries did not organize an annual exhibition of new paintings, the artists' societies continued to provide exhibitions in the spring or autumn, often open to both members and non-members, thus participating in the same system of artistic distribution and enlightenment as the civic art galleries. However by the end of the nineteenth century even the largest of these independent societies in Birmingham and Bristol were struggling to compete with their municipal rivals elsewhere.[134] The system unravelled in the twentieth century partly because the public became more interested in the art of the past and partly because the broad late nineteenth-century consensus on criteria of quality in contemporary art broke down under attack from successive waves of modernist critics, notably D.S. MacColl, Roger Fry, Herbert Read and their many associates.

Lastly the Autumn Exhibitions were competing with exhibitions held by dealers in Liverpool, although to some extent these exhibitions increased public interest in art and thus positively assisted the Gallery and its exhibitions. Of these dealers Thomas Agnew and Son was much the most important. This was a Manchester firm which moved to London in 1860. By 1870 it had opened its Exchange Fine Art Gallery in one of Liverpool's grandest new office buildings, the Liverpool and London Chambers next to the Town Hall. The commercial galleries generally preferred undemanding landscapes, genre paintings and watercolours rather than exalted history paintings. However in 1870 Agnew's had important works by Leighton, Gérôme and Alma Tadema, while in 1871 they were displaying four works by Millais including his great *Chill October*, which had been lavishly praised by all the critics for its imaginative feeling and noble pathos. There were also paintings by other well-established popular artists including Leader, Keeley Halswelle, Briton Riviere and W.P. Frith. In 1872 there were fewer masterpieces but the exhibition was still very popular. Millais's works were often the main feature in the 1870s. Like the Autumn Exhibitions Agnew's opened their displays in September with 'some of the largest and most notable pictures of the Academy Season'.[135] There was therefore direct competition between the two artistic attractions. 'The large dealers', commented the local press, 'do not care to have markets established beyond the influence of their own circle'.[136] Agnew's exhibitions in Liverpool continued until the end of the century, although in their later years they were dominated by watercolours. However in November 1890, shortly before the closure of the Autumn Exhibition, they exhibited Burne-Jones's four *Briar Rose* paintings in their Liverpool gallery.[137] These works, based on the *Sleeping Beauty* fairy tale, represented the search for perfect beauty in a hostile world. They were probably the artist's most popular works for which Agnew's had paid £15,000 long before their completion. The other leading Liverpool art dealer was Edward Grindley, whose shop, later known as Grindley and Palmer, was in Church Street between 1859 and 1906. He became a Conservative City Councillor in 1878 and thus was an influential competitor for the Autumn Exhibitions in the supply of paintings in Liverpool.[138] However after the closure of Agnew's in about 1909 there were few serious commercial art dealers in Liverpool until the brief appearance of the gallery run by Eric Rowan for Sam Wanamaker's New Shakespeare Theatre Club between 1957 and 1959, where works by Bacon and Bomberg were shown.[139]

In the twentieth century the Gallery's principal competitors in providing annual exhibitions were the Liverpool Academy and the Sandon Studios Society. The Academy, observing that the Autumn Exhibitions had little space for local artists, resumed its exhibitions in 1897, although, without its own premises, it had to move its exhibitions between the Royal Institution, Castle Street, South Castle Street and the Walker Art Gallery itself. By 1907 it had nearly a hundred members and associates, and its centenary exhibition at the Gallery included over 450 works. More serious competition came from the Sandon Studios Society which had been established by some of the artists teaching at the University's School of Architecture and Applied Arts. They had been made redundant when that school decided to confine itself to architecture in 1905. The Society enjoyed considerable lay support from the University, from University staff and from William Hesketh Lever of Port Sunlight, together with other members and patrons, while the Academy regarded itself as a strictly professional body. The Society had its own premises and exhibition space at the Bluecoat Chambers in central Liverpool. Until 1955 the Academy's exhibitions were largely confined to its own members and associates while the Sandon welcomed London and even French artists until 1939. The Sandon's orientation was strongly progressive with two exhibitions of post-impressionist paintings in 1911 and 1913, which also included work by Picasso, Matisse, Derain, Vlaminck and Rouault. Among its London exhibitors were Augustus John, Lavery, Tonks, Sickert, Paul Nash, Matthew Smith, Duncan Grant, Christopher Wood and Henry Moore.[140] The ideological differences between these two bodies and between them and the Gallery should however not be exaggerated. Of the fourteen original members of the Sandon Studios Society in 1908 nine also belonged to the Liverpool Academy and of these eight exhibited regularly at the Autumn Exhibitions.[141] In the 1920s Bowring, chairman of the Gallery's Arts and Exhibitions Sub-Committee, assisted the Sandon with appeals for money and with opening exhibitions.[142] The decline of the Autumn Exhibitions in the early twentieth century was only partly attributable to competition from the Academy and the Sandon. However, although these competing exhibitions may not have attracted many visitors, those visitors must have realized that there was a new and fashionable style in European art rather different from that prevalent in the Autumn Exhibitions.

The quality of the Autumn Exhibitions is hard to assess. They were certainly superior to the exhibitions of the Royal Society of Artists in Birmingham. They were rather larger but probably not much better than the exhibitions provided by the Royal Glasgow Institute of the Fine Arts, by the Royal Manchester Institution and the Manchester City Art Gallery.[143] The Liverpool organizers could claim that their careful selections of paintings made in artists' studios and at London exhibitions resulted in an exhibition more balanced and more representative of current artistic trends than any one of the London exhibitions, which inevitably reflected the stylistic preferences of their often partisan juries. Later critics complained that the Autumn Exhibitions were dominated by the conservative artists of the Royal Academy and had become a 'dumping ground' for the Academy with both local and independent artists largely ignored.[144] However Rathbone claimed with some justice in 1890 that the exhibition of that year will contain 'not only works of the artists of firmly established reputation but also of those who are working in advance of present ideas of art so that the next Autumn display will not only show art as it is but as it may be in the future'.[145] George Moore, a severe critic of academic art was impressed: 'Mr Rathbone I have always understood to be the life and soul of the Liverpool Art Gallery. It is owing to his enthusiasm and his industry that Liverpool is able to bring together every year so much various and interesting art. Without Mr Rathbone Liverpool exhibitions would drop into the ordinary jog-trot of other provincial exhibitions – a mere extension of the commercial system of the Academy'.[146] From a more conservative position the *Art Journal* commended the 'ample representation of the impressionist and of the mystical and poetical schools.'[147]

Moore was right about the importance of Rathbone. The Autumn Exhibitions were intended firstly to generate a profit which could be used for purchases for the permanent collection and secondly to show the work of the best established and emerging British artists. With a man of the personality and catholic taste of Rathbone in control these two perhaps incompatible objectives were successfully met. Under his influence the exhibitions were broad-minded and kept the regular visitor well informed about contemporary British art. Judging by the sales he was also good at finding marketable pictures. His successors lacked his ability to deliver these objectives. There were now too few works by well known or progressive artists, and the exhibitions were swamped with competent but unmemorable paintings. Declining sales also made the numerous marketable but unadventurous pictures harder to justify. It is true that there were also fresh challenges, not least from the champions of advanced art, together with a growing antipathy to Victorian Art and the lure of the cinema. The delivery of these objectives certainly became harder to achieve than under Rathbone and certainly beyond the abilities of later Committees and curators. Their increasing public hostility even to moderately modernist paintings lost the Gallery its position as the leader of contemporary art in Liverpool. For Lambert in the 1930s the annual Autumn Exhibitions, originally the Gallery's main concern, had become of much less importance than the permanent collection, but they were too much part of the city's social and cultural life to be discontinued arbitrarily. However the prolonged closure of the Gallery during the Second World War provided a good opportunity for their eventual abolition at its re-opening in 1951.[148]

Chapter 2

The Growth of the Collections
1871-1930

Annual attendance figures at the Walker Art Gallery in the late 1870s and 1880s regularly exceeded 400,000 visits and were occasionally over 600,000, although the Gallery was closed on Fridays and did not start opening on Sundays until 1891. Around 85% of these visitors came not to the paying Autumn Exhibitions but to the free permanent collection. However even by 1890 there was relatively little to see outside the exhibitions apart from a very few respectable but unexciting old master paintings by artists such as Lebrun and Panini together with about twenty notable eighteenth- and nineteenth-century works by Daguerre, Wright of Derby, Benjamin West, Fuseli, John Gibson, David Roberts, Leighton, Millais, Herkomer, Legros, Rossetti, Stanhope Forbes, Fred Brown and a few others. Displays at the Gallery were improved by loans from the National Gallery beginning in 1883, and by 1888 there were works by Turner, West, Lawrence, Etty, and a few other less distinguished British nineteenth-century artists, for which there was no space at Trafalgar Square. A cast gallery was another attraction. These attendance figures and many other promising statistics were published by the Gallery in a long booklet of 1888.[1] It revealed the enormous popular appetite for art outside London and must have been very influential in encouraging other town and city councils to establish municipal galleries of which over twenty had been opened in north-west England alone by 1914.[2] It also emphasized the need to extend the permanent collection. Its author, Charles Dyall, the Gallery's first curator, defended large exhibitions of contemporary art such as the Autumn Exhibitions from the charge that they debased popular taste due to the inevitable presence in them of many paintings of low quality. He argued that their very varied character attracted the general public who could easily distinguish good paintings from bad.[3] However he was clearly aware that a public gallery should also display permanently carefully selected works of exceptional quality.

Until 1929 the Gallery depended almost entirely on the profits made by the Autumn Exhibitions for the purchase of works of art for its collections. British local authorities depended until 1991 for most of their income on the so-called 'rates', a system of local taxation calculated as a proportion of local property rents. The Libraries, Museums and Arts Committee had to survive on the income from a rate set in 1852 at one penny (less than half one new penny) in the pound which produced about £12,000 annually in 1887. This rate did not rise to two pence until after 1900 and remained at that figure until after 1914. These amounts were low when compared with the income available for cultural purposes from local taxation in other major British cities, and there was virtually nothing available in Liverpool for buying works of art from the rates during the first fifty-five years of the Gallery's existence.[4] The causes of this municipal parsimony are unclear.[5] In 1859 there were only 14,744 municipal voters in the town but this figure increased considerably after the Municipal Franchise Act of 1869 and the new electorate seem to have been more reluctant in Liverpool – but not necessarily elsewhere – to pay for art through the rates than the more prosperous middle classes. Between 1870 and 1882 local government expenditure nationally more than doubled from £27.3 million to £55.5 million but most of this money was spent on education and on social improvement and certainly not on the arts. In Liverpool material deprivation was unusually serious and the Council remarkably ambitious in trying to alleviate it.

The Autumn Exhibitions made money for the Gallery in three ways. First there was a standard admission fee of one shilling (very approximately £3 today), reducing to sixpence (very approximately £1-50 today) or even to three pence towards the end of the exhibition and in the evenings for the benefit of the working classes who could not visit the exhibition during the day. This scale of charges remained unchanged until the late 1930s, although the periods and hours of reduced charges showed some variations over the years. It was by far the most important source of revenue as attendances were very high, averaging over 80,000 annually between 1877 and 1900, but falling sharply after 1910 and again after 1922. Secondly there were profits from the sale of catalogues. Thirdly commission was charged on the sale of pictures negotiated through the Gallery. Between 1877 and 1900, the best years for the exhibitions, total income for each exhibition averaged about £3,500 and total costs about £1,800.[6] However these figures could vary sharply from year to year and some sceptics suspected that not all the expenses and overheads incurred by the exhibitions had been included in the figures for their costs, thus artificially inflating the apparent profits.[7] G.H. Ball, a city councillor demanding municipal economy, criticized the profligacy of the Libraries, Museums and Arts Committee at a Council meeting in 1890 stating that 'the [Autumn] exhibition produced an artificial profit which they proposed to expend in the purchase of pictures'.[8] These profits, around £1,700 annually between 1877 and 1900, could either be spent immediately on acquisitions from the exhibitions for the permanent collection or carried over to future years to be used for the same purpose, although the town clerk seems to have had some reservations on the legality of these methods.[9] The Arts and Exhibitions Sub-Committee could therefore claim that the permanent collection was being increased at no expense to the Liverpool ratepayers.[10] The artists of paintings selected for purchase were expected to accept substantially less than the price they had fixed for insertion in the catalogue, and there was occasionally some undignified haggling. In 1890 Albert Moore refused the Sub-Committee's offer of £800 for his *Summer Night* because Merton Russell-Cotes had offered him £1,000 and he wanted £1,200 for the painting. Eventually Russell-Cotes withdrew his offer and Moore had to accept the £800.[11]

The popularity of the Autumn Exhibitions and the income derived from them began to fall in the twentieth century but costs of course did not fall leaving much less to spend on the permanent collection. The solution for the Sub-Committee lay in some creative accountancy. In principle at least the Autumn Exhibition accounts were kept separate from the Gallery's accounts. It seems however that after 1897 the published figure for the Autumn Exhibition income, on which the Gallery's purchase grant depended, was artificially inflated by including within it some revenue not entirely derived from the exhibitions, including cloakroom receipts, rent from the letting of rooms in the Gallery, admission fees to the permanent collection on the one 'paying' day each week, together with reproduction fees and photographic sales relating to the permanent collection. These 'miscellaneous receipts' amounted to over £500 annually by 1900 and by 1910 they accounted for most of the published profits of the Autumn Exhibitions. The chairman of the Sub-Committee's parent committee, the Libraries, Museums and Arts Committee, drew the Sub-Committee's attention to their questionable accountancy in a memorandum of 18 December 1912. He was not greatly concerned because the Sub-Committee was not deviating from the fundamental principle that works of art could only be bought from profits made by the Gallery, not from revenue derived from local taxation. However he did point out that since a large part of their income was no longer coming from the Autumn Exhibitions, there was no need to spend all of it on paintings from them.[12] The Sub-Committee however replied that £300 had been taken out of the Autumn Exhibition's income each year since 1890 to cover the Gallery's 'establishment charges' – or overheads – thus partially compensating for the allocation of the 'miscellaneous receipts' to the Autumn Exhibition income.[13] The Sub-Committee did however remove most of the 'miscellaneous receipts' out of the Autumn Exhibition accounts but still continued to buy nearly all their new acquisitions from these exhibitions, feeling no doubt that with the declining popularity of the exhibitions they must continue to buy from them to prevent their total collapse.[14] Despite all this ingenuity the amount being spent on new acquisitions was falling rapidly, from about £1,380 annually between 1900 and 1905 to about £770 annually between 1906 and 1912. With ever larger exhibitions their costs were rising from about £1,800 each between 1877 and 1900 to about £2,370 each between 1901 and 1912. Thus profits, after deducting the £300 due to the Gallery after 1890, were falling even faster than expenditure on new acquisitions, from about £1,320 annually between 1900 and 1905 to about £515 annually between 1906 and 1912.[15]

From the profits made by the Autumn Exhibitions the Gallery bought each year between 1871 and 1931 some three or four – and occasionally more – paintings and sculptures. The Council had pledged itself in 1871 to devote all these profits to acquisitions and Rathbone resisted later attempts to divert them to other purposes as a violation of a 'solemn covenant' between the Council and the artistic community.[16] This was the first systematic attempt in Britain to build up a representative public collection of contemporary art. The British Institution in London, the Royal Manchester Institution and the Royal Institution for the Encouragement of the Fine Arts in Scotland, all financed largely by wealthy patrons, had been buying contemporary art on a modest scale, but these were private bodies and their importance was declining sharply by 1850.[17] Some academies of art and art unions acquired contemporary art on a very modest scale. The Walker Art Gallery's programme of acquisitions was much more ambitious. Competition came from the Trustees of the Chantrey Bequest who began buying modern paintings and sculpture in 1877 for the future Tate Gallery. Birmingham's 'Public Picture Gallery Fund', dependent entirely on private generosity, started buying a few contemporary paintings for its future art gallery in 1871. In the 1880s the Birmingham, Manchester and Leeds City Art Galleries began more systematic purchasing. Manchester City Art Gallery with at least £2,000 each year and the Chantrey Bequest Trustees with about £2,500 were both slightly richer than Liverpool.[18] The idea for these annual acquisitions came originally from France where the government had for many years been acquiring modern paintings from the Paris Salons for French national and provincial galleries, but in Britain the initiative was local not national. Critics had for many years complained that high art in Britain suffered from receiving little of that official and church patronage common on the continent, especially in France, and many hoped that the new municipal art galleries would fill the gap.[19]

The growth of the permanent collection and the opening of the new Gallery in 1877 required the appointment of a curator. The post was advertised at a yearly salary of £300 which was immediately challenged in the Town Council by Arthur Forwood (1836-1898) a successful ship owner. Forwood was soon to become the leader of the Liverpool Tories and the great pioneer of the progressive and democratic Conservatism which dominated Liverpool politics for over seventy years. He perceptively asserted that at that salary they would not recruit a man 'competent to advise the arts committee as to the acceptance or purchase of works of art'. Picton however responded that the Libraries, Museums and Arts Committee did not want 'a man to control them in the selection of works of art. They wanted a man to be their servant not their master.'[20] The Committee were probably unwise to alienate Forwood, who joined the minority of councillors voting against the Gallery's purchase grant derived from the Autumn Exhibitions later that year and against the expansion of the Gallery in 1881.[21] The Committee drew up a short list of six from the 149 applicants and then reduced it to two contenders, George Harry Wallis, son of the keeper of the art collections at the South Kensington Museums and then in charge of the Bethnal Green Museum, and Charles Dyall, secretary of the Lyceum Club in Liverpool. At the Committee meeting Wallis received six votes and Dyall only two, but Samuelson, who had evidently promised the job to Dyall, threatened to resign if Dyall was not appointed and insisted that the Council should make the final decision. There it was agreed that Wallis knew much more than Dyall about art but Dyall had more experience in 'secretarial and financial business.' Samuelson repeated Picton's opinion that they did not want 'a man to be a great judge of pictures and did not want one to dictate to them on matters respecting which they thought they knew quite as much as he did.' Wallis eventually withdrew fearing the administrative load at the Gallery, and Dyall was appointed but only by 24 votes to 19. Wallis later became the highly successful first director of the Nottingham Castle Museum and Art Gallery, where he began his own autumn exhibitions in 1881, while his younger brother Whitworth became the greatest of all British municipal curators and directors at the Birmingham Museum and Art Gallery. Clearly many members of the Council were not convinced by Picton's and Samuelson's ideas and wanted a curator with more knowledge of art than Dyall possessed. The *Porcupine* commented: 'The committee did not want a man who was a great judge of pictures or to dictate to them. Happy committee who are so wise in their own conceit, but probably it may not be so happy for Mr. Dyall or for the town.' Dyall, 'a smart man of considerable local fame, and popular withal', began his career as an artist, worked on the great Manchester Art Treasures Exhibition of 1857, became a librarian at the Manchester Public Libraries and in 1863 was appointed secretary to the Lyceum Club, where he would have made many useful social contacts with the great Liverpool merchant families.[22] His *Address in Verse written by Mr Charles Dyall and delivered by him at the Conversazione of the Proprietors of the Lyceum on 9 November 1866*, together with a volume of his poems published in 1877, may have revealed him to the Council as a man of feeling as well as of business.[23] Dyall seems to have pleased his Committee. By 1897 his salary had reached £500 annually, the same amount which the newly appointed keeper of the Tate Gallery was then receiving.[24] The Committee's lack of foresight in not taking Forwood's advice became painfully evident following the death of Rathbone.

The Gallery's insistence that its curator should be a mere administrator was again seriously challenged in 1892 by the eminent critic George Moore, who wanted 'competent art directors', devoted entirely to the study of art, to replace the amateur councillors who then controlled municipal art galleries.[25] Rathbone responded arguing that democratic principles create local involvement:

> The people have supported it [the Gallery] because they felt it belonged to them. There have been two long and heated debates in the Council over the purchase of a single picture and that has created an interest in the town which is in itself an education in art.... An ideal autocracy might avoid making mistakes but it would have this danger...the public, having no voice in the purchase of pictures, would lose all interest.[26]

Moore exempted Rathbone from his attack on the 'Alderman in Art' and it was only after Rathbone's death in 1895 that Dyall's inadequacies became obvious. Exactly the same arguments were repeated on Dyall's retirement in 1904. The Libraries, Museums and Arts Committee recommended Carew Martin, secretary of the Royal Society of British Artists, for the job. He was a grandson of the artist John Martin and a nephew of E.H. Corbould, formerly drawing master to the royal family. He had studied in Paris and could speak French, Italian and German.[27] However, the Council refused to confirm the appointment. One member of the Committee had objected in principle to the choice of an art critic who might act on his own ideas and principles rather than those of the Committee. The *Burlington Magazine*, a scholarly periodical for connoisseurs, immediately published an editorial entitled 'No Critic Need Apply', pleading, as Moore had done, for an expert curator who would control most aspects of the Gallery's work. Eventually an art critic, Edward Rimbault Dibdin, was appointed but his powers were never much greater than those of Dyall.[28] In 1922 Lawrence Haward, the curator of the Manchester City Art Galleries, continued Moores's attack on committees of councillors in the language of the newly fashionable science of psychology: 'purchases may often be made in the artificial heat of momentary emotion by a committee acting under the influence of what the psychologists call herd-suggestion with funds drawn from the gate money taken at a popular exhibition.'[29] His reference to exhibition gate money was an unmistakable reference to the Liverpool Autumn Exhibitions.

Shortly before Dyall retired Harold Chaloner Dowdall (1868-1955), a Conservative city councillor, a future lord mayor and a close friend of Augustus John, tried to create a new post combining the curatorship of the Gallery with a new professorship of aesthetics at the University. He was assisted by two University professors, Richard Caton (1842-1926), a distinguished scientist, and Oliver Elton (1861-1945), holder of the King Alfred Chair of English Literature. The new post was to be funded by W. H. Lever, the great soap manufacturer at Port Sunlight. They hoped to attract the eminent critic D.S. MacColl to this post with a salary of £500. Dowdall emphasized that 'Birmingham was collecting a valuable lot of pictures free of charge because Wallis (their curator) was efficient and the rich citizens found that in following his advice they were backing winners and so gave freely.' However the City Council was hostile, Lever was hesitant and the plan failed.[30] Two years later MacColl became the keeper of the Tate Gallery. Dibdin had been trained as a lawyer in Edinburgh but had been working for the Queen Insurance Company in Liverpool between 1877 and 1904. He had however studied art as a young man and was the art critic of the *Liverpool Courier* from 1887 until 1904. His taste in art was distinctly conservative.[31] In his book on Frank Dicksee, a reactionary, but highly successful, contemporary British artist, he lamented that 'at the present time, the public taste, or the fashion, or whatever it is that regulates the fluctuations of opinion, is for pictures that have little in common with those of Mr. Dicksee. Classical feeling for design, romantic sentiment in art, are decried.'[32] Intelligent articles by him on the Gallery's collections appeared in the *Magazine of Art* in 1888 and in the *Pall Mall Magazine* of 1904. In the first he praised their 'catholicity', describing them as the best English municipal collections despite some recent populist acquisitions. In the second with his application for the curatorship in the post he expressed much more sympathy for the 'value of pictures in the education of simple folk'.[33] A long paper of the former year published his research on early art exhibitions in Liverpool, while in 1918 a scholarly article on Liverpool eighteenth-century artists established him as the leading expert on local art.[34] He wrote the only serious contemporary article on the eminent Liverpool 'New Sculptor', Charles John Allen (1862-1956).[35] He also had a respectable general knowledge of historic British art with modest books and articles on Gainsborough, Watts and Raeburn. He opposed post-impressionism in 1913, and as late as 1925 was still attacking the artists associated with the New English Art Club and the Slade School.[36] He exhibited watercolours at the Liverpool Academy and was President of the Artists' Club in Liverpool in 1896.[37] His expertise received some recognition from the Committee which resolved in 1912 that all recommendations for acquisitions should in future be accompanied by a report from the curator.[38] He could at least now comment even if he could not initiate or veto. However, Liverpool was far behind Birmingham in the development of an expert professional staff. There by 1904 all acquisitions originated with recommendations from the curator, Whitworth Wallis. They were never rejected by his Committee, and Wallis could if necessary buy pictures without reference to the Committee at all.[39]

Dibdin was succeeded by Arthur Quigley, a landscape painter, who had studied art at the Birkenhead and Liverpool art schools and had exhibited at the Liverpool Academy and at the Autumn Exhibitions. He had been president of the Liverpool Artists' Club and of the Liverpool Academy. He had been appointed assistant curator under Dyall in 1898 and on Dyall's retirement in 1904 he had offered to succeed Dyall at an annual salary of only £300, £100 less than the established amount of £400. The Council however rejected this enterprising idea and preferred Dibdin for the job at £400.[40] In practice Quigley had to act as curator for considerable periods while Dibdin was unwell. He was appointed acting curator on Dibdin's retirement in 1918 but was not promoted to curator until 1920 probably owing to his poor academic qualifications. By 1918 most municipal art galleries had accepted that their directors and curators required some specialist qualifications. Frank Rutter, the distinguished art critic and exhibition organizer, was appointed as director of the Leeds City Art Gallery in 1912, although his powers were as limited as those of Dibdin.[41] Quigley's appointment therefore is puzzling. The Committee may have blamed Dibdin for the collapse of the Autumn Exhibitions between 1910 and 1914 and may have felt that an entrepreneurial artist would be better than another scholar. Certainly Quigley was successful with the Autumn Exhibitions in the short run, and the Committee, who re-designated his post as director in 1927, clearly liked him. At his retirement in 1931 his annual salary had reached £875, and he left Liverpool for St. Ives, a painting colony, in his leaving present, a new car.[42]

Before the Gallery opened in 1877 about £3,000 had been spent on purchases from the six Autumn Exhibitions held between 1871 and 1876. Profits from these exhibitions had amounted to only about £1,000 but Rathbone and Samuelson had clearly been determined to demonstrate from the outset the fundamental importance of the permanent collection. They had always promised that the cost of acquisitions would be met entirely from the Autumn Exhibition profits and the deficit of about £2,000 was made up only in 1890.[43] Two of the most interesting of these early purchases, Sophie Anderson's *Elaine* and Louisa Starr's *Sintram*, were by women, although female artists were certainly not fashionable in the early 1870s. Rathbone continued to buy their work for the Gallery, which eventually became well known in feminist circles.[44] The Gallery's first notable purchase was Herkomer's *Eventide*, begun in 1876 and completed early in 1878. It was bought unfinished in April 1877 with £375 paid then and the remaining £375 on its arrival at the Autumn Exhibition of 1878. The Council was apparently undeterred by its violent expressionist perspective and by its grim social realist subject – a group of old women in the St James's workhouse.[45] Their next major acquisition in 1881 was Rossetti's *Dante's Dream*, his only monumental gallery painting and a supremely poetic and imaginative work at the other end of the Victorian stylistic spectrum from Herkomer's *Eventide*. It demonstrated, more clearly than *Eventide*, the difficulties arising from the decision only to buy important paintings from the Autumn Exhibitions. The Liverpool councillors admired it during their visit to the London studios in March 1881 but Rossetti had for many years refused to exhibit any of his paintings. Samuelson explained to the Town Council when justifying its purchase for £1,575 that Rossetti 'despised public opinion and ignorant criticism and could only be prevailed upon to allow his picture to be exhibited

[when] it had been bought at a high price.' The local newspaper reporter noted with some surprise that even after that explanation the purchase was 'ratified without challenge' by the Council.[46] In fact the negotiations for the purchase of the picture had collapsed in July when Rossetti became dissatisfied with private assurances that the Council would confirm the purchase of the painting once it had appeared in the Autumn Exhibition, and he relented only with great reluctance. The success of the tortuous negotiations over the acquisition was largely due to Thomas Henry Hall Caine, later the richest of all Victorian novelists, but in 1881 working in Liverpool in the building trade and writing on architecture. He greatly admired Rossetti's poetry, went to live with him in August of that year and acted as an intermediary between the Council and the lonely, dying artist whom Rathbone had offended.[47] He gave a lecture on the painting at the Gallery in November conceding that Rossetti's reputation depended on a few enthusiasts with access to private collections and on the work of his followers, most notably Burne-Jones, but also claiming that Rossetti was 'an artist who has probably done more to influence the direction of poetry and painting in our time than any man now living'.[48]

In 1884 the Sub-Committee wanted to buy Millais's *Isabella* (fig. 12) of 1849 which had just been bought in at the C.A. Ionides sale. It had been painted in the artist's early linear, detailed and realist style which he had long abandoned. Thus it could not be passed off as a normal Autumn Exhibition painting straight from the artist's easel. It was exhibited at the 1884 Autumn Exhibition but had been purchased in July six weeks earlier for only £1,050, a price 'so low that we do not like to name it', as the *Athenaeum* put it.[49] Thus the first three major paintings acquired for the Gallery were all effectively purchased before they were hung at the Autumn Exhibitions. However this practice of by-passing these exhibitions, although undoubtedly highly successful, was rarely repeated until the 1930s. The purpose of acquisition was both to improve the collections and to encourage major artists to exhibit at the Autumn Exhibitions. The second objective was as important as the first, and artists had to believe that only works hung at the Autumn Exhibitions would be considered for purchase, however much that restriction might limit the choice of paintings for the permanent collection.

Late in 1884 the extension to the Gallery had been completed nearly doubling its size to fifteen rooms. The new rooms were devoted to the Autumn and other temporary exhibitions thus leaving the permanent collection largely undisturbed, always on display and attracting more public attention.[50] Although Picton, Rathbone and Samuelson were not relying on local taxation for their purchases, every acquisition could be publicly challenged at meetings of the City Council. In 1888 Leighton exhibited his *Captive Andromache* (fig. 15) at the Autumn Exhibition. For M.H. Spielmann it was 'in itself a complete exposition of the art of painting'.[51] It was perhaps the one work in which Leighton resisted the superficial attractions of the aesthetic movement in order to compete directly with the grandest history paintings of the old masters. Samuelson and Rathbone had generally dealt with acquisitions but on this occasion Picton himself asked Leighton if he would sell his painting to the Gallery. Leighton replied that the first sketch for it dated from 1863, that it represented two years work and that it was worth £8,000. He had however priced it at £6,000 in the Autumn Exhibition catalogue, where it was five times more expensive than any other picture, and he would make a further reduction for a public gallery. In December the Libraries, Museums and Arts Committee unanimously agreed to buy it for £4,000, probably then the largest sum ever offered by a public art gallery for a work by a living artist – even more than the £3,150 paid by the British Institution in 1811 for Benjamin West's *Christ Healing the Sick* (Tate Gallery).[52] Picton told the Council that negotiations were well advanced to buy the painting, 'one of the noblest pictures ever painted by the English School'.[53] The prospect of the sale of his painting had persuaded Leighton, much against his own inclinations, to preside at the first meeting of the National Association for the Advancement of Art, a Liverpool initiative intended to improve the practice and appreciation of art throughout the country.[54] Early in December Picton formally welcomed Leighton to Liverpool where Leighton's presidential speech denounced English philistinism and praised French culture.[55] On 2 January 1889 Picton, then aged eighty-three and with only a few months to live, formally recommended the purchase of *Captive Andromache* to the Council. Robert Durning Holt (1832-1908), the leader of the Liverpool Liberal Party since 1878 and a future lord mayor, supported Picton stating that 'when it became known that one of the greatest historical pictures of the century was exhibited in Liverpool people would come to the city for the very purpose of seeing it'. Another Liberal councillor, Jeremiah Miles, commented that it was better to buy one important painting than a number of mediocre works, an intelligent criticism of the Gallery's acquisitions policy. However the purchase was rejected by the City Council by twenty votes to sixteen on the grounds that Leighton had apparently already agreed to the making of a photogravure of the painting in Berlin and that this might reduce the income available to the Gallery from copyright fees. Leighton was being treated as if he were a Council contractor manipulating the small print of his contract. Picton raged at the Council:

> He must say that he felt more humiliated and discouraged than he could express. He felt perfectly ashamed. He treated with Sir F. Leighton in all good faith backed up as he was by the unanimous expression in the Council on two occasions – on one occasion without a dissentient vote and on another with applause. If any members of the Council had any objections when the matter was first brought forward...why did they not say so and not allow him to go on thinking he had their approval and then

coming forward to give him a slap on the face? ... They were told that it was a great price to pay for a picture, but if they wanted a good thing they must pay for it. They could not get them on the 'cheap and nasty' system (hear, hear). The money which would be paid for the picture was not the money of the ratepayers who had not contributed a farthing towards it. The building was erected by Sir Andrew Walker...at a cost of nearly £40,000. The exhibitions had been held for 18 years and the Committee had realized out of them more than £30,000...He thought that this was a great thing to be proud of (hear, hear)...If the action which seemed likely to be taken were carried out he promised them that there would be no more art exhibitions...If the Council refused the offer...the city would be held up to ridicule and contempt from one end of the world to the other.[56]

Picton later felt that he had not presented the case for the acquisition well but his anger was understandable. Leighton after all was the one leading artist who had exhibited major paintings at the Autumn Exhibitions in the 1870s when few other academicians followed his example. No doubt Picton was convinced that the Conservatives had abandoned him out of political spite.[57] *The Liverpool Review*, representing the traditional Liberal emphasis on municipal retrenchment, praised the Council's decision. The money would have been better spent on 'workmen's dwellings'. The copyright issue was irrelevant but the painting was too expensive and anyway, although excellent for colour and design, it lacked 'feeling'.[58] Leighton's fair but rather patronising Liverpool speech of a month earlier about British cultural failings was re-printed in full in the Liverpool newspapers, and it is at least possible that its tone offended many members of the City Council. The Committee unsuccessfully disputed the right of the Council to veto a purchase not involving public money, but it did not in the end carry out its threat to terminate the Autumn Exhibitions.[59] The final humiliation came two months later when Manchester City Art Gallery bought the painting for the £4,000 vainly offered by Picton. At the Manchester City Council meeting of 6 March 1889 there were fifty-two votes in favour of the purchase and only six against.[60]

A year later the Sub-Committee invited Holman Hunt to send to the Autumn Exhibition his *Triumph of the Innocents*, effectively a *Flight into Egypt* with the 'spirits of the slain Innocents, his little neighbours of Bethlehem' accompanying the Holy Family. It had been completed in 1887 but had not been publicly exhibited, although a replica had been shown at a commercial gallery in London in 1885. Like Rossetti's *Dante's Dream* and Leighton's *Captive Andromache* it was a grand gallery painting difficult to sell to any private patron. Hunt's elaborate and highly symbolic religious paintings were far more popular than Leighton's more austere history paintings, but a photogravure of the *Triumph of the Innocents* had been published in 1887, and Hunt wanted £3,500, nearly as much as Leighton had asked for his *Captive Andromache*. Rathbone was now more cautious and used Hunt's popularity to raise over £2,000 from private subscribers thus reducing the total cost to the Council to a very manageable £1,500.[61] He demonstrated the same caution over Whistler's *Arrangement in Black and Brown: The Fur Jacket* (Worcester Art Museum, Massachusetts), a portrait of the artist's former mistress, Maud Franklin. It had been shown at the Grosvenor Gallery in 1877 but was then repainted by the artist for exhibitions in Amsterdam and Brussels in 1889 and 1890.[62] Whistler sent it to the 1891 Autumn Exhibition but increased the price from the £350, which he had demanded in 1889, first to £1,200 and then to £1,700, after discovering that Leighton wanted £1,800 for his *Perseus and Andromeda* at the same exhibition. He may have known that Rathbone, who would have liked to acquire the painting for the Gallery, had about that amount of money to spend on paintings at the exhibition. R.A.M Stevenson (1847-1900), the well-known critic and professor of art history at Liverpool University between1889 and 1893, tried to persuade influential Liverpool individuals to support the purchase on behalf of Rathbone. However Rathbone knew that with Whistler's controversial reputation among conservative artists and patrons he would have great difficulty in persuading the City Council to buy the painting at Whistler's price.[63] In the end he abandoned the portrait and the £1,700 was spent at the exhibition on seven quite different works. Rathbone fully understood the importance of securing major but inevitably expensive work for the new and largely empty Gallery. If he had he succeeded with the purchase of the paintings by Leighton and Whistler the Gallery would have started its life on a much firmer foundation.

Fortunately Rathbone's acquisitions policy also included the purchase of very cheap works by young and progressive artists, and he had the necessary insight to do it effectively. The Gallery bought Waterlow's *A Summer Shower* in 1874, Joseph Knight's *Showery Weather* in 1876, Stanhope Forbes's *A Street in Brittany* in 1882, Fred Brown's *Hard Times* in 1886, T.F. Goodall's *The Bow Net* in 1887, Hornel's *Summer* in 1892 and Charles Gere's *Finding of the Infant St George* in 1894. Thus within 20 years Rathbone secured for the Gallery important early works of the late nineteenth-century landscape revival movement, of the Manchester School, of the New English Art Club, of the Glasgow School and of the Birmingham School. At the time of the purchases Waterlow was 24, Knight was 39, Forbes was 25, Brown was 35 but still largely unknown, Goodall was 30 but known as a photographer rather than as an artist, Hornel was 28 and Gere was 25. The total cost of the seven paintings all bought directly from their artists was only £653. Waterlow's painting was the artist's first major success. Knight was founding the Manchester School in the 1870s and in 1877 his *A Tidal River* was one of the first purchases from the Chantrey Bequest. The acquisition of Forbes's painting encouraged him to become an open-air naturalist rather than a mere portrait painter. Gere's work was one of the earliest major paintings of the Birmingham school. The purchase of Brown's painting from the first exhibition of the New English Art Club provided the Club with a vital stimulus just when its future seemed very doubtful owing to the very low level of sales from the exhibition. Hornel's painting was the first work from the new Glasgow School to enter a public art gallery apart from commissioned portraits.[64] C.N. Hemy's *A Nautical Argument*, bought in 1877 for £250 might be added to the list. The artist was then aged thirty-six and did not become a member of the Royal Academy for another thirty-three years. It is clearly an imitation of the work of James Tissot, whose very popular paintings Rathbone would no doubt have liked but could not afford.

Rathbone was challenged in the City Council not only for trying to buy very expensive paintings by established artists but also over the acquisition of these very cheap works by young and progressive artists. In 1892 he proposed to buy from the Autumn Exhibition W.B. Richmond's classicist *Venus and Anchises* for £800 together with William Stott's *Alps by Night* for £300 and Hornel's *Summer* for £100. *Summer* was generally regarded as the most extreme of the eccentric Glasgow School paintings at the exhibition.[65] At the City Council meeting of 5 October two councillors denounced the two paintings by Stott and Hornel as 'mere daubs' and as 'rubbish', while Samuelson could only see in *Summer* 'an artifice for the introduction of a number of colours to make a harmony'. Rathbone replied that new movements in art were generally condemned in their early days but that the progressive Glasgow school had already been widely praised on the continent. Perceiving that it was the lack of naturalism in *Summer* that was under attack Rathbone admitted at the Council meeting that he had been 'a little staggered (loud laughter)' when he first saw it and that 'he had not been reminded of nature by the picture (loud laughter)' but it certainly 'pointed out to him facts in nature which he had never seen before'. At his suggestion a decision was postponed for a fortnight to enable all the councillors to see the paintings. At this second meeting where the fate of the two paintings was 'the principal subject of discussion', seventeen Liverpool artists presented a petition to the Council in their favour. Stott's painting now received general approval but opposition to Hornel's *Summer* was still strong. Rathbone threatened to resign if the Council voted against it. In organizing the Autumn Exhibitions he had 'to spend eight to ten hours a day in going about in a cab visiting the artists' studios and getting no lunch'. Samuelson derided Rathbone's threat to resign observing that Rathbone had made the same threat over the rejection of Leighton's painting. However some wavering councillors conceded that Rathbone's services were worth retaining at the cost of the purchase of *Summer* for £100 and the purchase was approved by forty three votes to five.[66]

Meanwhile there was extensive discussion of the merits of the two paintings in the Liverpool daily and weekly press. There were contributions both from Rathbone and from some Glasgow artists, among whom James Paterson was surprisingly unenthusiastic about Hornel's painting. Rathbone noted that 'his Committee had selected Richmond's picture – an excellent picture, easily understood of the people', but it was also right that 'the artists and students of the future capabilities of art should have their opportunities of studying its new developments, and of not being restricted within the limits of conventionality'. Rathbone emphasized the naturalistic elements in Stott's work rather than its poetic and visionary symbolism, while his reference to 'schemes of colour' in Hornel's painting and his comparison between it and a Persian carpet were as close as he came to describing Hornel's vigorous Japanese sense of design and pattern.[67] The critic of the *Liverpool Courier*, probably Edward Rimbault Dibdin, the Gallery's future curator, correctly noted the Japanese influence in Hornel's 'decorative methods' and in his 'gorgeous colour combination made more bizarre in effect by arbitrary use of dark lines'.[68] Rathbone was frequently accused of buying paintings which were abstruse and unintelligible either by virtue of their style as in Hornel's *Summer* or of their subject as in Segantini's *Punishment of Luxury*. His obituarists commented that 'Mr Rathbone's opinions on art matters and his leaning towards schools of painting which are not generally "understood of the people" were not always very cordially recognized,' and that 'his colleagues in the council were not always in accord with his tastes, but they were regarded by him as rude and unlettered barbarians more to be pitied than blamed, more to be educated than scolded.'[69] Even his niece Eleanor Rathbone, despite her respect for his achievements, observed that 'his choice of pictures for the public galleries sometimes tried the faith of his fellow citizens.'[70]

He and Samuelson countered these accusations by deliberately buying a group of unashamedly populist paintings. Among them were *Don't 'ee Tipty Toe* by John Morgan (bought in 1885), showing two children being measured to determine which is the taller, and *One of the Family* by F.G. Cotman (bought in 1880), in which the farmer's family at their meal are joined by their horse poking its head through the window. Even W.F. Yeames's famous *And When Did You Last See Your Father* (bought in 1878), ostensibly a respectable St John's Wood School painting with a subject taken from the English Civil Wars,[71] Henry Holiday's *Dante and Beatrice*, (bought in 1884), a deeply serious painting but also a lovers' tiff, and Frederick Goodall's *New Light in the Hareem* (bought in 1884), a baby with its white mother and black nurse in an oriental harem, are on the fringes of this group. Goodall's painting cost £1,000, Holiday's work £500 and Yeames's picture £750. These were substantial sums to invest in popular art. This policy, probably reflecting Samuelson's ideas but endorsed by Rathbone, was explained by the curator, Charles Dyall:

While endeavouring to secure works of the highest technical skill, the fact has not been lost sight of that the public, for whose edification and instruction the institution in a great measure exists, delight in subjects of a popular character, and, with this end in view, pictures have from time to time been added which, by appealing to common feelings and sentiments of our daily life, have afforded a fine moral lesson and given great pleasure to the numerous visitors to the Gallery who are uninitiated in the higher forms of art.[72]

This dual approach to the difficult problem of selecting acquisitions straight from the artist's easel for public art galleries, placing high and populist art into separate categories and buying examples of each category, may not have been invented by Rathbone and Samuelson, but with them it was an openly avowed policy carried out with considerable skill.

Considering Rathbone's interest in completing the sculptural programme for St George's Hall and the amount of public sculpture then being commissioned for Liverpool it is not surprising that the sculpture acquisitions for the Gallery from the Autumn Exhibitions were distinguished. While never aspiring to major statues by Rodin, as Manchester City Art Gallery had done, outstanding large bronzes by the leaders of the 'New Sculpture' movement were acquired, notably *Peace* by Edward Onslow Ford (bought in 1891) and *The Mower* by Hamo Thornycroft (bought in 1894). Frampton's outstanding symbolist plaster bust *Mysteriarch* was added in 1902, and the representation of symbolist 'New Sculpture' was strengthened with the purchase of Harry Bates's spectacular bronze, ivory, lapis lazuli and mother of pearl *Mors Janua Vitae* in 1920.[73] Bates's sculpture of 1899, bought for £750 from the Fine Art Society, probably acting on behalf of the sculptor's widow, was a welcome change from the usual pattern of acquisitions of new art from the Autumn Exhibitions and apparently reflected the Gallery's brief period of post-war prosperity. In 1895 the Gallery bought and funded the bronze casting of *Love and the Mermaid* by C.J. Allen, and it commissioned from him in the following year a marble bust of Rathbone. Sadly however the bust of Rathbone's wife by Dalou, the French sculptor who had been such a formative influence on many of these sculptors, did not pass to the Gallery.

Before 1914 contemporary foreign paintings were very rarely bought by British public galleries apart from a few works acquired by the Victoria and Albert Museum and by the Glasgow and Manchester City Art Galleries. However between 1871 and 1914 the Walker Art Gallery courageously purchased about thirteen European paintings more or less directly from the artist's easel. The most remarkable, Segantini's symbolist *Punishment of Luxury (or Lust)* of 1891, denouncing abortion and child neglect, was bought in 1893 for a modest £315. There were also Carl Gussow's excessively naturalistic *Old Man's Treasure* of 1876 purchased in 1879 for £500, Carl

Schloesser's Dusseldorf School *Village Lawyer*, bought in 1880 for £315, and Willem Geets' costume piece, *Awaiting an Audience*, acquired in 1886 for the same amount. Rather later Henri Le Sidaner's luminous *St. Paul's from the River* cost £200 in 1911 and less notable acquisitions included L.R. Garrido's *His First Offence*, another highly realistic genre scene, and Pilade Bertieri's *Lady in Black Furs*, an imitation of Boldini's portrait style. Garrido's work cost £80 in 1905 and Bertieri's painting cost £100 in 1914. Schloesser, Geets, Garrido and Bertieri all had brief European reputations and Gussow undoubtedly had a deep impact on the Berlin Academy in the 1870s. By 1914 the Gallery had also bought seven important modern American paintings including major works by F.A. Bridgman and W.L. Picknell, perhaps reflecting Liverpool's close trade links with America. These acquisitions, demonstrating the cosmopolitan ambitions of the Autumn Exhibitions, represented a brave attempt at internationalist patronage of living artists. They formed a striking contrast to the policies of the National Gallery, which was uninterested in any modern art, and of the Tate Gallery, which pursued a strongly insular policy at least until the Curzon report of 1915. Certainly by 1914 the permanent collections of the municipal galleries in Liverpool, Manchester, Dublin and Glasgow held much more contemporary foreign art than the great national galleries in London.[74] In retrospect it is clear that the Gallery had failed to spend its European money wisely except on the painting by Segantini. Rathbone had probably learnt a considerable amount about contemporary continental art, but his successors knew much less and certainly not enough to embark on this demanding enterprise, which did not survive the cultural nationalism of the First World War.

The Walker Art Gallery had been established in 1873 in the hope that it would attract gifts and bequests from the large collections of British and French nineteenth-century art owned by the wealthy merchants and manufacturers whose great houses ringed the city. These collections were described in great detail in a long series of over thirty articles in the *Athenaeum* between 1881 and 1887. In 1886 over a thousand paintings, drawings and watercolours from them were lent to the Walker Art Gallery for its *Grand Loan Exhibition*.[75] Exhibitions of this type were often held to inaugurate the many new municipal galleries then being built in north-west England in the hope that some of the lenders would turn their loans into gifts, although in practice this rarely happened.[76] The *Liverpool Mercury* listed the major lenders in 1886 as George Rae (1817-1902), the banker, with his works by Rossetti, Frederick Leyland with his paintings by Burne-Jones, Gilbert Moss with his watercolours, Ralph Brocklebank, the ship-owner, with his landscapes by Turner, A.G. Kurtz with his works by Leighton, Philip Rathbone with his paintings by Albert Moore, together with Charles Langton, Thomas Henry Ismay (1837-1899), George Holt, John Naylor (1813-1889) and Edward Samuelson.[77] From these collections Langton presented to the Gallery Poynter's *Faithful unto Death* in 1874, Kurtz gave Leighton's superb *Elijah* in 1879, the Brocklebank family donated paintings by David Roberts and Thomas Faed in 1893, Rathbone bequeathed an important group of early Italian paintings together with significant works by Albert Moore and Legros in 1895, while Ismay left Briton Riviere's *Daniel in the Lion's Den* to the Gallery in 1900. Holt's splendid collection was bequeathed to the Gallery by his daughter in 1944 and it remains in Sudley, the original family home in south Liverpool. A very few rather unfashionable paintings and sculptures were presented to the Gallery mostly at its request from the Naylor collection in 1967.[78] Otherwise only a few relatively insignificant works reached the Gallery from these important collections. Liverpool's artistic wealth was also demonstrated between 1872 and 1895 by the forty more specialized exhibitions of the Liverpool Art Club which was dominated by Rathbone. They included pioneering shows devoted to Hans Thoma, David Cox and modern Belgian art. The exhibition of 1881 included 340 late eighteenth-century and early nineteenth-century British paintings. Most of the exhibits came from local collections, but again very few ever entered the Gallery.[79] The completion of the new Liverpool Museum in 1860 was followed almost immediately by the gift to it of Joseph Mayer's great collection of antiquities. No such good fortune resulted from the building of the Walker Art Gallery seventeen years later. The owners of works by the mid-nineteenth-century 'Liverpool School of Painters', which included W. J. J. C. Bond (1833-1926), William Davis (1812-1873), John Newton, D.A Williamson (1823-1903), Robert Tonge (1823-1856), W.L. Windus (1822-1907) and others, might have been expected to be more generous. In 1904 the historian of these artists, H. C. Marillier, listed some thirty of these collectors of whom only three gave or bequeathed any part of their local paintings to the Gallery.[80] Samuelson, chairman of the Gallery's Committee for many years, gave only three paintings from his very large collection of Liverpool art.

Of course Liverpool's wealthy merchants faced other charitable demands. The new University received about £700,000 from them between about 1882 and 1914 making it the best endowed of the new universities apart from Manchester.[81] Between 1901and 1914 they gave £441,470 towards the building of Liverpool Cathedral, an enterprise certainly unparalleled elsewhere in Britain and probably in the world.[82] From 1873 to 1914 the Walker Art Gallery gained about £60,000 from them in buildings, cash and paintings. The ratios between these three amounts probably reflect fairly accurately the relative importance of higher education, religion and art for Liverpool's richer citizens. It is also possible that the origins of the Gallery in the philanthropy of a Conservative brewer still alienated the great Liverpool families with their traditional Liberal respect for the temperance movement. The controversy over the proposed Leighton and Whistler purchases cannot have increased the confidence of serious collectors such as Leyland in the idea that a local authority was a fit body to run an art gallery. The refusal of the committee to appoint a 'professional' curator at a proper salary may also have persuaded potential donors that this was not yet a well-run institution. In fact however the other English municipal art galleries also suffered from an absence of major donations from their wealthier inhabitants. The position in Scotland was very different and there Glasgow City Art Gallery received magnificent gifts and bequests from local collectors on a scale vastly greater than in any English city.

Among those who did support the Gallery was James Smith, a very successful, self-made Liverpool wine merchant and a 'well-informed and hearty Nonconformist Liberal'. He owned 'one of the largest wine businesses in Lancashire and the Midlands' and was a leading member of a Bordeaux firm of wine merchants. He was regarded as the 'best judge of claret in England'. He 'invested a large part of his fortune in works of art' but he also left £60,000 to Liverpool University and to the Liverpool Institute Schools.[83] In 1908 he bequeathed to the Gallery most of his large collection of sculpture by Rodin, Barye and the 'New Sculptors', etchings by Whistler and paintings by G.F. Watts, D.A. Williamson and Windus. They entered the collection in the 1920s.[84] He had bought two paintings by Watts from the sale of the artist's great patron C.H. Rickards in 1887 and then accumulated a further twenty-six partly through commissions placed directly with the artist and partly through purchases in the London sale rooms. He must have been among Watts's best customers during the last twelve years of the artist's life, paying him about £6,000 for some twelve paintings. These were often late versions of earlier compositions which Watts and his wife had to explain to their patron, and Smith bought better paintings in the auction rooms, above all the four great apocalyptic *Riders*, than in the artist's studio. This pattern of patronage was repeated with Rodin's sculptures which Smith at first bought through dealers and later directly from the sculptor, after securing an introduction to him in 1903. Rodin was very popular with British patrons, among whom Smith was not the first, but provincial wine merchants rarely bought such demanding classical subjects as *The Death of Athens*. Rodin discussed possible changes to this sculpture with Smith in his studio and explained to him: 'I could not reduce the size of the plinth very much because unfortunately it is the subject. It is the mountain which accompanies the living mountain which is the young girl's body, and which animates it in the way it does'. This first version cost Smith about £500, about the same amount that he was paying for many of his paintings by Watts. A second version was later bought by the great Ruhr steel magnate August Thyssen, who was very much more typical of Rodin's international clientèle.[85]

Between 1924 and 1932 George Audley (died 1932) gave or bequeathed a wide ranging group of late-Victorian paintings by Clausen, Albert Moore, Leighton, Wyllie, Sargent, Tuke, Pettie, Hook, and others, together with a few earlier paintings by William Collins, Augustus Egg, F.R. Pickersgill, Wilkie and Poynter. His five paintings by Clausen, mainly early works, Moore's *Shells*, Leighton's early *Italian Crossbow Man*, Wyllie's very early *Blessing the Sea*, Tuke's *The Promise* and Wilkie's *Bathsheba at the Bath* were all important and distinctive works. There were over eighty paintings altogether which significantly enriched the Gallery's British holdings. Like Smith he was a self-made man in the alcohol business – in his case whisky and beer rather than wine. He moved to Southport in about 1905 and retired from business in 1920 at the age of fifty-six with £180,000. Then 'the collection of pictures became his great hobby'. He frequented artists' studios but he was not 'in touch with any modern art movements which he was quite unable to appreciate.' The 1920s were of course an excellent time for the purchase of Victorian paintings which were then falling rapidly in price. The residue of his collection, some 98 works, was sold at his death in 1932 by auction and only fetched £1,314.[86] Unfortunately the Gallery seems to have had no contact with Frank Hindley Smith, another Southport collector and a friend of Roger Fry.[87] His magnificent collection, rich above all in impressionist paintings, was given and bequeathed to various British public galleries, especially the Atkinson Art Gallery in Southport and the Fitzwilliam Museum in Cambridge, but nothing came to Liverpool.

Throughout this period there were also a few distinguished gifts and bequests of individual pictures, which, although then not particularly well regarded, have since become more highly valued. Wright of Derby's *The Annual Girandola at the Castel Sant'Angelo, Rome* (fig.10), presented by Robert Neilson in 1880, was the first major eighteenth-century painting to enter the Gallery. Fuseli's *Return of Milton's Wife* and *Milton when a Boy Instructed by his Mother*, formerly owned by William Roscoe, were presented by his descendant Sir Henry Roscoe in 1914. There were also John Martin's *The Last Man* donated by Richard Heap in 1888, Brett's *Stonebreaker* bequeathed by Mrs Sarah Barrow in1918, Madox Brown's *Coat of Many Colours* commissioned by George Rae and given by Mrs William Coltart in 1904 and Leighton's *Perseus and Andromeda* bought for £1,000 in 1909 for presentation to the Gallery by Sir William Hartley (1846-1922), the jam maker.

In 1893 the famous early Italian and Netherlandish paintings collected by William Roscoe nearly a century earlier were placed on loan in the Gallery by their owners, the Liverpool Royal Institution. The Institution had acquired them in 1816 following Roscoe's bankruptcy and had opened the collection to the public as the first permanent exhibition of works of art displayed in Britain with the avowed intention to improve public taste.[88] The Town Council had been unsuccessful in its attempt to take over the Institution's art gallery and collection in 1850, although the Institution itself admitted that its gallery, which was regularly open to the public and was free of charge on Mondays, had never been popular. In the late 1880s Martin Conway, professor of art history at Liverpool's University College and an expert on early Italian and Netherlandish art, had unsuccessfully tried to link the gallery with his courses and to make it a public institution.[89] In 1899 Dyall commented that 'the Roscoe Collection has been located in Liverpool for more than fifty years, and although known to a few connoisseurs and art devotees the general public were hardly aware of its existence.'[90] In 1891 a section of the Royal Institution's art gallery was converted into a chemistry laboratory for the Institution's schools and in 1892 the entire school building was sold to the City Council to be part of a new nautical college. The Institution's schools closed in 1892 and its responsibilities for higher education were gradually transferred to the newly founded Liverpool University. The period of loan for the Institution's paintings was set at 40 years in 1908 and effective responsibility for their display and conservation passed to the Gallery. Roscoe had formed his collection between about 1804 and 1816 not as works of art but as illustrations of the history of early Renaissance art, but, whether by luck or judgment, it included among its earlier paintings some masterpieces including above all Simone Martini's *Christ Discovered in the Temple* (fig. 1) and Ercole de' Roberti's *Pietà*. The Institution's collection also contained some later old master paintings, most notably an early painting by Poussin, which were included in the loan. In 1905 five early Italian paintings bequeathed by Rathbone joined the Institution's group and together they made the Gallery the most important English municipal collection. The immediate impact of these superb paintings seems however to have been no greater at the Walker Art Gallery than at the Royal Institution's gallery. Plans for a new building 94 feet long and 45 feet wide to be erected next to the Walker Art Gallery intended exclusively for the display of the Institution's paintings were drawn up but never implemented. After a special exhibition of them and the publication of a new catalogue they were hung tightly packed together in a downstairs gallery with poor lighting, and in any event by 1893 popular taste had moved on from gold backgrounds, Botticelli and 'squint-eyed' saints.[91] In 1928 however a new catalogue of the Royal Institution's collection was published by the Gallery.[92] Primitivism again became fashionable and Roscoe's pictures ceased to be curiosities and became masterpieces.

Local artists frequently complained that the Gallery rarely exhibited or bought their paintings.[93] Marillier's book on nineteenth-century Liverpool art of 1904 complained that by then only around twenty works by Merseyside artists had been bought by the Gallery. A further twenty oil paintings by local artists were bought from the Autumn Exhibitions.[94] Following the lavish celebrations for the seven-hundredth anniversary of the granting of the city's first charter and inspired by Picton's volumes on local history, the Gallery mounted an enormous historical exhibition of Liverpool art in 1908.[95] Dibdin, who had already published some articles on Liverpool painters, did the necessary research.[96] By 1906 he had devoted two rooms in the Gallery to paintings by Liverpool artists. In 1910 Violet Hunt, already a famous novelist and soon to be notorious for her affair with Ford Madox Ford, gave many sketches by her grandfather, Andrew Hunt (1790-1861), a successful Liverpool drawing master. She also presented a few works by her father, Alfred William Hunt (1830-1896), a watercolourist much influenced both by the Pre-Raphaelites and by Turner. John Elliot (died 1917), a Conservative Birkenhead tobacco merchant, left to the Gallery part of his substantial collection of Liverpool School paintings by William Davis, William Huggins (1820-1884) and others in 1917.[97] James Smith bequeathed his paintings by D.A. Williamson and by Windus to the Gallery in 1908 although they did not enter the collection until 1923. He had met Windus in about 1865 and they became intimate friends. He was apparently Williamson's first important patron, perhaps also in the 1860s. He wrote a moving and personal account of their lives and work, noting that Windus 'possessed a charming manner, was a brilliant conversationalist with a tenacious manner and a vivid imagination'[98] Paintings by local artists and with local connections began to be bought on a modest scale (fig.13). In 1910 the *Horse frightened by a Lion* by George Stubbs, who had been born in Liverpool, was bought at Christie's for only £22.50. His pastel and gouache portrait by Ozias Humphry, once owned by Joseph Mayer, had been bought in 1893. In 1906 editorials in the newly founded *Burlington Magazine* encouraged the acquisition of local material by provincial art galleries and deplored the promiscuous 'crowd of second-rate things at the Walker Art Gallery'.[99] Although paintings by nineteenth-century Liverpool artists could have been bought at any time before about 1960 for even less than £22.50 – allowing for inflation – the Gallery's enthusiasm for them waned after 1918. The large exhibition of 1908 had attracted fewer than 7,000 visitors and serious interest in Liverpool art did not revive until Mary Bennett joined the staff in 1956.

Dibdin seems also to have influenced the diversification of purchasing policy to include two new categories, art pottery and prints, probably acquired in support of the Autumn Exhibitions, which widened their scope in these directions at the same time. Material in these areas had the attraction of being cheaper than paintings. Between about 1906 and 1916 around one hundred ceramic vases, bowls, panels, small sculptures and even an umbrella stand designed by Christopher Dresser were bought from manufacturers as diverse as Doulton and Company, Martin Brothers, Pilkington's Tile and Pottery Company, the Ashby Potters Guild, Josiah Wedgwood and Sons and the Royal Staffordshire Pottery. Among the last purchases were vases and figures from the Copenhagen Royal Porcelain Manufactory purchased in 1916 probably as a gesture in support of Anglo-Danish friendship during the First World War. However, unlike many other British art galleries, the Walker Art Gallery never engaged further with decorative art. It came into the Gallery under the auspices of the Arts and Crafts movement, which saw no real distinction between fine and decorative art. The modest holdings left the Gallery for the Liverpool Museum some fifty years later in support of a rationalization of collecting policy which gave the Museum control of applied art. Between 1906 and 1916, also under Dibdin, prints by over eighty living artists were purchased. The new policy reflected the very considerable popular and professional success of the art potters and the great print mania which only collapsed in 1929 with the economic depression. Few of the etchers and engravers involved were of great eminence or originality, but in 1911 the Gallery bought a number of colour woodcuts from the section in the Autumn Exhibition of that year devoted to the Society of Graver Printers in Colour. These included works by Charles Mackie, William Giles, Sydney Lee and Edward Louis Lawrenson. Prints of this type could rarely be found in other public collections until after 1918.[100]

Again perhaps in order to buy more objects from a declining purchase fund, modern watercolours were increasingly bought. These included *Our Lady of Snows* by Edward Reginald Frampton in 1916, *The Sleepless D*aisy by Annie French in1907 and two by William Russell Flint in 1909 and 1916. Between 1911 and 1923 there were three by Robert Anning Bell, who had taught at the University's short-lived art school. The Gallery remained immune from the growing interest in early English watercolours although it had received a few from James Smith in 1896, and there were some gifts and bequests including the majestic but faded *Fall of the Clyde, Lanarkshire: Noon* by Turner presented by the Holt Family in 1909. The National Art-Collections Fund's first gifts to the Gallery were two watercolours by John Baverstock Knight in 1910, which were followed in 1916 with the gift of a landscape in the style of Girtin.

Reginald Grundy, a respectable if conservative art critic, reviewed the collection in 1913:

> The earlier purchases for the Gallery were indeed largely dictated by a spirit of compromise which resulted in half of them being of a purely popular character and the other moiety of works of artistic excellence. Since the present regime with Alderman John Lea as chairman of the Arts Committee and Mr. Dibdin as expert adviser, the Philistine element seems to have been overpowered and recent additions are marked by a sane, somewhat conservative, but thoroughly enlightened taste.

However, he went on to say that the recent rapid fall in the amount of money available for purchasing works of art had placed the Gallery behind Glasgow, Manchester and Birmingham City Art Galleries as patrons of new art.[101] Grundy's apparently surprising conclusion that the standard of the Gallery's purchases had improved after Rathbone's death in 1895 reflects partly no doubt his wish to ingratiate himself with the new administration at the

Gallery, but principally his contempt for the populist paintings acquired by Rathbone and Samuelson. H.M. Cundall, another conservative critic, had reviewed Rathbone and Samuelson's acquisitions more sympathetically in 1895 but he deplored the absence of historic British pictures, a concern that was to dominate discussions of the Gallery's policies in the twentieth century.[102]

Modernist critics were understandably less generous. In the context of the disputed purchases of the paintings by Hornel and Stott in 1892 George Moore in *The Speaker* and D.S. MacColl in *The Spectator* denounced the Gallery's permanent collection as a rather miscellaneous reflection of the low standards of the Royal Academy exhibitions and of fashionable London dealers. They wanted the Gallery to buy works by Manet and Whistler and by Barbizon, Hague School and impressionist artists.[103] Liverpool critics soon followed. In 1901 and in 1904 Dowdall attacked the selection of paintings for the permanent collection on the grounds that 'it is the opinion of many competent critics that the work associated with the Royal Academy at the present time is not likely to take any prominent place in the permanent progress of art'. He favoured instead the purchase of paintings by Watts and Charles Shannon.[104] Lea wrote privately to him:

> There is an unwritten law that the artists shall benefit by the purchase of pictures out of the [Autumn] exhibition, and you can quite well understand that if the committee were to go to Agnew's and purchase say a Watts as named by you for a large amount that the following spring the visiting deputation would be directed to Agnew's for works to form our own exhibition. In many cases the hope of a sale secures us the picture.[105]

Many years later Dowdall wrote to Vere Cotton about his reformist plans:

> D.S. MacColl backed me up in the Spectator and Sir Wm [Forwood, the Chairman of the Libraries, Museums and Arts Committee] was mildly sympathetic but they were too strong for me. Prominent R.A.s, who are past their not very distinguished prime and losing their market, butter up the local committee and the Autumn exhibn who in return buy a worthless picture and meet criticism by invoking the prominent R.A.s whose names are well known and whose pictures are popular with the semi-educated public.[106]

Writing in 1909 in a book sponsored by the progressive Sandon Studios Society, Frank Rutter, an art critic with advanced ideas, compared the Gallery's recent purchases unfavourably with those at Manchester and Leeds City Art Galleries. For him the Gallery had 'followed the fleeting fashions of the day instead of securing works with enduring artistic qualities.'[107] He probably meant that the Gallery had abandoned the realism and naturalism of the Newlyn artists and of the New English Art Club in favour of the more decorative and symbolist style represented by Boughton's *Road to Camelot*, Burne-Jones's *Sponsa de Libano*, Abbey's *O Mistress Mine*, Evelyn De Morgan's *Life and Thought*, George Frampton's *Mysteriarch*, J.J. Shannon's *Reverie* and Millie Dow's *Eve*, all bought between 1896 and 1906. Later in 1927 Rutter condemned the policies of all British municipal art galleries except those at Birmingham, Aberdeen, Dublin and Glasgow, while in 1933 he observed that in the twentieth century Bradford, Leeds and Manchester City Art Galleries had been buying paintings from the progressive New English Art Club rather than from the more reactionary Academy.[108] Manchester and Leeds had abandoned their annual exhibitions of new paintings for sale long before Liverpool terminated its Autumn Exhibitions and could concentrate instead on their permanent collections without considering the needs of temporary exhibitions. For John Rothenstein in 1930 the Walker Art Gallery was 'the most militant and opulent provincial stronghold of the most debased kind of popular-academic art.'[109]

It was not just modernist and progressive observers who criticized the Gallery's acquisitions. In 1904, as part of his plea that the Gallery should buy local art, Marillier described many of the Gallery's actual purchases up to that date as 'clap-trap' art or more simply as 'rubbish'.[110] The influential Manchester Pre-Raphaelite patron Charles Rowley, who detested impressionism, claimed in 1911 that 'at Liverpool they have for years gone for the dregs of fashionable work at the Royal Academy.'[111] Similarly in 1912 and in 1924 Councillor Herbert Rathbone criticized both the general standard of the permanent collection and the methods by which it was acquired. He was a son of Philip Rathbone, greatly interested in education and for many years chairman of the Museums Sub-Committee of the Libraries, Museums and Arts Committee. He could not therefore be ignored but the Gallery's only real defence was the familiar argument that paintings had to be bought from the Autumn Exhibitions in order to encourage artists to exhibit in them. The curator further argued that purchasing contemporary rather than historic art was an adventurous but justifiable policy. The Gallery could not however deny that by 1912 it was concentrating on paintings exhibited at the Royal Academy and on the work of 'academic' and 'arrived' artists. It also failed to recognise that the Royal Academy was becoming more conservative and that the Gallery had to collect more widely. Quigley seems to have been unusually hostile to modernism. In 1924 he warned that 'it is well known how malcontents and extremists in art-circles, operating now for over a quarter of a century, have brought about a dislocation in outlook among the younger artists and the public generally.'[112] The Gallery had allowed the initiative in the visual arts to pass to the University and the Sandon Studios Society where town and gown met.

The Impressionists were not entirely ignored at the Gallery. By 1912 its curator was regularly submitting to the Sub-Committee lists of his recommended purchases from the Autumn Exhibitions, reflecting his increased importance in the administration of the Gallery.[113] The Autumn Exhibition of 1924 was unusually wide-ranging. In May Quigley and Lea had visited Paris where their selections for the exhibition included Alfred Sisley's *Landscape with an abandoned cottage* priced at £483 and Camille Pissarro's *Red Roofs* priced at £460.[114] The two artists had died many years earlier and the paintings had evidently been obtained from dealers or from the artists' families, an unusual practice at the Autumn Exhibitions. Quigley compiled a list of some thirty-five paintings and recommended that the Sub-Committee should select their purchases from his list. He had optimistically estimated that about £1,250 was available that year for new acquisitions. The two impressionist paintings were both on his list, together with two pastels by Lhermitte presumably invited from the artist himself, who was still alive. The listed works varied in price between about £35 and £1,200, making the paintings by Sisley and Pissarro among the curator's more expensive recommendations. He however felt that there was 'no available work of outstanding merit' at the exhibition and that the best were only as good as 'some of our lesser important possessions'. By 1924 profits from the Autumn Exhibitions were falling rapidly and it was perhaps unsurprising, with their curator's unenthusiastic assessment of the pictures exhibited, that the Sub-Committee decided to confine their acquisitions to one small watercolour by Muirhead Bone for which they paid just £40. It was one of the cheapest items on Quigley's list.[115] Even in the last years of the Autumn Exhibitions the Sub-Committee was not usually as parsimonious as this, but clearly the enthusiasm for buying contemporary art from them was diminishing rapidly.

About £51,000 had been spent on acquisitions for the Gallery from the profits of the Autumn Exhibitions up to 1914, slightly less than the £64,000 spent by the Manchester City Art Gallery before that date with its annual grants from its Council, but probably more than any other provincial gallery.[116] It is difficult to offer an objective assessment of the quality of the paintings acquired by Rathbone and his immediate successors. Calderon was an important member of the St John's Wood School and some of his scenes from modern history are interesting. However, by any reasonable standards, it seems hard to justify the £800 spent in 1886 on his *Ruth and Naomi*, which can fairly safely be regarded as one of Rathbone's typical purchases, neither specially important nor by any means insignificant. Rathbone recorded his own reaction to the painting:

> Ruth and Naomi is a picture worth study; it gives the impression that the painter has had a distinct intention and has carried it out. It is no mere

group of models placed to make a tableau vivant as so many subject-pictures are; each of these figures is doing the work she is supposed to be doing. The earnest tender entreating look of Ruth requires no word to translate it, and the pitying sympathetic yet respectful attitude and expression of the servant maid is very happy ...[Mr Calderon's] work is generally instinct with a depth of feeling and richness of humanity which are gifts of genius and which no education can give.[117]

But Calderon was not a genius and the review of the painting in *The Spectator* is just:

It is our friend the conventional long robed sacred figure picture ... and from its own point of view very well painted too. It is very clean, very bright, and very inoffensive...It is essentially trivial in its main conception, and incomplete in its details; nor can one accept from a technical point of view its smooth, slab brushwork as good painting, its thin brightness as good colour or its conventional arrangement as good composition.'[118]

However the plebiscite organized by the *Pall Mall Gazette* named Calderon's painting as the best religious painting at the 1886 Royal Academy Exhibition,[119] and most purchasing policies concentrating on contemporary work generally follow contemporary prejudices. This was a work reflecting late nineteenth-century classicism and idealism appropriate for a gallery which could not afford work by Leighton. A representative acquisition from the period after Rathbone's death in 1895 would be Gotch's *A Pageant of Childhood* bought for £500 in 1899. Contemporary critics noted its stylistic and iconographic affiliations – fifteenth-century Florentine art, late poetic Pre-Raphaelitism, French symbolism of the 1890s, Art Nouveau, feminism, a decorative and formalist emphasis together with the late nineteenth-century British interest in childhood and pageants.[120] Surely all this was worth the £500 which the Gallery paid for the painting. Gotch was an interesting artist starting as a Newlyn School naturalist before specializing in 'imaginative symbolism'.[121] Standards soon declined and the purchase for £300 in 1907 of *The Admonition* by Henry Woods, a late and very weak example of the neo-Venetian School, was far less defensible and specifically condemned by Rutter in 1909.[122] Liverpool's achievement should not however be judged too harshly. Newcastle had no art gallery at all until the Laing Gallery opened in 1904 thanks to a gift of £30,000 from Alexander Laing, who, like Walker, had no interest in art. At that date it did not own a single painting. Hull opened its art gallery in 1900 but by 1903 it only owned four paintings.[123] By these standards Rathbone and Samuelson had done very well indeed.

Between 1884, when the Gallery's first extension was completed, and 1931 the permanent collection had increased from about three hundred to over two thousand items. Dibdin and Quigley frequently complained in the Gallery's annual reports about their increasing difficulties in finding room to display more than a small number of these works and about the work required to re-hang the permanent collection after each Autumn Exhibition. They must have looked enviously at the enormous horseshoe gallery added to the Museum in 1901 as part of the City Council's new technical college. The solution was plainly a second and larger extension. Slum property on the north side of the Gallery was easily acquired, and in 1912 Thomas Bartlett, a bachelor, bequeathed £10,000 specifically for this project together with large gifts to the City's hospitals, university and cathedral. Nearly all the Gallery's serious benefactors were in the alcohol business and he was a wine and spirit merchant.[124] Audley and Bowring each provided a further £10,000 in 1925. In 1933 Lord Wavertree, the third son of Andrew Barclay Walker who had died in 1893 leaving over three million pounds, left £20,000 in his will to the Gallery. However, thanks to other much smaller donations and accumulated interest payments, only a part of Wavertree's Bequest was needed for a huge extension completed in 1933. It eventually cost about £60,000, increased the Gallery's display space by over a half and provided it with a substantially remodelled entrance hall. The Liverpool architect Sir Arnold Thornely (1870-1953), best known for the baroque Port of Liverpool building at the Pierhead and the classical Stormont Parliament Buildings in Belfast, was appropriately modest in his fashionably restrained Beaux-Arts classicism of the period. The layout of the extension which added six large galleries and links between the old and new buildings was straight-forward and the scale in keeping with the existing galleries. Only the Prince George Gallery, the Gallery's largest space with its barrel roof, aimed for grandeur suitable for openings and concerts.[125] Compared with the splendour of Lord Leverhulme's recently completed Lady Lever Art Gallery at Port Sunlight, which was surely a major, although never publicly acknowledged, encouragement for change at the Walker Art Gallery, the extension and remodelled entrance hall were designed for a modest budget. Like the original building the extension was functionally efficient and it maximised gallery space. It also made good use of an irregular, steeply sloping site. The committee and curators after Rathbone may not have mounted progressive Autumn Exhibitions or made splendid acquisitions but the extension galleries, the largest addition to a municipal gallery in the twentieth century, were a considerable achievement. The director also now had a spacious office with an adjacent space for his secretary and administrative staff constructed in one of the original ground floor galleries.

Later generations might have abandoned the Autumn Exhibitions, which by 1931 were already in very sharp decline, and spent Wavertree's money on paintings to hang undisturbed in the existing smaller gallery. Although the exhibitions were discontinued only six years after the completion of the extension, the size alone of the new Walker Art Gallery would always encourage an emphasis on loan exhibitions even at some cost to the permanent collection, and in that sense the decision to concentrate on buildings rather than on works of art was of critical importance.

Chapter 3

The Making of the Modern Walker Art Gallery

The modern Walker Art Gallery was created between 1931 and 1951 by two remarkable but very different men, Vere Cotton (1888-1970) and Frank Lambert (1884-1973). In 1910, after leaving Cambridge, Cotton obtained a job as tutor to the two sons of Hugh Rathbone, a cousin of Philip Rathbone. Hugh Rathbone, a very successful Liverpool grain merchant, was then trying to prevent the total collapse of Rathbone Brothers, the principal and historic Rathbone company, which had played a large part in the growth of Liverpool's trade and commerce in the eighteenth and nineteenth centuries. Their downfall was perhaps the most spectacular event in the 'decline of the liberal plutocracy' – that is the decline of the radical or liberal non-conformist merchant families who had dominated the Gallery and Liverpool in the nineteenth century.[1] Hugh Rathbone's main problem was the reluctance of the grandsons and great grandsons of the company's founders – Philip's nephews and great nephews – to work in the business in the early twentieth century, and he immediately saw that his sons' tutor might do the work which they declined.[2] Thus Cotton joined Rathbone Brothers in 1911 at an annual salary of £100 with a promise of an eventual partnership if he proved satisfactory. Apart from distinguished military service in the First World War he remained with Rathbone Brothers until 1960, as a partner from 1919 and as senior partner from 1939. By 1911 the great firm had declined to become effectively a small private Liverpool bank advising its clients on investment and taxation. However the family was still large and powerful, and in 1922 Cotton married Elfreda Moore, a granddaughter of Philip Rathbone. He did not seek expansion for the bank, and when Bertram (or Larry) Rathbone joined the firm in 1934 he was able to devote less time to it, but it did give him local company directorships and useful contacts among Liverpool's wealthier citizens.[3] His interests lay in Liverpool's major cultural institutions. In 1922 he joined the Liverpool Cathedral Executive Committee, which – not the bishop, dean or chapter – was statutorily responsible for the design and building of the great cathedral. He was their secretary from 1933 until 1961 and wrote the official and very detailed guide to the cathedral. In 1926 he was elected to the Council of Liverpool University. He became the University's Treasurer in 1939, the President of the Council in 1942, Pro-Chancellor in 1948 and Chairman of the Development Committee from 1946 until 1954, the four most important non-academic posts at the University.[4] He travelled extensively throughout his life and had a good knowledge of art galleries around the world.

In 1931 Cotton, then not yet a city councillor, wrote to the *Liverpool Daily Post* condemning the Gallery's permanent collection as 'utterly unworthy of the second city of the Empire'. Recognizing that European masterpieces were now too expensive he proposed the formation of a well-balanced collection of British paintings and sculpture, an objective largely unknown to British art galleries at that time. He wished to 'build up by purchase and gift a really representative collection of the British School with one or two sections specially favoured'. He proposed the appointment of a committee of outside experts as well as of city councillors to assess the quality of the existing permanent collection and to make recommendations for its improvement and expansion. He suggested that some of the least significant existing paintings should be sold. Above all he insisted that the Gallery's new director should be an expert in 'art scholarship and gallery administration', who would be given substantial freedom in the choice of acquisitions.[5] No doubt he was thinking of a director of the calibre of Whitworth Wallis who virtually created the Birmingham Museums and Art Gallery between 1885 and 1927 or of Sydney Cockerell who transformed the Fitzwilliam Museum in Cambridge between 1908 and 1937.[6] Cotton certainly knew and greatly admired Cockerell's work.

Cotton was successful where earlier attempts to reform the Gallery had failed principally because his campaign to reform the Gallery was public and a new director was about to be appointed. There was a very extensive and favourable response to his letter to the *Liverpool Daily Post*, and correspondence in the paper about the failures of the Gallery lasted over a month. The *Daily Post* itself wrote a judicious editorial broadly supporting his campaign.[7] It culminated in a letter sent to the City Council by about eighty leading Liverpool figures stating that the Gallery was 'inadequately fulfilling its purpose' and that there should be 'a more sympathetic and tolerant attitude towards new ideas'.[8] Henry Cole was no more impressed by Cotton in 1931 than he had been by Herbert Rathbone in 1924 and at the official presentation ceremony in December to the retiring director, Arthur Quigley, he referred to 'ill-informed statements with regard to the Gallery on the part of self-constituted critics based for the most part on ignorance of the conditions of public administration'.[9] Quigley himself wrote an official report defending the collection but conceding that work by more progressive artists, identified by him as Augustus John, Tonks, Steer, Conder, Henry Lamb, Duncan Grant, Paul Nash, Epstein and Stanley Spencer, should be bought together with some French impressionist and post-impressionist paintings.[10] Works by all these British artists apart from Lamb and Tonks were indeed acquired over the following twenty-five years. Dibdin, Quigley's predecessor, supported Cole and opposed Cotton's insistence that the director rather than the Arts and Exhibitions Sub-Committee should effectively run the Gallery. He argued that the Sub-Committee could not constitutionally abdicate their responsibility for its management and that there were then no generally recognized British credentials or qualifications in 'art scholarship and gallery administration'.[11] However Dibdin did not appreciate that the new widespread uncertainty over standards of taste and over judgements of quality in art, promoted by the rejection of Victorian and much traditional art by Roger Fry and his associates, encouraged local authority committees and the general public to more readily accept the authority of an expert director.[12]

In retrospect Cotton's judgment on the collection was too harsh but it reflected the accepted fashionable 'advanced' ideas of the 1920s on academic and narrative later Victorian art. His idea of a balanced survey collection had been much discussed in the context of European art at the National Gallery and elsewhere as far back as the nineteenth century, but the idea was largely new to the collecting of British art. Most of the major regional art galleries had begun by buying contemporary British art straight from the artist's easel but some had also bought older work by living artists. As early as 1881 Birmingham City Art Gallery had purchased *Arab Shepherds* painted in 1842 by W.J. Muller (1812-1845) for the enormous sum of £2,730. In 1884 the Walker Art Gallery had acquired Millais's *Isabella* of 1849 (fig. 12) and the following year Manchester City Art Gallery bought Ford Madox Brown's *Work*, begun in 1852, for £400. Manchester continued to buy both contemporary art and the art of the immediate past, especially Pre-Raphaelite and New English Art Club paintings. Birmingham, like the Fitzwilliam Museum, concentrated more strictly on the early Pre-Raphaelites, on William Blake and on a few other late nineteenth- and early twentieth-century British artists. Joseph Chamberlain himself, the great pioneer of local government in Birmingham and beyond, had contributed £105 to the purchase of Muller's *Arab Shepherds* and he strongly opposed the purchase of works by living artists. In 1893 he observed:

> My view is that it is a mistake to use the funds to buy the pictures of living artists unless their position is so absolutely assured as to make the purchase a certain investment...[I fear that the works of living artists] will not hereafter be considered representative and a small collection like ours should, as far as possible, consist of works having real representative value.[13]

The Walker Art Gallery felt constrained, partly for moral reasons, partly for strictly business reasons, to buy paintings by living artists because those artists, by exhibiting their work at the Autumn Exhibitions, created the purchase funds used by the Gallery for acquiring paintings. Manchester, relying on its guaranteed £2,000 annually from its Council, and Birmingham, with generous private sponsorship, emancipated themselves from contemporary art, Birmingham quite rapidly, Manchester much more slowly. It took Liverpool another forty years. Neither Birmingham nor Manchester nor Cambridge however was greatly interested in British art before 1800 although Manchester had bought three paintings by Richard Wilson between 1897 and 1905. The Tate Gallery, which had been officially designated as the National Collection of British Art only in 1919, did not have its own purchase grant, although the Victoria and Albert Museum, founded primarily in order to display exemplary continental art, showed a new interest in historic British art in the early twentieth century.[14] Cotton will of course also have known the hugely successful Lady Lever Art Gallery at Port Sunlight, only about six miles from Liverpool, with its rich but idiosyncratic collection of British late eighteenth- and nineteenth-century art. Purchasing there however had largely ceased in 1925 with the death of its founder, Lord Leverhulme, and its holdings of British art reflect his enthusiasms rather than a balanced overview. The Walker Art Gallery was by 1927 well aware of its lack of historic British art. The unsigned preface to the catalogue of the permanent collection of that date observed: 'There are gaps yet to be filled – particularly by examples of the eighteenth and nineteenth centuries, and the Committee will welcome gifts of worthy examples of the periods named to help in making good these deficiencies.'[15]

In fact the Gallery had been buying opportunistically but not very successfully a few inexpensive historic paintings from local sources. *Lady and Child*, attributed to Kneller but now catalogued as an early eighteenth-century British School portrait, was bought in 1879 for £35. Two paintings attributed to Constable, two to William Collins and two to Landseer had been purchased in 1881. Only the two sensitive studies by Landseer have regularly been on public display in recent times. In 1925 this policy of occasional casual purchases reached a disastrous climax with the acquisition from a leading Liverpool dealer of a *Portrait of a Lady*, thought possibly to be by Raeburn but in fact probably recently painted, for the unusually large sum of £315.[16] Even the press recognised the over-optimism of the attribution and its acquisition seriously damaged the Gallery's reputation. Cotton's originality lay less in his rejection of contemporary art, in which he was merely bringing the Gallery in line with general practice outside Liverpool, but far more in his desire for a representative survey of British art from the Tudors to the present day.

Frank Lambert was appointed director in 1931. At £800 his salary was a considerable improvement on the £650 which he had been earning as director of the Leeds City Art Gallery.[17] However the short list for the post only included Sydney Davison, the curator of the Lady Lever Art Gallery, G.P. Dudley Wallis, curator of the Whitworth Art Gallery in Manchester and Lambert himself.[18] Other possible candidates for the post were probably deterred by the huge workload involved in the administration of the Autumn

Exhibitions. John Rothenstein, later a distinguished director of the Tate Gallery, apparently applied but was rejected at a preliminary interview at which he remembered having being unable to utter a word.[19] Lambert, a career museum curator deeply immersed in the procedures of English local government, was the first professional director or curator at the Gallery. Previously the Gallery had relied on local artists, critics and historians. In 1908, shortly after leaving Cambridge, he had joined the staff of the Guildhall Museum in London and he remained there, apart from military service during the First World War, until 1924. He directed important excavations of Roman material at the old General Post Office and of significant medieval and post-medieval objects at Moorfields, many of which are now in the Museum of London. He described and analyzed these discoveries in various articles published in scholarly journals including *Archaeologia*, and he could be described as London's first professional archaeologist.[20] The London Museum, founded in 1912 with substantial funding from central government, soon became London's leading archaeological museum, and it was probably for this reason that Lambert left the Guildhall Museum to become curator of the Stoke-on-Trent Museum and Art Gallery. There he found a small collection of paintings which inspired a new interest in fine art. In 1925 he clashed sharply with Dibdin at the Exeter meeting of the Museums Association. In his speech there Dibdin, in his most reactionary mood, had denounced the Tate Gallery for hanging paintings by members of 'that so-called advanced clique associated with the New English Art Club and the Slade School.' Lambert was the only member of the audience to challenge Dibdin, asserting that this 'clique' was painting masterpieces which if not bought now would be unaffordable fifty or a hundred years later.[21] Between 1927 and 1931 he was director of the Leeds City Art Gallery, where again he was the first director with previous museum experience. Here his assistant was the remarkable Ernest Musgrave, whom he promoted. Rothenstein, Lambert's successor at Leeds, described Musgrave as 'resourceful, imperturbable, conscientious, courteous and above all dedicated.' In 1946 Musgrave became a very successful director at Leeds and was probably the only British art gallery director to have begun his career as a uniformed warder. He always remained a very close friend of Lambert and of Lambert's wife, who was working at Leeds City Art Gallery when Lambert met her.[22] Lambert had begun his career as an archaeologist; he had studied the geology of the Isle of Wight in some depth; at Stoke he had been concerned primarily with ceramics; only at the age of 43 had he turned to fine art exclusively. He was clearly a successful and experienced administrator with a wide knowledge of history and art rather than an academic specialist and polemicist like Rothenstein, who had taught art history at American universities and had a doctorate in the history of British art from London University. Indeed Rothenstein characteristically blamed him for leaving important British historic and old master paintings in the cellars at Leeds and for hanging in their place trivial Victorian anecdotal pictures. On his arrival in Leeds in 1932 Rothenstein described the Gallery as 'utter dereliction' and insisted on the immediate redecoration of every room.[23] This criticism was hardly fair as Lambert disliked most Victorian narrative paintings as much as Rothenstein did, and he had asserted his modernist affiliations by exhibiting Epstein's *Genesis* very prominently in 1931.[24] He had also become an extension lecturer at Leeds University and sought to engage the visitor at the Gallery with public talks, as he was to do at Liverpool. He never had Rothenstein's knowledge or contacts, but at Liverpool he had the necessary perception and education to select paintings within parameters established by Cotton and was sufficiently efficient, experienced, diligent and tactful to steer the Gallery and its staff in the entirely new direction specified by Cotton, while still achieving his personal programme. For his part Cotton insisted that the director, not the chairman and certainly not the Committee, must run the Gallery.

> Not the least important duty of the Chairman is to see that the Director's authority is upheld...It should be axiomatic that no purchase or gift or bequest, on which the Director reports adversely, should be accepted by the Committee, and conversely that no purchase which he emphatically recommends should be turned down by it.[25]

This was important evidence that power over the Gallery was shifting decisively away from the Committee and towards the director. The first of Lambert's two presidential addresses to the Museums Association of 1947 and 1948 contained a highly intelligent account of the development and philosophy of modern art marred only by some prejudice against Victorian art, while the second was more practical and controversial. In deploring excessive specialization among curators, in demanding more concern for display rather than acquisition and in favouring the placing of most paintings, except masterpieces, among the decorative arts of their periods, it anticipated many later twentieth-century ideas.[26] Mixing the fine and decorative arts, as Leverhulme had done at Port Sunlight, was then seen as an effective way of capturing the imagination of the visitor which was of real concern for Lambert.

Cotton himself joined the City Council shortly after the publication of his letter of 1931. He became a member of the Libraries, Museums and Arts Committee in 1934 and its chairman in 1939. Although Cole remained as chairman until 1939 Cotton was sufficiently influential to take 'the leading part in carrying out the reforms which he proposed', as Lambert himself put it.[27] Similarly in his obituary of Cotton a later director, Hugh Scrutton, wrote of these reforms: 'Such things take time and the efforts of many people but it is right to give Colonel Cotton the place of honour in the long campaign.' Although Cotton ceased to be chairman of the Committee and a member of the City Council in 1955 he remained active as a co-opted member on the Committee, chairing a meeting of the Mayor Bequest Selection Committee, at which two sculptures were acquired by the Gallery, only a month before he died in 1970.[28]

In 1929 the Council, recognizing that the profits from the Autumn Exhibition were now completely inadequate to provide picture purchase grants for the Gallery, established for the first time a modest annual grant of £750 for this purpose, and in 1933 about £14,400 from Lord Wavertree's bequest formed an additional fund for the acquisition of works of art. Wavertree also gave the Gallery some notable paintings by local artists, three portraits probably of the Collinson family by the young Romney and some racing pictures including *The Start of the St Buryan Races, Cornwall*, an early work by Munnings. The annual purchase grant fluctuated downwards during the economic depression of the 1930s and the Second World War, but stabilized at £1,000 between 1945 and 1951. With the six new galleries built between 1931 and 1933 Cotton and Lambert had the space, the money and the commitment to form their new permanent collection of the best available historic British art. With the new galleries completed Lambert made the first serious attempt in the Gallery's history to hang the permanent collection chronologically, clearly demonstrating the gaps identified by Cotton. Manchester and Birmingham City Art Galleries had achieved chronological arrangements of their collections in 1898 and 1913 respectively.[29]

Cotton and Lambert did not intend to abandon contemporary art entirely but their purchases of important twentieth-century paintings concentrated on earlier works with well-established status and historical importance. Sickert's *Old Bedford* bought in 1945 and his *Bathers, Dieppe* bought in 1935 had been painted 52 and 33 years before their acquisition. Steer's *The Wye at Chepstow* was purchased in 1936 but painted in 1905, and his *Corfe Castle and the Isle of Purbeck* of 1908 was acquired in 1935. Gilman's *Mrs Mounter* (fig. 17), bought in 1945, and his *Interior with Flowers* were both 27 years old when bought, while Bevan's *Under the Hammer* and Gore's *The Garden, Garth House* had been painted 19 and 41 years before their acquisition. Conder's *Newquay* of about 1906 was purchased in 1939 and Mark Fisher's *Harlow Mill* of 1912 was bought in 1939. Even Lowry's *Fever Van*, bought in 1943, had been painted in 1935. For acquisition purposes modernity meant mainly New English Art Club and Camden Town paintings belonging stylistically to the early twentieth century. Lambert preferred to build up a distinguished group of pictures which well convey to the visitor the achievements of British artists in the early twentieth century rather than to attempt to acquire more advanced and progressive work for which there was no political support, probably not even from his chairman. Lambert's favourite painting was Gilman's *Mrs Mounter* – for him a 'masterpiece of modern portraiture' – perhaps because it both celebrates a very English housekeeper with a large brown earthenware teapot and also shows the influence of French post-impressionism at its most creative.[30] Buying paintings with established reputations was not cheap. *Mrs Mounter* cost £550, the two works by Sickert £1,600 together and Steer's *Wye at Chepstow* £650 towards which the National Art-Collections Fund made a contribution of £100. This was one of its first substantial grants to the Gallery and evidence perhaps that it had forgotten the Gallery's refusal to accept Sickert's *The Pork Pie Hat* of 1898 (Johannesburg Art Gallery) from it as a gift in 1913.[31] Lambert may have remembered his observation of 1925 that masterpieces by members of the New English Art Club would be unaffordable fifty years after they were painted.[32] In 1936 he wrote a very lucid and sympathetic article on impressionism and its very different impact on Steer and Sickert.[33] Only Lowry's nearly new *Fever Van* was inexpensive at £31.50 with copyright. The Contemporary Art Society's gifts of Ginner's *Le Quai Ensoleillé, Dieppe* in 1950, Spencer's *Villas at Cookham* in 1938 and Paul Nash's *Landscape of the Moon's Last Phase* in 1944 greatly contributed to Lambert's ambition to represent leading British artists of his time even if on occasion with modest works.

Lambert and Cotton could not abandon the old tradition of buying new paintings from the Autumn Exhibitions and elsewhere, although Cotton would probably have liked to do so. He had never believed that art galleries should be patrons of art and denounced, like Joseph Chamberlain fifty years earlier, the practice of buying paintings straight from the artist's easel.[34] He observed in 1951: 'during the 1930s some important acquisitions had been made but the Committee were still devoting much of their resources to acquiring pictures straight from the artist's easel'.[35] These included Augustus John's *Two Jamaican Girls* and his *Scottish Canadian Soldier*, a popular subject in 1940. Sickert's *Summer Lightning*, a painting inspired by Victorian illustration, was bought from the artist in 1932. Manchester City Art Gallery had bought Sickert's disturbingly realist *Mamma mia Poveretta* in 1911 and the Atkinson Art Gallery in Southport had purchased his *Theatre of the Young Artists, Dieppe* in 1923, but *Summer Lightning* was the first work by Sickert to enter the Walker Art Gallery. Other works bought 'straight from the artist's easel' were Duncan Grant's *Farm in Sussex*, Lucien Pissarro's *Cerisiers en Fleur* and Ethel Walker's *Spanish Gesture*. John's two paintings were expensive at £450 each. The new fashionable hard-edged realism was represented by Fleetwood-Walker's *Amity*, James Cowie's *Intermission*, Algernon Newton's *Townscape*, Richard Eurich's *Ship Inn*, McIntosh Patrick's *Springtime in Eskdale* and Laura Knight's *Spring in St John's Wood*. Cowie's *Intermission* with its striking use of black was perhaps his masterpiece and McIntosh Patrick's painting was and remains enormously popular. Laura

Knight's street scene cost £400, McIntosh Patrick's landscape £225, Newton's townscape £200 and Lucien Pissarro's cherry trees £136.50. A similar work by Pissarro's father would have been priced at over ten times that amount. The rather intense near life-size groups by Cowie and Fleetwood-Walker, a Birmingham artist, seem inexpensive at £120 and £150. From the 1933 Autumn Exhibition Lambert bought *Sonia*, the first of three bronze busts he was to acquire by Epstein, the artist who had been publicly ridiculed by Lord Wavertree in 1926. He never really gave serious consideration to modern sculpture with the exception of works by Epstein.

Although Cotton may have disapproved of these acquisitions they demonstrated higher standards in the purchase of contemporary art than the Gallery had displayed since Rathbone's death. Despite some hints of surrealism none of these paintings were 'advanced' or 'progressive' works when they were bought between 1932 and 1951. In 1934 Lambert had, like Quigley a few years earlier, promoted the familiar idea that buying cheap avant-garde art provided better value for money than purchasing more generally accepted work because progressive artists often became well-known and expensive in time.[36] Cotton however never seems to have accepted this idea, and in practice both men were cautious in implementing this dangerous theory which became standard practice in many museums of modern art later in the century greatly inflating their reserve collections. The Walker Art Gallery and other British galleries have often been blamed for not acquiring impressionist, post-impressionist or even cubist, surrealist or futurist paintings in these early years. However at the 1927 Autumn Exhibition the paintings by Renoir and Monet at £4,250 and £3,000 were by far the most expensive works on display and well beyond the Gallery's resources, while in the 1930s Samuel Courtauld was paying between £800 and £8,000 each for his impressionist and post-impressionist works. In 1936 Lambert himself described these paintings as only affordable by millionaires, while in 1947 he noted that Picasso was 'already both fashionable and exceedingly expensive.'[37] Cheaper paintings by lesser artists were of course available but Lambert and Cotton also needed the support of their own Committee, which only approved the purchase of Sickert's *Old Bedford*, very expensive at £1,000 in 1947, by seven votes to six.[38] In the City Council itself even Gilman's beautiful and rather traditional *Interior with Flowers* aroused 'sharp controversy' in 1945.[39] Manchester and Leeds City Art Galleries bought much more progressive or 'advanced' art than the Walker Art Gallery in these years. Under Philip Hendy between 1934 and 1945 Leeds bought surrealist paintings by Sutherland and Wadsworth, primitivist works by Christopher Wood and abstract sculptures by Henry Moore and Barbara Hepworth, both born in Yorkshire. In 1947 and 1948 Manchester City Art Gallery bought two largely abstract paintings by Ben Nicholson which would have certainly met concerted opposition among Liverpool councillors many years later.

There was however one serious omission in Cotton and Lambert's purchases of modern art. In 1909 Chaloner Dowdall, the retiring Lord Mayor of Liverpool and a persistent critic of the Gallery's conservative acquisitions policy, asked his friend Augustus John to paint the customary official mayoral portrait commissioned each year by members of the City Council. The fee was £100. John included in his full-length life-size portrait the diminutive figure of the mayor's footman dressed as a ceremonial sword-bearer and brandishing a huge sword.[40] Many visitors and critics at the 1909 Autumn Exhibition saw John's magnificent portrait (probably rightly) as an attempt to ridicule civic dignity, and when Dowdall sold the portrait in 1918 the Gallery did not try to buy it. John was now famous and the price secured by Dowdall, £1,450, was then far beyond its resources. The purchaser, E.P. Warren, died in 1928 and the portrait was exhibited at the small 1932 Autumn Exhibition, where it must have dominated the displays. The Gallery could have bought it at any time until 1938 when the National Gallery of Victoria at Melbourne purchased it for £2,400.[41] This amount was however very much more than Cotton and Lambert ever paid for a modern painting, and they rarely used the Wavertree Bequest for modern art.[42] Furthermore the purchase would have both undermined their policy of assembling a representative collection of British art and aroused the hostility of traditionalist members of the City Council. In 1954 the Gallery contributed towards the costs of bringing the portrait back to England for the Augustus John exhibition at the Royal Academy, and it was also displayed separately at the Gallery.[43] The Conservatives were still in power in Liverpool and Cotton was still the Gallery's chairman, but perhaps civic pride was at last no longer an issue.

In their ambition to build up a more representative coverage of pre-Victorian British art Lambert and Cotton acquired older British paintings with considerable success – although inevitably at higher prices than contemporary art even after the financial slump of 1929. When the Gallery reopened in 1952 it presented an impressive survey of British art from the Tudors through to the present. There were gaps but no other regional gallery could offer such a convincing coverage. Given the modesty of the Gallery's resources many of the great names were inevitably missing and some purchases have not stood the test of time. It would be hard to find a more appropriate work to launch the modern English school than the portrait of the authoritarian Henry VIII, based on Holbein's lost Whitehall picture, which the Gallery bought in 1943. The identity of the sitter and the period of British history are immediately recognisable by virtually every visitor, although at £3,360 the portrait was expensive. Thanks to E. Peter Jones who gave in the same year *Queen Elizabeth: the Pelican Portrait* by Nicholas Hilliard, or by an artist very close to him, the collection has one of the great Elizabethan portraits. The seventeenth- century coverage is rather thin with just three important pictures, However one of the three works is a lively full-length late portrait of *Charles II* painted 'ad vivum'(or from the life) by Kneller, bought in 1952, which establishes another clear historical landmark in the survey. Scrutton strengthened it in his early years most notably with William Dobson's *The Executioner with the Head of John the Baptist* after Mattias Stom which has been described as 'the only English Caravaggesque picture known.'[44]

Enthusiasm for eighteenth-century British art had swept Britain and America in the 1880s and the fashion proved remarkably resilient. With outstanding paintings by Wright of Derby, Fuseli and Stubbs, subject painting of this period was already well covered and Lambert wisely built on this strength. He was right to describe Richard Wilson's *Snowdon from Llyn Nantlle* (fig. 8), bought in 1935 for only £950, as 'one of the masterpieces of its artist and its kind, almost Chinese in the monumental simplicity of its design,' and he was intensely proud of it although he remembered Cotton describing it as rather boring.[45] The gift of Wilson's *Valley of the Mawddach and Cader Idris* by James and Robert Rankin in 1937 added a second outstanding landscape by this artist. Four more paintings by Stubbs were acquired. These included a version of his rather poignant *A Monkey*, reworked in 1799 and bought in 1950, together with the characteristic *Molly Longlegs* (fig. 7) and *Gnawpost and two other colts* given by Lewis's Ltd in 1951 thanks to the intervention of their chairman, Lord Woolton.[46] Stubbs might have been even better represented if James Cross, a Liverpool alderman, had offered *Haymakers* and *Reapers* (Tate Gallery) to the Council at a more modest mark up on the £20 he had paid for them in North Wales in 1934, but his proposed profit was too great to be acceptable to his fellow councillors. Until the Tate Gallery bought paintings by Stubbs extensively in the 1960s and 1970s the Liverpool group of his work was unequalled in any other British Gallery.

Even modest eighteenth-century portraits remained highly priced in the 1930s and 1940s, and Cotton and Lambert's purchases did not always give particularly good value for their limited resources. They saved the Council's annual grant until in 1933 it had reached £3,000 and then spent more than half of it on Raeburn's *Mrs Anne Graham*, a 'tender and sensitive portrait of an elderly woman' in Lambert's words which had been part of the distinguished collection of the Liverpool chemical industrialist Gaskell Holbrook II (1846-1919) and had been lent by Agnew's to the 1933 Autumn Exhibition.[47] In 1940, rather following the fashion of the time but with justification from the artist's Lancashire connections, they acquired *Mr and Mrs William Atherton* by Arthur Devis, a characteristic conversation piece of the 1740s. This modestly dressed middle-class Preston couple contrasts strikingly with Zoffany's well known rather flashy *Family of Sir William Young*, sporting van Dyck fancy dress, which had been included by its owner Sir Philip Sassoon in his very influential *English Conversation Pieces* exhibition of 1930. In 1937 it cost £3,500, less than half its price at Christie's in 1928. This was the same price paid by the Gallery for Hogarth's *Garrick as Richard III* in 1956 and for Derain's *L'Italienne* in 1959. Not until 1960 with Rubens's *Virgin and Child with St Elizabeth and the Child Baptist* (fig. 4) did the Gallery ever pay more for a work of art. Representative portraits by Ramsay, Lawrence and Hoppner were added and in 1950 the *Liverpool Daily Post and Echo* presented a portrait by Gainsborough of Sir Robert Clayton characteristic of the work of the artist's Bath period. Inevitably buying with inadequate resources involved some speculative purchases with doubtful attributions. A portrait of Lord Loughborough is no longer thought to be by Reynolds but rather by Mather Brown, and a *Card Party* attributed to Hogarth is now catalogued as a copy after Gawen Hamilton. The absence of any oil paintings by Turner was remedied with gifts from F. J. Nettlefold in 1948 of his early *Linlithgow Palace* and from Lady Holt in 1946 of a late *Landscape*. A modest *Seashore with fisherman near a boat* by Constable was purchased in 1949 to represent the other great landscapist of the early nineteenth century. In the early years of Scrutton's directorship, while Cotton was still a powerful figure at the Gallery, the policy of developing a survey collection of British art continued. Acquisitions in 1956 included the fascinating unattributed *Portrait of George Delves and a female companion* dated 1577, once at the Delves family home, Doddington Hall in Cheshire. This was an opportunist purchase from a Chester bookseller which had to wait nearly forty years for the necessary conservation to put it into an exhibitable state. There were also Cornelius Johnson's *Portrait of a Lady* of 1633 and Hogarth's masterpiece *Garrick as Richard III*. Hogarth's *Portrait of a Lady* and Reynolds's *Miss Elizabeth Ingram* were bought in 1964. After 1964 British picture prices began to rise steeply under the impact of Paul Mellon's purchases and Scrutton switched resources elsewhere in particular to the Impressionists and Post-Impressionists.

Two distinct tastes are perhaps discernible in these acquisitions. It seems that Lambert had a fairly austere eye which admired carefully composed and thoughtfully painted pictures whether old or new, while Cotton was probably more concerned with the social and historical context of a work and preferred more flamboyant paintings. Their partnership imposed a much needed discipline on the collection and their ambition of presenting a survey of British art from Tudor times to their own made the collection far more intelligible and enjoyable for the visitor with little knowledge of British art history. Unfortunately, with no physical expansion of space at the Gallery since the 1931-1933 extension galleries, the clarity of their vision became rather obscured by the very crowded picture arrangement originated in the 1970s in order to display a substantial proportion of the collection. The eighteenth-century and earlier purchases were generally funded from the Wavertree Bequest reflecting the donor's well known distaste for modernism in any form.

Lambert and Cotton both felt that there was more than enough Victorian and Edwardian art in the Gallery, and additions were entirely by bequests or gift except for the purchase of works by Walter Crane and Robert Anning Bell. Both artists had close links with Liverpool. However as soon as Cotton became chairman of the Libraries, Museums and Arts Committee in 1939 he and Lambert started to accumulate vast holdings of material by the great Victorian designer and sculptor Alfred Stevens, who was given his own gallery in the reopened Walker Art Gallery of 1951. Presumably Stevens's work, together perhaps with portraiture, belonged to the 'one or two sections' to be 'specially favoured' within the proposed representative collection of British art. Cotton and Lambert were probably inspired by enthusiasm at the Tate Gallery and at the Victoria and Albert Museum for this artist, whose work was thought to reflect Italian Renaissance principles rather than the art of his own time. The huge marble saloon mantelpiece together with the enormous dining room doors and buffet from Dorchester House in London were bought following the demolition of the house in 1929, although none of this material went on display at the Gallery until the 1970s. After the war they rescued the decorative wall and ceiling work from Deysbrook House in the Liverpool suburbs on the demolition of that house in 1946. Lambert also spent much time during the war buying smaller sculptures, drawings and paintings by Stevens from elusive private collectors at rather inflated prices.[48] The leading expert on Stevens, K.R. Towndrow, commented that the Gallery possessed no original work by Stevens in 1939, but that by 1951 it had 'one of the most important and representative groups of Stevens material in the country.'[49]

Following the example of his predecessors Lambert bought a few paintings of Liverpool interest. *Liverpool Town Hall in 1806*, which records the illuminations to mark the visit of the Prince Regent and the Duke of Gloucester to the town, and *A Sailing Ship in the Mersey* of 1811, were both by Robert Salmon, a very precise almost biedermeier marine artist from Whitehaven who worked in Liverpool and Boston, Massachusetts. They suited Lambert's taste for carefully composed pictures. He was particularly pleased with Huggins's *Portrait of a Man* of 1842 which he purchased from a pawnbroker near the Gallery for £20 in 1945. Mrs Roscoe's bequest in 1950 of a group of portraits and other material connected with William Roscoe included Lawrence's *Thomas William Coke of Holkham* and an evocative portrait by Ibbetson of Hugh Mulligan, the Liverpool engraver and anti-slavery poet, with a clay pipe. Work by living local artists, bought on a very modest scale, was well represented by *The Enemy Raid, May 3rd 1941* by George Grainger Smith. Substantial gifts could not be expected during the economic depression of the 1930s and the Second World War, but with the new concern for the permanent collection shown by Cotton and Lambert the situation soon greatly improved. Cotton was extremely active during the early 1950s in persuading local businesses to buy pictures chosen by the Gallery and then to present them to the Gallery. The Royal Insurance Company, Lewis's, the *Daily Post* and *Echo*, Owen Owen and the P. H. Holt Trust were among the companies and charities persuaded to help in this way.

In 1944 Emma Holt bequeathed to the city the collection of British and French art formed by her father, George Holt, together with Sudley, the family's house in the Liverpool suburbs, its grounds of about thirty acres and £20,000 for their maintenance.[50] The Holts, like the Rathbones, were very successful Liverpool Unitarian and Liberal ship owners and merchants, and their companies had worked together very closely in the 1860s and 1870s.[51] Holt himself developed Liverpool's trade with Brazil on a considerable scale. His collection was not only rich in nineteenth-century British and French paintings, including two of Turner's greatest late works, *Schloss Rosenau* (fig. 14) and *The Wreck Buoy*, but, unlike many other similar collections formed by Liverpool merchants, it also included notable late eighteenth-century portraits by Reynolds, Gainsborough, Romney and Raeburn. Holt spent around £51,000 on his art collection between about 1868 and his death in 1896. Generally he preferred artists of the generation before his own, but he was an important patron of J.M. Strudwick in the early 1890s. He bought most of his paintings from Agnew's and other dealers rather than from the Liverpool Autumn Exhibitions. The bequest of this collection certainly transformed the Gallery's holdings of British art, and, with its sixty notable British paintings dating from between 1750 and 1870, it effectively rescued Cotton's scheme for a representative collection of British art. For the first time the Gallery owned paintings by Opie, Bonington, Mulready, Callcott, Dyce, G.H. Mason, Patrick Nasmyth and others. Indeed some of the best paintings from the bequest were temporarily brought from Sudley into the Gallery to reinforce its early British holdings during the reopening celebrations of 1951. In scope, size and cost George Holt's collection was very similar to that formed by the Liverpool banker John Naylor who spent about £61,000 on his collection between the 1840s and his death in 1889. There however the similarity between the two men ends. Naylor spent a further £285,000 on his country house and grounds near Welshpool and lived there as a leisured country gentleman.[52] Holt lived in his fairly modest Liverpool suburban villa with simple utilitarian furniture, working long hours every day in his office before retiring at the age of seventy. He was probably the single greatest benefactor of Liverpool University giving a total of about £29,000. He was offered the chairmanship of the Arts and Exhibitions Sub-Committee on Philip Rathbone's death in 1895 – clearly a rather transparent attempt by the Sub-Committee to persuade him to leave the collection to the Walker Art Gallery. He refused the post and bequeathed the collection to his only child, Emma. She never married and the absence of heirs may in part explain her splendid gift. The Gallery left the collection at Sudley, the family home, thus providing the only surviving example in north-west England of a Victorian merchant's art collection in its original setting.[53] The collection was accompanied by the dealers' bills and other documentation which allows the development of Holt's taste and preferences to be traced and the economics of collecting to be studied in detail. Regrettably no attempt was made to secure any of the original furnishings when they were sold. This would have prevented later not entirely successful attempts to refurnish the house.

Thanks to Cotton's diplomacy the unsatisfactory situation in which the most important European paintings in the Gallery were on long-term loan was finally resolved. In 1948 the Liverpool Royal Institution presented to the Gallery William Roscoe's collection and its other old master paintings.[54] Cotton as Pro-Chancellor of Liverpool University, which had taken over the Institution, played the leading role, and the gift was immensely significant for the reputation and strength of the permanent collection.[55] For the Gallery, still closed to the public after the war, these 'years of austerity' were in fact its golden years. Never before, and certainly never since, has an English municipal art gallery received such magnificent gifts as during the Cotton years.

Meanwhile paintings returned to the Gallery from Avening Court in Gloucestershire, from Galltfaenan in Denbighshire, and from Croxteth Hall and Knowsley Hall in Lancashire, where they had been sent for safety during the war. The best paintings acquired between 1935 and 1945 went immediately to a special exhibition of them at the National Gallery, which then toured Britain, greatly improving the Walker Art Gallery's reputation and emphasizing its new policies under Cotton and Lambert.[56] The Ministry of Food, which had taken over the Gallery on the outbreak of war in 1939, did not finally vacate the Gallery until September 1950. The first opportunity for the display of the Gallery's pictures therefore occurred in the suburbs at Sudley which was opened to the public in April 1949. Floors were strengthened, a small public library was installed, some objects from the bombed Liverpool Museum were included and some paintings from the Gallery's historic collections were displayed alongside the main attraction, George Holt's superb pictures. In the first six months there were nearly 40,000 visitors. Later developments at Sudley during the 1970s included the display there of a group of Holt family portraits given by Anne Holt in 1974 and of much of the Gallery's collection of nineteenth- and early twentieth-century sculpture, especially the smaller works. A modest loan exhibition programme also contributed to the popularity of this important neoclassical villa situated in Liverpool's most prosperous suburb.

During the summer of 1949 Cotton and Lambert, together with the director of the Museum and the city architect, visited twenty-four museums and galleries in Sweden, Denmark and Holland within a fortnight, inspecting them all 'literally from cellar to roof' for ideas for the refurbishment and re-display at the Walker Art Gallery. The City Council's Finance Committee twice rejected their application for the necessary expenses but finally relented.[57] Lambert had already spent three weeks in Sweden for the same purpose in 1946.[58] They observed that especially in Sweden museums and galleries were principally intended for research and higher education, not for 'sight seeing', and that all the staff even at the smaller institutions, where budgets were much more generous than in Britain, had high academic qualifications. Lecture rooms, libraries, archives and slide collections were widespread. Art galleries needed a conservation and a photographic studio. Air conditioning was very desirable but expensive. Temporary exhibitions were not allowed to encroach on space used for the permanent collection. Wall coverings were generally light in colour. Artificial and natural lighting were studied in detail and the problems of roof lighting discussed.[59] A Sub-Committee was appointed to consider their report and make formal recommendations, which were accepted by the Council in January 1950. The Ministry of Food had left the building in a deplorable state of disrepair and about £31,500 was required for the work involved.

Previously all the Gallery's building costs had been met by private benefactors while the permanent collection itself had been almost entirely assembled from gifts, public subscriptions and the profits from the Autumn Exhibitions. Very little could now be recovered from the government in the form of dilapidations as the Gallery had not technically been requisitioned but had been lent to the government by the Council in a gesture of patriotic solidarity in September 1939. Cotton had conciliated the Labour opposition in the Council by making the re-opening a part of the celebrations for the Festival of Britain of 1951, a favourite project of the Labour government, on which large sums were spent by the Liverpool City Council.[60] However in Liverpool elements of the Labour party were still unhappy. At the Council meeting in which Cotton asked for confirmation of the expenditure the flamboyant local Labour Member of Parliament Bessie Braddock protested that the money should have been spent on social housing. The Tory councillors accused her of seeking political advantage from cultural issues and she called one of them a liar. The mayor ordered her removal from the council chamber and the police eventually had to escort her out. Her husband John Braddock, who had been a member of the Libraries, Museums and Arts Committee for a considerable period and was now leader of the Liverpool Labour Party, felt bound to support her. He commented: 'This was a vast expenditure to make the Art Gallery tenable again. If the labour and materials could be used to make habitable some slum houses they had no right to spend the money'.[61] In practice Labour in Liverpool supported the Gallery at least as generously as the Conservatives, but their social consciences always made their councillors hesitant. The Braddocks had probably never forgotten the 'invasion' of the Gallery in 1921 by the National Unemployed Workers' Committee, for which John Braddock, one of the organizers although not one of the participants, had been prosecuted. The demonstrators in 1921were primarily seeking publicity for their cause and do not seem to have had any objection to the Gallery itself, except perhaps as a public institution principally used by the middle and upper classes.[62]

The necessary permission was obtained with some difficulty from the Ministry of Health to proceed with the work on the Gallery. Structural work cost £18,300; painting and decorating amounted to £5,700; new furniture and lighting came to about £7,500.[63] These were very large sums in the age of austerity when art galleries were a very low priority. The entrance hall was re-planned to include comfortable chairs and a bookstall. Two 'rest rooms' were furnished for tired visitors. A sculpture landing was created above the entrance hall with new windows providing some side lighting as well as the more usual overhead lighting. The new windows, cut at Lambert's suggestion, may not have suited the neoclassical austerity of the portico, but they made the landing a much more congenial space, and the city architect felt that the views from them towards St George's Hall were adequate compensation.[64] Lay lights (or glass ceilings) were installed throughout the eleven galleries of the original building, providing even and more subdued daylight illumination directed on to the paintings as well as some protection for the paintings from rapid changes in temperature and humidity. They reduced the volume of space to be heated and softened the rather institutional look of the rooms. The galleries in the extension of 1931-1933 were adapted to form a temporary exhibition suite. New and effective specially designed artificial neon lighting, concealed in long rectangular reflectors hung from the ceilings, was installed throughout the Gallery. Radiators were extensively re-sited. A large gallery was converted into a photographic and restoration studio and provided with the necessary fittings and equipment. Most of the Gallery was re-decorated with light colour schemes appropriate to the paintings in each room, a plum-coloured paint for the eighteenth-century pictures and grey-green for the modern works. Some galleries had slightly patterned carpets.[65] Special display arrangements were made for the drawings, furniture, paintings and sculpture by Alfred Stevens. Overall the changes, much indebted to Scandinavian taste, were modest and aimed at making the galleries seem friendly.

Gallery publications were taken very seriously. As well as a good range of postcards, a general guide and pamphlets about aspects of the collection, there was a series of *Walker Art Gallery Picture Books* each containing twenty reproductions of different types of paintings. A large ground-floor gallery was converted into a lavish lecture hall with new seating and stage, with sophisticated projection apparatus in a separate high-level room and with a new pulpit for the lecturer. A later generation would have installed a café rather than a lecture hall but this was the great age of the art-history lecture illustrated by slides. Before the war Roger Fry had given two-hour lectures to paying audiences of over 2,000 in London.[66] Now celebrities such as Kenneth Clark and John Rothenstein could lecture in the new hall at the Walker Art Gallery. Sheila Somers, appointed as Deputy Keeper and Lecturer in 1955, was an excellent speaker combining popular appeal with academic weight, and she attracted large audiences.[67] Through her the new generation of art historians from the Courtauld Institute, Margaret Whinney, John White, Michael Kitson, Michael Jaffé, Peter and Linda Murray and others came up from London to give lectures. Between 1954 and 1960 there were regular series of lectures providing a chronological survey of European art from the Renaissance to the twentieth century organised in collaboration with Liverpool University and given partly by Gallery staff and partly by distinguished visiting lecturers. Attendances were very high at first but had fallen so considerably by 1960 that the project was abandoned. The lecture hall was increasingly used by outsiders, although Walker Art Gallery curators were still giving art history lectures there in the 1970s, often in association with Liverpool University, and the Gallery's Education Department used it for formal talks and teacher conferences until 1988. Television of course destroyed the public art-history lecture but the lecture hall does emphasize the Gallery's post-war high academic seriousness after the social emphasis of the pre-war Autumn Exhibitions. There was a mission to instruct as well as to amuse.

All the design and building work at the Gallery was substantially complete by March 1951, that is in less than two years after Cotton's and Lambert's exploratory visit to the continental galleries and only seven months after the final departure of the Ministry of Food. In any circumstances this would be a notable success for an ambitious and elaborate project controlled by a local authority committee, for whom bureaucratic protocol rather than art is generally the priority. In the prevailing post-war conditions of rationing, shortages, regulation and inflation it was an amazing achievement, reflecting perhaps the new optimism of the Festival of Britain and of a new belief in scientific and artistic progress. The principles of Cotton and Lambert's arrangement of the Gallery's works of art remained largely unchanged until 1988, although some watercolour displays were removed while the rooms devoted to Alfred Stevens, to Liverpool artists and to the Walter Stone collection of paintings by sporting artists were dismantled with the pictures integrated into the general chronological sequence. The original nineteenth-century part of the Gallery, which the visitor enters first, contained the permanent collection displayed broadly chronologically but with some exceptions to allow for associations between particular groups of works of art and to allow large paintings to be shown in large rooms and small paintings in small rooms. The large extension of 1931-1933 contained space for loan exhibitions and exhibitions from the Gallery's reserve collections together with rooms for restoration, photography and Museum collection storage. The huge annual autumn exhibitions no longer disrupted the hanging of the permanent collection, now greatly improved by the splendid acquisitions of 1939-1951, which were all now on display in Liverpool for the first time. Alderman Ernest Cookson, the acting chairman of the Libraries, Museums and Arts Committee during Cotton's temporary absence as lord mayor, recorded that 'the re-opened art gallery has attracted widespread admiration and is a fitting monument to the Director, Mr F. Lambert.'[68] 60,000 visitors came to the Gallery during the first two months in which it was open.[69] In 1953 the prestigious *Burlington Magazine* devoted an editorial to the Gallery, describing its Italian paintings as rivalling those in the Ashmolean and Fitzwilliam Museums, and its 'storehouse of English academic and Pre-Raphaelite art of the last century' as 'probably unsurpassed'.[70] Resources had been concentrated on the undamaged Gallery rather than on the heavily bombed Liverpool Museum, which did not re-open until 1964, causing resentments at the Museum which lasted at least until 1986. In the year ending in April 1953, the first full year during which the Gallery was open, the City Council spent about £23,700 in running costs on it. Of this amount salaries and wages accounted for about £13,000.[71] In 1937 total running costs had been about £12,600.[72] It was not an expensive amenity.

Lambert had re-established the Gallery's status with only one other professional or managerial member of staff, his deputy director. In that post he inherited Charles Carter who went on to run Aberdeen Art Gallery and Museum. Carter was followed by G.L. Conran, whom he appointed in 1936 at the age of twenty-four. Conran left in 1938 to become director of Southampton Art Gallery and he later became director of Manchester City Art Gallery.[73] John Paris, who had studied at both undergraduate and postgraduate level at Oxford, occupied the post between 1938 and 1949, apart from military service during the war. He wrote a short book on English watercolours in 1945 and, on leaving Liverpool, became a successful director of the National Gallery of South Africa between 1949 and 1962 before moving back to England to become director of the National Army Museum.[74] These were bright young men reflecting the new reputation of the Walker Art Gallery. Paris was replaced by Ralph Fastnedge (born 1913) who began in October 1949 just as the work needed to re-open the Gallery was starting. Fastnedge had studied both at Oxford and at the Courtauld Institute of Art and was the first former Courtauld student to work at the Gallery.

The Institute had opened in 1931 as a part of London University, and one of its principal objectives was the provision, for the first time, of advanced teaching in the history of art for curators in British art galleries. Teaching of this type had long been available on the continent, and it was said that Campbell Dodgson, Keeper of Prints and Drawings at the British Museum from 1912 until 1932, was the only British fine art curator taken seriously in German academic circles until after the Second World War. Until Anthony

Blunt became its director in September 1948 the Institute had some difficulty in attracting students of the right academic calibre, and it had virtually closed during the war, but it remained the only place in England offering full-time undergraduate and postgraduate degrees in art history until the early 1960s. Apart from the Tate Gallery, the national and university art galleries regarded it with some suspicion probably due to professional jealousies.[75] However, many provincial galleries, more aware of their lack of art-historical expertise, welcomed its graduates on to its staff. Fastnedge who became the Director of the Lady Lever Art Gallery must have been among the first of its students to attain a senior post in any British art gallery. Sheila Somers was one of Blunt's research students at the Institute working on Poussin's patrons when she joined the Gallery staff in 1955.[76] Of the six curators appointed between 1955 and 1961 four had studied at the Courtauld Institute, and most, but by no means all, the curators appointed subsequently had also studied there. The preferred pattern of study, followed for example by Timothy Stevens who became assistant keeper of British Art in 1964 and later director in 1971, was an undergraduate degree at Oxford or Cambridge followed by a postgraduate qualification at the Courtauld Institute.

A tradition of preferring specialist to generalist curators was established in Liverpool despite Lambert's scepticism over its merits, which was shared in the major municipal galleries.[77] Three of the six curators appointed between 1955 and 1961 were women, a remarkably high proportion at a time when women were often found in decorative art departments but much more rarely as curators of fine art. Fastnedge's appointment certainly reflected the new professionalism which Lambert and Cotton wished to introduce at the Walker Art Gallery. He and Somers were largely responsible for establishing the reputation of the Gallery as a centre of scholarship. He started work on a new detailed catalogue of the Gallery's very important Italian and Netherlandish paintings, and he began to publish articles on them in the *Burlington Magazine*, the leading English academic art history journal.[78] Sheila Somers's notes on these paintings were very useful later to Michael Compton in his work on the new *Foreign Schools Catalogue* of 1963. Fastnedge also published extensively on the collection in the *Liverpool Bulletin*.[79]

The *Bulletin* was another of Cotton's initiatives intended to raise the academic standing of the Gallery, of the Liverpool Museum and of the Liverpool City Library.[80] The Liverpool Museum had launched a scholarly bulletin in 1898 but it proved short-lived.[81] The first number of the new *Bulletin* appeared in 1951 with an editorial board headed by Cotton and with Fastnedge as editor. The Glasgow Art Gallery and Museums had launched *The Scottish Art Review* in 1946 and Leeds City Art Gallery had begun their *Leeds Art Calendar* a year later.[82] Cotton however was not far behind and he was aiming at a more scholarly and less general periodical than was promoted in Glasgow and Leeds. He wrote in the introduction to the first volume: 'The *Bulletin* will have a dual function. It will keep the public in touch with the growth and development of the three institutions, but, what is more important, it will provide a medium for the publication of the results of research carried out on the material which they contain by independent scholars and by members of the staff'.[83] Thus it reflected the same high-minded intellectual attitude evident in the creation of the grand lecture hall. Some important articles were published in it not only by Fastnedge but also by other members of staff. There were Mary Bennett's article on William Windus of 1958-9 and her follow-up pieces to her Pre-Raphaelite exhibitions of the late 1960s. Hugh Macandrew's article on Roscoe and Fuseli of 1959-60 was followed by Michael Compton's paper on Roscoe as a collector in 1960-61. The quality of the articles, covering acquisitions, new discoveries about the collections, local artists and collectors, was varied, and the 'independent scholars' wanted by Cotton proved hard to find. John Woodward's article of 1954 on some recently acquired royal portraits was exceptional.[84] Publication became less regular in the 1960s, and in 1970 the Walker Art Gallery Numbers were merged with the Gallery's Annual Reports, which were expanded to include very detailed accounts of every acquisition. The value of the articles, still nearly all by the staff, was improved with new research on J.H. MacNair, Paul Delaroche, R.B. Kitaj, J.A. Koch and G.A. Wallis, artists then unfamiliar except in academic circles.[85] However, with the take-over of the Lady Lever Art Gallery in 1977, for which no extra fine art curators were recruited, the pressure on staff time became too great and publication of both the Annual Report and the *Bulletin* ended. It was generally felt that publication of detailed catalogues of the collections should have a higher priority. The *Walker Art Gallery Monographs* were another scholarly venture launched by Cotton in 1951 on the re-opening of the Gallery. They were to be detailed accounts of artists well represented in the collection. *Walker Art Gallery Monograph Number One* was devoted to the work of Alfred Stevens but Stevens's reputation was waning, and this proved to be both the first and the last volume in the series.[86] The same format was however followed by the successful *Scottish Masters* series published by the National Galleries of Scotland in the 1980s. Following the achievement of national status and of greater resources in 1986 the new National Museums and Galleries on Merseyside established a Scholarship Committee, composed of trustees with a special interest in research. They seriously considered launching a new multi-disciplinary scholarly bulletin.[87] However some trustees doubted that a new *Liverpool Bulletin* could succeed, arguing not unreasonably that the staff should rather be encouraged to write for existing national and international academic journals within their own specialisms. Such articles would be more widely read and would promote the careers of their writers more effectively than articles in a 'house' journal.

The overall quality of a new Liverpool journal would be uneven and contributions from distinguished outsiders would remain difficult to obtain. However it still seemed to some at the Gallery that these eminent trustees now commanding large budgets lacked the vision of Alderman Cotton, a mere Liverpool private banker in an age of austerity thirty five years earlier.

However in the gradual professionalization of its staff the Walker Art Gallery lagged well behind most of the other major provincial galleries, especially in recruitment. At Leeds Frank Rutter, the founder of the Allied Artists' Association and a distinguished art critic, became director in 1912. He was followed by Solomon Kaines Smith who had lectured at Cambridge University and at the National Gallery and had written books on Greek art, on Wright of Derby and on John Crome. After Lambert's brief period as director John Rothenstein, who had a doctorate in the history of art from London University and had written a biography of Eric Gill, became his successor. He was followed by Philip Hendy who had catalogued the paintings at the Isabella Stuart Gardner Museum in Boston and had been curator of paintings at the Museum of Fine Arts there. Hendy was able to combine his directorship with the Slade professorship of fine art at Oxford over ten years. In 1927 Kaines Smith moved on to the Birmingham Art Gallery and Museum, where he was succeeded in 1945 by Trenchard Cox, who had studied art history in Paris and Berlin. Rothenstein, Hendy and Cox later became directors of the Tate Gallery, the National Gallery and the Victoria and Albert Museum. At Manchester David Baxandall moved on to direct the National Galleries of Scotland.[88] No director or curator at the Walker Art Gallery had qualifications or experience comparable to those of these figures. It was therefore all the more remarkable that the Gallery emerged in 1951 as a major national as well as local institution.

Chapter 4

The Struggle for State Aid, 1860-1986

The rapid expansion of public services in nineteenth- and twentieth-century Britain, and elsewhere in Europe, was usually provided by local authorities with some supervision and subsidy from central government. Thus nineteenth-century British provincial police forces received a grant of a quarter (later a half) of their costs in return for some control by the Home Office in London. Henry Cole, effectively the first director of the Victoria and Albert Museum, then known as the South Kensington Museum, had tried unsuccessfully to provide government grants to provincial museums and art galleries in the 1860s.[1] In 1877, the year in which the Walker Art Gallery was completed, J.T. Bunce, the editor of the *Birmingham Post*, argued in the influential Liberal *Fortnightly Review* that London already had generous artistic provision and that loans from the national collections and government grants to the new provincial art galleries and museums were now the new priority.[2] Three years later Bunce was answered by the great collector and curator J.C. Robinson. Robinson knew British regional collections well as he played some part in originating the travelling exhibitions which the South Kensington Museum sent out to the provinces and he later collected Italian sculpture for the Birmingham art gallery. In 1880 he wrote three letters to *The Times* on state aid for provincial art galleries. They represent the 'official' attitude of the cultured metropolitan élite which, although rarely stated with Robinson's brutal candour, has never essentially changed:

> The great provincial centres are...calling on the State to help them in their efforts to create local museums and galleries of art. They find it comparatively easy to erect spacious buildings but most difficult to stock them with suitable specimens...We have in London Imperial art museums and galleries of the highest rank, and the State has of late established others on a similar scale in the minor metropolitan centres, Dublin and Edinburgh. Are we to go further in this direction – in other words are Manchester, Glasgow, Birmingham, Leeds and a number of other important centres of population to have art museums created at the same high level? I am convinced...that the only result of attempts on the part of our provincial centres to form comprehensive collections of original works on the metropolitan model would be the amassing of a considerable amount of miscellaneous second-rate material of the curiosity-shop order, among which the few really important specimens, accidentally or otherwise acquired, would be practically buried and lost sight of.

Referring to the collections of the Liverpool Museum he sneered: 'In our own country Liverpool is a great emporium but art students and antiquaries would scarcely expect to have to visit the city of quays and warehouses to inspect Roman consular diptychs'. He suggested that Liverpool might exchange its original works of art for a large supply of casts, copies and reproductions. However he knew that French practice scarcely supported his dismissive attitude towards provincial art galleries. Indeed he admired the collections of old master paintings and drawings at the Lille and Montpellier museums, although he deplored the presence of two of Perugino's greatest works in isolation at Lyon and Caen. He conceded that where local art galleries already had a substantial collection of historic art they might be allowed to acquire closely related works to form a coherent, distinctive group, but otherwise they should confine their purchases to contemporary and regional art and to copies and reproductions. Thanks to recent massive purchases by the new American collectors and by the German art galleries the art of the past had simply become too expensive to permit the formation of new public collections devoted to it.[3]

The Builder however, with its strong commitment to social improvement, represented a very different tradition. Later in 1880 it published an article entitled 'National Art Museums for the Provinces'. Looking at Germany rather than France it argued that British provincial art galleries should have the same national status as the German National Museum at Nuremburg or the Bavarian State Collections at the Alte Pinakothek in Munich. Loans to municipal art galleries from the South Kensington Museums, which were favoured by Robinson provided that important works were not involved, were useful, but 'the temporary nature of these exhibitions has always been a principal drawback to their utility'. The London and regional art galleries should be controlled by a single government minister 'whose sole duty should consist in the supervision and fostering of the art interests of the community throughout the country'.[4] This was the national museums and art galleries service demanded by some influential provincial curators in the 1970s and 1980s.

By 1882 there were substantial public art galleries either already built or under construction in Glasgow, Liverpool, Salford, Manchester, Birmingham and elsewhere. In 1881 and in 1882 the issue of state subsidies for them was debated at some length in the House of Commons. Jesse Collings, chairman of Birmingham's Free Libraries and Art Gallery Committee and, like Bunce, closely associated with Joseph Chamberlain's great programme of municipal improvement in Birmingham, moved resolutions in the House of Commons in favour of substantial government grants to provincial museums and art galleries. He wanted grants from the Department of Science and Art to enable provincial galleries to buy decorative art. He wanted more extensive loans and even gifts from the national art galleries and museums to provincial galleries, noting for example that some of the huge collection of watercolours by Turner at the British Museum could easily be allocated to the regional art galleries. Foreseeing opposition from the aristocratic trustees of the London art galleries he, like the writer of the article in *The Builder*, suggested that they should be replaced by direct control from a new government department of culture. Much of his support came from Radicals like himself who disliked the indifference of the wealthy to the diffusion of art among the new industrial towns. His resolutions were seconded by John Slagg of Manchester who claimed, rightly, that the French government was very generous to its regional museums. W.S. Caine of Liverpool described the success of the Walker Art Gallery, countering the argument that provincial cities should do more for their own galleries. Gladstone himself entered the debate as prime minister and urged caution, especially over grants to provincial galleries for the purchase of original works of art and over the abandonment of the trustee system. He did not see how limits could be placed on the number and size of present and future regional galleries all demanding grants, a problem which was to disrupt progress on this issue over at least the next century. A.J. Mundella, the Liberal minister then in charge of the South Kensington Museum, observed that the government was already doing much for regional art galleries through temporary loans from that Museum. George Howard, speaking for the National Gallery, reported that the Gallery had just made a substantial loan of its paintings to the Walker Art Gallery.[5] To reinforce this parliamentary pressure a deputation from forty towns and cities, led by Collings and including Picton on behalf of Liverpool, visited Earl Spencer, then President of the Council with a general responsibility for education, on 8 March 1882. Picton did not ask for money from the government but he did request loans of works of art from the National Gallery, the British Museum and the South Kensington Museums, pleading also for some central state authority over these institutions.[6] Collings's resolutions were defeated in parliament. The loans did materialize, partly thanks to the National Galleries Loan Act of 1883, but the ministry of culture did not and the grants were on a very modest scale.

During the summer of 1882, reflecting perhaps Joseph Slagg's comments, the eminent art critic and exhibition organizer Joseph Comyns Carr was sent to France by the *Manchester Guardian* in order to report on French provincial art galleries primarily for the benefit of the Manchester Town Council which was then establishing its own art gallery. The long introduction to his book compared the new British regional galleries very unfavourably with their much older French counterparts:

> But these museums of provincial France are not merely municipal. From the circumstances of their origin [by Napoleon] they also enjoy the advantages of State assistance and control...The principle which connects the

museums of the great cities of the departments with the central machinery of government is deemed essential to the progress and development of art. And it is this principle, as we must remember, that still needs to be enforced among ourselves. The right of the large centres of industry to a share of the national art treasures has hitherto been urged with but little effect.[7]

Carr argued that state regulation and subsidy gave French provincial art galleries a national status which attracted important gifts from local collectors and encouraged local councils to provide substantial buildings and distinguished curators for them. Although French principles of arts administration and practice enjoyed considerable if often reluctant esteem in Britain, Carr's pleas were as ineffective as Collings's resolutions in the House of Commons. After this brief debate of 1877 to 1882 the issue of state aid for provincial art galleries did not receive serious discussion for the next ninety years, apart perhaps from some pleading in its favour in the first serious reference book on British provincial art galleries published in 1888.[8] There was however one significant benefit for the regions. Mundella did enable the South Kensington Museum to offer not only travelling exhibitions but also grants in support of the purchase by provincial art galleries of copies, casts and replicas. These grants had been available to 'South Kensington' art schools since the 1860s and in 1881 they were offered to provincial art galleries. Eventually they were extended to include original works of art. They amounted annually to around £1,500 early in the twentieth century, £1,000 in the 1930s, £2,000 in the mid-1950s, £25,000 in the early 1960s, £500,000 in the late 1970s and rather over £1,000,000 in the early 1980s. They were increased dramatically from £2,000 to £15,000 in 1958 in order to cover paintings as well as drawings, watercolours and sculpture. These grants, covering up to half the total cost of the work in question, were of great importance in convincing local councils that money spent on acquiring works of art would attract substantial government grants for works of high quality. However, even with the assistance of other funding bodies such as the National Art-Collections Fund (now known as the Art Fund), provincial galleries often struggled to find the other half.[9] The Walker Art Gallery secured grants of £183 and £104 in 1887 and 1892 principally in support of its casts gallery, but nothing more until 1960.[10]

In Britain there was a sharp demarcation between national and local control. Outside London historic buildings and their collections generally went national – as in France – to the Ministry of Works (later the Ministry of Public Buildings and Works, later still English Heritage) or to the National Trust, but museums and art galleries were always local institutions in the care of city, town or county councils with no state funding or control. After the Second World War central government spending on the arts increased much more rapidly than local government expenditure in this area. Rather than any deliberate policy or party programme this probably reflected the popular success of the Council for the Encouragement of Music and the Arts during the Second World War and its transformation into the Arts Council of Great Britain, together with the practical need to reinstall the national collections and repair their buildings. There was also undoubtedly a greater post-war cultural awareness among ministers and senior civil servants than among local councillors and council officials. Indeed it seems that there was a general deterioration in the quality of vision and scope of thought in local government in twentieth-century cities partly owing to the retreat of the traditional governing classes into distant suburbs, partly to greater reluctance on the part of local business men to serve on local councils and partly to increasing centralization in political life.[11]

The major preoccupation for the Walker Art Gallery and for the other large regional museums and galleries was therefore the expectation that central government would eventually provide substantial financial assistance for them, as well as for the great national collections in London, Edinburgh and Cardiff, in return for some element of government supervision. This policy had been recommended by the Miers Report of 1928 and by the Markham Report of 1938, which observed that 'there is only one body in the country strong enough, wealthy enough, and having at its call sufficient expert guidance to bring better direction to [provincial museums and galleries] and that is the government'. This indeed was and remained the fundamental issue. However, Markham's plain language, expressing the need for both some central government finance and control for provincial galleries and some contempt for their existing management, was palatable neither to central nor to local government. Sadly later reports were much more cautious. Lord De La Warr, the President of the Board of Education, was sympathetic until war intervened in 1939.[12] Immediately after the war the Museums Association, which represented provincial rather than national or university museums and galleries, published their document: *Museums and Art Galleries: A National Service: A Post-War Policy.* This document recommended the establishment of a Museums and Art Galleries Grants Board on the same lines as the University Grants Committee. The Board with two sections, one for museums and one for art galleries, would assess schemes for their improvement, allocate grants, impose conditions and carry out inspections to ensure the maintenance of high standards at all institutions.[13] As President of the Museums Association between 1946 and 1948, Lambert was negotiating a 'short bill' which would authorize an initial government grant of £250,000 to provincial museums and galleries to be channelled through this new Museums and Galleries Grants Board. The measure was being promoted by the Arts Group of the Parliamentary Labour Party whose secretary, Dr Barnett Stross, explained in November 1947 that municipal galleries were being very badly treated by comparison with national institutions. He observed that the Arts Council had neither the mandate nor the resources to establish a better balance and that the new Board was needed to provide national assistance for regional art galleries and museums. The editorial of the July 1948 issue of the *Museums Journal* announced that the Museums Association would discuss the 'hoped-for government aid to museums' at its August conference. But there in his presidential address Lambert reported that the progress of this bill had been delayed and in fact it was never presented to parliament. If provincial galleries were ever to achieve any reasonable parity with their London counterparts the best moment for success was the brief period of post-war idealism and of the associated new public support for the arts. Stross and Markham continued to plead for financial assistance from the Treasury for provincial museums and art galleries in the House of Commons at least until 1964 but they were unsuccessful and the opportunity was lost.[14] Proposals very similar to those advanced by Stross were recommended in many official reports over the following fifty years but their partial implementation was always very reluctant and never generous.[15]

As chairman of Liverpool University's Development Committee between 1946 and 1954, Cotton saw enormous sums of money pass from the Treasury in London through the University Grants Committee to provincial universities which enabled them to achieve some sort of parity with the universities of Oxford, Cambridge and London. In 1949 his committee published William Holford's report recommending the redevelopment of about 76 acres of central Liverpool for the university at a cost of over £5.6 million.[16] He must have wondered why similar 'centres of excellence' could not have been created by central government among England's regional museums and art galleries – and why a year later he had to struggle so hard to raise a mere £31,500 to enable the Walker Art Gallery to re-open. He had been at first rather hostile to governmental intervention in the affairs of municipal galleries,[17] but in 1955 at a dinner celebrating the opening of an exhibition in London of the Gallery's new acquisitions Cotton made a speech pleading for assistance from central government to provincial galleries in the acquisition of works of art of exceptional quality. He deplored 'artistic centralization' and the lack of resources in regional museums and galleries which should be 'centres of research and scholarship'. He apologized to his audience for his frequent repetition of this theme.[18] He wrote more formally to *The Times* in the same year:

> [There are at least six provincial art galleries] which by any standard, the range and importance of their collections, the training and scholarship of their staff, the quality of their publications, their readiness to lend and the facilities which they offer to students and the public are in all but one

respect national institutions...[that is] that the nation contributes nothing whatever to their maintenance and nothing to their growth except relief from duty on acquisitions from deceased artists.[19]

Thus Cotton was widening the scope of the government grants he was requesting, but at the same time he was strictly confining the number of provincial art galleries eligible for these grants to the six most important institutions. He was well aware that from Gladstone onwards governments feared the sheer number of provincial art galleries, many quite small, which might ask for financial assistance. In the following month the Museums Association wrote formally to the Chancellor of the Exchequer asking him to consider state aid to municipal museums and galleries. It received a negative reply referring to 'this essentially local problem' and refusing even to recommend any substantial further assistance to provincial art galleries from their local authorities. The Association described this answer as insulting and it certainly represented the lowest point in the quest for government assistance to municipal galleries.[20] In 1958 Sir Mortimer Wheeler, the great archaeologist and former director of the National Museum of Wales, interrupted the placid annual meeting of the Museums Association, demanding that the government should set up a new official body analogous to the University Grants Committee to distribute money to provincial museums and galleries and describing the existing official body, the Standing Commission on Museums and Galleries, established in 1931, as the 'Recumbent Commission'. He pointed out that the aggregate age of its eleven members was 776 and his derisive title for it was not forgotten.[21] In 1944 Markham had, for the second time, pleaded for the Commission to include a representative of the provincial museums and galleries, only to be told that this was unnecessary as the Commission's functions 'relate primarily to the various national institutions not the provincial institutions.'[22] In 1960 the Financial Secretary to the Treasury asked the Commission to compile a useful survey of provincial museums and galleries but in advance he effectively ruled out government supervision or grants. He described regional galleries, rightly, as the 'Cinderella group in the family of arts', and plainly Cinderella was not going to the ball in his coach. The survey, chaired by the Earl of Rosse, noted that outside London and Edinburgh the Walker Art Gallery, together with the Glasgow City Art Gallery, the Ashmolean Museum in Oxford and the Fitzwilliam Museum in Cambridge had been 'built up to national standard'. This at least indicated that the other major municipal collections were at a lower level, a distinction that later official reports were reluctant to make. The survey also reported without further comment that throughout most of Europe except Britain a system of grants and inspection from central or regional government had been established for major provincial galleries.[23]

In 1954 Cotton had joined the Arts Council and his 1955 speech was quoted at length in the Council's *Annual Report*. The Council strongly supported his plea for financial assistance from central government for important acquisitions by provincial galleries but stated that this assistance could not come through the Council.[24] It was however an obvious anomaly that Liverpool's orchestra and theatres could receive central government funding through the Council, but that the Gallery could not. Local authorities were only beginning to accept general responsibility for music and drama in the 1950s and could therefore demand Arts Council grants as a condition of their own subsidies. Public art galleries had however been very generally supported and controlled for over fifty years by local authorities who had therefore less bargaining power with the Arts Council in this area. There were furthermore fewer provincial theatres and orchestras than art galleries needing Arts Council support. Little was lost immediately as Kenneth Clark, then the Council's chairman, remarked:

> Our main claimants, Covent Garden, Sadler's Wells and the leading orchestras, used up practically all our grant. As a result our meetings had that negative and despondent character which has now spread to every branch of a bankrupt country.[25]

Provincial orchestras were (and are) not far behind London orchestras in quality and funding, but with museums and galleries the gap was (and is) enormous. In 1974-5 the Arts Council gave £162,000 to the Royal Liverpool Philharmonic Orchestra which of course also benefited from grants from the local authorities on Merseyside. In the same year the Gallery's total expenditure was only about £242,000. The Arts Council financed – with, in some cases, local support – the mostly new so-called 'independent' galleries, the Ikon Gallery in Birmingham, the Arnolfini Gallery in Bristol, the Museum of Modern Art in Oxford, the Whitechapel Art Gallery in London, Kettle's Yard in Cambridge and others. They were situated in comfortable parts of southern and central England and within easy travelling distance from London; they concentrated on contemporary art and generally had no permanent collections.[26] Although they were called 'independent' very few of them could have survived without the support of the Arts Council, which favoured them probably because, unlike many of the local authority galleries, they strongly encouraged modernist contemporary art and could be largely controlled by the Council. This was to provide competition not assistance to municipal and other galleries.

Although the Arts Council had always been intended to support existing cultural institutions rather than to provide its own music, drama or art, this principle was reversed in its own art department, which believed in 'direct provision' – that is it provided its own exhibitions and occasionally some grants in support of other exhibitions, but very little general financial institutional support. N.M. Pearson observed in 1982:

> For reasons which are far from clear in the forties and fifties when the Arts Council was dismantling the direct provision operated...in the Second World War it was accepted that the art department should continue to create and provide exhibitions. An argument was made that no other organization was able to provide such a service – but an equivalent argument could have been made for...other departments.[27]

The Arts Council could, for example, have set up its own orchestras playing the music of which it approved and making modest grants from its small remaining music budget to existing orchestras. With its 'independent' galleries this is precisely what it did in the visual arts. However if the Walker Art Gallery and other regional art galleries received only fairly modest support for their own exhibitions from the Arts Council, they did benefit greatly from the exhibitions, often of very high quality, circulated by the Council, by the Victoria and Albert Museum and occasionally by the other national museums. The high standards of these touring exhibitions could persuade the regional galleries to produce similar exhibitions from their own resources, although this form of state aid in kind could also have precisely the opposite effect. It could encourage provincial galleries, especially the smaller ones, to rely on exhibitions from London rather than organizing their own loan exhibitions and displaying their own permanent collections. Indeed the possible detrimental impact of the Arts Council's touring exhibitions on the development of exhibitions originating in the provinces was recognized in the early 1980s by one of their own committees chaired by Gerald Forty, formerly head of fine art at the British Council. Some cynical observers noted that the Victoria and Albert Museum and the Arts Council only began to emphasize the unfortunate effects of their exhibitions on local initiatives just when they were starting to withdraw or reduce these exhibitions in the late 1970s and late 1990s. The Arts Council also felt that many of the exhibitions organized by the regional art galleries were not sufficiently innovative and stimulating to justify extensive support from its own limited funds. Similarly the Council's 'Housing the Arts' fund could in principle support municipal galleries but rarely did so, apart from an entirely exceptional grant of £200,000 to Leeds City Art Gallery for its major refurbishment of the late 1970s and smaller grants in this period to the Laing Art Gallery in Newcastle and to Stoke City Art Gallery.[28] As part of a major review of arts funding in 1984 known as the 'Glory of the Garden', the Arts Council provided new grants totalling well over £500,000 to the larger municipal galleries primarily in order to improve their facilities for loan exhibitions.[29] Of this sum £197,000 was allocated in 1985-6 and its Art Department reported: 'The main success of the year was the opening phase of a strategy for realizing the largely untapped potential of England's municipal galleries. This extensive network has generally been so under-resourced that most galleries cannot engage in active exhibition programmes.'[30] Two years later about £440,000 was awarded to the larger local authority galleries. Sandy Nairne, then the head of the Council's Art Department, commented later that 'this was the only bit of "Glory" that actually seemed to work' but it could not be carried far enough.[31] Indeed even after the 'Glory of the Garden' review the Arts Council was still awarding larger sums annually to the 'independent' galleries than to the great municipal galleries.[32] The Arts Council could have grasped many years earlier that long-established local authority galleries could display exhibitions more effectively and more economically than the 'independent' galleries. In fact this change of policy came too late for the Walker Art Gallery which achieved national status in 1986. Even these new grants were, however, modest in scale and in 2001 the next major report into provincial galleries could still observe: 'There has been substantial indirect funding for theatres and orchestras in the regions (through the Arts Council) for many years on a scale that the major regional museums and galleries have never enjoyed, despite being entitled to be regarded as cultural institutions of equal status in the regions.'[33] At no time in this period did the Arts Council seriously promote the development, care or housing of the permanent collections of regional galleries. In the provinces their essential concern was towards facilitating the display of contemporary art.

In 1971 Lord Eccles, the new Conservative Arts Minister, commissioned yet another inconclusive report on provincial art galleries, the Wright Report. 'Willy' Wright was the senior civil servant in his department and a forceful personality.[34] His Report's financial statistics were startling. In 1971 the amount that local authorities in England and Wales were spending on their 468 museums and galleries was less than half the amount they were spending on swimming baths and much less than half the sums allocated by central government to the eleven national museums and galleries in London and Cardiff. Its recommendations, encouraging local authorities to support their art galleries more generously and to improve their scope and efficiency, were very familiar from earlier reports and studies. However Wright did favour direct government subsidy through a new central museums body or council to a 'limited number of centres of excellence', a significant advance on the refusal to contemplate such grants in the Rosse Report of 1963. These 'centres of excellence' would establish high standards in every field for themselves and support other smaller galleries in their areas in order to raise levels of achievement generally. Their staff would have levels of pay and conditions of service comparable with those in the national art galleries and there would be a frequent interchange of staff between the two sectors. [35] The principle of 'designated museums', as they were later called, was an important advance as significant art galleries are distributed very unevenly across Britain, and an essential first step is to identify those with collections, buildings, staff and other facilities making them worthy of central government subsidy. In December 1973 the Walker Art Gallery was already applying to become a 'government assisted provincial centre of excellence'.[36] In 1974 it published a survey of visitors showing that over a third of them came from outside Merseyside.[37] The Wright Report's recommendations were usefully summarized in 1976 by Lord Redcliffe-Maud, who went on to observe that none had been implemented.[38] Hugh Jenkins, Eccles's Labour successor as Arts Minister, also observed that Wright, who retired in 1976, did not do much to implement the findings of the committee which he chaired.[39] Eccles's own comments on the Report of the Drew Committee, which six years later covered much the same ground as the Wright Committee, revealed that he had not grasped the distinction between small local galleries and major regional galleries, that he had the traditional Conservative dislike of government interference in local government and that he had effectively disowned the conclusions of the Report which he had commissioned: 'Much as non-national museums require more support we must not allow their essentially local character to be endangered for the sake of a tidy structure created to assess nationwide government grants and to provide a uniform system of pay and conditions for work in the museum service.'[40]

Sir Arthur Drew was like Wright, a successful civil servant but of rather higher cultural standing. He was a trustee of the British Museum and became both chairman of the Museums and Galleries Commission, which was mainly concerned with the national museums and galleries, and president of the Museums Association which primarily dealt with local museums and galleries. The report of his committee repeated the plea for government funding of the major regional galleries in the Wright Report. It recommended that over half their costs should be met by central government in return for commitments from their local authorities that staff salary scales should be substantially raised, that high standards of display and conservation should be maintained and that outside experts and independent representatives should be involved in the municipal committees running these galleries. Only about seven regional galleries would qualify for this generous treatment and while there may have been joy in Sheffield there might have been anger in Hull. The Report also produced new figures to reinforce the Wright Report's indictment of the current low level of local government spending on museums and galleries. In England and Wales local authorities were spending about 0.15%, rising to 0.22% in the north-west, of their total expenditure in this way – that is a total of about £22 million of which about £13.5 million would be recovered from central government through the Rate Support Grant.[41] By 1978 Liverpool was in serious economic decline but much more prosperous cities to the south and east were also neglecting their art galleries. The government rejected the Drew Report's recommendations as it had the Wright Report's ideas. Perhaps it felt that if city and county councils had such a low opinion of their own galleries there was no reason for it to take a more generous view.

The most significant form of state aid to local authority museums and galleries was directed through the area museum councils or services which from 1959 onwards were gradually established throughout Britain. They provided subsidized conservation, display, transport and some other facilities principally for the smaller galleries and institutions in their area which individually could not afford these specialist services. They were independent companies limited by guarantee, funded partly by charging their customers for work done, partly by subscriptions from the local authorities and other institutions in their areas owning substantial collections, and partly by central government, which after 1963 contributed about half of their total expenditure. Their directors were appointed by the local authorities in their regions. As all authorities were contributing to the costs of the service regardless of their museum spending levels or needs there was pressure to spread the benefits as widely as possible. Following the recommendations of the Museums and Galleries Commission they were generally based in the larger galleries of each area.[42] Thus for example Bristol City Art Gallery, the principal innovator in this development, had by 1975 two conservators in its studios working for the Gallery itself and two working for the Area Council – with considerable benefits in shared expertise and equipment for all the galleries in south-west England.[43] The Wright Report of 1973 recommended that the Area Museum Councils and Services should be expanded into 'Provincial Museum Councils' with wider responsibilities and greater financial resources from central government.[44] Two years earlier Richard Harrison, closely associated with the area councils in Yorkshire, had published an article criticizing their performance. He saw the causes of their difficulties in professional jealousies, in low subscriptions and in local government indifference to museums and art galleries.[45] But later in the 1970s there were in many areas significant improvements, and the grant from central government to all the area councils and services rose from £10,000 in 1963 to about £132,000 in 1973, to £1,040,000 in 1977 and to around £2,500,000 in 1984.[46]

The North West Museums and Art Galleries Service held its inaugural meeting in 1962. It first selected Manchester City Art Galleries for the conservation of oil paintings and Liverpool Museum for archaeological conservation. However in 1973 it centralized all its activities in Blackburn where it developed new studios and recruited new staff in its own building, a former private house. It decided that its art conservation should be based at Blackburn not at the Walker Art Gallery or at the Manchester City Art Gallery, and that it should not share their facilities and staff. Setting up a centralized service at Blackburn isolated the organization from involvement with the major galleries and museums in the region and consolidated the widely held view that it really existed for the small museums and art galleries. This was a grave mistake by both the service and the larger art galleries as here was a satisfactory conduit for central government money which increased substantially during the 1960s and 1970s. The cause of this unfortunate decision in favour of Blackburn and of the very slow growth of the Service generally probably lay in the indifference of most local authorities to their museums, a passionate concern to preserve local autonomy and a lack of trust and of ambition on the part of all the professional staff involved. Although the Area Councils were principally concerned with the smaller provincial galleries and collections, their conservation needs, together with those of the Walker Art Gallery's paintings, could have justified new and much needed updated conservation studios in Liverpool with specialized staff and equipment. A survey of 2000 estimated that there were at least 17,270 easel paintings in the museums and galleries of North West England.[47] It was a great opportunity missed.

Liverpool City Council was a founding member of the North West Museums and Art Galleries Service. Scrutton together with the director of the Liverpool Museum supported involvement but reported that they 'did not entirely share this enthusiasm [for the area councils and services]'.[48] In 1967 Scrutton told John Willett that the committee structure for the Service was 'too cumbrous and the result not very inspiring.'[49] He noted the opinion of Robert Rowe, the progressive and energetic director of the Leeds City Art Gallery: 'Robert thinks that serious restoration jobs will always have to go to London and for this reason has no interest in the Area Council Service schemes so far as Leeds is concerned.'[50] There was a general feeling, possibly only partly justified, that the area councils and services lacked the resources, staff and credibility to be of use to the larger art galleries, which feared that their existing conservation facilities might be used by other galleries in the area without adequate payment to them either from central government or from the other galleries.[51] The Service resolved the dilemma that most of its services were not used or needed by the largest art galleries and museums in its area by giving an identical amount annually to each of them which, subject to certain guide lines, could be spent essentially at their discretion. These grants usefully increased the Walker Art Gallery's resources enabling it to acquire new picture racking at the Lady Lever Art Gallery, to put on display the monumental white marble fireplace by Alfred Stevens from Dorchester House, in store for over forty years, to facilitate the paper conservation programme and similar activities. Any co-operation with other galleries was far more difficult. The Walker Art Gallery tried to establish a paper conservation studio in co-operation with the Service and the Whitworth Art Gallery in Manchester, which owned watercolours, drawings and prints of great importance. However even this modest initiative, which was to be based at the Whitworth Art Gallery, failed. By 1969 the total expenditure of the North West Museums and Art Galleries Service was only about £37,000 of which central government provided about £18,500. By 1979 there were five art conservators working at Blackburn and total expenditure had risen to about £425,000.[52] The Service at Blackburn did valuable work for some of the smaller collections in the area with very limited resources but, isolated from Manchester and Liverpool, it could never provide the truly regional solution required in the area. Arguably the Service was too ambitious in offering such a full range of technical and conservation services and should have focused on fewer activities. It also had great difficulty in offering affordable services to the many impoverished small art galleries in the area which still favoured much cheaper freelance conservators. Its pursuit of perfection could be the enemy of any significant improvement. In 2003 it became the North West Museums, Libraries and Archives Council focused on education rather than on conservation or display and a few years later it was closed entirely. There were perhaps two wider messages in this failure. Firstly regionalism received only very modest support from the government and from the regions. Secondly, as the Markham Report had observed back in 1938, the improvement of regional art galleries required firm government direction. The Victoria and Albert Museum grant fund in support of acquisitions proved a much more successful channel of central government assistance to provincial art galleries than the area museum councils. Both these two vehicles of state aid provided half the cost of the services concerned, but the former was wholly controlled by the national museums and art galleries while the latter relied on local initiative and co-operation.

The future of the large regional galleries was much discussed at two conferences in Sheffield in 1958 and 1966. The first, attended by Scrutton and Cotton, was convened by the City Council there with the provocative subject: 'The Nation's Art Treasures'. It was intended to protest at the government's recent allocation of important works of art from Chatsworth House, accepted by the government in place of tax, to the National Gallery and other London galleries and museums rather than to Sheffield itself, only a short distance from Chatsworth, or to any other regional gallery. It was well attended by provincial art gallery staff and by members of their city councils together with other eminent figures in public and academic life. *The Times* reporter noted however that only Cotton could offer detailed recommendations.[53] Cotton insisted that those regional galleries with notable permanent collections, well-trained staff, good city-centre buildings and acceptable facilities for conservation and research should be eligible not only for paintings accepted in place of tax but also for government grants to enable them to buy any work of art for which an export licence had been refused on account of its importance.[54] The Walker Art Gallery's chairman was also present and his Arts Sub-Committee formally joined in the protest against the allocation of the Chatsworth paintings and other works to London. [55] Beyond that nothing was achieved other than a rather reluctant but very important acceptance by the Treasury that works of art accepted by the government in lieu of tax could be allocated to the major regional galleries as well as to the national galleries. Cotton's success over this issue may not have seemed very significant in 1958, but it greatly assisted the Gallery in its acquisitions of the 1970s and 1980s.

The second Sheffield conference eight years later concerned the same subject but in a wider context. This was the 1966 Museums Association Annual Conference, where the principal theme was the relationship between the national and regional art galleries and museums. Jennie Lee, who had visited the Walker Art Gallery in 1965 as the first Minister for the Arts in the euphoria of the new Labour government, spoke at some length. She was arts minister for over six years, far longer than any other holder of the post. She was a major political figure, enjoying the support and confidence of the prime minister and of most of the Labour party. She more than doubled not only cultural central government arts spending generally but also expenditure on the national museums and galleries in London. At Sheffield, while conceding that there was considerable provincial resentment at the concentration of central government resources on London galleries, she also stated that she had 'set my face firmly, as far as London is concerned, against any lowering of London standards'. Thus her frequently expressed determination to move some of this money out of London was very hard to achieve. In 1966 she had at first decided to allocate Gauguin's *Harvest: Le Pouldu*, accepted by the government in place of tax, to Manchester City Art Gallery, a clear response to the demands of the 1958 Sheffield conference, but had finally given it to the Tate Gallery after pressure from its director, Norman Reid, whom she knew well, and from 'mutual friends', that is the London art establishment. Reid delivered a personal letter to her flat the evening before the decision was to be made. No episode reveals more clearly the disadvantages of provincial galleries in their struggle for government support. Lee devoted most of her speech in Sheffield to supporting local arts centres and regional arts associations. Most of the new money which she raised for the provinces was spent on these new populist initiatives together with regional theatres. She placed great emphasis on youth and novelty and probably found municipal art gallery committees and staff unexciting, elderly and conservative. Central and local government had supported art galleries and museums for many years; in her terms these were the 'old arts'; she wanted the 'new arts', above all music and theatre, which in any event she preferred to the visual arts. She wanted ambitious, imaginative and newsworthy schemes while provincial art galleries wanted, above all, better housekeeping.

Back at Sheffield in 1966 Michael Levey, later director of the National Gallery, speaking on behalf of the national galleries, conceded that the large regional galleries should have a 'semi-national character', enabling them to acquire major works of art through central government, and that provincial staff salaries and conditions of service should be improved to permit a greater interchange of staff between the national and regional galleries – although he became rather more cautious when speaking on the same theme as director at the Museums Association Conference of 1975. In 1966 Scrutton seems to have been shocked by the complacent acceptance of the existing situation by most speakers, who merely favoured greater assistance from national to provincial museums and galleries. Between 1960 and 1965 directors of provincial art galleries had discussed at length substantial state funding for their institutions but few believed that anything would happen. Scrutton now pleaded for full national status for the larger regional art galleries and for redressing the existing huge difference in collection quality between London and the regions by positive discrimination in favour of regional galleries at the expense of national galleries in the allocation by the government of newly acquired works of art. He believed that substantial assistance could be given by Whitehall to municipal galleries without control over those galleries passing to central government and cited the example of university funding as evidence. He concluded by saying that 'I alone of the set speakers at the Conference feel that a revolution is necessary in the relations between the national and the municipal institutions.'[56]

Of course Scrutton's revolution never came although Thomas Greenwood, the Labour chairman of Liverpool's Libraries, Museums and Arts Committee optimistically observed in 1966: 'The year has been marked by much debate on the question of Government aid for the arts in the provinces. The methods by which this aid will be given, and the forms it will take, are undecided. But what seems certain is that the government will increase its support for all the arts in our city as in others...Clearly in any such policy the Walker Art Gallery must be one of the key factors.'[57] Wider support came from Francis Cheetham, the influential director of the Norwich Museums, who contributed two articles to the *Museums Journal* in 1966 and 1968 pleading for a national museums service on French lines in Britain, with the larger regional museums and art galleries receiving substantial financial support and regulation from central government.[58] In 1968 Denys Sutton reviewed the condition of provincial art galleries in an editorial in *Apollo*, the most influential art periodical after the *Burlington Magazine*.[59] He saw considerable advantages in central control by the Ministry of Education but in the end he was so impressed by the vitality of Birmingham Art Gallery and Museum that he concluded that 'the disadvantages that stem from ministerial control are greater than any gains.' It is doubtful that he would have made the same judgment ten years later.

Undoubtedly if the major provincial art galleries were ever to secure substantial central government funding it would have been either immediately after the Second World War or in the late 1960s under Lee, who was admired by two such different figures as Roy Strong and John Pope-Hennessy.[60] Ben Shaw, the dominant Labour politician on the Merseyside cultural scene between the 1960s and the 1980s had, thanks to his business connections in Northern Ireland, seen the transformation of the Ulster Museum, formerly municipal, when it gained national status in 1962, and he was as convinced as Cotton on the Conservative side that the Walker Art Gallery must seek funding from central government. In August 1968 Scrutton discussed the issue with Michael Walker, an assistant secretary in the section of the Department of Education and Science concerned with the arts. Walker told him that Lee had only recently become seriously interested in museums and galleries rather than in arts centres. She had earlier rejected a proposal from the North West Economic Planning Council that the Walker Art Gallery and the Hallé Orchestra should have national status, fearful that her department would have to establish a 'pecking order' among provincial cultural institutions. Now the dismal economic climate no longer permitted increased government spending in any direction. She had pleaded in vain for a National Museums Capital Fund to promote expansion throughout the country. Walker went on to say that the director of the British Museum, whom his department regarded as the spokesman for all museums and art galleries, was not very forceful and that the Museums Association was ineffective.[61] The Museums Association, the only representative body for British museums and art galleries, had consistently supported state aid to municipal galleries. At its Liverpool conference of 1970 its Council had circulated a discussion paper entitled: *A Museum Service for the Nation: the Case for State Help for Selected Major Museums throughout Great Britain*, almost exactly repeating its document of 1945.[62] However the Association enjoyed little support in the national and university museums and art galleries and only rather modest influence in art galleries anywhere. It could never decide whether it was a professional association, a teaching institution, a trades union or a local authority organization and in trying to perform all these functions did none of them very well. Weight of numbers in its membership inclined it to represent the smaller municipal museums and galleries which had little hope of central government funding.

Andrew Faulds, who became a Labour Party spokesman on the arts after the Conservatives won the general election of 1970, attempted to carry on Lee's policies with the Labour Party's *A Practical Arts Policy* of 1973.[63] Her scheme for a capital fund to improve art gallery buildings was to be implemented, and the larger provincial art galleries were to be designated as 'regional national art galleries' with close links to the existing national museums and galleries. However he was not appointed as Arts Minister when the Labour Party regained power in 1974, and it was not until Labour gained power again in 1997 that the Designation Scheme of 1997 and the Designation Challenge Fund of 1999 provided some regular but still fairly modest government funding for the larger provincial galleries. Fortunately by then the Walker Art Gallery was a national institution with nearly all its costs met from national taxation.

Chapter 5

The Years of Growth

Lambert retired in 1952 and his post was advertised at a salary of £1500. This was £300 more than he had been receiving since 1947 and nearly double the £800 which he had received on his appointment in 1932. There was considerable discussion and close voting in the Libraries, Museums and Arts Committee about the exact levels of the salary scale.[1] It was only £100 less than the director of the Tate Gallery was then receiving. Cotton was plainly hoping for that new director expert in 'art scholarship and gallery administration' which he had demanded back in 1931. The dramatic improvements in the permanent collection, the refurbishment of the Gallery itself and the ending of the Autumn Exhibitions, which were administratively very demanding, no doubt encouraged applications for the post. David Baxandall, director of Manchester City Art Gallery and Dr Mary Woodall, keeper of the Department of Art at the Birmingham Museum and Art Gallery must have been the front runners although the director of Aberdeen Art Gallery and the assistant director of the Fitzwilliam Museum in Cambridge were also short-listed.[2] These were much more impressive candidates than the two men who had competed against Lambert in 1931, but the absence of any staff at any level from the major national collections was also very evident. The great divide between the national and provincial galleries was already in place. Directors moved then – but more rarely later – from provincial to national galleries. Junior staff continued to do the same. Five curators at the Birmingham Art Gallery and Museum moved to national museums and galleries between 1965 and 1975 and the Walker Art Gallery suffered less spectacularly in the same way. However few staff at any level moved in the opposite direction.[3]

Fastnedge naturally applied for the vacant directorship in 1952 and so did Hugh Scrutton (1917-1991), then the director of the Whitechapel Art Gallery, who was appointed. Scrutton's gallery, much admired for its engagement with the deprived of London's east end, had recently held notable loan exhibitions, covering the Pre-Raphaelites in 1948, Mark Gertler in 1949, W.P. Frith in 1951 and contemporary British realist artists in 1952, but it had no permanent collection. One of Scrutton's exhibitions, covering the work of twelve living British artists ranging from Duncan Grant to Prunella Clough, received high praise as late as 1960.[4] Scrutton himself had been responsible for forming a new 'Friends' organization to assist the Gallery.[5] At thirty-four he was much the youngest of the candidates who, apart from Fastnedge, were all over forty. In formal study and work experience he was the least well qualified of the short-listed candidates. He had studied at Cambridge but had no qualifications in art history and had visited very few of the major Italian cities. After military service during the war he had worked for a year as a volunteer in the Department of Prints and Drawings at the British Museum in 1946 under A.E. Popham, 'an admirable scholar and master of dry, ironical wit, spoken in the high accents of Bloomsbury' in Kenneth Clark's words.[6] It was probably Popham and his colleagues who showed Scrutton the importance of research and scholarship in museums and art galleries. Scrutton then admired El Greco, impressionism, cubism, Roger Fry's formalism together with, more specifically, Cézanne, Picasso, Paul Nash, Matthew Smith, Graham Sutherland and Ben Nicholson.[7] His appointment however indicated that the selection committee were in fact looking for youth and new ideas rather than for experience in running a large provincial art gallery or for any deep knowledge of art history. Later that year Baxandall, who had been buying modernist paintings and sculpture by Léger, Ben Nicholson and others at Manchester, was appointed director of the National Gallery of Scotland, and Mary Woodall soon became a very highly regarded director at Birmingham.

Elizabeth II became queen a few days after Scrutton's appointment, and his first task was to commission the required formal portrait of her for Liverpool Town Hall, which already contained grand full-length portraits of most British monarchs from George III onwards. A progressive bearded young director from a gallery in working-class London was not well qualified for the job. He knew and admired the work of John Napper, who had painted some murals at the Whitechapel Art Gallery in 1950, and recommended him for the commission. However Napper's huge portrait, over three metres high including the frame, was generally – and probably rightly – condemned on its arrival in Liverpool in early May 1953. Scrutton defended Napper's portrait vigorously and David Piper, an assistant keeper at the National Portrait Gallery, wrote in its support in the *Liverpool Daily Post*, although this no doubt seemed like mere professional solidarity.[8] Napper had tried to combine the conventions of state portraiture with impressionist light, colour and brushwork. Sargent or his imitators might have succeeded but not Napper. Napper had been a pupil of Gerald Kelly before the war and he was then teaching at St Martin's School of Art with pupils including Frank Auerbach and Leon Kossoff. Although a successful society portraitist, especially of 'girls in pearls', he was not experienced in the grand portrait tradition that was required. Scrutton's budget for the portrait, £1,000, was inadequate to attract the leading Royal Academicians who were highly accomplished in this field and could still attract very large fees for formal portraits in boardrooms and country houses. In 1911 the City Council had commissioned a portrait of George V on his accession to the throne from Luke Fildes, and they were very displeased when Fildes told them that their fee of £550 was only adequate for a replica of his state portrait. The City Council's Finance Committee, effectively the city's governing body, rejected Napper's portrait and commissioned a new portrait with the traditional baroque curtain and column for the Town Hall from Edward Halliday (1902-1984) who had been born and trained in Liverpool and was emphatically a professional portrait painter.[9] The Finance Committee however did not control the Gallery and could not prevent Scrutton from hanging his portrait over the main stairs.[10] There it remained until 1989, marking Scrutton's brave attempt to establish a new tradition in formal municipal portraiture. It was not perhaps surprising that Scrutton's plea to take over control of all the paintings in the town hall was rejected.[11] It was not until 1967 that the City Council at last demonstrated its confidence in the Gallery's competence by entrusting this historic collection of portraits of monarchs, mayors and other local worthies by Thomas Lawrence, Thomas Phillips, Henry Pickering and others to the Gallery's care.[12]

Back in 1931 Cotton had felt that the Gallery should concentrate on British art as important continental paintings were too expensive. However in 1947 Birmingham City Art Gallery with Mary Woodall as their keeper of art bought at auction Orazio Gentileschi's superb *Rest on the Flight into Egypt* for only £525 without the use of a dealer, and this may have encouraged Cotton and Lambert to be more adventurous.[13] In 1950 they bought for £1500 *The Betrothal*, a sensitive and moving portrayal of a young couple by a follower of Rembrandt who specialized in themes of this type.[14] After Lambert's retirement, an early self portrait by Rembrandt from the collection of Charles I (presented by Ocean Steamship Company (P H Holt Trust)) and a notable early sixteenth-century Flemish tapestry (presented by Martin's Bank Ltd) entered the collection in 1953 as part of the group of gifts made by Liverpool banking, insurance and shipping companies largely thanks to Cotton's influence with local businesses. The National Art-Collections Fund's donation of a splendid *Virgin and Child* by Murillo in the same year and of an atmospheric *River Scene* by Salomon Ruysdael in 1955 further encouraged collecting in this area. Until 1956, while not ignoring British art, Scrutton purchased interesting but generally minor Venetian, Neapolitan and Netherlandish seventeenth- and early eighteenth-century decorative paintings by Bor, Ferri, Solimena, Dughet, Tacconi, Pittoni and others. This policy very much reflected the taste of the period, although perhaps his most memorable early purchase was quite different, a self-portrait by Mengs from the Panshanger Collection, costing only £480 in 1953.[15] The most notable Italian painting was Solimena's *Birth of the Baptist* at £270 acquired the same year.[16] He preferred to buy modestly priced pictures cautiously from London dealers such as Colnaghi and Agnew rather than from the auction rooms.

The early acquisitions were frequently given new frames designed and made by Robert Sielle, a much admired London frame-maker who worked for the Tate and National Gallery. His frames were very simple and untraditional in design, often combining edges of highly burnished gold and matt textured colour or fabric chosen to harmonise with the painting, but their scale was often on the heavy side. Sielle reframed the *Self portrait* by Mengs and *The Magdalen* by Bor. Scrutton also ordered from him new frames for many paintings already in the collection ranging from the sixteenth-century Netherlandish *Rest on the Flight into Egypt* to Matthew Smith's *Black Hat*. Like many of his contemporaries he felt that the traditional carved and gilded frame could be an impediment to the enjoyment of a painting and was seeking a more modern alternative. It was the last example of a long tradition of contemporary-style frames for old masters before the taste for period-style framing took over in the 1960s. Under Scrutton the process of softening the visual appearance of the galleries continued; some were hung with wallpaper and later with fabrics, and the entrance hall was given a contemporary colour scheme while preserving the 1930s fittings.

An editorial of 1955 in the prestigious *Burlington Magazine* praised Scrutton's acquisitions but was less enthusiastic about the Gallery's purchases of more modern art, observing enigmatically that 'since Liverpool has never been exactly famous for its patronage of modern art no doubt the Director is obliged to tread delicately on this slippery ground'.[17] In fact Scrutton and his successors, conscious of the Autumn Exhibition acquisitions to which the *Burlington Magazine* was referring, never spent large amounts on contemporary art. Paintings generally were very inexpensive in the 1950s and early 1960s, but until 1956 Scrutton only had an annual purchase grant of around £1,000 and about £1,000 from the Wavertree Bequest. His achievements were considerable although in retrospect he perhaps lacked the ambition that the National Art-Collections Fund hoped would be encouraged by their gift of the work by Murillo, and above all he did not aim high enough. Like many directors he did not consider rigorously the contribution his purchases would make to the visitor's experience and how they related to the existing collection. His acquisitions generally were less impressive than those made at the Birmingham City Art Gallery and made a much smaller impact on the collection. Directors enjoy buying and Scrutton was no exception but it did lead perhaps to too many minor acquisitions. At first he could not carry over any part of the annual grant from the City Council to the following years, but in 1964 a 'cumulative purchase fund' permitted the accumulation of funds for major acquisitions.[18] He showed the same reluctance to concentrate resources on a few exceptional works when he moved on to sculpture and impressionist and post-impressionist paintings. In 1966 he observed rightly that as gallery acquisitions 'objects of the second class in the arts, although deeply interesting to specialists, cut no ice with anyone else'.[19]

By 1947 Birmingham City Museum and Art Gallery already had an annual purchase grant of £5,000.[20] In 1957 the Walker Art Gallery's annual grant from the Council was increased to £3,000. By then the Wavertree Bequest had been very nearly exhausted. Between 1956 and 1962 Scrutton and the Museums Association carried out three surveys of the purchase grants available to the larger provincial art galleries. The figures are probably not strictly comparable as regular income from trusts and friends' organisations may not always have been included, and in some cities modest but significant amounts will have been allocated for museum rather than art gallery purposes. These are the figures: Aberdeen in 1956, £2,905, in 1958, £3,950, in 1962, £3,500; Birmingham in 1956, £6,900, in 1958, £12,200, in 1962, £22,000; Glasgow in 1956, £1,700, in 1958, £2,500, in 1962, £6,500; Leeds in 1956, £2,860, in 1958, £2,500, in 1962, £7,500; Liverpool in 1956, £1,800, in 1958, £3,000, in 1962, £5,000; Manchester in 1956, £4,400, in 1958, £5,000, in 1962, £5,400; Sheffield in 1956, £2,500, in 1958, £2,500, in 1962, £2,500. In 1962 the Tate Gallery was already spending about £75,000 each year on the purchase of works of art and the National Galleries of Scotland about £27,000. The dates are significant because these were probably the last years in which important works of art could be bought very cheaply, and in Liverpool the new money permitted the acquisition in 1956 of Hogarth's *Garrick as Richard III* for £3,500 which transformed in a spectacular fashion the modest holding of British eighteenth-century art built up by Lambert and Cotton.[21] It was of course one of the very few works which can safely be described as creating the British School of Painting both for its subject matter and for its style and technique.

The dramatic increase in the purchase fund can probably be attributed to the new policies of the Labour Party which had gained control of the Liverpool City Council for the first time in 1955. Cotton, as a Conservative, had to resign as chairman of the Libraries, Museums and Arts Committee. Despite his enormous achievements he had failed to persuade his party to provide reasonable acquisition funds and he had only been partially successful in another equally important area – the recruitment of more staff. In 1952 there was a professional staff of two, a director and a deputy director, the same level of staffing that the Gallery had in the nineteenth century with many fewer pictures, although now it had the services of a freelance paintings conservator. Fastnedge had been appointed deputy director in 1949 at a salary of £635 after the offer of £595 failed to attract suitable candidates. A new post of senior administrative assistant was created in 1953 and Sheila Somers came in July 1955 as deputy keeper and lecturer at a salary of £675.[22] A review of staff and work at the Gallery was carried out by the town clerk's establishment office in 1956, and while Labour were in power between 1955 and 1961 three more new posts at keeper or assistant keeper level were created and filled, together with a new post of schools officer. A second freelance paintings conservator working part time was also recruited. Thus by early 1961 there were four curatorial posts, as well as a deputy director and a director, and this level has never been exceeded. Despite the generous pay enjoyed by the director, salaries lower down the hierarchy, especially for the assistant keepers, were modest and remained so until national status was achieved in the late 1980s. In 1957 Michael Compton moved from Leeds City Art Gallery to the Walker Art Gallery as a senior assistant keeper, improving his salary from about £500 to about £700.[23] By 1960 assistant keepers were only receiving between £610 and £765 annually while senior assistant keepers were earning between £880 and £1,065.[24] In the same year the salary scale for senior assistant keepers in the national galleries in London ran from £1,217 to £1,915. The gap between national and Liverpool salary scales contracted modestly in the 1960s and 1970s. The senior assistant keepers in Liverpool were re-designated as keepers and received higher salaries. By December 1972 these keepers were earning between £2,994 and £3,324 while salaries for senior assistant keepers in the national galleries ran from £2,597 to £4,424 and salaries for keepers from £5,350 to £6,260. Assistant keepers in Liverpool were then receiving between £1,803 and £2,388, easily explaining the rapid turnover in staff at that level in the 1970s.[25] Generally starting salaries were reasonably good but pay scales were very short. The director's salary, which had been almost exactly the same as that earned by the director of the Tate Gallery in 1951, was little more than half that amount by the end of 1972.[26] The demand for qualified art historians to teach in art colleges, polytechnics and universities at high salaries, following the establishment there of art history departments, also made recruitment difficult. The post of keeper of foreign art was advertised publicly twice in 1967 at a modest but respectable salary of £1,665 and the only application came from the assistant keeper.[27] An assistant schools officer post was created in 1966 and more conservators arrived in the early 1990s with national status and a new conservation department no longer directly controlled by the Gallery. However it was essentially in the late 1950s and early 1960s that the Gallery, thanks to Scrutton's determined efforts, was able to achieve respectable staffing levels. In 1960 the Gallery's total expenditure was around £65,000 of which salaries accounted for about £28,000.[28] In 1964 total expenditure was approximately £98,000 with salaries at about £52,000.[29] In a period of low inflation the figures for 1960 were nearly treble the amounts for 1952 and the figures for 1964 were more than quadruple the amounts for 1952, the year of Scrutton's appointment as director. This was his most remarkable achievement.

    The principal immediate reason for these substantial increases in staff numbers was the pressing need to compile a complete new inventory of the very large permanent collection of about 8,000 works including over 1,700 paintings, and to gather together systematically the documentation for each work.[30] The new inventory also had to reconcile what the Gallery was recorded as owning with the material it physically held, and to identify war losses together with items in the building which were not its property. Mary Bennett, who joined the staff in February 1956 from the William Morris Gallery in Walthamstow, devised a detailed record card for each work of art on which was recorded not only every feature of its physical appearance and structure but also, as far as possible, information about it from Gallery and local records as well as from books, articles and other published and unpublished sources. Her record card was later much plagiarized in other art galleries. To achieve this result every work of art had to be carefully examined, back and front. Each work of art also had its own file in which all types of related material, old and new, correspondence, photographs, photocopies, research notes, comments by outside experts, transcripts of telephone conversations, could be securely placed. Every work was re-measured, re-numbered and entered into a new inventory book. Mary Bennett herself covered the British oil paintings and sculpture over a period of about five years while Hugh Macandrew (1931-1993), who arrived in 1957 after reading history at Edinburgh University and a spell as a volunteer at the Tate Gallery, was responsible for the more numerous but more easily handled prints, drawings and watercolours. He left in 1962 and later specialized in prints and drawings both at the Ashmolean Museum and at the National Gallery of Scotland. Compton dealt with the few but very important foreign paintings. At the same time a determined effort was made to photograph first all the more significant paintings, watercolours, drawings and sculptures and then finally the entire collection. All these procedures may seem to be basic and standard public art gallery good practice, but not all national galleries and very few provincial galleries had achieved by the 1980s the level of documentation attained at the Walker Art Gallery by about 1962. Unlike many documentation projects it was finished within a remarkably short time and to an extremely high standard, so that proper management of the collection was possible. From the public's point of view the greatest immediate benefit of the new inventory was perhaps the rediscovery of *Ruins of Holyrood Chapel* by the pioneer photographer and painter Daguerre, which judging by post card sales became an immediate favourite with the visitor.

Apart from establishing exactly what the Gallery owned the main purpose behind this great effort was to facilitate the compilation and publication of detailed and well-researched catalogues of all parts of the collection and to manage it efficiently. Numerous such catalogues of the old master paintings then owned by the Liverpool Royal Institution, including those formerly owned by William Roscoe, had been published in the nineteenth century, and in 1928 Maurice Brockwell wrote a new catalogue of them for the Walker Art Gallery.[31] The Gallery believed it had an obligation to make available as widely as possible full information on its entire collections and that proper curatorial understanding of its holdings increased the value of the collection both for visitors and students. Publication of these catalogues frequently showed the limitations of curatorial knowledge and often led to significant new information and attributions. Among these was the identification of Charles Le Brun, Louis XIV's court artist, as the painter of the

Atalanta and Meleager from the French royal collection which had been presented to Liverpool in 1852.[32] Good fully illustrated catalogues also enabled the validity of new acquisitions to be questioned far more rigorously. This project was not new. In April 1912 Thomas White began compiling a detailed catalogue of the entire permanent collection at a salary of £3 per week. He worked alphabetically and by February 1916 he had only reached artists with names beginning with the letter K. His diligence and expertise were much praised by the curator but the Gallery's Sub-Committee dismissed him in April. His work was completed by the curator and assistant curator in the following year thanks to the leisure available to them after the suspension of the Autumn Exhibitions during the First World War. Eventually the Libraries, Museums and Arts Committee decided that the catalogue was too expensive to print and it was never published.[33] However White's documentation survived in the Gallery's files and formed a basis for later work. For curators of the 1950s, 1960s and 1970s cataloguing was seen as their first duty after acquisitions and loan exhibitions, which outside London could only be afforded on a modest scale. Of course there was still general responsibility for conservation, display, storage, loans and education, but these functions were increasingly being hived off to specialists, who generally performed these duties more effectively than curators had ever done. Fastnedge and Somers had been doing serious research on the earlier foreign paintings since the early 1950s, and they had first established the Gallery's reputation for scholarship. Scrutton too must share the credit. He often said that he was no scholar but he never doubted the importance of research. Lastly in the early 1960s Mary Bennett established the Gallery's reputation for research into Victorian art particularly the Pre-Raphaelite brotherhood, then a very unfashionable area of expertise, which it has never lost.

Research on the entire collection was enormously assisted by the growth of the Liverpool City Library which adjoined the Gallery on its west side. A few months after Scrutton's appointment, the City Council had selected George Chandler as its new city librarian. Chandler believed in Picton's great idea, which amazed some of his colleagues, that in his libraries 'all standard books should be there no matter how seldom some of them might be read'.[34] By 1950 the City Library had about one million books. 200,000 had been lost in the war but many had already been replaced. Chandler worked on Picton's principle and he was soon buying 'practically every English book'. The Hornby Library within the City Library already held a large collection of engravings and rare books of which many were illustrated or related to the history of art. In April 1955 the City Library opened a new art library containing about 40,000 volumes in one of the Gallery's large ground-floor rooms with direct access to the Library itself. Chandler had recruited Keith Andrews (1917-1991) as the specialist art librarian at a salary very generous by the standards of the Walker Art Gallery.[35] Andrews, born Kurt Aufrichtig

1. Simone Martini (about 1284-1344)
Christ Discovered in the Temple, 1342
Panel, 49.6 x 35.1 cm
Courtesy National Museums Liverpool (the Walker)
Formerly in the collection of William Roscoe; presented by the
Liverpool Royal Institution in 1948

2. Joos van Cleve (active 1511-1540/41)
Virgin and Child with Angels, about 1525
Panel, 85.5 x 65.5 cm
Courtesy National Museums Liverpool (the Walker)
Formerly in the collection of Charles Blundell; bought in 1981 for £225,000 (tax remission)
from the Trustees of Colonel Sir Joseph Weld with the aid of the National Heritage
Memorial Fund, the Art Fund, the Victoria and Albert Museum Grant Fund,
the Special Appeal Fund and other donors

3. Francesco Primaticcio (1504-1570)
Ulysses winning the Archery Contest, about 1550
Red chalk heightened with white on light red prepared paper, 24.3 x 32.4 cm
Courtesy National Museums Liverpool (the Walker)
Formerly in the collections of William Roscoe and Charles Blundell; bought in 1991 for £245,000 with the aid of the Art Fund and the Friends of the National Museums Liverpool

4. Peter Paul Rubens (1577-1640)
Virgin and Child with St Elizabeth and the Child Baptist, about 1632
Oil on canvas, 180 x 139.5 cm
Courtesy National Museums Liverpool (the Walker)
Bought in 1960 for £50,000 with the aid of a £25,000 special Treasury Grant and of contributions from the Art Fund, various local trusts, companies and individuals

5. Nicolas Poussin (1593/4-1665)
Landscape with the Ashes of Phocion, about 1648
Oil on canvas, 116.5 x 178.5 cm
Courtesy National Museums Liverpool (the Walker)
Acquired by the twelfth Earl of Derby between 1776 and 1782; bought in 1983 for £1,150,000 (tax remission) from the Trustees of Lord Derby's Heirlooms Settlement with the aid of the National Heritage Memorial Fund, the Art Fund, the Victoria and Albert Museum Grant Fund, and other donors

6. William Hogarth (1697-1764)
David Garrick as Richard III, 1745
Oil on canvas, 190.5 x 251 cm
Courtesy National Museums Liverpool (the Walker)
Bought in 1956 for £3,500, using the Wavertree Bequest and with the aid of the Art Fund

7. George Stubbs (1724-1806)
Molly Long-legs with her Jockey, 1761-2
Oil on canvas, 101 x 126.8 cm
Courtesy National Museums Liverpool (the Walker)
Presented by Messrs Lewis, Liverpool, on the occasion of the re-opening
of the Walker Art Gallery in 1951

8. Richard Wilson (1713-1782)
Snowdon from Llyn Nantlle, 1765-66
Oil on canvas, 101 x 127 cm
Courtesy National Museums Liverpool (the Walker)
Bought in 1935 for £950

in Hamburg, had come to England as a refugee in 1934 and had been working in a London antiquarian bookshop with no university degree or librarianship qualifications, although he did attend evening lectures at the Courtauld Institute twice each week. It was an excellent appointment and later, as keeper of prints and drawings at the Scottish National Galleries, he created that department's international reputation.[36] In Liverpool he lamented that owing to the vagaries of the Dewey classification system he was also responsible for books on sport, and he stayed for only two and a half years. His successors however included Antony Symons who left in 1970 to become the Tate Gallery's first professional librarian. There Symons developed a modest catalogue collection into 'a resource without parallel elsewhere in the field of modern and contemporary exhibition catalogues'.[37] Andrews and Symons were not only collecting art books in many languages on a large scale, including for example a 1672 edition of Bellori's *Le Vite de'Pittori*, but also prints by Schongauer, Delacroix, Daumier, Whistler and others. Andrews published an article in the *Liverpool Bulletin* on some early lithographs in the City Library.[38] Leeds followed Liverpool's example with an art library and print room within its art gallery.[39] In the early 1960s the Liverpool Art Library moved out of the Walker Art Gallery into the City Library itself, but certainly by the late 1970s it was probably superior to any other English art library outside London, Oxford and Cambridge. Andrews and Symons were very remarkable men, and the Gallery staff gained enormously both from the Library they formed and from their personal knowledge of art history. It seems that Andrews applied unsuccessfully for Fastnedge's job as deputy director in 1957 intending no doubt to carry on the scholarly tradition created by Fastnedge and Somers. Nor were the Gallery staff idle themselves. Leaving the city's Art Library to acquire books and periodicals they concentrated on exhibition, sale and permanent collection catalogues, specializing in Liverpool and Manchester sale catalogues, together with art gallery reports and bulletins. These were collected in exchange for the Gallery's own publications from other galleries throughout the world. By the 1980s the Gallery's library enjoyed the same pre-eminence in its more modest field as the city's Art Library.

With detailed primary documentation complete and a splendid art library growing within their own building the writing of detailed catalogues of the permanent collection moved ahead rapidly. Compton had been appointed as a senior assistant keeper with specific responsibility for writing a catalogue of the foreign paintings. The other candidate for this post later became director of the Courtauld Institute.[40] Compton left only two and a half years later to be director of the Ferens Art Gallery in Hull with a draft catalogue complete but still requiring substantial editing. This was carried out largely by John Jacob (1929-2001), the deputy director who had joined the Gallery in 1957 from York City Art Gallery, with the help of Hugh Macandrew, and the catalogue was finally published in 1963 with a companion volume of plates in 1966.[41] Birmingham City Art Gallery had published a catalogue of their paintings in 1960 written by John Woodward, with the help of John Rowlands, Malcolm Cormack and Ellis Waterhouse. They had a stronger art-historical team but their catalogue, mainly concerned with British paintings, was selective while the Walker Art Gallery aimed to include every work held however apparently unimportant. Compton benefited greatly from the extensive earlier research of Fastnedge and Somers, especially on the very important early paintings. He could also rely on the wide European perspective of Andrews who had a detailed knowledge of continental art-historical literature.[42] Although his catalogue had a few rather speculative attributions and showed a lack of interest in the nineteenth-century academic paintings, his achievement was very considerable in this pioneering effort, and it established a pattern for future catalogues. In 1967 and 1968 exhibitions of all the Gallery's old master drawings and prints and of all its early English water-colours and drawings had been held to enable visitors and the staff to assess these interesting and unusual, but far from comprehensive, collections. The accompanying catalogues, containing much more detail than is generally found in exhibition catalogues, were intended to be a first stage in the compilation of more detailed catalogues.[43] Sadly research was only pursued on the foreign works. A more sober, detailed and comprehensive catalogue of all foreign works of art in the collection, now broadened to include sculpture, drawings, prints, silver, porcelain and tapestry as well as paintings, appeared in 1977 with every item illustrated. A supplement in 1984 covered acquisitions made between these two dates.[44] It was not easy for the three authors concerned to do justice to such a large and varied collection but these catalogues provided a foundation for the eventual compilation of more specialized catalogues covering distinct sections of the collection. Work on a detailed catalogue of the British oil paintings had also begun but this was a much more difficult assignment. There were probably fifteen times more British than foreign pictures, and the development of British art history was at a very primitive stage. Initially it was planned to give the pictures very concise entries but, with increasing curatorial ambition and the growing interest in nineteenth-century British painting, this approach became outdated. To make progress it was decided to break down the British holdings into more manageable parts. A volume for the paintings in the Holt Bequest at Sudley first appeared. Mary Bennett then covered all the paintings by Merseyside artists together with every local portrait and landscape in a new fully illustrated catalogue published in 1978, a very remarkable achievement at a time when, if British art history was still unfashionable, the study of painting in the regions had scarcely begun.[45] For the first time it explored the importance of a large group of paintings usually pejoratively described as being of 'local interest' and highlighted the rich diversity and achievement of painting and patronage on Merseyside from the mid-eighteenth century. A second volume on Merseyside sculpture, watercolours and miniatures was planned, but in 1978 the Gallery took on the Lady Lever Art Gallery and priorities had to be re-assessed. Accordingly a similar new inventory of the Lady Lever holdings was begun and a series of eight detailed catalogues of works of art in the Lady Lever Art Gallery were published between 1983 and 2000. Mary Bennett's specialist knowledge resulted in a very thorough catalogue of all the Pre-Raphaelite works at the Lady Lever, Sudley and Walker Art Galleries in 1988.[46] This catalogue illustrated not only the wealth of Pre-Raphaelite holdings spread between the three collections but also the benefits of bringing the collections together.

The publication of detailed catalogues of permanent collections is rarely financially profitable but the Gallery was able to use a modest and unrestricted bequest from Frederick Bowring to cover its costs. Income from the sale not only of catalogues but also of more remunerative cards, slides and reproductions were paid back into the bequest creating a publications fund. Reproduction fees from the publishers of art books and of illustrated books of all types, which were rapidly increasing in number and size in the 1960s and 1970s, were paid into the same fund enabling it to support not only Gallery publications but also other important projects, including in 1984 a grant of about £25,000, half the sum required, towards the purchase of the Lancashire County Sessions House, a huge court building immediately next to the Gallery. The publications counter at the Gallery never expanded into anything resembling a bookshop, which was not commercially viable. However a coffee bar, opened in 1957, did grow into a café after a few years but without the sustained commercial success of the publications department. It closed in 1974 for practical reasons, and food and drink did not become available at the Gallery again until 1984 when a local catering firm started to provide modest refreshments in the entrance hall using the same 'contracted-out' system which had been employed during the Autumn Exhibitions. It was generally felt that eating and drinking humanized rather than trivialized the austere grandeur of Thornely's architecture, and the service was taken over by the trading company of the National Museums and Galleries on Merseyside in 1996.

This intensive work on the permanent collection involved the hundreds of paintings from the reserve collections which had been loaned to a wide variety of municipal offices, public and semi-public institutions and commercial companies throughout Merseyside and beyond. By 1927 there were already 661 works on loan to municipal bodies alone and by 1954 the total figure was 854 paintings. These loans required much work by curators, conservators and technicians in selecting appropriate works for different locations, in hanging, moving and recalling pictures at the request of borrowers, in checking their condition and restoring any damage, as well as research on their status, attribution, subject and provenance. Borrowers however wanted 'bright modern pictures,' not the 'third-rate Victorian and Edwardian paintings,' generally on offer.[47] Satisfying the more eminent of these borrowers could be difficult. The director of the Leeds City Art Galleries was nearly dismissed from his post for refusing to continue the loan of some watercolours to a sunny room in his local Judges' Lodgings.[48] In 1957 all paintings in Liverpool on long-term loan were recalled for a complete review of their condition and suitability for loan.[49] In 1958 an annual charge of one pound for each painting was imposed, although schools were exempt.[50] The figure remained unchanged for at least twenty years but in practice the money was hard to collect. The loans were however important in providing a use for the reserve collections and thus deflecting suggestions for their sale or disposal. Other major municipal galleries were selling important but unfashionable Victorian paintings at this time, and the threat in Liverpool was probably very real. In 1954 a special meeting of the Libraries, Museums and Arts Committee decided that no sales should take place but that storage and care should improve.[51] In 1958 the sale of 'pictures surplus to requirements' was considered by the Arts Sub-Committee. The town clerk advised that any paintings bought by the City Council, or given to it without specific conditions prohibiting their disposal, could be sold and the proceeds given to the Gallery.[52] Fortunately it was agreed that further consideration was necessary and in practice nothing was done, probably thanks to constructive inertia from Scrutton. As late however as 1968 Alderman Macdonald Steward, the Conservative leader of the City Council, whose wife was a co-opted member of the Committee, was asking the town clerk if the Gallery's paintings could be sold – no doubt as part of the great Conservative drive of the late 1960s for town hall efficiency.[53]

In his London speech of 1955 pleading for more central government assistance for provincial galleries, Cotton had suggested that the immediate priority was for help for these galleries to acquire paintings which had been bought in Britain by overseas buyers but which had been temporarily refused an export licence on the grounds of their exceptional importance, in order to give British galleries time to raise the necessary money for their purchase.[54] In 1959 the Nelson-Atkins Museum of Art in Kansas City bought Rubens's *Virgin and Child with St Elizabeth and the Child Baptist* (fig. 4) of about 1633 for £50,000 from the Duke of Devonshire. The attribution, provenance and significance of the painting were not in doubt. An export licence was temporarily refused. The National Gallery were not interested in buying the painting. In the euphoria following the Conservative election victory of 1959 the Treasury had increased the Tate Gallery's annual purchase grant from £7,500 to £40,000 and the National Gallery's grant reached £125,000 only three years later. It was therefore not entirely surprising that the Treasury felt able to offer a special grant of £25,000 to any provincial gallery able to raise the remaining £25,000 within the three months specified in the provisional refusal of the export licence. This imaginative gesture by central government has never been repeated. Liverpool, Manchester and Southampton City Art Galleries attempted to raise the money but only Liverpool was successful. The City Council approved a special grant of £4,000 and allowed the Gallery to anticipate the next year's purchase grant, thus giving the Gallery £10,000 to put towards the required matching funding. Manchester City Art Gallery's committee rather tactlessly asked for £20,000 from its Council. The Council's Finance Committee reduced this amount to £10,000 and the Council itself reduced it further to £250.[55] The remaining £15,000 required by the Walker Art Gallery was given by Liverpool business, individuals and trusts, thanks to Cotton's fund-raising skills, together with grants from the Calouste Gulbenkian Foundation, the Pilgrim Trust and the National Art-Collections Fund. Thus about 60% of the total amount came from outside Liverpool, and for major acquisitions this percentage would rise sharply over the next twenty-five years. The purchase, which received exceptional and favourable press coverage, dramatically increased the reputation of the Gallery both in Liverpool and in the rest of the Britain.[56] In the same year as the acquisition of the painting by Rubens, Scrutton widened his purchasing interests to include twentieth-century European art with the acquisition of two respectable but not exceptional paintings by Vlaminck and Derain costing together over £6,000.[57] The National Art-Collections Fund refused a grant for the unusually classicist work by Derain, probably believing it to be too expensive, and certainly in comparison with British eighteenth- and nineteenth-century paintings these pictures were not cheap.[58]

Encouraged by the success of the Rubens venture an appeal was launched in March 1961 to the 'large industrial and commercial concerns on Merseyside' for funds to support further acquisitions. In 1951 Cotton had noted that the Gallery could no longer expect large gifts and bequests from wealthy individuals and that it should look to business instead.[59] The Walker Art Gallery's aims in 1961 were specific. It wanted to buy work by 'some of the great modern masters of the past hundred years so that the story told by the Gallery's splendid collection of old masters should be brought forward and the link made with our own times'.[60] This of course simply repeated Cotton's contention of 1931 that the Gallery's purchasing policy had so far been too narrowly focused on rather conservative aspects of British contemporary art leaving a huge gap between about 1800 and 1960 in the Gallery's holdings of British and Continental art. There was some truth in this assertion although the Gallery already held works by Corot, Daguerre, Delaroche, Scheffer, Gérome, Doré, Frère, Rodin, Rosa Bonheur, Legros, Segantini, Gussow, Le Sidaner, Liebermann, Monticelli, and others, together with a very important and unusual group of late nineteenth-century American paintings including works by Sargent, Boughton, Picknell, Abbey and Bridgman. Indeed if there were gaps in the Gallery's collection they lay much more in the eighteenth or twentieth century than in the nineteenth century. However for the purposes of this appeal the 'great modern masters of the past hundred years' were not Gérome or Legros or even Rodin and Segantini but principally the French Impressionists and Post-Impressionists, artists who had had a profound influence on painters whose work had been bought by Cotton and Lambert, notably Sickert, Gilman and Gore. Most successful British and American businessmen admired their bright colour, loose brushwork and generally undemanding subject matter. The Liverpool company director Morton Oliphant collected their work and supported the Gallery's appeal for funds to buy their pictures. Birmingham City Art Gallery had already bought notable paintings by Sisley, Courbet, Camille Pissarro, Cassatt and Degas between 1948 and 1960. The Walker Art Gallery's appeal, re-launched in 1968, raised nearly £120,000 in nine years. More than half came in the first few months. This success, together with Scrutton's ingenious use of tax concessions to increase the effective value of the funds at his disposal, was widely admired, particularly by his fellow directors who saw it rightly as a highly original initiative. The first appeal's £77,000 together with £52,900 from other sources such as the National Art-Collections Fund and the Victoria and Albert Museum Purchase Grant Fund was spent on eight works costing altogether £129,900. Several of the works had substantial tax discounts so the £77,000 secured pictures then valued at well in excess of £250,000. The success of the appeals certainly played some part in encouraging the great London galleries to transform their collections and buildings largely through private generosity over the rest of the century.[61] Cotton, 'that formidable raiser of funds and inspirer of gifts', could appeal in the 1960s to a small close-knit group of Liverpool business leaders controlling their own companies, survivors in part from Liverpool's earlier 'Liberal Plutocracy.'[62] Some were collectors and most had a wide interest in art.[63] Paintings by Courbet (£7,000), Cézanne (£32,400), Monet (£16,200), Seurat (£13,500), Degas (£50,000) and others were bought with the assistance of money from the Appeal.[64] Cézanne's harrowing *The Murder*, one of his early dark and violent paintings inspired by Zola's novels, was very untypical of his work and style, but it seems to have been popular in Liverpool. Scrutton's very personal response to works of art is reflected in his appreciation of this painting: 'That slatey-blue near monochrome, slightly and subtly varied to give definition to the darkness, is the real substance of the work of art.'[65] He even saw a rather unflattering connection with Liverpool: 'It seems fitting that Liverpool – a great nineteenth-century city in whose past grim and terrible incidents lie buried – should now own this slate-blue painting, which is so powerfully evocative of the depth of human nature.'[66] He was proudest of a small sketch by Seurat, a notable preliminary study. The acquisition of Degas's *Woman Ironing* (fig. 16) demonstrated his skill in exploiting the tax concessions available for sales by private treaty. Unable to persuade the executors of Mrs. Pleydell-Bouverie to withdraw the picture from a Sotheby's auction he agreed with the executors an offer which in effect became the auction reserve. Not unexpectedly, given the substantial tax liability, it was bought in and sold to the Walker for £50,000, about a third of its market value. This was apparently one of the first occasions on which this particular tax saving mechanism was used by a provincial gallery at an auction.[67]

However the impact of the pictures he acquired nearly fifty years ago is still hard to assess. As other aspects of nineteenth-century French art are re-valued the special importance attached to impressionist and post-impressionist paintings in the 1950s and 1960s seems less justifiable. Was Monet's *Seine at Bennecourt*, showing the breakup of the ice on the river, by the great painter of sunlight really a prudent acquisition at £16,200 from Wildenstein's in 1962?[68] Wildenstein's were then the leading dealers in the work of this rather uneven artist, and perhaps the Gallery could not reasonably have hoped for a better example of his work for this small amount. The National Art-Collections Fund declined to contribute towards the cost of this painting and John Moores, who had little interest in the Gallery's historic collection, refused any assistance with the purchase of Cézanne's *The Murder* despite his enthusiasm for this artist's work.[69] This initiative remains however the only attempt by a regional gallery to make good a perceived 'gap' in its collection with funds from local donors. The national museums and galleries were able to rely on central government to help with their 'gaps'. Probably Lambert who believed that impressionist paintings were already too expensive in the 1930s was right. Some Gallery staff tried to persuade Scrutton to consider twentieth-century art, particularly works by the German Expressionists, which were still moderately priced and more readily available. On the other hand no other municipal gallery or museum proved able to raise such large sums from business sources for the acquisition of works of art.

The appeal fund was not re-launched in the 1970s although from time to time commercial support was obtained for specific purchases, notably *The Ashes of Phocion* by Poussin (fig. 5) and *The Virgin and Child with Angels* by Joos van Cleve (fig. 2). Cotton had died. Most of the contributing firms had lost their autonomy, and their new local managers rarely had the power or the inclination to assist the Gallery. Control of Liverpool's historic banks, shipping companies and insurance companies was passing to London boardrooms. The new post-war factories and businesses had head offices far from Merseyside. Economic decline on Merseyside was unmistakeable.

Although gifts from individual collectors and their families declined as Liverpool's great mercantile families moved or faded away, they remained significant. In 1952 the ship owner Sir Ernest Royden gave four royal portraits to the Gallery including one by Highmore. In 1953 Geoffrey Tillotson presented a portrait of Thomas Sprat, the great Bishop of

Rochester, by John Riley which was then thought to represent Bishop Tillotson, an ancestor of the donor. In the following year another local businessman Major Philip England presented the elegant full-length portrait of the heiress of William ninth Earl of Derby, Henrietta Maria Lady Ashburnham, by Dahl, probably at Cotton's instigation. In 1955 Mr and Mrs S. Samuels, leading Liverpool collectors, donated *Man of Aran*, a bronze bust by Epstein. In 1953 C.F.J. Beausire had given to the Gallery a notable early landscape by Loutherbourg probably again at Cotton's request. He 'wished to present the picture to the City as being the centre of his business successfully carried on by his family for three generations.'[70] In 1960 his family gave at the Gallery's request the bronze *Falling Warrior* of about 1956-7 by Henry Moore, then still a controversial artist in the provinces. It had cost them £3,000.[71] In fact Beausire collected not modernist sculpture but eighteenth-century furniture, French paintings and above all English watercolours. In 1972 he bequeathed to the Gallery some forty-five watercolours including fine works by celebrated artists including Turner, Cox, Edward Lear, J.F. Lewis and David Roberts. Even more remarkable were some magnificent large exhibition watercolours by Copley Fielding, an artist adored by Ruskin and admired in the France of Charles X, but entirely ignored in the twentieth century.[72] This was the greatest gift received by the Gallery for many years and probably no single subsequent gift has matched it. The Gallery has never treated watercolours with the respect they deserve partly because its own collections of watercolours, although of considerable interest, do not match those at the two Manchester public galleries or those at the Birmingham and Leeds City Art Galleries. Beausire wished to change this attitude and tried to make his gift conditional on a promise that the Gallery would always have 'a substantial number of watercolours on display'. The Gallery resisted this obligation but did commit itself to providing a space for the display of watercolours as soon as possible. A small gallery was briefly allocated for changing displays of works of art on paper in the early 1980s, and the pledge to Beausire was renewed on the acquisition of the old master drawings from Charles Blundell's collection in 1995.[73] A room specially designed for works of art on paper and for textiles was eventually planned in 1998 but soon abandoned, and the commitment to Beausire has never been fully honoured.[74]

Cotton worked hard on fund-raising for the Gallery until his death in 1970, but the most important figure there after his resignation as chairman in 1955 was Ben Shaw (1907-1986). Labour lost control of the City Council in 1961 but regained it in 1963 and thereafter power in Liverpool and Merseyside oscillated between the two parties with Labour dominant for most of the time. Shaw was effectively the Labour member of the Liverpool City Council and later of the Merseyside County Council with responsibility for the arts just as Cotton had been for the Conservative party. The two men were however very different. Shaw was a Liverpool Jewish business man of

Russian extraction who was very successful in the clothing trade. He first joined the Libraries, Museums and Arts Committee in 1957 when he was already over 50, although he had been active in the Labour party before the war. He was immensely hard working, enthusiastic and loquacious but with only a fairly modest knowledge of the arts, except perhaps in an educational and political context. He strongly supported the socialist principle that the workers deserved cultural provision of the highest quality and he liked pictures. Intensely proud of Liverpool and Merseyside, he always believed that the Walker Art Gallery was of national significance and that it should receive national funding not only in recognition of this fact but also to enable its collection and activities to be developed to the standard that he felt Merseyside deserved. Like Cotton he was probably not a major figure within the hierarchy of his own political party, and notoriously Council leaders of all political parties rarely took the chairmen of their Arts Committees very seriously. However he worked very hard to convince his political leaders of the importance of the Gallery and to impress his own energy and enthusiasm into the Gallery staff, all much younger than him. However like Cotton, in spite of his persuasive charm, he never secured from the Council the additional funds needed for an effective gallery.

In October 1963 he and Scrutton spent two weeks together visiting the art galleries and museums of eight American cities, and Scrutton must have felt that he had escaped the dominance of Cotton only to fall under the control of Shaw. From his American tour he and Shaw discovered that 'their galleries are...part of the social life of their cities in a sense much more pronounced than we can claim,'[75] and in 1965 he formally proposed the formation of a 'Friends of the Walker Art Gallery'. The idea had been discussed in 1960 by the Arts Sub-Committee of which Shaw had recently become deputy chairman. Drawing on his experience in forming the Friends of the Whitechapel Art Gallery ten years earlier Scrutton rightly advised the Sub-Committee that they must choose between a low annual subscription of about a pound which, after expenses, would yield very little financial benefit to the Gallery, and a much higher subscription of about three pounds which would attract very few members.[76] In the proposal of 1965 the organisation was to be called 'Contact' and would be primarily intended to keep members informed about Gallery activities not to raise money.[77] 'Friends' of museums and galleries had been well known in continental Europe for many years and the Fitzwilliam Museum in Cambridge had founded its Friends in 1909 in imitation of the 'Friends of the Louvre'.[78] The idea was slow to spread to British municipal galleries and museums. In 1912 Frank Rutter, the director of the Leeds City Art Gallery, together with Michael Sadler, the vice-chancellor of the University and an important modernist collector, founded the Leeds Art-Collections Fund, effectively a 'Friends' organization, in order to provide money for acquisitions by the Gallery.[79] In 1912 and in 1916, very low points in the Gallery's history, the curator, Rimbault Dibdin, had proposed the formation of a group of 'art collectors and connoisseurs' to assist the Gallery with acquisition and public relations.[80] Dibdin's successor, Arthur Quigley, was less sure in 1924, fearing that a Friends' organization might be too radical and modernist.[81] Glasgow Art Gallery and Museums founded their Friends association in 1944 with a minimum annual subscription of only one shilling (very approximately £1-50 today).[82] In 1948 Bristol City Art Gallery established a very successful 'Friends' organization which concentrated on buying contemporary British art for the Gallery.[83] The Tate Gallery had established its 'Friends' in 1958 with a high subscription and, like Bristol, had stated that their principal purpose was to raise money in support of its purchase funds. By 1963 they had raised over £85,000 but even in 1967 there were still only two thousand members.[84] Eventually in 1973 Shaw, now chairman of the new Arts, Culture and Libraries Committee, was able to form a very inclusive 'Friends' organization covering both the Walker Art Gallery and the Liverpool Museum that he had long wanted.[85] Its low annual subscription did indeed provide very little money to the Museum and Gallery, but, thanks to the enterprise of its voluntary committee, substantial sums were raised by means of many fund-raising schemes. The Friends ran an extremely lucrative lottery in the late 1970s in partnership with the Everyman Theatre and the Royal Liverpool Philharmonic Orchestra until they had to withdraw from it due to problems with Value Added Tax. Unexpectedly therefore the contributions of the Friends towards purchases were substantially higher than those provided by the Council.

In 1963 the annual purchase fund from the City Council rose to £10,000 and remained at that level or rather less until the shift to national status in 1986, but inflation and rising picture prices reduced its real value dramatically. Sculpture was seen by many curators including Scrutton in the early 1960s as offering better value than paintings. Peter Cannon-Brookes, who was appointed keeper of art at the Birmingham City Art Gallery and Museum in 1965, made some notable acquisitions there of baroque sculpture.[86] Scrutton valued sculpture for adding visual interest and historical context to displays of paintings of the same period or school.[87] He favoured sculpture dating from before 1800, which was then largely unrepresented in the Gallery's collections. However sculpture of this period presented difficult problems of attribution and dating. Outside the great figures and by comparison with paintings it had been little studied by art historians, particularly the methods of its production. Scrutton inevitably had to place great, and perhaps too much, reliance on the opinion of dealers for independent expert advice. In 1966 the purchase of an ivory *Meleager* for £2,500 had to be abandoned at the last moment due to doubts about its value and status.[88] He became a close friend of Andrew Ciechanowiecki, Cyril Humphris and David Peel, all then emerging as leading sculpture dealers in London. In 1961 he bought two nearly life-size limewood south-German saints of about 1720-1730, the first baroque sculptures to enter the collection. They are interesting as probably part of an altar group but otherwise of rather modest distinction.[89] In 1963 a group of about ten rather miscellaneous and unimportant bronzes of all periods between the sixteenth and twentieth centuries were bought, but this year also saw, with John Jacob's encouragement, the purchase of the outstanding sixteenth-century wooden figure of a warrior saint now attributed to the Master of Elsloo, perhaps Scrutton's most distinguished sculpture acquisition.[90] It was bought not from Bond Street but from an auction held at Scarisbrick Hall, just outside Liverpool, and had almost certainly been acquired for the Hall in the late 1830s by A.W.N. Pugin, its great architect. When exhibited at Sint-Truiden in 1990, Paul Williamson described it as a 'magnificent and until recently virtually unknown lifesize figure.'[91] Scrutton was further encouraged by the bequest of Frederick Mayor which came into effect on the death of Mayor's sister in 1960. It provided about £37,500 for the acquisition of seventeenth- and eighteenth-century works of art 'of the highest quality'. The Liverpool Museum could also use the money but in practice spent very little.[92] The bequest provided most of the money for a bronze *Cupid holding Laurel Wreaths*, then attributed to Étienne Le Hongre and bought in 1964 for £3,750, together with a large north-Italian terracotta *Virgin and Child* acquired in 1967 for £6,000.[93] Although Scrutton observed correctly that by 1967 sculpture was ceasing to be cheap his later purchases were more ambitious. They included a characteristically brilliant and vertiginous *Homage to Sculpture* by Francesco Bertos, which had been in the memorable Arts Council *Italian Bronze Statuettes* exhibition of 1961, and an excellent signed bust by Giuseppe de Levis. There were also two marbles, a charming *Education of Christ*, then attributed to Antonio Perolo and recommended by John Pope-Hennessy, Director of the Victoria and Albert Museum, together with an important figure from a tomb probably from the studio of Arnolfo di Cambio.[94]

Scrutton always discussed his acquisitions with his staff but understandably took little notice of dissenting voices over his own proposals. With a small purchase fund there was little room for initiatives from individual curators. However in 1958 he did approve the proposal of Hugh Macandrew, then working on Roscoe, to acquire where possible old master drawings from William Roscoe's great collection which had been sold by auction in 1816. In this way some at least of Roscoe's drawings could be reunited with his early Italian and Northern paintings already in the Gallery. Over the years a handful of drawings by Fra Bartolommeo, Breughel, Claude, Guercino and others were acquired.[95] Eventually in 1995 the purchase of the drawings from Charles Blundell's collection, which contained many drawings owned by Roscoe, carried this policy very much further.[96] Drawings were rarely bought for their own sake but could be acquired as preliminary studies for paintings already in the collection. In 1964 the Gallery was offered two black and white chalk studies for Frederic Leighton's *Elijah*. A discussion with Scrutton at tea about these and about the value of preparatory studies for explaining to visitors how pictures are created led to their purchase. From then on preparatory drawings were often bought when they appeared on the market and were actively sought from the descendants of artists, notably from the Clausen family, who very generously donated a large group of work connected with the Gallery's paintings. Prices were normally very affordable. Around £200 was the usual price for a good red chalk drawing by Holman Hunt in 1967.

Scrutton would freely admit that he had very little interest in the cultural history of Liverpool and Lancashire but he recognised that it could not be totally ignored. He purchased in 1957 *Burd Helen* by William Windus (1822-1907), an important Liverpool Pre-Raphaelite picture, from Colnaghi.[97] From time to time the descendants of the great nineteenth-century Liverpool families offered the Gallery, either as gifts or for modest sums, pictures and sculpture that had been acquired by the founders of the family fortune. Scrutton would usually accept the offers if there was enthusiasm amongst his staff. In 1967 the Naylor family presented a group of material including a small version of Ary Scheffer's *Temptation of Christ*, which had been bought by the Liverpool banker and developer John Naylor in Paris in 1855, together with a group of marble portraits of the family by B.E. Spence (about 1823-1866), a Liverpool sculptor based in Rome.[98] The Gallery declined the offer of Delaroche's *Napoleon crossing the Alps* since it already possessed another version of the painting. Naylor's version was later acquired by the Louvre.[99] Perhaps the most unexpected work to be acquired locally was the over-life-size marble *Death of Virginia* by Giacomo de Maria carved between 1806 and 1810. It had been purchased in 1820 in Bologna by Le Gendre Starkie, a Lancashire collector, and was on loan to Townely Hall Art Gallery in Burnley, where it was threatening the stability of the hall floor. It cost £200. Occasionally acquisitions of local interest would be made as a result of specific staff research activity, notably some Liverpool school pictures bought by the banker George Rae and a group of marble reliefs by John Gibson from the collection formed by the Sandbach family. They had remained in the family's vast gothic home Hafodunos Hall after it had become a boarding school. The Sandbachs were Gibson's most sympathetic patrons and shared with him a Liverpool background.

Scrutton's last years in Liverpool were difficult. The Council's priority was the rebuilding and fitting out of the war-damaged Liverpool Museum which, apart from the capital costs, involved significant increased annual running costs. Local politicians were pre-occupied with the newly fashionable arts associations, and the Merseyside Arts Association was established in Liverpool. They were also concerned with creating a stunning new modern

Liverpool, and the Gallery's finest display space, the Prince George Gallery, was given over to a vast model of Liverpool showing the triumph of the motorway sweeping all before it. The air-conditioning plans were suspended, and the Gallery was essentially on a stationary or declining budget.

It would be unfair to say that Scrutton lost interest in the Gallery but, despite having more money to spend, there were no purchases in his later years to match the paintings by Hogarth and Rubens bought in his earlier years. He tried to exploit the potential of the tax advantages of private treaty sales and attempted to negotiate the purchase of pictures from the estate of Captain Spencer Churchill at Northwick Park which were sold at Christie's in 1965 and from that of Oliver Vernon Watney of Cornbury Park which were sold at Christie's in 1967. But he could make no progress, despite the fact that while tax rates were at 70% or more, the financial advantages of a private treaty sale to a public institution were very considerable. He attempted to buy two panels by Francesco Granacci and others illustrating the life of John the Baptist in the Labia sale at Sotheby's on 24 June 1970. They were companions to a panel bequeathed to the Gallery by Philip Rathbone in 1895, but he could not raise the funds for a serious bid.[100] Both were bought by the Metropolitan Museum in New York. He continued to buy Italian baroque and rococo paintings, most notably a pair of doors painted with allegorical figures of merit and abundance attributed to Francesco or Gian Antonio Guardi for £25,000 and a large *Diana and Endymion* from the studio of Solimena for £9,000, which he particularly liked. Neither could compare in quality with his earlier purchases and they were not cheap.

In 1969 he was president of the Museums Association and the Association's annual conference was held in Liverpool. Much thought was given to the presentation of the Gallery and he arranged for the picture display, which had been quietly becoming more crowded, to be reduced in numbers. An important and preferably provocative temporary exhibition was needed but funds were limited, and the Gallery decided to display its own works. A tightly packed display in the Gallery's largest space, the Prince George Gallery, of about one hundred paintings, mostly huge, and of some five sculptures, all from the Gallery's reserve collections, was arranged. The title was *The Taste of Yesterday* and most of the works were academic nineteenth-century paintings, then still very unfashionable. The majority had not been on display since the 1930s.[101] A detailed and fully illustrated catalogue was published. Although Scrutton did not think very highly of them himself, his younger colleagues, many art historians and even the general public, all greatly influenced by John Betjeman and other enthusiasts for Victorian art, were becoming increasingly interested in paintings of this type. The authoritative *Burlington Magazine* praised the Gallery:

[It had mounted] a large properly catalogued exhibition of items from the permanent collection that have not been on view for years...This is not an exhibition that has any great aesthetic revelations, but it is of exceptional interest. The title is 'The Taste of Yesterday', but, for anyone who does not accept current values as sacrosanct, the show by implication is also about the taste of today and about how galleries are run.[102]

The display was brief but the Gallery had committed itself to the public display of a substantial part of its large holdings of later Victorian and Edwardian art. This could only be achieved by hanging pictures in some rooms from floor to ceiling, frame to frame, just as the hundred paintings in the *Taste of Yesterday* display had been shown. There was some historical justification for this policy as nineteenth-century exhibitions and displays were usually hung in this way. Rather later this 'period' approach to hanging paintings was praised on aesthetic grounds. But there were deeper issues. In the past curators had seen their function as selecting very precisely for their public the best pictures from their collections and displaying them in splendid isolation in a single well-spaced row. Now curators were less sure that they could or should choose paintings so prescriptively for their public or that they had any right to stand between the public and its collections. Taste was always subjective and fluctuated greatly from period to period and from person to person. Therefore as many paintings as possible from the permanent collection should be crammed onto the walls, and a well-informed public should make their own choices. Some of the paintings were hard to see but surely that was better than confining them to storage. The result was demanding for the less knowledgeable visitor, who might be bewildered by the amount and variety of the works of art on display, but a marvellous and rich feast for the eyes of the initiated. It was also making the political point that the Gallery believed that more of its collection should be on display and that additional space was urgently required. The Gallery was a pioneer in this new policy. It was élitist but also democratic. This disarmed critics and accordingly it was imitated if rather cautiously.

Looking back on his work at Liverpool Scrutton particularly deplored the opposition within the City Council to his proposed purchases of progressive and controversial works of art. It seems that Conservatives did not support these acquisitions because they were conservative artistically as well as politically, and that Labour members were hostile because they favoured social realism not abstraction. In 1958 he had recommended the purchase of a *Still Life* by William Scott (fig. 18) at a price of £247. The Arts Sub-Committee first deferred the purchase and then rejected it. No voting figures are given in the minutes of their proceedings so presumably the vote was unanimous.[103] Scott had by then an international reputation and the painting was acquired a year later by the Musée National d'Art Moderne in Paris. Its official title is now *Liverpool Still Life* to commemorate the Liverpool episode.[104] A year later Scott won a £500 prize with his *Blue Abstract* in the John Moores Exhibition and Moores presented it to the Gallery. Scrutton was not the only provincial gallery director to suffer in this way. In 1950 the City Council in Manchester voted by eighty-four votes to twenty against the purchase of Ben Nicholson's *Still Life 1950* for £500, although eventually Baxandall, the progressive director of the City Art Gallery, was able to acquire it through private subscribers.[105] In 1963 Scrutton's proposal to buy ten paintings from the John Moores Exhibition was only approved by nine votes to eight after he had dropped a work by Bridget Riley, now recognised as an outstanding artist of her generation, from his list and after Shaw, the chairman, used his casting vote.[106] As late as 1969 the purchase of *18.1.69* (the painting's date of execution) by John Hoyland, one of the leading British abstract painters of the 1960s, was approved by six votes to three by the Arts and Recreations Committee, but Scrutton abandoned the acquisition to appease the opposition.[107] Worse still Scrutton was deterred from even proposing some more daring purchases for fear that the Council would have 'regarded me as a joke'.[108] In fact most city councillors both respected and admired him, and it was this that enabled him to raise staff numbers and salaries and to increase greatly the council's annual grant for acquisitions. It must however be said that his patrician instincts and background did not always enable him to have such a high opinion of some of them.

Throughout the 1960s Scrutton's control over the Gallery's administration increased, but it was something of a Pyrrhic victory. Most routine decisions at the Gallery no longer needed the approval of committees of councillors who were, for example, no longer present at interviews for the selection of staff below the level of deputy director. The Conservatives gained power in 1967 promising above all business efficiency.[109] Streamlining, initiated by the town clerk Sir Stanley Holmes, led to the original twenty-three committees being reduced to ten, but the numbers of departments and of heads of departments were not cut. A large Arts and Recreations Committee, the standard solution of the time, was created to control not only art galleries, museums and libraries but also parks, swimming baths, cemeteries and sports centres, an ancestor of the 'leisure services committees' which soon came to dominate most municipal art galleries. Meetings were inevitably acrimonious as previously independent chairmen fought for their departments. Scrutton found the new order very difficult. These new multi-purpose committees were intended to establish priorities for spending between their many functions. Thus they could for example decide whether money should go to swimming baths or art galleries. In practice they often had little interest in the arts and could rarely distinguish between serious educational purpose and casual spare-time amusements. After Holmes's changes the management consultants, McKinsey and Company, were asked to re-structure and amalgamate departments. The new language of quantifiable needs, standards, shortfalls and performance criteria was scarcely appropriate to art galleries. A strong emphasis on 'corporate planning' reduced the authority of specialist committees and professional staff, who were to be controlled by a powerful policy committee and by a new dominant chief executive.[110] Senior appointments within leisure service departments throughout the country no longer favoured professional specialists but generalist managers.[111] Lord Montagu of Beaulieu, vice-president of the Museums Association, observed in the debate on the Drew Committee's Report that, as larger committees acquired wider responsibilities, art gallery directors moved lower in civic hierarchies:

> Museums do not get a voice on committees or the access to chairmen which they deserve. It is inevitable if a committee has to choose between building a new swimming pool for the kids, an incinerator to burn the rubbish, raising their own staff salaries or voting more money to the local museum that unfortunately it is always the museum that comes off worse.[112]

Not every councillor was convinced by the new management plans under which departments were amalgamated and the number of chief officers reduced. Margaret Simey, a Labour councillor of long standing deeply concerned with social services, described with some distaste the new cult of management and the contempt of the McKinsey 'yuppies' for the British local government system and for its councillors and officials, whom they addressed, to her horror, by their first names. However she did not deny that the general level of administrative efficiency in Liverpool City Council did improve.[113] Following concerns put forward by the Gallery Mckinsey and Company finally recommended:

> Control of cultural activities...is presently linked with recreation but we consider that this link would result in too narrow a basis for determination of priorities. The Arts and Recreation Committee would be faced with choices between acquiring paintings or additions to museum collections and providing children's playgrounds and other recreational facilities. If Liverpool is to have a museum and art gallery of national standard allocation of funds to this purpose should be a matter of overall city policy.[114]

Given the standard municipal solution of a single 'leisure services' department this was remarkably enlightened, especially from management consultants. In practice however the General Purposes Committee became the 'parent' committee for the Gallery, which thus effectively slipped further down the committee hierarchy. As part of this re-structuring, the directors of the Gallery and of the Liverpool Museum together with the chief librarian joined the town clerk's (or chief executive's) department and reported to the deputy town clerk (or director of administrative services), Alfred Stocks. There was inevitably some further loss of independence and influence. Fewer committees with wider responsibilities resulted in less supervision by councillors over the salaried staff and less dialogue. The gradual transfer of power away from the committee to the director, which had begun with Philip Rathbone's death in 1895, was completed. However, the old municipal tradition of close co-operation between Gallery staff and a few influential councillors interested in art was in serious jeopardy. To some extent the Gallery had escaped from the control of elected committees only to fall under the sway of senior council officials. Stocks however proved to be a very benign and imaginative manager. With the enthusiasm of the time for amalgamation and streamlining it was the best possible achievable arrangement. The new system did allow the Gallery to continue operating as effectively an autonomous department with a chairman and it permitted some direct access to a committee. This relatively independent status, rarely achieved at other regional art galleries, enabled it in 1974 to slip easily out of the City Council and into the County Council.

In 1964 Scrutton had been short-listed for the post of director of the Tate Gallery. He had a good chance of success since the front runner was much distrusted by the chairman of the selection board. Furthermore Scrutton was the only candidate with extensive experience as the director of a large public art gallery, and his Gallery had, like the Tate Gallery, a substantial permanent collection and a programme of loan exhibitions concentrating on contemporary art. However the post went to Norman Reid, the deputy director at the Tate Gallery, who was then primarily seen as an administrator.[115] Scrutton must have felt deeply disappointed. In 1970 he was more successful with his appointment as director of the National Galleries of Scotland. There he replaced Baxandall whom he had beaten in the contest for the directorship of the Walker Art Gallery eighteen years earlier. He was succeeded by Timothy Stevens, and the Gallery had for the first time a director with both considerable administrative experience, a real familiarity with the local art scene and a wide-ranging knowledge of the history of art.

Chapter 6

The County Council and the Lady Lever Art Gallery

There can be no reasonable doubt that the early 1960s were very good years for the Gallery. The mood of post-war idealism was still strong and the age of austerity had ended. By 1964 the annual grant for purchases had reached £10,000. In addition the Special Appeal Fund and the Mayor Bequest provided a total of over £100,000. Expenditure on the Gallery was rising rapidly. In 1960 a generous grant from central government had enabled it to buy an important work by Rubens with the expectation that similar grants would follow. With six curatorial posts, including those of the director and deputy director, the Gallery was well staffed, and staff salaries were rising rapidly. The director was being paid more than any other comparable art gallery official outside London.[1] The air conditioning of three galleries was completed in 1963. The *Foreign Schools Catalogue* was published in 1963 revealing with much scholarly detail the richness of the collection. The Ford Madox Brown exhibition of 1964 showed that the Gallery could select, organize and catalogue an important historic exhibition with great success. The biennial John Moores Exhibitions had established themselves by 1963 as the leading national exhibitions of contemporary British art. By 1967/68 attendance figures at the Gallery reached over 234,000 visits.

The Pre-Raphaelite exhibitions continued into the late 1960s and the John Moores Exhibitions did not start to falter at least until the mid-1980s. There were some remarkable acquisitions in the 1970s and early 1980s in very difficult circumstances. In the same period air-conditioning was extended into three further galleries after very long delays and two full-time conservators were appointed. Well researched catalogues of the Gallery's collections continued to be published by the staff and outsiders. Above all the Gallery assumed responsibility for the Lady Lever Art Gallery in 1978. But after 1965 if there was no actual fall in the Gallery's fortunes the pace of progress greatly declined. Annual attendance figures at the Gallery peaked at 278,000 in 1972 but later they were static or falling varying from 168,000 to 235,000 between 1977 and 1985. The national galleries in London, Edinburgh and Cardiff were moving ahead very rapidly. Two simple statistics will illustrate the contrast. In 1946 the annual allocation from taxation for the purchase of works of art for the Tate Gallery was £2,000 and for the Walker Art Gallery it was £1,000. In 1964 the Tate Gallery had £60,000 and the Walker Art Gallery £10,000. The widening gap was perhaps not unreasonable considering the Tate Gallery's national responsibilities. In 1979 however the Tate Gallery received over £1,000,000 and the Walker Art Gallery just £5,300.[2] Staffing levels reveal the same contrast. Excluding warders and shop and café staff the National

Gallery had 25 employees in 1955, 38 in 1975, 83 in 1985 and 198 in 1995.[3] Approximate comparable figures at the Walker Art Gallery are 14 in 1955, 26 in 1975, 32 in 1985 and 42 in 1995. The gap had become a gulf.

It is not easy to find causes although the steep economic decline of Liverpool and a dramatic drop in its population were certainly significant. For most of the period after 1955 the Liverpool City and Merseyside County Councils were controlled by Labour. In 1963 Bill (or William) Sefton, later Lord Sefton of Garston (1915-2001), became leader of the local Labour party on the death of John (or Jack) Braddock. Sefton was born in Liverpool, the son of a docks capstan driver and the first of his family to leave the docks. He was trained as a plumber and joined the City Council in 1953 after five unsuccessful attempts. He was eventually made a life peer by James Callaghan in 1978.[4] Sefton was a strong supporter of the enticing vision for a new modern Liverpool then being offered by the city planners, although Braddock had remained sceptical that these plans would solve Liverpool's economic problems. Nothing now was allowed to stand in the way of the delivery of the new Jerusalem. Sefton was even prepared to accept the demolition of the Albert Dock, Liverpool's finest industrial building. It was the lowest point for Liverpool's Victorian and Edwardian heritage and for the institutions associated with its past. In spite of the Beatles Liverpool's public reputation outside the city could not have been much lower. Politically Sefton, a Bevanite, was to the left of Braddock who had become increasingly right wing after a Communist youth. Both were local dictators, and both men could and did intervene in the Walker's affairs with considerable effect.

Ben Shaw, the principal Labour figure in the various city and county committees controlling the Gallery after the Conservatives lost power in 1955, was deeply committed but lacked Vere Cotton's art-historical knowledge and fund raising contacts. After Cotton the Liverpool Conservatives provided no regular spokesman for the arts. However, with the establishment of the Merseyside County Council John Last emerged as the leading Conservative councillor for the arts. He worked for John Moores's Littlewoods Company from 1969 until 1993. He stood unsuccessfully for parliament three times and, unlike Shaw, had ambitions to play a role in the arts outside Merseyside. He had Shaw's enthusiasm and more influence with his party nationally, but probably no more with his party locally.

After 1965 the professional staff in the Gallery certainly advanced both in technical expertise and in practical experience. The causes of the Gallery's difficulties between 1965 and 1986 related more to circumstances than to individuals. Merseyside's economic base was faltering as traditional employment in the docks and ship building contracted sharply. Sir Terry Leahy, born in Liverpool and for many years chief executive of Tesco, was a close but also impartial observer of the economic scene: 'Liverpool has had a difficult time. It was very exciting in the 1960s with music and culture, but the 70s and 80s were very depressing.' The pressure on local public resources from theatres threatened with closure and from new arts organisations, especially the arts association and the area museum service, grew far faster than the Council's income. The direct costs of the Committee controlling the Gallery were also rising. The urgent need to extend the Central Library to enable its book stock, stored in warehouses across the city, to be kept together in William Brown Street was seen very reasonably by the Liverpool City Council as its priority. This objective enabled the Library to hand back to the Gallery some of the space that it had occupied since the war. Capital funding for Gallery air-conditioning had to wait until the Library extension had begun. Local government became more subservient to central government with fewer areas where it could control the nature and extent of its expenditure. Those few areas included art galleries, and as the levels of discretionary spending were reduced, so there was more hostile scrutiny over it by councillors and officials, who often no longer had Cotton's wide vision and interests. As a proportion of their total outlay local councils were still spending very small sums on art galleries, but, as a fraction of that expenditure over which they had any real control, cultural costs had become a significant item. Within the Gallery's budget, excluding inescapable expenditure on staffing, heating, lighting and similar items, there was similarly only a tiny discretionary amount available. Hence the frequent budget cuts demanded invariably led to the trimming of the purchase fund. The Gallery felt that reducing the curatorial staff would jeopardize the cataloguing programme which was beginning to bear fruit. In Liverpool the Liberals were gaining power by denouncing wasteful expenditure on prestigious projects, most notably a proposed monumental civic centre designed by Colin St John Wilson to house municipal services which was seen as of little value to most Liverpool citizens. In practice the Liberals generally exempted the Walker Art Gallery from these attacks but their success made the other two parties reluctant to spend money on anything except basic services. Lastly, after the 1960s, public art galleries became increasingly dependent for their income not on taxation but on sponsorship, donations and commercial activities, especially shops, cafés, publications and fees charged for the reproduction of their paintings. London and Edinburgh galleries, situated in centres of wealth and influence, benefited greatly and easily from these new sources of revenue, but galleries in poorer, provincial and unfashionable areas had no real access to this new money.

In 1971 the new Conservative Government decided to reform local government in large cities on regional lines by creating another tier of local government, the new metropolitan county councils. A new Merseyside County Council would administer the area from Southport in the north down to Liverpool in the south and from the Wirral in the west to St Helens in the east. Within this area five new metropolitan borough or city 'district' councils, generally created from amalgamations of the old smaller borough councils, would form a 'lower tier', dealing with local affairs. Although Liverpool City Council became one of these 'lower tier' councils, it supported the creation of the new County Council.[5] Crucially however education, by far the most important function of local government, was placed into this 'lower tier', and did not fall under the control of the new metropolitan county councils.

Furthermore although the Redcliffe-Maud Report, on which these reforms were based, had proposed a large new Merseyside Metropolitan Region including most of west Cheshire,[6] the area eventually allocated to the new Merseyside County Council was much smaller. Warrington, Widnes, Runcorn and Ellesmere Port were placed in Cheshire not in Merseyside, while Wigan was allocated to Greater Manchester and Skelmersdale to Lancashire. Thus the new Merseyside County Council was a relatively small local authority with a correspondingly modest income, especially compared with Greater Manchester. For the most part Parliament decided on the allocation of local government functions between the new metropolitan county councils and the borough or city 'district' councils. However, museums and art galleries were one of the few exceptions, although libraries, traditionally often linked with them, were allocated to the new 'district' councils, much to the annoyance of the Liverpool city librarian. Within each county council area the city, borough and county authorities could themselves decide which of them should control the art galleries in their areas. A county council and a city or borough 'district' council could both support the same gallery either through a joint committee of the two councils or with one of these councils actually controlling the gallery. The Wright Report of 1973, although discussing local government re-organisation, sadly made no recommendation on this issue, probably because there was no consensus among the fifteen joint authors.[7] However in describing the Report's findings to the Museums Association Conference of 1973 Lord Eccles on behalf of the government made the important statement that he would prefer the 'upper tier' county and metropolitan county councils to control the museums and art galleries in their area. This indeed was the advice formally given to local authorities by the Department of Education and Science.[8] Eccles pointed out that where the 'lower tier' city and borough 'district' councils retained their art galleries, council tax payers in their areas – or ratepayers as they then were – would probably have to contribute to the cost both of a county council and of a borough or city council museums and art galleries service.[9] This indeed proved to be the case in Manchester where the City Art Gallery remained with the City Council although the Greater Manchester County Council set up its own museums and art galleries department which gave large grants to the Whitworth Art Gallery and to museums in the county.[10] Similarly in Birmingham, Sheffield and Leeds, the major city art galleries stayed with their city councils and did not pass to the new West Midlands, South Yorkshire and West Yorkshire County Councils. Andrew Faulds, a

Labour Party arts spokesman from 1970 until 1974, deplored the absence of even any discussion of a county structure for art galleries in the West Midlands and the lack of any involvement by the Greater Manchester County Council in the financing and control of Manchester City Art Gallery.[11] Among the non-metropolitan county councils Bristol stayed with its city council rather than moving to the new Avon County Council and only in Leicestershire and in Norfolk did the county councils absorb important city art gallery collections.[12] Manchester, Birmingham, Leeds and, to some extent, Sheffield were prosperous cities confident that they could continue to look after their art galleries without support from surrounding areas. Poor relations between the new metropolitan county councils and the old city councils in these areas often discouraged the city councils from handing over their art galleries to the county councils and even from any co-operation with them over funding or services.[13] The directors of the galleries in these four cities were apparently not convinced that there were substantial advantages in moving from city to county control. The creation of the metropolitan county councils represented the best chance to achieve change and rationalisation offered to major regional art galleries in the twentieth century, but it was largely an opportunity lost.

The outcome in Newcastle and Liverpool was very different. All the art galleries and museums within the new Tyne and Wear County were to be administered by the new County Council. Legal ownership of these art galleries and museums however was retained by the old city and borough councils. This encouraged the smaller institutions to accept a new centralized structure which involved some loss of local identities but also greater efficiency and wider access to specialized skills. Secession remained possible but was never seriously considered partly because all the councils were controlled by the Labour party thus preserving personal relationships and eliminating political rivalries.[14] John Thompson, the director of Newcastle's Laing Art Gallery, strongly supported this solution.

A different result was achieved on Merseyside. There the new County Council would take over, own and administer the museums and art galleries within Liverpool itself, but outside Liverpool the important collections at the Williamson Art Gallery in Birkenhead and at the Atkinson Art Gallery in Southport were to remain under the control and ownership of the Wirral Metropolitan Borough Council (for Birkenhead) and of the Sefton Metropolitan Borough Council (for Southport). The decision over the Liverpool collections and buildings was never seriously discussed in any meeting of the city council or its committees, probably because the three political parties together with the city and county councils were all in agreement. In 1973 Stevens recommended to Alfred Stocks, the Liverpool City Council deputy chief executive and his immediate superior, that the Gallery should pass to the new County Council principally because it was used by visitors from across Merseyside and so should in fairness be paid for by the whole of Merseyside. He also felt that the Gallery would suffer under an impoverished city council faced with many social and economic problems, and he hoped that a move to a larger authority would eventually facilitate national recognition and funding. He also did not want to risk sharing a committee again with leisure responsibilities such as swimming pools and parks. Stocks accepted this advice together with similar recommendations from the Liverpool Museum and from the Royal Liverpool Philharmonic Orchestra. Stanley Holmes, the Liverpool City Council chief executive, who was generally a supporter of the arts, saw his future with the County Council and so he also favoured a take-over by the new County Council. On one occasion, in response to a speech about the loss of the Gallery to Liverpool, he replied by assuring the speaker that the County Council would not be moving the Gallery out of Liverpool. The Liberal Party had gained control of Liverpool City Council. The removal of its cultural institutions to county control suited them as their priority was the reduction of local taxation. Perhaps fearing that the Liberals were unbeatable in Liverpool many leading Liverpool Labour councillors turned away from the city towards the county. Bill Sefton, who had lost his Liverpool seat to the Liberals, moved from being leader of the Liverpool City Council to becoming leader of the Merseyside County Council. Ben Shaw graduated from chairmanship of the City Council's Arts, Culture and Libraries Committee to chairmanship of the County Council's Arts and Culture Committee. There was a genuine belief amongst the councillors leaving Liverpool that the county, however limited in size and range of functions, could contribute to solving the region's problems. There was a feeling of mission which gave the new organisation a sense of purpose. It would not be primarily concerned with Liverpool's appalling social problems and might therefore be more interested in the arts. A director of one of the Regional Arts Associations made the same point more cynically: 'They [the new metropolitan county councils] basically had a lot of money and nothing to do, so naturally they got involved with the arts'.[15] This was not entirely true on Merseyside where even the new County Council suffered from the area's economic decline. The move of many of the leading politicians and senior council personnel to the new county ensured that there was no radical change in the way business was conducted, and critically the budgets set by Liverpool for the Museum and Gallery continued much as before. The director ceased to be director of the Walker Art Gallery and became director of the Merseyside County Art Galleries and a chief officer again, a status that had been removed in the McKinsey reorganisation. The Gallery and the Liverpool Museum were managed once more by their own committee with a chairman reporting to the full council.

The refusal of the smaller museums and art galleries on Merseyside to move to the new County Council was largely due to strong opposition in the new Wirral Borough Council. Thus the Birkenhead and Southport galleries were deprived of Liverpool's expertise and experience, and the creation of a unified art galleries and museums service on Merseyside was prevented. The local authorities, particularly the director of the Atkinson Art Gallery in Sefton, were not entirely hostile to the idea and were still considering an integrated museum and art gallery service with Liverpool in September 1974.[16] However in July 1975 the Wirral Borough Council announced that 'it was not interested in further discussions with regard to the provision of an integrated museum service or the introduction of specialized art gallery services on a county-wide basis.'[17] In December of that year Last argued that the Williamson Art Gallery should have been handed over to the County Council partly because the Wirral Borough Council had appointed 'a bath superintendent' to run it. The leader of the Wirral Council replied that Last had shown 'a singular lack of appreciation of the integrated nature of the Leisure Services Department of Wirral, and totally ignores the fact that the officer with direct responsibility for the division of the department which covers libraries, art galleries and museums is an experienced and highly qualified man with an encyclopaedic knowledge of his subject.'[18] Like many other councils Wirral distrusted increasing control from London, but it disliked any interference from Liverpool far more, and these events should have provided a warning against the very persistent idea within government circles that assistance and guidance from the large regional museums, the so-called regional 'hubs', were the best way to improve the smaller provincial galleries in the area.

In 1974 the Gallery's budget was set at £242,000 of which about £173,000 was spent on salaries and wages. This was about two and a half times the figure for 1964 but, allowing for inflation, represented much slower growth than in the ten years before 1964. By 1974 annual expenditure at the Liverpool Museum (by then the County Museums) at £592,000 was more than double the amount for the Gallery, even excluding spending at Speke and Croxteth Halls which the Museum controlled. Croxteth Hall alone accounted for £148,000 and heavy expenditure there inhibited growth both at the Museum and at the Art Gallery until 1986 when the house and park after prolonged negotiation were returned to Liverpool.[19] Croxteth Hall, situated about five miles east of Liverpool, together with about 500 acres of its extensive surrounding estate, were accepted on behalf of Liverpool City Council by Bill Sefton, then its Labour leader, from the executors of the last Earl of Sefton who died in April 1972. The executors received planning permission to develop most of the rest of the estate for housing. The house and land passed to the control of the Museum which was already responsible for Speke Hall and its grounds. In 1974 they were therefore inherited by the County Council, and the Museum developed the land at Croxteth as a country park and the house, like Speke Hall, as a visitor attraction.[20] The Liverpool City

Council allocated £25,000 to the Gallery at its request to buy some of the Sefton family pictures and £10,000 to the Museum to buy some furnishings. The executors at the Gallery's suggestion offered most of the family portraits to the Government in lieu of taxes. Unfortunately only three pictures were accepted as being of sufficient quality by the Government's advisors in spite of the family's long connections with Liverpool and in spite of the need for a display of the Hall's historic contents when it opened to the public.[21]

The most unexpected work in the collection and one of the three pictures accepted was a very large German romantic watercolour of William Tell by J.A. Koch of 1799, perhaps reflecting the Whig principles of the family.[22] More predictable was the 'acceptance in lieu' of the stunning full-length portrait of the first Countess of Sefton by Gainsborough (fig. 9), which, first exhibited at the inaugural exhibition of the Royal Academy in 1769, is certainly the finest eighteenth-century portrait associated with Merseyside. The third painting accepted was *The Earl of Sefton and Party Returning from Grouse Shooting with a View of Glen Lyon, Perthshire* painted in 1841 by Richard Ansdell (1815-1885), born and trained in Liverpool. With the £25,000 special grant the portraits and other pictures unsuccessfully offered in lieu of taxes were bought from the executors. In 1973 the remaining works of art and other furnishings were sold in a Christie's sale at Croxteth, where a few more paintings were acquired.[23] The Gallery could not however afford the most famous picture at the sale, *The Waterloo Cup* also by Ansdell, which it had earlier tried unsuccessfully to buy privately from the executors. The subject, a famous local hare coursing meeting on land owned by the Seftons with the local gentry and many Liverpool worthies present, made the painting vital to the Gallery both as a local artist's masterpiece and as a social document. Humanitarian considerations had made it very politically incorrect, but at the Christie's sale the great collector Paul Mellon was eventually outbid by a flamboyant Bond Street dealer who arrived at the sale by helicopter. The price was £89,250, far more than any other painting by Ansdell had ever reached. In 1975 the Gallery, assisted by the economic recession of that year, was able to buy it for about the same price. The Gallery's attempt to use the 'acceptance in lieu' system demonstrated its shortcomings when dealing with an historic family collection of mixed quality. Material of outstanding regional interest was apparently not within the canon of British art as defined by those national galleries which advised the government on the operation of the system. If all the family portraits had been accepted the Gallery would have been able to bid at the Christie's sale for exceptional works by Liotard and Angelica Kauffman, which had been owned by the Seftons since the eighteenth century. However ultimately Lady Sefton bequeathed to the Gallery all the pictures she had removed from Croxteth to her London home, including an important group of sporting paintings by Ben Marshall, John Ferneley and others, together with a few pictures she had bought herself, most notably an impressionistic *In the Garden* by James Charles. Her executors also agreed to offer in lieu of taxes any of the pictures the Gallery wanted from Abbeystead, the family's great north Lancashire sporting estate. Fortunately a more understanding attitude was taken by the government's advisors on this occasion and all were accepted including John Skeaping's *So Clever*, a greyhound which had won the Waterloo Cup in 1971 for the last Earl, as well as further family portraits by Ansdell. Lady Sefton also specifically allowed the Gallery to sell pictures it did not want from her London home, and the proceeds of their sale made a very useful contribution to the purchase of Poussin's *Ashes of Phocion*. The Sefton paintings added a new significance to two large groups of sporting pictures of generally rather lower quality already in the Gallery's collection, Lord Wavertree's racing pictures and Walter Stone's sporting paintings bequeathed by his sister Mary in 1944 at Vere Cotton's instigation. These holdings were further strengthened by Lieutenant Colonel John Raymond Danson (1893-1975)'s collection of work by his Liverpool ancestor the animal artist Charles Towne (1763-1840), accepted in lieu of tax by the government in 1979 at the Gallery's suggestion. His family business, F. C. Danson & Co, had been Liverpool's leading average adjusters. These extensive holdings seemed appropriate for Liverpool, the home of the Grand National. When the Liverpool Museum eventually opened Croxteth Hall to the public, the Hall did provide useful display space for a substantial group of the Gallery's sporting paintings, for some of the Sefton portraits and for many Victorian and Edwardian paintings from the Gallery's stores. The plans to have a proper display of sporting art at Croxteth have yet to be realized.

    The County Council also inherited from Liverpool City Council Speke Hall, a spectacular and romantic fifteenth-century half-timbered house on the banks of the Mersey, which by the 1950s had become engulfed by Liverpool Airport, industry and housing. Speke Hall had passed to the National Trust in 1943 under the will of Miss Watt but, as it lacked any significant endowment, the Trust was reluctant to accept it. Liverpool City Council stepped in, offered to manage it, open it to the public and signed a 99-year full repairing lease with the National Trust. Initially the hall was managed by the City Estates Department, but in the late 1960s it passed to the care of the Liverpool Museum who understandably wished to improve the presentation and visitor facilities. A structural survey revealed that it required huge expenditure just to make it safe, and, even after significant grants from the National Trust and other private and public sources, it proved a major and unavoidable financial commitment for the new County Council. The cost of maintaining Speke and Croxteth Halls, with their parks and gardens, and of opening the latter to the public, severely limited the County Council's ability to develop the Gallery or pursue other new ventures such as the Maritime Museum. Croxteth and Speke were on the edge of some of Liverpool's huge and very grim working-class housing estates, and this clearly justified heavy expenditure there. Thus the problem of Liverpool's social deprivation, apparently circumvented with the take-over by the County Council, came back to compete with the Gallery's needs once more.

Many other regional art galleries and museums had taken over responsibility for the large country houses on the edge of their city boundaries. Encroaching urbanisation and industrialisation had been persuading the families owning these houses to abandon them ever since the end of the nineteenth century. Local authorities needed their parks for public recreation. In some cases the city art gallery established itself wholly or partially within the country house, as in Towneley Hall at Burnley, formerly the family home of the Towneleys and acquired by Burnley Council in 1901. The merits of country-house museums and art galleries run by local authorities remain controversial, but responsibility for Speke and Croxteth Halls undoubtedly diverted the County Council away from its responsibilities for the care of its art collections, and the return of Speke to the National Trust and of Croxteth to Liverpool City Council in 1986 was probably in the long-term interests of all concerned.

Under the County Council the Gallery was not only competing for funding with Croxteth and Speke Halls but also with Liverpool Museum itself, which after its partial re-opening in 1964 was now rapidly expanding, attracting many more visitors than the Gallery and employing many more staff. Its shipping department grew into a new Maritime Museum opened to the public at the Pier Head in 1980 with five permanent and twenty temporary staff. It was certainly badly needed. Rotterdam had opened a modest maritime museum in 1874; a very substantial new maritime museum had been completed in 1936 in Stockholm; the Hull dock offices were converted into a museum in 1974. Aided by substantial local bequests and the Merseyside Development Corporation the Liverpool Maritime Museum expanded rapidly, and by 1985 it had 40 permanent and 54 temporary employees, staffing levels similar to those at Croxteth. Growth on this scale left little money for the Walker Art Gallery. Although the need to invest in capital-funded projects was readily accepted by the County Council, government limits and control on the way capital was used meant that there would never be much money for the Gallery.

The mood at the County Council was however expansionist and the major achievement of the Gallery under its control was the takeover of two outstations. First came the former mortuary chapel of St James's Cemetery.[24] It had been designed together with the cemetery itself in 1827 by Liverpool's greatest architect, the younger John Foster (about 1787-1846), who transformed an old quarry into a site of great dramatic grandeur dominated by the chapel in the form of a Greek temple. It is now his only complete surviving building and of great importance to Liverpool's architectural heritage. After its inauguration it soon acquired important monuments to Liverpool's leading citizens by Gibson, Gott and Chantrey, and it probably has no parallel in any English industrial city.[25] The building had been used by the adjacent Anglican Cathedral for many years as a store. Public access became possible after the Cathedral's completion. A new roof and improved security arrangements were provided. There was a precedent in Bristol where the City Council had re-opened a redundant church as St Nicholas's Church and City Museum in 1973.[26] Local authorities are generally cautious in ecclesiastical projects, but both Bill Sefton and the Conservative Sir Kenneth Thompson (1909-1984), who succeeded Sefton as the leader of the County Council, supported the acquisition. Thompson, born in Liverpool, had been a Liverpool councillor before the war, and, when he first entered parliament for Liverpool Walton in 1950, he remained at first a member of Liverpool City Council. He became responsible for the Victoria and Albert Museum as a parliamentary secretary in the Ministry of Education between 1959 and 1962. His national and local political experience made him an extremely effective leader, and he had a much wider vision than most Merseyside councillors. The Gallery added a few church monuments rescued from local redundant churches, thus partly converting the building from a chapel into a museum, and re-named it 'The Oratory'. John Ritchie, the environmental county planning officer and a fervent believer in architectural conservation, greatly assisted the Gallery with the restoration of the building and with obtaining grants for it. Later as director of development and chief executive of the Merseyside Development Corporation, the government agency largely responsible for Merseyside's commercial and cultural renewal after the Toxteth riots of 1981, he became the principal figure in the development of the Albert Dock which housed the Maritime Museum and the Tate Gallery in Liverpool.

The Gallery's second and much more important acquisition changed its character fundamentally. The Lady Lever Art Gallery, about six miles from Liverpool on the Wirral, had been founded by William Hesketh Lever, the first Lord Leverhulme, in the centre of Port Sunlight, built by him as a model village for the workers at his huge soap factory at the end of the village. It opened to the public in 1922 in a new purpose-built 'Beaux-Arts' classical building and contained his enormous collections of British late eighteenth- and nineteenth-century paintings and sculpture, of eighteenth-century English furniture, of Wedgwood pottery and of Chinese seventeenth- and eighteenth-century porcelain. There were also smaller but very fine groups of French and British tapestries, English embroideries, ancient and European sculpture, Greek vases, Edwardian paintings, English watercolours and old-master drawings. Comparisons are always difficult but by any reasonable standards it was among the five or six most important English art galleries outside London, certainly rivalling the Walker Art Gallery and surpassing it in the quality of its building. It was a magnificent example of the belief in the value of art as an essential element in the local philanthropy of the successful late nineteenth-century industrialists in north-west England.

Lever had established the Gallery with its own trustees and its own very generous endowments, both entirely separate from his soap manufacturing company, Lever Brothers. However by 1975 inflation had greatly reduced the real value of its original endowments and of the income derived from them, which became insufficient to cover its running costs. These endowment funds stood at about £156,000 and the annual income at around £20,000, while the Gallery's expenditure on salaries and wages alone was over £40,000. Lever's grandson, the third Lord Leverhulme (1916-2000), was the chairman of the Trustees and he made up the balance of about £30,000 each year from his family trusts. Now, with annual inflation running at about 20%, he and his co-trustees wanted to make more permanent arrangements for the long-term care of the Gallery. Some paintings, including important works by Rubens (now at the National Gallery of Scotland and the Metropolitan Museum of Art, New York), had been sold about twenty-five years earlier. However these sales and the furniture disposals made at the same time had only demonstrated the futility of sales by public institutions, as notable but unfashionable works were sold for very low prices. Unilever, the successors to Lever Brothers, were approached for help but declined suggesting that further sales should be held. Lord Leverhulme had no wish to repeat the earlier experience, recognising that disposals did not offer a long-term solution. Early in 1976 he approached Stevens and Shaw informally through his land agent Frank Williams, enquiring about the possibility of involvement by the Merseyside County Council. Williams, both a close personal friend and a Conservative county councillor, was able to reassure him about the policies of the Council. He was an admirer of the Walker Art Gallery and had confidence in its ability to treat the Lady Lever Art Gallery appropriately. In June Leverhulme wrote formally with the backing of Shaw and Stevens to Bill Sefton, then the leader of the County Council, offering the galley to the Council. Negotiations were prolonged by discussions over the future of the current charitable trusts governing the Gallery. In the event it was agreed that the County Council should become their sole trustee. Leverhulme was not interested in being involved in the Gallery's routine management but, wishing to ensure that it preserved its unique character, he understandably wanted to retain some influence over the display and care of the collection after its transfer to the County Council. The Council were to receive both the Gallery's original endowment and a commitment from Lord Leverhulme that his family trusts would continue their support at the same amount in perpetuity. At first it was proposed that a few of the trustees should join the Council's Arts and Culture Committee in some capacity, but there were legal and technical objections to this solution. In the end a consultative committee, which was chaired by Leverhulme and included some of his trustees and some county councillors, was established. It could offer advice to the Arts and Culture Committee on certain issues related to the running of the Gallery and had absolute control over the deployment of the collection away from the Gallery and over acquisitions for the Gallery. Essentially the Lady Lever Art Gallery was to be managed by the Walker Art Gallery and the first Lord Leverhulme, its founder, was to be its presiding genius.

Broad agreement between the County Council and the Lady Lever Art Gallery trustees was finally reached in March 1977.[27] It was Shaw's finest achievement. His most difficult moment came when he had to show Sefton around the Gallery and to persuade him that the Council must acquire it. Without Sefton's approval there could be no deal. The two men together with Stevens walked around the Gallery. Shaw did his best to engage Sefton, who remained stonily silent throughout the tour. The lack of the slightest response was visibly alarming Shaw. As Sefton was leaving, having made no comment, Shaw nervously plucked up the courage to ask his leader for his reactions. Sefton succinctly and in a dead-pan voice replied that he knew the Gallery from previous visits, that it had of course to come to the County and that he had only come that day to check it was as good as he remembered it. He added that he always thought the impeccable craftsmanship of the furniture explained why the British were such good engineers and then left, leaving Shaw speechless on the Gallery steps. Only a few weeks later Labour lost power in the County Council elections and Shaw was replaced by John Last as chairman of the Council's Arts and Culture Committee, while Sefton was replaced by Thompson as Leader of the County Council. Shaw had taken considerable trouble to ensure that Last and Thompson were in agreement as at the Oratory. The two parties followed their usual bipartisan cultural policy and the Conservatives formally ratified the agreement in March 1978.[28]

Preserving the Lady Lever Art Gallery was the County Council's most important and bravest cultural decision. There was probably less popular support for it than for the creation of the Merseyside Maritime Museum. Many councillors however rightly felt that this was exactly what the new County Council had been set up to do. In taking over the Walker Art Gallery in 1974 the Council had acquired the instrument and the expertise it needed to run the Lady Lever Art Gallery to high standards. Certainly if the Walker Art Gallery had remained with Liverpool City Council in 1974 it could not easily have rescued another gallery outside Liverpool. It is impossible to guess what might have happened if the County Council had refused to assist the Gallery. Wirral Borough Council might have provided grants sufficient for the Gallery's most immediate needs, but it had neither the expertise nor the resources to provide a long-term solution for a Gallery of international importance.

Ralph Fastnedge, who had been Frank Lambert's last deputy director at the Walker Art Gallery, had tactfully been retired from the post of curator at the Lady Lever Art Gallery shortly before the transfer negotiations started. His assistant, John Macdonald, generously stayed on briefly as acting curator to facilitate the transfer. Thanks to his enthusiasm, the Gallery's very low attendance figures had begun to improve with many more visitors coming in groups. Ron Delamere, gallery factotum in the best sense of the word, craftsman, gallery and collections manager and much more, continued in his post for some years. As far as possible the Walker Art Gallery's curatorial, conservation and administrative staff expanded their responsibilities to cover these functions at the Lady Lever Art Gallery which was to be fused with the Walker Art Gallery. As the Walker Art Gallery had no significant decorative arts curatorial skills, an additional assistant keeper, Penelope Eames, was recruited both for this area and to be the curator at Port Sunlight.

Recalling the acrimony over the unforeseen enormous repair bills that the County Council was paying at Speke and Croxteth Halls, the Walker Art Gallery commissioned a structural survey of the building. This identified serious problems with the roof which lacked an insulating layer between the concrete of the structure and the asphalt that made it watertight. Following Ritchie's advice Port Sunlight was formally designated as a 'conservation area' in 1978, enabling the Council to qualify for higher government grants for repair and maintenance work at the Lady Lever Art Gallery than would have been available for a 'listed' building. Re-roofing and other repair work was approved in November 1978 and was in progress by April of the following year.[29] Improving security levels to the standards achieved at the Walker Art Gallery and at Sudley by recruiting more warding staff involved the County Council in further expense, which however proved fully justified when the pipe carrying the main water supply into the Gallery burst in the early hours of one morning, and prompt staff action prevented a major disaster.

It was decided that the Gallery should as far as possible return to its appearance when it first opened to the public in 1922, subject to conservation requirements. Visitors probably noticed few changes but steadily more paintings, sculpture and furniture were placed on display, more rooms were opened to the public and much labelling was renewed. Some internal modernist architectural features of the 1960s were quietly removed, notably the suspended plaster saucers which obscured the leaded-light inner domes of the sculpture rotundas. Many rooms were re-decorated. Behind the scenes however considerable progress was made with vast improvements to the storage, conservation, documentation and photography of the collections. Each of the many stored pieces of furniture received its own tailored cover. Loose prints and drawings were mounted and placed in new boxes. The Wedgwood pottery was re-inventoried as part of a programme of preparing a new inventory of the whole collection. The skills and experience that the

Walker Art Gallery had acquired on its own massive re-documentation were usefully redeployed at the Lady Lever Art Gallery. In 1982 Lucy Wood, who wished to become a furniture specialist, was appointed as curator at the Gallery where the eighteenth-century furniture was unequalled outside the Victoria and Albert Museum. It proved to be a happy choice. She wrote two massive catalogues of the furniture, the second with the help of a Leverhulme Trust Fellowship, and she has become one of the leading furniture historians of her generation. In 1980 an exhibition of masterpieces of both fine and decorative art from the Gallery was held at the Royal Academy in London to celebrate the fiftieth anniversary of the formation of Unilever, the exhibition sponsors. It also included a large section covering Port Sunlight Village, and the catalogue, written by a panel of experts, involved much new research into the Gallery's collections and into the building of the village.[30] Its success introduced the Gallery to the huge and articulate population of south-east England and by 1991 annual attendance figures at the Gallery, which between 1945 and 1976 had fluctuated between 12,000 and 41,000, had climbed dramatically to over 96,000 visitors. The Walker Art Gallery, in its case to the Council in support of the acquisition of the Gallery, had rightly emphasized its tourist potential, and, together with the village, it became increasingly popular with tourists visiting nearby Chester.

While the first Lord Leverhulme had included in his new Gallery a Tudor-style tea room in the basement and good visitor facilities, he did nothing to explain to visitors the scope of the collection or his objectives in forming it. His tastes were varied including ethnography collected on his world-wide business travels and masonic regalia reflecting his personal involvement with this movement. Although his enthusiasms were wide-ranging he did not assemble a balanced collection covering British fine and decorative art. He did not collect, for example, British silver and porcelain. After 1945 the highly individual character of the collection had been softened by reducing the displays and by lending significant groups of material, in particular ethnography, Egyptology and the ancient Greek vases, to other museums in north-west England. An attempt was made to make the public displays conform to a more conventional art-historical narrative. As part of the new inventory these loans were recalled in 1978. Extra display space and a proper introduction to the collection and its remarkable founder were needed, but no part of the main exhibition floor could be spared for them, and access to the spacious basement was restricted. However, very soon after the Gallery acquired national status and much improved funding in 1986, work began on transforming access to the basement from within and without the Gallery and on creating there additional galleries together with a new café, shop and entrance. Misguided efforts to close the ground floor entrance were successfully resisted with the support of Lord Leverhulme.[31] A permanent display devoted to the very personal tastes and career of its founder enabled hundreds of masonic, ethnographic, ceramic, textile and architectural objects, together with his large collection of shells, to be shown for the first time. Each object was conserved and mounted. Fabrics similar to those which he commissioned lined the walls, and the showcases which he selected housed many of the exhibits. Very high performance modern showcases were used for the most sensitive items. The paintings which the first Lord Leverhulme had bought to advertise his soap filled one room. Outside experts provided advice on selection, display and labelling and contributed to a scholarly volume describing his taste and patronage.[32]

The Walker Art Gallery gave priority to the Lady Lever Art Gallery's collections in its research programme. Highly detailed and scholarly catalogues were published on the foreign works of art in 1983, on the ancient sculptures in 1986, on the Greek vases in 1987, on the English embroideries in 1992, on both the Victorian and Edwardian paintings and on the English commodes in 1994, on both the eighteenth-century paintings and on the British sculptures in 1999 and lastly on the upholstered furniture in 2008.[33] Works in the Lady Lever Art Gallery were also prominent in the catalogue of 1988 covering all the Pre-Raphaelite collections there, at the Walker Art Gallery and at Sudley.[34] Nearly all these publications were written by members of staff, and they represented the most sustained programme of research ever devoted over about twenty-five years to any provincial art gallery in Britain. The third Lord Leverhulme was very enthusiastic about the cataloguing programme. It would have been very warmly supported by the first Lord Leverhulme, who had meticulously kept detailed documentation on his collections and had commissioned a catalogue of them in three monumental volumes in the 1920s.

When the first Lord Leverhulme gave most of his enormous collections to the Lady Lever Art Gallery in 1922 he retained for his private collection two important paintings by Millais, *Cymon and Iphigenia*, which showed the influence of Etty on his early work, and *Apple Blossoms* (or *Spring*) of 1859, demonstrating clearly the artist's transition from Pre-Raphaelitism to Aestheticism. Thanks to the close relationship established by the Walker Art Gallery with the third Lord Leverhulme, *Apple Blossoms* was bought for the Lady Lever Art Gallery in 1986 with help from the National Heritage Memorial Fund, and *Cymon and Iphigenia* was accepted in lieu of inheritance tax on his estate after his death in 2000 and allocated to the Lady Lever Art Gallery, thus further enriching the Gallery's Pre-Raphaelite collections.[35] In addition to giving the portraits of his grandparents by Luke Fildes and a number of other items when the Gallery passed to the care of the County Council, he bequeathed to the Gallery the infamous and highly unflattering portrait of his grandfather, the first Lord, by Augustus John. His grandfather had cut out the head and concealed it in a safe. Now every visitor to the Gallery could judge between artist and sitter.

Acquisitions for the Walker Art Gallery in the final years with Liverpool and under the County Council were not easy. Apart from the problem of a static purchase grant and escalating art prices the Gallery had many more paintings and sculpture worthy of display than space in which to show them and a Gallery extension was a very distant prospect. In practice Scrutton's acquisitions often forced a work of comparable quality off the walls into store. The Gallery decided to concentrate on major acquisitions that would make a real difference to the visitor's enjoyment and experience. Apart from the occasional opportunist cheap purchase and works that rounded out the history of local culture it tried to preserve its limited resources for the occasional memorable purchase. There were never going to be the funds to put together a comprehensive overview of British Art, let alone European Art, and it stopped worrying about the glaring gaps that had so bothered earlier curators. For the staff the Frick Gallery in New York with its small exceedingly well chosen collection was the ideal. Purchasing policy would be rather less promiscuous, less self indulgent, and more sharply focused. The number of purchases, excluding local material, dropped dramatically. The Gallery also believed that, if its claim to national funding was going to be taken seriously, it needed to aim higher with its acquisitions.

The Gallery's very limited resources suggests that this ambitious approach was naive, but unexpectedly the 1970s and early 1980s turned out to be good years for acquisitions. The annual purchase grant from the County Council was around £3,000 between 1974 and 1979 rising to about £5,000 in 1980. It was very substantially below the best levels achieved under the City Council in the 1960s particularly if the serious inflation of the 1970s is taken into account. However the inauguration in 1980 as a public body of the National Heritage Memorial Fund with generous funds and a very positive attitude in its early years made the ambition of regional galleries to acquire memorable pictures at last achievable. The Victoria and Albert Museum Grant Fund also grew significantly. Between 1963 and 1974 the maximum that they gave to the Gallery in one year was £10,000. In four of the years between 1974 and 1985 its grants exceeded £40,000, peaking at £150,000 in 1983 for Nicolas Poussin's *Ashes of Phocion*. It was a very serious force for acquisitions and constructively helpful. The National Art-Collections Fund (later known as the Art Fund) became very much more involved in supporting acquisitions by regional museums. Modest funds from local sources were still necessary to unlock large grants from these national bodies. This was achieved by strict control of the small annual grants available from the Council and by diverting the remaining money in the Gallery's Special Appeal Fund, about £43,000 in early 1976, and in the Mayor Bequest, worth about £63,000 at the same date, away from French impressionist paintings and baroque sculpture.[36] The brief but very successful lottery run by the newly formed Friends also provided critical help, together with some assistance from businesses connected with Merseyside.

The Finance Acts of 1930 and 1956 had permitted the remission of any death duties, capital transfer tax, inheritance tax or capital gains tax payable on the sale of works of art by their owners provided that these works were sold to a public art gallery. The price paid by the gallery was usually reduced by three quarters of the amount of the tax remitted with the remaining quarter passing back to the former owner or his family as an incentive or 'douceur'. This was entirely different from the 'acceptance in lieu' procedure, used at Croxteth Hall, under which owners and executors effectively paid their taxes in works of art rather than in cash, with the works of art then handed on by the government to public galleries. Until the 1970s municipal galleries had not greatly profited from this tax concession partly through ignorance of the procedures involved and often through the reluctance of executors to go to the trouble of private treaty sales. In 1968 however Scrutton not only used this procedure for the purchase of Degas's *Woman Ironing* (fig. 16) but he also initiated the process by approaching the owner's executors and indicating to them the financial advantages available both to them and to the Walker Art Gallery. During the 1970s the auction houses, particularly Christie's under Christopher Ponter, and some dealers, notably Agnew's, increasingly appreciated that private treaty sales involving the 'douceur' and the 'acceptance in lieu' procedure made sound financial sense for some estates, particularly with the punitive tax rates then in force.

With the Gallery's very low purchase grant it could effectively only buy important paintings if they carried significant tax discounts. Apart from making limited funds go further the County Council, grant-giving institutions and generous benefactors felt more attracted towards works that in effect carried a substantial government subsidy. The first acquisition, in 1978, was Montagna's very moving and intimate *Virgin and Child with St John the Baptist* formerly owned by Ludwig Mond, a great Cheshire industrialist and the National Gallery's greatest benefactor. The price after tax concessions was £126,287. The vendors, the executors of the late Sir Thomas and Lady Merton, later facilitated the allocation to the Gallery of a large drawing of a young man by Luca Signorelli, which had been accepted by the government in lieu of capital transfer tax.[37] In 1981 came the first purchase (£225,000 after tax concessions) made with the help of the National Heritage Memorial Fund, Joos van Cleve's *Virgin and Child with Angels* (fig. 2), combining Netherlandish naturalism and early Renaissance classicism. It came from the great collection formed between about 1770 and 1840 by the Blundells at Ince Blundell about eight miles north of Liverpool.[38] The Gallery already owned much of the eighteenth-century sculpture from this house. Two years later the Fund provided most of the money necessary for the Gallery to buy Nicolas Poussin's *Landscape with the Ashes of Phocion* (fig. 5), one of his great brooding classical landscapes of 1648-1651, conceived in his most heroic and stoic mood. It came from the Earl of Derby's collection at Knowsley Hall some seven miles east of Liverpool. Even after tax concessions it was the most expensive painting (£1,150,000) ever bought by the Gallery, and local businesses and charities contributed generously to ensuring that this outstanding picture remained on Merseyside. Had the Heritage Memorial Fund been in action earlier, Rembrandt's startling *Belshazzar's Feast* (now National Gallery) and Koninck's panoramic *Landscape* (now Rijksmuseum, Amsterdam) both sold from Knowsley in the 1960s might have remained on Merseyside. The British collection also benefited from the Fund's help, notably for Ford Madox Brown's tiny *Waiting: An English Fireside* of 1854-5, bought in 1985.[39] It represented a delicate blend of domestic realism and religious symbolism and had once belonged to the artist's Liverpool patron, the tobacco merchant John Miller. On much the same scale Elsheimer's exquisite *Apollo and Coronis*, which came to the Gallery in lieu of inheritance tax from the estate of the fourth Lord Methuen, is even more emotionally charged with its moving depiction of love and remorse. That this extraordinary picture came to Liverpool owed much to the assistance of George Holt, a member of the distinguished ship-owning Liverpool Unitarian family which by happy chance had married into the Methuen family. For many years a co-opted member of the Gallery's governing Committee, Holt acted as a bridge between the old businesses and families of Liverpool and the Gallery. He bequeathed his pictures including two popular paintings by Atkinson Grimshaw, long on loan, and a striking *Lottie and the Baby* by Orpen to the Gallery in 1993. Perhaps the most unexpected acquisition was a portrait by Tissot of the wife and children of Chapple Gill, a successful Liverpool cotton broker, sitting in their suburban home. It was bought from a descendant who called in at the Gallery. This sympathetic record of late Victorian domestic leisure by an artist who specialized in that theme was purchased in 1979. Thus the Gallery, without sacrificing its commitment to quality, concentrated on paintings with Merseyside connections which could justify both to itself and to its benefactors their acquisition, assisted wherever possible by reduced prices through tax concessions. Sadly however the Gallery could not afford some important paintings formerly owned by the Blundells, nor some notable old master prints from Roscoe's collection, which came on to the market in these years.

The 1970s and 1980s were difficult times for Liverpool clubs and charitable organisations, which had often played a significant role in local cultural life, and some were forced to close. In 1970 the Gallery acquired from the Sandon Studios Society, a pioneer of modernist art in Liverpool, most of its art collection including watercolours by Herbert MacNair (1868-1955), a friend of Charles Rennie Mackinstosh. MacNair, who had worked in Liverpool, became an artist of special interest for the Gallery.[40] On the winding up of the University Club, material by Robert Anning Bell (1863-1933), who had taught at the University, was added to the Gallery's collection. The outstanding gift was Alexander Munro's sensitive bust of the great social reformer Josephine Butler (1828-1906) from the Diocese of Liverpool at the closure of the Josephine Butler Memorial Home in 1975. After the collapse of the Liverpool Academy in 1981 the Gallery acquired all its minute books and records going back to the early nineteenth century, documents of great importance for the cultural history of the city.

The Gallery naturally continued to add to its collection of Liverpool artists and attempted to do so more systematically than had sometimes been the case in the past. Some family portraits by William Caddick (1719/20-1794) and his son Richard (1748-1831) published by Dibdin in 1918 were acquired. *Sweethearts and Wives*, a nautical farewell on the Mersey and the masterpiece of John J. Lee (active 1860-1867), the rarest of the Liverpool followers of Pre-Raphaelite detail and vivid colours, was bought in 1980 for £28,500. The acquisition of photographs began. These included *The Ark Royal*, the most memorable image of Edward Chambré Hardman (1898-1988), the city's outstanding twentieth-century photographer. There were also photographs by Cartier-Bresson, taken on his visit of 1962, in which Liverpool's inhabitants are captured in his inimitable way. Prints by Whistler and Wadsworth connected with their visits to the city were purchased. Perhaps the most enchanting acquisitions made were the panoramic watercolour views of Liverpool, depicting a spacious elegant town with its numerous churches and open spaces, shown by Michael Angelo Rooker at the first Royal Academy Exhibition in 1769.

Many art galleries in the region did not hesitate to sell works of art which did not appear to fit in with what was then conceived to be their 'collection policies', documents suddenly fashionable in the 1970s. The Gallery attempted to persuade institutions to be cautious, pointing out the importance of items listed for disposal. It did not on every occasion succeed, and it sometimes bought material of this type, notably the American Harriet Hosmer's marble *Puck* from the Kendal Museum in 1976 and George Augustus Wallis's *Landscape near Rome* from the Smith Art Gallery in Brighouse in 1971.[41] The same year and nearer home it persuaded Bebington Corporation to transfer to Liverpool institutions what was left of the collection bequeathed to it by Joseph Mayer (1803-1886), Liverpool Museum's greatest benefactor.

After seeking a new international status in the 1950s and 1960s many of the larger English regional art galleries reverted to a more local and less ambitious attitude in their acquisitions, displays and exhibitions. By the 1970s even Birmingham Museum and Art Gallery, which had earlier achieved an academic and artistic ascendancy among English municipal art galleries from three very remarkable directors, Whitworth Wallis, Trenchard Cox and 'Mighty Mary' Woodall, began to concentrate its efforts on its own region and its own public.[42] Similarly Bristol City Art Gallery's acquisitions became more modest and more local in the late 1970s.[43] In Manchester the change occurred after the departure of Timothy Clifford as director in 1984. The sophisticated internationalism of Fritz Grossmann's exhibitions of German art and of European Mannerism in the 1960s and of Clifford's acquisitions in the 1970s and 1980s did not survive. Similarly Robert Rowe's retirement as director of Leeds City Art Gallery in 1983 was marked by rather narrower horizons there.

The immediate cause of this new parochialism lay in dwindling resources but there was also a search for a clearer sense of identity which could be found in close links with the local community more easily than in seeking a wider national or international role. The Walker Art Gallery profited from this new regionalism in its acquisitions, but the richness of its artistic hinterland resulted in improved not reduced quality. In other respects it strongly resisted this trend. The Gallery had engaged with community art from the 1960s and had often found there limitations rather than commitment.[44] The veneer of optimism in the many government reports on provincial museums and galleries had grown very thin by 2001.[45]

After 1970 the Walker Art Gallery began to rely heavily on government grants and tax concessions for acquisition, for major improvements and repairs to buildings and even for an ambitious project of research into local collections and public sculpture funded by one of the numerous 'job creation' programmes of the later 1970s. A grant from the government-funded Museums and Galleries Commission secured the Sessions House for the Gallery. Conservation area grants had proved critical for the repair of Lady Lever Art Gallery. These grants, available from a large number of public agencies created in Whitehall and later in Brussels with ever changing acronyms, reflected a profound change in the financing of many public institutions, especially noticeable in impoverished regional art galleries. No longer were governing bodies and directors given even reasonable budgets to spend at their discretion. If they wished to do more than merely exist they were compelled to compete with each other and with other similar cultural organizations for subsidies awarded by many official or semi-official funding bodies on the merits of each project or acquisition and on the strength of the documentation supporting them. The new system has often been associated with the Conservative administration of Margaret Thatcher in the 1980s but in fact it was favoured by all governments of this period. In theory it encouraged galleries to consider carefully and justify publicly their priorities before spending public money and resources, while it could ensure that only the best schemes received funding at all. In practice it simply transferred power away from the professional staff and lay elected committees appointed to manage galleries and towards these very varied governmental agencies, which often had considerable expertise but rarely great knowledge of local conditions and needs. In a real sense these government grants and tax concessions were national funding and national status by the back door. They did not encourage responsible and creative local administration and came at a very heavy price.

Chapter 7

Nationalisation and the Great Liverpool Art Boom

The Gallery's quest for national status and funding was achieved not by the implementation of the numerous official reports which had recommended them but by a remarkable and largely unexpected government decision made in the context of further changes to local government.[1] In their election manifesto of early 1983 the Conservatives pledged themselves to abolish the Greater London Council and the six metropolitan county councils, Greater Manchester, Merseyside, South Yorkshire, Tyne and Wear, West Midlands and West Yorkshire. Although these councils had been created by a recent Conservative government they were now regarded as a 'wasteful and unnecessary tier of government.' The services which they provided would in future become the responsibility of the borough or city councils within each county or of joint committees of these borough or city councils. Under these proposals the galleries and museums managed by Merseyside County Council would either be run by a joint committee of the city and borough councils or be returned to the borough or city in which the museum or gallery was physically located. In its detailed 'White Paper' of October 1983, *Streamlining the Cities*, the government, astonishingly, recognized the national importance of the Walker Art Gallery, and proposed that it should pass into the care of the Tate Gallery which would receive increased funding for this extra responsibility. The government expected that the Tate Gallery trustees would establish committees with substantial local membership to run the Gallery. The proposal had some logic as the Tate Gallery was then establishing a branch gallery in Liverpool at the Albert Dock. The future of the Walker Art Gallery's three outstations was not stated. The Lady Lever Art Gallery would presumably pass to the Wirral Borough Council while Sudley and the Oratory would return to Liverpool City Council or all three might become the responsibility of a joint committee. Similarly there was no special assistance for the Liverpool Museum, by then renamed the Merseyside County Museums, with its three outstations, the Maritime Museum, Speke Hall and Croxteth Hall, which would all also pass into the care of Liverpool City Council or again to a joint committee. The Tate Gallery trustees however refused to accept responsibility for the Walker Art Gallery.[2] Whatever the Tate trustees and their director might have felt about the Government's plan for the Walker their decision encouraged intense lobbying of the government by many cultural organizations, by the arts media and by many influential individuals to recognize that the Liverpool Museums and the Lady Lever Art Gallery were also of national importance.

Five months before the publication of the 'White Paper' the Labour party had regained control of Liverpool City Council after nearly ten years of Liberal dominance. Largely under the control of Militant, an extreme left-wing faction, they were determined to pursue an ambitious house-building programme and other schemes of social and educational improvement, even if this meant confrontation with the Conservative government in London.[3] The City Council was therefore never going to have much money left for any new cultural spending, and co-operation between the Council and central government over the future of museums and galleries in Liverpool was unlikely.[4] If the Liverpool Museum, the Walker Art Gallery and their outstations in Liverpool had returned to the Council they would have been very low priorities, and the quality of their displays, conservation, exhibitions, acquisitions and curatorial work would have almost certainly deteriorated. Indeed as the provision of museums and galleries are not statutory obligations for local authorities, the Council might well have resisted the return of the galleries and the museums on any terms. While a joint committee might have seemed a more congenial solution it offered no guarantee of the necessary support for the galleries or museums by the councils represented on the committee and no certainty of reasonable funding even at the current level. Richard Wilding, the civil servant in charge of the Office of Arts and Libraries, the government department responsible for the arts, noted that, owing to the power of Militant, the City Council option was impossible and he soon discovered that the Merseyside borough councils were not interested in forming any joint committee. He concluded: 'finding no other practicable solution for the Merseyside bodies, we decided simply to nationalize them.'[5]

Naturally Merseyside County Council fought the Government's abolition plans to the last. In its determination to make it as hard as possible for the Government to proceed with its abolition it vetoed any communication and supply of information between its staff and Whitehall. The Gallery found itself in an impossible situation torn between loyalty to the County Council and the new opportunity for gaining national status and funding, an ambition shared equally by successive Gallery chairmen of all political parties, in particular Ben Shaw on the Labour side for more than thirty years. As at the time of the establishment of the metropolitan county councils, there was little leadership from the Museums Association and now the political situation in Liverpool created deep and general concern over the dangers that threatened Merseyside museums and galleries if any part of them was returned to Liverpool City Council. On 4 January 1984 Lord Gowrie, the Minister for the Arts, visited the Walker Art Gallery, Sudley, the Lady Lever Art Gallery and the Liverpool Museums where he met, in addition to the directors, Ben Shaw the chairman, George Holt (for Sudley representing the Holt family) and Lord Leverhulme (for the Lady Lever Art Gallery). They all put forward arguments for keeping the Walker Art Gallery and its associated galleries together. On 28 March 1984 the Office of Arts and Libraries wrote both to Stevens and to Richard Foster, the director of the Museums, asking for detailed information about their institutions. The government was changing its attitude and was willing to accept much more responsibility for them after the abolition of the County Council. On 11 April Lord Gowrie announced the government's revised intentions in the House of Lords. There was now to be 'central funding' for the Walker Art Gallery, the Lady Lever Art Gallery, Sudley, the Oratory and the Liverpool Museum. The Maritime Museum was added to this list later in the year but the government refused to accept responsibility for the Museum's two other outstations, Croxteth Hall and its park and Speke Hall, arguing that they were country houses not museums or art galleries and should be returned to Liverpool City Council and to the National Trust respectively. This was indeed their eventual destiny facilitated by some extra government grants. The government had allocated about £17 million annually for the Merseyside museums and galleries and for some nine other smaller similar institutions elsewhere in England, all likely to suffer severely from the abolition of the metropolitan county councils. The Merseyside County Council's veto on contact with the government was reluctantly relaxed and information about Merseyside's museums and galleries was passed to the Office of Arts and Libraries. John Last, the former Conservative chairman of the County Council's Arts and Culture Committee, was able to arrange an informal meeting on 6 June 1984 at which Lord Gowrie told Stevens and Foster that the government would set up a board of trustees to administer these museums and galleries. It would be similar to the boards running the national museums and galleries in London and would thus be appointed and funded by central government. Under the original plan the Tate Gallery would have had to cover the Walker Art Gallery's annual budget, which was then slightly under £1,000,000. The annual expenditure of the Walker Art Gallery and of the five extra museums and galleries now added to the list for nationalization came to a total of about £4,000,000, partly already met by the Government from its Rate Support Grant. To this had to be added the costs involved in setting up the new statutory body and in establishing the necessary administrative departments to cover all the work previously done for the museums and galleries by the County Council, notably personnel services, buildings management, financial control, public relations and legal and architectural matters. In addition money for the further development of all the museums and galleries, especially the Maritime Museum, and for aligning the pay and conditions of the staff with civil service standards would be needed. Furthermore a realistic purchase grant for new acquisitions, which under the County Council had been very low, had to be agreed. For the local taxpayers on Merseyside the new offer was very beneficial. National status removed the burden of maintaining and developing the Merseyside museums and art galleries from local taxation to the state. Of course local control over them was lost but, sadly perhaps, this was never a serious concern for local politicians. As the demise of the County Council became inevitable discussions with the Office of Arts and Libraries began, and detailed arrangements for the takeover of Merseyside's museums and galleries in April 1986 were made. On 16 December 1985 their annual government grant for 1986-7 was announced. At £8,745,000, including a purchase grant of £750,000, it was far above all expectations on Merseyside. There was no doubt that the Government wanted the new national institution to be a success and continued to be very supportive in the early years notably over the Conservation Centre.

It is not clear how and why Government moved from a modest link-up with the Tate Gallery for the Walker Art Gallery to a new generously funded National Museums and Galleries on Merseyside. Museums and galleries in Greater Manchester and Tyne and Wear, threatened financially by the abolition of the metropolitan county councils, also received compensating but modest government grants. Neither Lord Gowrie, the minister for the arts, nor Michael Heseltine, the 'minister for Merseyside,' who both had a deep affection for Merseyside, was close to Margaret Thatcher. The Treasury was apparently unenthusiastic. On the day before the announcement of the greatly increased grants on 11 April 1984 *The Times* stated that the chief secretary to the Treasury had rejected Lord Gowrie's plea for an extra £40 million to make up for the arts funding lost by the abolition of the metropolitan county councils, even after arbitration from the prime minister's cabinet committee on the abolition.[6] Some evidence points to Lord Carrington as the saviour of the Walker Art Gallery. Despite being a Tory grandee with some left-wing sympathies – as well as a deep interest in the arts – he remained one of Mrs Thatcher's most trusted advisers, especially after the Falkland Islands disaster in which his resignation as foreign secretary saved her reputation. His country house was close to Chequers and it seems that at a Boxing Day party there in 1983 she approved the massive rescue plan despite her personal commitment to reduce government spending and despite the risk that the other major regional galleries and museums would demand similar generous treatment. Certainly such a controversial and unexpected decision could only have been taken at the highest level, and by a prime minister very concerned about Liverpool's future. The Government may also have felt that as it had already invested so heavily in Liverpool, particularly through the Merseyside Development Corporation, there was a strong economic argument in favour of developing the museums and galleries which might generate income from tourism. In the history of state assistance to regional art galleries in the twentieth century it is an outstanding landmark and led the way to further more modest intervention, notably the so-called 'Renaissance in the Regions.'

As well as fighting the Government's abolition plans the County Council had to deal with a Government determined to control local expenditure through 'rate-capping', that is placing an annual limit on the size of local taxation. Although the County Council was, like Liverpool City Council, controlled by Labour it was not dominated by Militant and the extreme left.[7] There had been important changes amongst its political leaders. Bill Sefton, its first Labour leader, had gone to the House of Lords as Lord Sefton of Garston and Sir Kenneth Thompson the first Conservative leader had died. Ben Shaw had stood down as chairman of the County Council's Art and Culture Committee in 1983 after over twenty years as Labour party spokesman for the arts to become the final chairman of the County Council. He had been replaced by his deputy chairman James (or Jim) Riley who had worked for Cammell Laird, the Birkenhead shipbuilders. Although without Shaw's knowledge of the gallery world and its politics he proved the ideal chairman for the difficult situation. He understood the contradictory position in which the Gallery found itself and was relaxed about the exchange of information and ideas between the Gallery staff and the Office of Arts and Libraries, despite his leader's ban on any contacts of this nature. Being a political realist he knew that the Government had the power to impose its will and that, to secure the best possible deal for the galleries and museums, details of their expenditure and activities had to be passed to the government to permit arrangements for their future management to be made. The smooth transition between local authority and national control owed much to his influence.

In the search for additional funding for the County Council in 1985 consideration was given to the possibility of a sale of a part of the Gallery's collection to the Council's Superannuation Fund, which would then lend it back to the Gallery.[8] The Gallery staff compiled a list of those works of art bought directly by the Gallery without assistance from grant-giving bodies or individuals, who might object to the sales. A precedent had been set by the British Rail Pension Fund which had invested heavily in works of art. The obvious objection to the Council's proposals was that ultimately the paintings would have to be sold to provide pensions for local government staff on Merseyside, and the Gallery would then probably not be able to afford to buy them back. The Council sought expert legal opinions which indicated that, while it might have the necessary powers to sell the paintings, its freedom to use the proceeds was likely to be restricted and the idea was quietly abandoned.

It might seem that the creation of the National Museums and Galleries on Merseyside followed logically from the grant of national status to the art galleries in Edinburgh in 1850, in Dublin in 1854, in Cardiff in 1907 and in Belfast in 1958. These cities gained their national galleries largely from a new recognition of rising national identity in their areas, not primarily from the importance of their collections. The clearest example is Cardiff, where the extremely modest Cardiff municipal collections became the National Museum of Wales as part of Lloyd George's campaign within the ruling Liberal party in favour of Welsh identity and of some Welsh autonomy. Nineteenth-century European nationalists had believed that a national gallery and museum were a necessary part of nationhood. On Merseyside however national status was granted by a government for very different reasons. It resulted directly from the government's determination to abolish a regional 'wasteful and unnecessary tier of government' and the need to solve a practical problem of finding a future for the outstanding Merseyside collections. It was an assault on regional identity rather than a celebration of it. On Merseyside the word national is used in the Italian sense to mean a regional art gallery of such importance that it should be administered by central government. But this was an entirely new concept in Britain. In Cardiff and Edinburgh it is reasonably clear that the word national in their titles refers to the Welsh or Scottish not to the British nation, although both galleries now have collections of European importance.

Following existing practice at other national museums and galleries the expenditure of the large government grant for the Gallery became the responsibility of an unpaid board of trustees appointed by the government. In all art galleries power had been gradually moving away from governing boards and committees towards salaried professional staff, but, while in local authority galleries this had been a largely smooth and uninterrupted process, there was considerable but rather spasmodic opposition to it among the more expert boards in the national museums and galleries. There were also significant peculiarities in Liverpool. First the chairman was not elected by the trustees themselves but appointed by the government. This procedure, which had already been adopted by other national museums and galleries, greatly enhanced the power of the chairman, who often had never been an ordinary trustee. Secondly, there could be up to twenty trustees, and at any one time there were usually about seventeen. Other national museums and galleries – with the notable exception of the British Museum – had generally fewer than ten or twelve. In a large board or committee the sense of personal involvement in decision making is less strong, dissidents are reluctant to insist too strongly on their own ideas and trustees with special interests do not have the time to explain their concerns. Individual trustees were not allocated to represent the various departments and did not have any 'pastoral' responsibility for particular groups of staff. Thirdly, the trustees were composed of two rather different groups fairly equal in number, one based in London and one living on Merseyside. Even within these two groups there was a great variety of social, educational and occupational backgrounds. This certainly led to a balanced representation of different viewpoints, but it also made any concerted and independent action within the Board difficult to achieve. Fourthly, the first two chairmen had very substantial business experience and great skill in achieving general agreement among the trustees around policies promoted by the director, but neither claimed great personal expertise in artistic matters and were inevitably heavily dependent on the professional staff for ideas and policies. Lastly, attendance levels at trustee meetings were not always high. The chairman expressed his concern over this problem in 1990 and 1995, although he might have given more consideration to the travelling required by the London trustees and to the presence of some trustees at meetings of committees of the Board.[9] For all these reasons central authority became stronger and to a considerable extent the board of trustees assumed an advisory rather than a managerial role. Trustee revolts, acrimony between staff and trustees and concerted opposition to policies agreed between the chairman and director were rare, and the turbulence characteristic of many other boards of trustees at other national galleries in this period was largely unknown. This general acquiescence on the part of the trustees reflected a broad harmony of approach throughout the institution in its early years but later had rather different results. The first batch of trustees included the director of the Courtauld Institute of Art, an artist, an art critic, an architectural historian and a leading authority on gallery environment as well as rather fewer specialists in other fields covered by the National Museums and Galleries on Merseyside. This generally reflected practice on other national trustee boards, but the professional bias in favour of art did not last more than about ten years. The government also tactfully appointed as trustees two former chairmen of the County Council Arts and Culture Committee, John Last and Ben Shaw, together with George Holt, a co-opted member of the earlier city and county council arts committees and a link with the old Liverpool shipping families. As new trustees were appointed – usually on the advice of the director or chairman – there was inevitably a tendency to choose those unlikely to oppose existing policies with too much vigour, and it would probably be true to say that these new trustees sometimes lacked the practical experience in the artistic world of their predecessors.

The most immediate result of nationalisation was the merger of the Gallery and the Museums to form the National Museums and Galleries on Merseyside under a single director. At first the Office of Arts and Libraries did not decide between having a single director or two directors, one for the Museums and one for the Gallery, leaving the trustees, when appointed to make this decision. The Office then changed their policy in early 1986, now insisting on a single director. The choice was to be between Stevens and Foster and the unsuccessful candidate would be deputy director. There was a legal requirement for a single 'accounting officer' responsible to Parliament for the expenditure of public money. The National Museum of Wales provided an example of a multidisciplinary institution combining the National Gallery for Wales and the National Museum with a single director who was the accounting officer, and Birmingham Museums and Art Galleries were a good example of a successful multidisciplinary local authority service. On 3 February a selection panel composed of Shaw and Last as former chairmen of the County Council's Arts and Culture Committee, Ray O'Brien as chief executive of the County Council, Richard Wilding and the newly appointed chairman of the trustees, Sir Leslie Young, selected Foster as director and Stevens as deputy director. Young had a very distinguished career in industry and in public service on Merseyside, but no members of the panel had any professional experience of museums or galleries. It was not therefore surprising that when four weeks later a group of those trustees already appointed gathered together there were serious misgivings about the nature of the appointments from two trustees. It was explained to them that they and the rest of the board could not have been involved in the selection process as it was necessary to carry it out very rapidly. Neither questioned the selection panel's preference for Foster over Stevens. One however immediately asked whether 'in practice Stevens would continue to be in charge of the Walker Art Gallery'. Young replied that 'in his view line management responsibility through a single director was of fundamental importance', but added that 'Stevens would continue to have particular responsibility for the Walker Art Gallery'. The other trustee had a very different concern. He felt that Stevens as deputy director, far from running the Gallery, would be 'largely involved in administration' and that therefore an assistant director would be needed to administer the Gallery. Young repeated that 'the concept of a single director with the sort of structure now envisaged was necessary to support an effective operation'. He was confident that in due course Foster and Stevens could amicably settle their own ranges of responsibility. Both trustees knew that relationships between directors and specialist heads of departments in composite museums are always demanding and often difficult.[10] Stevens had no difficulty with the concept of a single director and he accepted that his role as deputy director and head of the Walker Art Gallery could not be defined until the staff structure for the new organisation had been agreed. Foster at no time made any attempt to define Stevens's role with him.

Stevens believed that the generous government settlement indicated that the Government wanted an active forward-looking institution that played its part in national affairs. He wanted a radical change in culture. The civil service team who came to Liverpool in 1986 to carry out a staff inspection and to advise the trustees on the new staff structure favoured the formation of strong semi-independent departments each covering one of the disciplines represented in the new organization. The specialist heads of these new larger and fewer departments would be the dominant figures in the director's management team. Until 1989 this was the usual form of governance among composite multi-disciplinary national museums. Stevens favoured this approach while Foster, wishing to preserve the existing structure, preferred to regard the organisation in terms of buildings rather than in terms of the curatorship of material. Stevens saw the staff inspection as a unique opportunity to establish a fresh vision for the new institution, to discard out of date staff structures and to reduce drastically the number of departments. The inspectors agreed with his plan for a centralised conservation department and for combining the fine and decorative arts into a strong single department, and these proposals were indeed eventually largely implemented. Elsewhere the advice of the civil service team was largely rejected. In the event the heads of the curatorial departments became a third tier of management reporting through a line of keepers to Foster, who strongly disliked any form of delegation.

Foster acted timidly as is well illustrated by his refusal to accept Stevens's recommendation that Amico Aspertini's *Virgin and Child with Saints* should be bought for the Gallery. It came from the collection of Liverpool's great cultural leader, William Roscoe, whose collection formed the core of the Gallery's holdings. Roscoe, who attributed it to Ghirlandaio and Michelangelo, regarded it as the best picture in his collection. Stevens contacted the perceptive acting keeper of art at the National Museum of Wales, Mark Evans, who earlier had spent some six years at the Walker Art Gallery as an assistant keeper. He bought this masterpiece by this remarkable Bolognese artist for his Museum for less than £350,000, and found that grants were readily available. What made the situation particularly galling for the Gallery was that it did have the funds necessary to acquire by far the best picture associated with Roscoe not already in a public gallery. The whole purpose of seeking national status was that pictures such as this could be acquired for Merseyside. At the end of August 1987, following the debacle over the use of the Sessions House and what he perceived as a general lack of progress, Stevens followed the Aspertini to the National Museum of Wales. There as keeper of art he supervised the renovation and extension of the art galleries, which doubled in size.

Much to Stevens' disappointment none of his curatorial team received promotion. Between 1988 and 2000 three senior appointments were made to the Gallery's staff from outside Liverpool. New blood is of course welcome, a vast amount was achieved in these years but many at the Gallery observed that a similar policy of outside recruitment at senior levels was not pursued at the Liverpool Museum or at the Maritime Museum.

After Stevens's departure the director and trustees favoured a policy of centralization, effectively merging the Museum and Gallery. At nationalisation the museum was allocated an annual £3,197,000, the maritime museum £2,263,000, the Gallery £2,617,000 and the administrators £668,000,[11] demonstrating clearly the strong position achieved by the museums, but the figure for the Gallery, which included the Lady Lever Art Gallery, was still about one hundred times greater than the 1953 figure before allowing for inflation. Very soon separate budgets for the institutions were abandoned. The trustees did not form an art gallery committee. Unified conservation, education, design, security and marketing departments were established. There was a single purchase fund instead of the separate and very large allocation of £550,000 for the Gallery originally agreed.

Merging museums and art galleries was fashionable. In 1963 Leeds, Liverpool, Sheffield, Manchester, Newcastle, Bristol and Bradford all had separate art galleries under their own specialist directors with rather attractive annual salaries varying between £1,365 (at Newcastle) and £2,785 (at Liverpool).[12] By 2000 all these galleries except the one at Manchester had been merged with the local museums, despite the opposition of many of their directors.[13] In the 1950s T.J. Honeyman, the charismatic director of the Glasgow Art Gallery and Museum, had pleaded unsuccessfully for the separation of the two institutions on the grounds that the objectives of British provincial museums were too narrowly educational.[14] Manchester retained its own art gallery only because the museum there was run by the University. But art galleries and museums have very different objectives. Kant and many others have rightly insisted on the 'disinterestedness of aesthetic pleasure'. Museums, however, are rightly more concerned with more utilitarian but equally important purposes, education, technology, craft skills, materials and the study of history. In merging with museums art galleries rightly feared a dilution of their separate identity.

In 1989 Stevens was replaced by Julian Treuherz, the keeper of fine art at Manchester City Art Galleries, but only as keeper of art galleries not as deputy director. With his lower status he generally only attended trustee meetings during the discussion of items directly relating to his functions. Heads of departments must have wide autonomy and independence to be effective. Observing these events from Tate Liverpool where he was curator and then director between 1987 and 2000, Lewis Biggs commented: 'The amalgamation of the Walker with Liverpool Museum in 1986 effectively demoted its leadership: Stevens...left'.[15]

By 1984 the population of Liverpool had been declining sharply for many years and it was about half the figure for 1931. The city had become smaller than Sheffield or Leeds and about half the size of Birmingham. However it has been estimated that between 1984 and 2010 over £225 million at 2007 values were spent in Liverpool on capital projects involving the improvement and building of art galleries, museums and institutions closely related to them. To this enormous sum could be added the £24 million spent on providing a new art school for Liverpool in 2007-8. There may be some exaggeration in these figures but they probably represented the largest single spending spree on the development of buildings for the visual arts and museums ever undertaken in any provincial English city over a relatively short period.[16] It was all the more remarkable in that the years between 1990 and 1995 and between 2007 and 2010 were periods of deep economic depression. The larger of the projects were the conversion of a substantial part of the Albert Dock into the new Tate Gallery Liverpool, the conversion of the Midland Railway Goods Offices into the National Museums Liverpool Conservation Centre, the extensive improvements to the Liverpool Museum, renamed the World Museum, the conversion of old university buildings into the Victoria University Gallery and Museum, the erection of a new Bluecoat Gallery and the refurbishment of the adjoining Bluecoat buildings, the building of the new Museum of Liverpool and the construction of a new centre for the Foundation for Art and Creative Technology, which is devoted to the art of video and film.

The new Tate Liverpool reflected the concern felt by many national museums that their collections and activities were entirely based in London and that the regions were being ignored. The Science Museum created its outstations in York and Bradford. The National Portrait Gallery organised significant long-term displays at country houses including Bodelwyddan, not far from Liverpool. The Tate Gallery's initiative received a warmer welcome in Liverpool than in some other regional galleries, because the Walker Art Gallery saw very clearly the city's desperate need for visitors and tourists interested in art and perceived the Tate's arrival as a great advantage. The Albert Dock, an exceptionally important industrial building, was being converted for leisure use by the Merseyside Development Corporation at the government's expense, thus providing much of the funding for the new Tate Liverpool. Tate Liverpool opened in 1988 with Richard Francis, a former assistant keeper at the Walker Art Gallery, as its first director. It has since attracted an average of around 600,000 visitors each year although the joint activities between the Walker and the Tate envisaged by Stevens did not materialise.

Although the Tate Gallery had been considering establishing a new gallery in Liverpool before 1981 there is no doubt that the principal causes for this enormous expenditure on arts projects in Liverpool were the Toxteth riots of that year and the resulting conviction in London and Brussels that Liverpool was an area of dereliction in the new prosperous Western Europe of the 1980s. Car factories had been built to solve this problem in the 1960s. Now it was the turn of art and museums. The riots succeeded where postwar idealism had failed. Only a very small proportion of the huge amounts spent originated in Liverpool or Merseyside. The money came primarily from governmental institutions and agencies, most notably the Heritage Lottery Fund, the European Regional Development Fund, European 'Objective One' funding and the North West Development Agency, set up by the government in 1999. There were much more modest contributions from private trusts, businesses and individuals, some based outside Merseyside. This was not the self help which had characterized the earlier development of Merseyside's art galleries and museums. It was enlightened despotism and the important decisions were taken outside Liverpool.

There were other reasons for these vast new capital developments. Especially with the establishment of the Heritage Lottery Fund in 1992 money became more easily available for art gallery building and design projects than for the acquisition, conservation and cataloguing of works of art. There was a widespread feeling, not at all favoured in the Walker Art Gallery, that art galleries had 'enough' paintings and sculptures, and that the priorities now were well-designed spaces and facilities in which to display them. National art galleries gradually took over responsibility for their own buildings from the government's Property Services Agency in the late 1980s and early 1990s. Trustees generally were thus given more interest in these buildings with their fine nineteenth- and early twentieth-century architecture, which was then once more attracting favourable critical attention. At the new National Museums and Galleries on Merseyside most of the available money went to the Liverpool Museum.

The Walker Art Gallery made modest but useful gains from this astonishing largesse. More reliable and sensitive controls on the air conditioning were installed permitting the Gallery's early paintings to move northwards into the extension galleries of 1931-1933 and facilitating a complete re-arrangement of the permanent collection in 1988, the first since 1951.[17] Treuherz had a particular interest in the physical appearance of the Gallery. Thanks to these new resources the entrance hall and six galleries were lavishly re-decorated. The Gallery had generally, but not invariably, favoured neutral and unobtrusive background colours which did not compete with the pictures. These were now replaced by stronger colours and patterns which were thought, not entirely correctly, to reflect more closely the original design of the Gallery itself and the style of many of its paintings. The bare 'unfurnished' look, the fine-art 'purism', characteristic of the Gallery gave way to a luxurious, less Spartan approach, more reminiscent of nineteenth-century country-house displays. This more flamboyant attitude to display had been popularised first by the 'country house museum' movement of the 1960s and 1970s and then by Timothy Clifford at the Manchester City Art Gallery and at the National Gallery of Scotland in Edinburgh. New showcases had 'period' decoration. An overall effect was aimed at rather than one that sought to navigate the visitor through the displays. Extended descriptive labels replaced the old room guides. The Gallery had become responsible in 1989 for decorative art generally, not just for the collections of it at the Lady Lever Art Gallery, and therefore some furniture and other decorative art could easily be found for the Walker Art Gallery.[18] However the large decorative art collections in the Liverpool Museum and the staff responsible for them were not moved to the Gallery which remained essentially devoted to fine art, and a fully integrated department was not achieved. The Prince

George Gallery, long the main space for temporary exhibitions, and two adjoining galleries were air-conditioned and given a new goods lift to form a self-contained suite for temporary exhibitions. The new sculpture conservation department was able to commission in China a replica of Warrington Wood's huge statue of Liverpool which replaced the original much-decayed version over the Gallery's pediment.[19] New storage racks were installed. A lecture theatre was created in the Sessions House. The Gallery's commitment to the detailed cataloguing of its collections was greatly encouraged by the formation of a trustees' scholarship committee and many new catalogues and publications emerged.[20] The new Conservation Centre provided generous space, equipment and staffing for the restoration of the Gallery's paintings, sculpture, prints and drawings. Higher salaries for both conservators and curators permitted the long-term retention of junior staff which had been impossible under local authority pay scales. Sudley was refurbished and given a passenger lift, although much material of Liverpool interest there was removed from display. Sadly regular public opening of the Oratory was abandoned in 2000.[21]

What was not done however was the provision of new galleries for the display of the Gallery's permanent collection, which was its greatest physical need. After 1945 much purpose-built Gallery space had been allocated to meet other pressing requirements. Even by1986 four ground-floor galleries were not used as public galleries. Liverpool City Libraries still occupied most of one following bombing in the Second World War. Another was used as a print room and offices for the administrative staff. A third was used for lectures, other educational activities and occasional exhibitions. A fourth was mostly occupied as curatorial offices. On the first floor one gallery had been converted into a conservation studio and another into a café and store. In 1965 Hugh Scrutton had submitted a report to Liverpool City Council's Arts Sub-Committee entitled 'Pressure of Space'. He was concerned that larger and more frequent exhibitions were severely reducing the space available for the permanent collection.[22] He also wished to display more of the Gallery's huge collection of Victorian and Edwardian paintings and sculpture which was becoming increasingly fashionable. There was also of course a growing collection of large important contemporary paintings from the John Moores Exhibitions. By 1970 Scrutton believed that new galleries should help to provide space for 'as many as 1,400' oil paintings on permanent display rather than the existing 450.[23] In December 1965 the Arts Sub-Committee established a Special Sub-Committee to consider this issue.[24] Vere Cotton suggested that the space over the far end of Clayton Street and between the original Gallery of 1874-1883 and the extension of 1931-33 should be filled in at first-floor level to create two new display galleries.[25] In 1967 the city architect approved this idea in principle and suggested that a new goods lift and loading bay should be installed adjacent to and beneath the new galleries.[26] Estimates and plans were provided for the scheme but its implementation depended on a decision over an extension to the Liverpool City Library. When that scheme eventually received funding the Gallery's project was abandoned partly because the development of land behind the Sessions House seemed to be a better and more cost-effective solution to the demand for more space. A scheme very similar to the abortive 1967 project was successfully developed at the near end of Clayton Street between 1997 and 2001 as part of the creation of the exhibition suite in the extension galleries. The link between the original Gallery and the extension of 1931-33 was widened but only a very modest amount of extra display space was achieved. Some extra space for the permanent collection in the extension galleries had been made available first in 1974 by moving the conservation studio to the gallery occupied by the café which was eventually relocated to the Entrance Hall,[27] and secondly in 1996 by moving the conservation studio to the new Conservation Centre. In 1988 at the cost of about £200,000 the ground-floor lecture hall was converted into a sculpture gallery designed by Charles Ryder with about one hundred and fifty pieces crammed together in the best Walker Art Gallery tradition.[28] The former print room and administrative offices re-opened with a display of decorative art in 2004. None of these improvements solved the problem of the fundamental shortage of space for the sympathetic display of the picture collection.

Between 1986 and 1989 serious consideration was given to a long-term lease of St George's Hall, the huge architectural masterpiece designed between 1841 and 1856 by H.L. Elmes and C.R. Cockerell. It was built to house both law courts and concert halls, but by 1984 it was largely empty following the opening of new Crown Courts in Castle Street. It stands only about 50 metres from the Gallery and its vast and cavernous basements could have formed excellent display spaces for both the Gallery and the Museum, as well as providing room for storage and conservation. However, its owners, Liverpool City Council, had other ideas and the cost of its long-term use for Gallery and Museum purposes was estimated at about £17 million. Even in the financial euphoria of the creation of the National Museums and Galleries on Merseyside in 1986 this seemed a very large sum. After renting the building and opening it to the public in 1988 and 1989, the trustees largely lost interest in it, although they were still considering the use of the basement in 1996.[29] The City Council have struggled to find any serious use for it, and many felt that the trustees had given up too easily and that a splendid opportunity to give a sympathetic use to one of Liverpool's outstanding buildings had been lost.

Space for new display galleries had been made available by the acquisition in 1973 of the car park adjacent to the Gallery's extension galleries and behind the Sessions House.[30] In 1984 the empty Sessions House, a splendid building designed by F. and G. Holme between 1882 and 1884, was bought from Lancashire County Council for £55,000[31] with all the funding coming from the Gallery's Bowring Bequest Fund and the Museums and Galleries Commission. Between 1983 and 1987 ambitious but practical plans were drawn up to move to the Sessions House all the Gallery's activities except public display, paintings storage and craft workshops, so that all its purpose-built galleries could be used again for the public display. The two court rooms would be converted into a large lecture theatre and a conservation studio. Space for the library, for the print room and for the very extensive documentation files and archives together with offices for all members of the staff could be found elsewhere in the Sessions House. An underground passage would connect the two buildings.[32] A new building directly adjoining the extension galleries might be erected on the car park, thus providing yet more public display space. Mill Lane, separating the Sessions House from the Gallery, was closed as a public thoroughfare and practical arrangements were made to permit access for vehicles to the backs of the two buildings.

However the County Council decided to use the Sessions House not for Gallery purposes but for displays of photographs and other graphic material illustrating the history of the urban working-class on Merseyside, and it opened to the public as a Museum of Labour History on 24 March 1986, a week before the abolition of the County Council.[33] The Labour majority on the Council could well argue that most social-history displays of the early 1980s ignored working-class life, but this omission should have been resolved much earlier through the Arts and Culture Committee. From its foundation the Gallery and its managing committee had experienced interference by the whole council, usually on acquisitions or its exhibition programme. It had learnt to live with it and did so on this occasion. The Council's Labour party did have a serious point, and their enforced establishment of a Museum of Labour History, against Foster's advice, permanently changed the Museum's policy towards working-class history. Many observers however regarded this venture as a political parting shot by a section of the local Labour party, directed against the Conservative government and its plans to abolish the Council. It cost the County Council about £100,000. At the first meeting of the trustees of the new National Museums and Galleries on Merseyside on 3 March 1986 John Last, the principal Conservative representative for the arts on the former County Council, suggested that the future of the Labour History displays should be reviewed within the next year.[34] The earlier conversion scheme enabling the Sessions House to be used for the Gallery's purposes was approved in principle by the trustees in 1988.[35] However the City Council and others objected to the closure of the Museum and the trustees did not dismantle it and close the Sessions House to the public until November 1991.[36] In 1993 the Museum re-opened near the Pier Head with considerable alterations and a less politically contentious name, the 'Museum of Liverpool Life'. In 1997 there were plans to erect a glazed link building between the Sessions House and the Gallery and to convert part of the Sessions House for display purposes but these were abandoned as too ambitious.[37] Despite these problems by 2002 the underground passage was in place, parts of the Sessions House had been gradually converted to house the print room, a modest lecture theatre, archives storage and education offices, although most of it remained empty. No new galleries have been erected on the car park. In the two other British national galleries outside London, Cardiff and Edinburgh, new display rooms were provided on a large scale between 1975 and 2000. This never happened in Liverpool. Even after the modest improvements of 1974 to 2002 it still remained true that the Gallery had less display space in 2002 than it had in 1939.

These useful gains for the Gallery were achieved at a considerable price, the imposition of admission charges between 1997 and 2001. The Gallery had levied charges on visitors to some of its exhibitions but never before on entrance to its permanent collection, except at the Lady Lever Art Gallery under the Merseyside County Council for the benefit of the Purchase Fund. The Conservative government of Edward Heath had compelled the national museums and galleries to introduce charges in 1974 but these were lifted by the Labour administration of Harold Wilson after only a few months. However in the late 1970s it became apparent that nationally funded museums and galleries, unlike local authority galleries, were only able to reclaim much of the new value added tax levied on their expenditure by imposing admission charges. In 1984 the National Maritime Museum introduced entrance fees and most of the other national museums, but not the national art galleries, followed their example over the next twelve years. The National Museums and Galleries on Merseyside had followed the practice of the old Merseyside County Council in imposing charges at the Maritime Museum but elsewhere resisted admission fees until the meeting of the trustees of 15 January 1997. There on the advice of the director charging at all its museums and galleries was approved by ten of the eleven trustees present.[38] The annual government grant was then falling but the immediate cause of this new policy was an ambitious programme of improvements at the Liverpool Museum and, to a much smaller extent, at the Walker Art Gallery, then scheduled to take place between 1998 and 2001 at a total cost of about £34 million. The final cost was about £44 million of which about £6 million was spent at the Gallery. The Heritage Lottery Fund provided over £32 million.[39] These figures would have been considerably larger without the value added tax reclaim permitted to museums and art galleries with admission charges, and the money raised by charging would help to provide the small proportion required from the Merseyside trustees after the substantial contributions from the Heritage Lottery Fund and the European Regional Development Fund.[40] The admission charge was set at £3 at all the museums and galleries but some relief was given to local residents by permitting all visitors to re-use their tickets without any further payment on subsequent visits at all or any of the museums and galleries within a year.[41] Children, students and pensioners gradually received exemptions after assurances that the value added tax reclaim would not be reduced.[42] Implementation of charging was delayed until July 1997 to enable Chris Smith, the new Labour Secretary of State for Culture, Media and Sport, to react. He pleaded for the postponement, at least, of admission fees, but he could not offer enough new money to achieve even some delay.[43] The effect of charging for admission on attendance figures at the museums was not too severe, but the Gallery, which had attracted over 200,000 visitors annually in nearly all the past thirty years, received only 124,000 visits in 1997 and 117,992 a year later. Galleries rely on brief casual visits to a much greater extent than museums. Some doubt was thrown on these statistics by speculation that imprecise methods of counting visitors before the imposition of charges had exaggerated their numbers by up to 40%.[44] However, even casual observation between 1997 and 2001 revealed many empty galleries. Sir Denis Mahon, a great collector and a passionate opponent of art gallery admission charges, withdrew his proposed bequest to the Gallery of three important Italian seventeenth-century paintings by Guercino, Pier Francesco Mola and Luca Giordano.[45] Locally he was denounced by some as a London art connoisseur meddling in the affairs of a Merseyside gallery.

In 2001 the government made the necessary adjustments to enable the value added tax to be reclaimed and admission charges were removed in December. By 2003 attendance figures were back up to 219,000, but still well below the 278,000 achieved in 1972, and they fell again later in the decade. Meanwhile the capital spending programme of 1997-2002 had claimed another victim. Before 1993 the grant for purchasing works of art at all the national museums and galleries had been fixed by the government separately from the grant for all other purposes. By 1998 however, as part of a movement for giving trustees and directors more independence from government control, they could allocate any or no part of their total income to buying works of art. Theoretically the purchase grant for the Museums and the Gallery at Liverpool remained at £750,000 from 1986 until 1997, although money had been taken out of it to pay for other projects, most notably the repair of the Gallery roof in 1990.[46]

There had been many important acquisitions for the Gallery. There was an attempt to fill the gap left by the Gallery's failure to buy British modernist art of the 1930s with the purchase of works by Ben Nicholson and Ceri Richards but generally the policy of concentrating on works with Merseyside connections was continued, notably the significant if rather conventional portraits of the West Lancashire landowners, Fleetwood Hesketh and his wife by Wright of Derby which were bought for £880,960 after tax concessions. The trustees evidently liked this well established policy of concentrating on acquisitions with local associations which had been very successful from political necessity under the County Council. At a meeting in 1991 they had to choose between the Hesketh portraits, a superb drawing by Primaticcio, *Ulysses winning the archery contest in the presence of Penelope's suitors* (fig. 3), from William Roscoe's collection, and two fine ideal paintings, *Bathers* and *Moonlight* by Claude Joseph Vernet. Despite some expert advice to the contrary they rejected the Vernet paintings.[47] By far their most important and dramatic purchase followed on from the acquisition of the drawing by Primaticcio for £245,300 with help from the National Art-Collections Fund. In 1995 the Gallery bought the 328 old master drawings collected by Henry Blundell (1724-1810) and his son Charles at Ince Blundell Hall near Liverpool for £3.2 million after tax concessions.[48] About half of these came from the great collection formed by Roscoe whose splendid early Italian and Netherlandish paintings formed the core of the Gallery's displays. Indeed the Blundells and Roscoe were by far the most significant Liverpool collectors in the late eighteenth- and early nineteenth-centuries. The Gallery had been buying drawings from Roscoe's collection as they appeared on the market since the 1950s.[49] Now there were drawings by Mantegna, Tintoretto, Parmigianino, Primaticcio, Correggio, Domenichino and Rubens and, even if not all were of the highest quality, together they transformed the Gallery's holdings in this area and kept together one of the last surviving large British collections of old master drawings in private hands. With eighteen months' research leave Xanthe Brooke, the curator of European Art, was able to catalogue them in detail despite the wide range of artists, schools and periods involved. In 1998 a selection of them were exhibited in the Gallery and at the British Museum in London.[50] Generous grants for the purchase were again received especially from the National Heritage Memorial Fund, without whose help the acquisition would have been impossible, and the National Art-Collections Fund. Two further important items from Ince Blundell were secured. Richard Wilson's *Landscape with Phaeton's petition to Apollo*, commissioned by Henry Blundell, passed to the Gallery under the acceptance in lieu procedure in 1999. Two years later, with the aid of the Heritage Lottery Fund and National Art-Collections Fund, the spectacular amber and ivory cabinet probably made in Danzig around 1700 was purchased for £539,755. Regrettably however neither the moving *Coat of Many Colours* by a follower of Rembrandt, which had been in the Derby Collection at Knowsley since the early eighteenth century, nor the very remarkable *Procession of the Magi* by the Master of St Bartholomew from Ince Blundell now in the Getty Collection in Los Angeles were acquired when they came on the market.

Indeed the drawings were the last outstanding fine art acquisitions. Between 1986 and 1997 the purchase grant for the Museums and Gallery had fallen from over 8% to less than 6% of the total grant. In February 1998 the director advised the trustees to reduce it to £250,000, less than 2% of the total grant, and in practice it fell much lower still as the costs of the capital spending programme at the Liverpool Museum rose by over £8 million. The motives for this drastic reduction were the need to fund these improvement works and to maintain public programmes and marketing initiatives. There was evidently considerable opposition by some trustees to this decision, and it was eventually agreed that this reduction in the purchase grant should apply only until the end of the capital spending then scheduled for 2001 but in practice achieved only some years later.[51] Purchase grants at all national galleries and museums were under huge pressure in the late 1980s and 1990s and usually fell. However most institutions prudently kept sufficient funds in place to enable them to secure the necessary support from the National Heritage Memorial Fund and the National Art-Collections Fund for outstanding acquisitions, which as national institutions they had to make every effort to secure. In Liverpool this period marked the end of the policy, initiated by Vere Cotton and Frank Lambert in the early 1930s and expanded in the 1950s, that the Gallery should aim to collect major historic English and European paintings. Although, ironically, with the tax concession regime and the establishment of the National Heritage Memorial Fund and of the Heritage Lottery Fund, the financing of major acquisitions had never been easier, the Walker Art Gallery preferred a less ambitious policy focusing on the purchase of decorative and inexpensive contemporary art.

Chapter 8

The John Moores and the Peter Moores Exhibitions

The most influential figure in the Walker Art Gallery's affairs in the last half of the twentieth century was Sir John Moores (1896-1993) the hugely successful local business man and Merseyside legend. He persuaded Liverpool City Council to embrace contemporary art in a manner that gave the Gallery a unique character among its municipal rivals. His younger son Peter built on his achievement and between them they gave Merseyside and north-west England an opportunity to see and enjoy contemporary British art unrivalled outside London. Both were active sponsors whose contribution went well beyond simply providing funds.

From a working-class background Moores had by 1924 founded the Littlewoods Football Pools Company with two friends while he was working for the Commercial Cable Company.[1] As the Cable Company did not permit its staff to take on any outside employment Littlewood, the birth surname of Colin Askham, one of the partners, was used for the new enterprise. Lack of immediate success coupled with heavy losses persuaded his partners to sell out to Moores. With the aid of a very supportive family Moores turned the business round with astonishing speed, although at first he had to continue working for the Commercial Cable Company. By the mid-1930s he had established the Littlewoods mail order and chain stores companies, thus becoming a millionaire. His commercial empire, which included much more than these core businesses, remained under family control and management until it was sold after his death. Although he had passed much of his wealth to his children in the late 1940s to avoid death duties he was widely regarded as one of the ten richest men, and at one time as the second richest man, in England.[2] In 1992, a year before his death, his companies had a turnover of over £2,700 million and made profits of over £97 million.

In 1930 he moved with his family to a modest but comfortable house in Formby, about ten miles north of Liverpool, his home until his death. Although not a native, Liverpool became the focus of his life. He entered local politics becoming a Conservative member of Liverpool City Council between 1933 and 1940. There he met and formed a lasting friendship with Jack and Bessie Braddock, then well to the left of the Labour party, who were later to be dominant figures on the Council. The Second World War gave him the opportunity to exercise his genius for management to the full. To support the war effort he switched with great success his largely clerical workforce into parachute and barrage balloon manufacture and also into engineering. At its peak his organisation had around 30,000 local employees and was well known as a caring and sympathetic employer. He was a generous supporter of local good causes that interested him personally, especially children's charities, youth clubs, the art college, universities and the Tate Gallery in Liverpool.

Moores first started taking lessons in painting in 1947 while on holiday in Bermuda and it became a consuming preoccupation and delight until his death. One of his teachers was William Stevenson, then a very highly regarded Principal of the Liverpool Art College. Stevenson later joined the Littlewoods Design Department and designed the company's headquarters building in central Liverpool, for a time the tallest building there. Moores often went on painting holidays and later had a studio attached as an annexe to his office. Like many business men of his time he greatly admired the art of the French Post-Impressionists and often copied their work, particularly that of Cézanne. His copy of Van Gogh's *The Blue Cart* hung in the office adjacent to his own. He was a friend of George Kennerley (1908-2009), the Chairman of Vernons Pools, another Liverpool football pools company. Kennerley had built it up virtually from nothing on behalf of Vernon Sangster, and it became the principal competitor of Littlewoods Pools. Kennerley was a highly competent artist of great flair and exuberance who exhibited at the Royal Academy and with London galleries. He gave one of his paintings to the Walker Art Gallery in 1952 and the Gallery purchased his *Irises (Homage to Van Gogh)* from him in 1970. He was a close associate of William Scott and made an important collection of twentieth-century paintings especially the work of Matisse, Soutine, Marquet, Jawlensky and de Stael. Moores had no artistic friendships of this type, and he was not interested in collecting, not even, despite the dealers' best efforts, the post-impressionist paintings which he admired. There were a few pictures in his office and home, most notably a *Still Life* by Morandi given to him by his family together with Anthony Donaldson's *Three Portraits of You*, the second-prize winner at the 1963 John Moores Liverpool Exhibition, which he later gave to the Gallery, and a painting by Therese Oulton, bought by him from the 1985 John Moores Exhibition, but he was far from being a compulsive buyer. Moores did not follow the familiar policy of acquiring art for the work place, although a competition won by Patrick Glynn Heesom for a large sculpture outside his new headquarters had been run in 1965. Only once, from the 1978 John Moores Exhibition, did Littlewoods acquire a significant group of paintings for display in the JM Centre, the company's headquarters.

In 1955 Moores submitted a small still life to the open section of the Liverpool Academy Exhibition at the Walker Art Gallery. It was very conspicuously signed by him in large letters and the entire selecting jury of the Academy knew the identity of the artist. They rejected it and Moores immediately organized his own exhibition of many of the rejected paintings in one of his buildings in central Liverpool, apparently attempting to discredit the verdicts of the Academy jury.[3] Although his exhibition was not successful it probably suggested to him the idea for the John Moores Exhibitions, which were, in part, intended to attract young artists who found it difficult to display their work in the rather conservative exhibitions then provided by the Royal Academy, by other similar institutions and by London dealers. His first contact with the Walker Art Gallery however was not auspicious. Scrutton wrote to him on 29 August 1955 asking for money for acquisitions. Moores refused in a letter beginning 'Dear Sir' and characteristically concluding with absolute honesty: 'I'm very interested in art, but only in a very modest way'.

Rather surprisingly it appears to have been the councillors and not the Gallery who made the first move towards reviving interest in British contemporary art beyond Merseyside. This was somewhat unexpected as there was little popular demand for modern art in Liverpool, which never attracted large numbers to the Gallery. Most councillors felt as uncomfortable with contemporary painting and sculpture as their predecessors in the last days of the Liverpool Autumn Exhibitions. The rejection by the City Council of a modern purchase approved by the Art Committee was far from a thing of the past, but the councillors saw temporary exhibitions as being a very different matter and not subject to the same restrictions. In December 1955 Scrutton was instructed by the City Council's Libraries, Museums and Arts Committee to submit a report to them on proposals for reviving the pre-war Autumn Exhibitions.[4] He was evidently horrified by the idea and with Frank Lambert's help provided an indictment of these exhibitions for the Committee in March 1956. Standards were low. Despite admission fees and commission on purchases the last three Autumn Exhibitions in 1936, 1937 and 1938 had made losses. In 1938 there were only 14,000 visitors. An enormous amount of administrative work was required. The display of the permanent collection and work on it was severely disrupted. Much smaller Autumn Exhibitions might be possible but losses could still be expected and substantial amounts of money would be needed to buy paintings from them in order to encourage eminent artists to submit their work.[5]

Only eight months later he was able to provide the Committee with details of a new exhibition, and he recommended it to them as an improved substitute for his proposed new small Autumn Exhibition – but with the reservation that it would still absorb a vast amount of staff time. As with the old Autumn Exhibitions all artists could send in paintings and sculpture for display but now each artist was limited to two works and selection by the jury would be far more rigorous. Only about 300 works would be shown. Prizes, a new departure, totalling £4,000 would be awarded to encourage artists to submit despite their slim chances of inclusion and despite the imposition of modest handling charges on each work sent in. Thirteen of these prizes would be open only to artists under 36. Free transport would be offered to artists in London who took their work to a collecting centre there. Winners of the six larger prizes for the open and junior sections would be required to give their winning paintings or sculptures to the sponsor, Moores, who would normally pass them to the Gallery. Some additional paintings, selected jointly by the Gallery and Moores, would be purchased. These provisions would provide exhibitions and purchases of a much higher standard than the old Autumn Exhibitions could achieve. Artists would price their works and no commission would be charged on sales. In practice, as with the later Autumn Exhibitions, there were relatively few sales, apart from those to local public art galleries or to the Arts Council. About thirty well known artists would be invited to send two works to the exhibition. These works would escape both scrutiny by the jury and handling charges, following earlier practice at the Autumn Exhibitions. These 'invited' artists could win a prize and some did. A small admission charge for visitors, eventually fixed at one shilling with sixpence for children and students (very approximately £1-00 and 50 new pence today), would also help to cover costs. To inspire confidence the jury would be composed of the leading critics, gallery directors, art historians and artists of the day, who were tempted to come to Liverpool by Moores's generous jury fees. By striving to introduce a robust selection system and aiming at a radically smaller show the Gallery was wisely making a determined effort to exclude the many modest paintings that had overwhelmed the fewer distinguished pictures in the later Autumn Exhibitions. Works on paper which had been an important feature of these exhibitions were not permitted as part of the attempt to produce a more disciplined, concentrated and less diffuse show. This was now all possible thanks to Moores's sponsorship. The Gallery's first sponsors had been in alcohol – Walker, Wavertree, Bartlett, Smith and Audley – or in shipping – Rathbone, Holt and Bowring. Now it was the turn of football pools, chain stores and mail order. Moores would pay all costs directly attributable to the exhibition except the salaries of Gallery staff while they worked on it. The Gallery would give him the handling charges to help cover the costs of transport from London and from the Liverpool agent and of course it would provide the space for the exhibition without charge.[6]

Undoubtedly the exhibitions promoted Moores's company's public image but this was essentially private not commercial sponsorship. These were the John Moores Exhibitions not the Littlewoods Exhibitions, and his personal involvement both gave the project its early impetus and later sustained the series. Moores's offer to sponsor this biennial competitive exhibition of British painting was well timed as it came when there was little sympathy for contemporary art from the public or the press, and not much more in most municipal art galleries. It gave the Gallery exhibitions which made it a major force in the encouragement of contemporary British art. Not the least of their achievements was that they changed the public perception of the

Gallery. In the late 1950s it was an unheard-of partnership between a local authority – particularly a Labour local authority – and a very wealthy dedicated capitalist, who owned football pools and chain stores and had a major stake in Everton Football Club. For this reason Moores had been careful to secure support for the exhibitions at a very early stage from his old friend John Braddock, the leader of the City Council and the Liverpool Labour Party. Scrutton was at first hesitant over the detailed arrangements for the exhibition, and in early October 1956 Braddock phoned him urging him to proceed while negotiations were still in progress.[7] Moores rather uncharitably never forgot Scrutton's sensible initial caution, believing that Scrutton thought that he wanted to promote an 'exhibition of Sunday painters' not the work of professional artists.

Moores was proud of Liverpool and concerned with its well-being. Shortly before the first exhibition opened he wrote to the *Sunday Times*:

> Living in the provinces as I do, I am one of those deeply concerned with the plight of provincial museums and art galleries. But I have often thought that decline had something to do with the concentration of art shows, art criticisms and the like in London. Surely, to be a living thing, a provincial gallery must play a real part in the cultural life of the town it serves, and not merely be a pale and distant reflection of what is going on in the metropolis. It is because I believe this that I am collaborating with the Walker Art Gallery, here in Liverpool, to organise an art exhibition open to any artist working in Britain, coupled with the offer of substantial prizes. When leading artists exhibit this autumn at the Walker Art Gallery – the exhibition opens on November 9 – the Gallery will be serving the very purpose for which it was designed, and act as a focus for the cultural life on Merseyside. What we are planning in Liverpool can be started elsewhere. It is far better, in my view, for provincial galleries to seek and gain support from local patrons than to receive a grant of money from the government. Anonymous subsidies are not the way to generate locally the 'climate of discernment' of which your art critic wrote so sensibly last week.[8]

In principle Moores was right about local private patronage. However the economic decline of Merseyside, particularly of locally owned businesses, coupled with the rise there of multinational companies with little commitment to Merseyside culture, made his proposals unrealistic, although they were followed magnificently rather later by his son Peter. The exhibition's aims set out in the catalogue of the first exhibition remained essentially the same for the series:

1. To give Merseyside the chance to see an exhibition of painting and sculpture embracing the best and most vital work being done today throughout the country
2. To encourage contemporary artists particularly the young and progressive.[9]

The first John Moores Exhibition was judged to be a success and the series was launched. 181 works rather than the 300 predicted were shown from a total submitted of 2059. Alan Bowness, then a lecturer at the Courtauld Institute and later both director of the Tate Gallery and principal founder of Tate Liverpool, commented on the first exhibition in the *Observer*:

> By a happy but improbable piece of collaboration, John Moores of Littlewoods Ltd and the Walker Art Gallery have mounted what is, despite the abstentions, the most considerable representative show of contemporary British painting that has been seen anywhere for some years...One must warmly commend a most interesting exhibition, extremely well presented in what must be now one of the country's most attractive galleries. It is much to be hoped that Mr. Moores will be encouraged by this bold venture in patronage to establish the John Moores Exhibition on a permanent basis.[10]

A. C. Sewter, who taught art history at Manchester University, wrote in similar terms of the first exhibition in the *Manchester Guardian*:

> Several of the more ambitious provincial art galleries have attempted to organise exhibitions aiming at a representative selection of 'the best and most vital work being done today throughout the country' in painting and sculpture; none of them however has succeeded so well as the John Moores Exhibition...The John Moores Liverpool Exhibition may quite possibly prove a landmark in the history of British art comparable with the birth of the New English Art Club.

Sewter gave the reasons why the exhibition has succeeded: substantial prizes and a distinguished selection panel. 'It is clear that the generous participation of Littlewoods has enabled Liverpool to present an exhibition of national significance which normal municipal art gallery methods and finance could not suffice to achieve.'[11]

The exhibitions were never as successful as the Autumn Exhibitions in attracting visitors, but with the changed nature of Liverpool, particularly the growth of rival attractions and a declining population, this is not surprising. The 1957 exhibition had nearly 11,000 visitors while the 1938 Autumn Exhibition had 14,000.[12] Attendance figures climbed to just over 26,000 for the 1967 exhibition but there were considerable fluctuations between shows. A survey of 1965 threw up some revealing information about the source of the visitors. 36% came from Liverpool, 24% from other parts of Merseyside, 39% from elsewhere in Britain, 1% from abroad. Scrutton found the large number of visitors from beyond Merseyside hard to believe but, even if over stated, it is evidence of the wider reputation of the exhibition and of the Gallery. Nor did he point out, as more recent curators might have done, the economic benefits to Liverpool from this influx of visitors from outside Merseyside. Visitors were also classified by occupation. Not all responded but 29% were art teachers, designers, art students or otherwise connected with art, 17% came from professional or business backgrounds including white collar workers, 16% were school children, 6% were school or university teachers, 3% were manual workers and 3% were housewives. Visitors were also asked about their familiarity with the Gallery. 25% were frequent visitors, 50% came occasionally, 25% were first-time visitors, while 87% of all visitors came especially to see the exhibition. This last figure reinforced the Gallery's view that the temporary exhibition programme was a major attraction for visitors particularly for those coming for the first time. Visitor satisfaction was also tested and as might be expected those critical of contemporary art were far more articulate than the admirers. However 69% found the exhibition worth seeing while 27% did not and 4% had mixed feelings. Scrutton remarked on the hostile reaction to modern art by the public and yet their strong wish to see it. He thought 'the John Moores Liverpool exhibitions are doing exactly what the Art Gallery is here to do in the modern field – to confront artists with their public.' With hindsight it might have been wiser to have free admission. However income from visitors to offset the Gallery's own expenses was important for funding other exhibition projects. The Gallery was then running on a very small budget with a tiny staff, which explained Scrutton's initial caution about the Gallery's capacity to deliver a hugely complex exhibition.

The exhibition format was refined and adjusted over time, particularly during the early years. After 1957 artists could submit only one work not two. A French section with a complex prize system was part of the 1959 exhibition but the idea of a foreign section, derived from the later Autumn Exhibitions, was not repeated. Handling sculptures as well as paintings proved to be well beyond the Gallery's technical capacity, and sculpture, never submitted in large quantities, was excluded with regret after the 1961 exhibition. As contemporary paintings grew larger in the 1960s pressure on exhibition space became intense so a maximum size, 3m high and 2.1m wide, was introduced without objections in the press – unlike the later restriction on depth. The second exhibition in 1959 had sixteen 'invited artists' whose work was eligible for prizes and an 'hors concours' group of six painters. This last group were not eligible for prizes because, as the catalogue explained 'their distinction is such that they may be said to be above the battle'. Neither of these groups was subject to scrutiny by the jury so around 14% of the 158 works exhibited were predetermined. The invited section was dropped for the next show and the 'hors concours' section after 1967. Although the 'hors concours' artists did give the exhibition some well-known names such as Bacon, Freud and Kokoschka, the quality of the work sent in was sometimes disappointing. Some artists who had exhibited 'hors concours', notably Victor Pasmore, continued loyally to submit paintings which might be rejected by the jury. The division of the entries into an open section and junior section (under 25 years old), which was abandoned in 1959 but reinstated in 1961 (with a new age limit of 36), finally disappeared in 1965. The exhibition had settled down to being mainly about the work of artists in their late twenties and thirties so the division into junior and open sections made no sense. In this it was different from the nineteenth-century Autumn Exhibitions which attracted artists of all ages. The change to an exhibition entirely chosen by the jury, without the comfort of 'invited' and 'hors concours' artists, which had ensured a significant number of familiar names, was a brave move towards a truly open exhibition. This marked it apart from the Royal Academy summer exhibitions where the work of academicians could not be rejected by the jury.

The most striking difference between the John Moores Exhibitions and the Autumn Exhibitions was the offering of monetary prizes. It was an unusual step, although Liverpool Town Council had funded them at the Liverpool Academy from 1828 until 1857 when controversy over their award to Pre-Raphaelite painters had led to the virtual collapse of the Academy. The very uncertain prospect of provincial sales has rarely been sufficient to persuade successful London artists to exhibit outside the capital. Moores, rightly in the Gallery's view, wanted the first prize winner to have enough money to do something different and exceptional. In spite of extensive research the prizes were taxable as it was deemed that the artist had sought a prize by entering. Ever the shrewd publicist Moores sensed that prize winners would be covered in the news pages as well as the arts section of a paper. In addition he thought rightly that an exhibition with prizes would have greater visitor appeal. A prize was also a good incentive for any journalist. A leader in the *Daily Telegraph* complaining about the award of the second prize of £3,000 in 1978 to *Untitled No 9 1977* by William Turnbull, a very beautiful painting in shades of white, would not have been written if a monetary prize had not been involved. Although the concept of prizes in the arts has become acceptable again in recent years, notably with the Turner Prize at Tate Britain, and the National Portrait Gallery's BP Portrait Award with first, second and third prizes and runners up, it was not quite acceptable or correct in progressive circles in the 1960s and 1970s, which disliked any competitive element in life. Writing in *Art and Artists* in

1979 Hugh Adams thought 'the very concept of prize-winning paintings is wrong'.[13] Juries sometimes found it difficult to award an outright first prize. Tense negotiations between Moores and the jury, with the exhibition secretary, the director of the Gallery, as the intermediary, could follow. With one exception the total prize money remained at around £4,000 until 1969 when it rose to £6,500. The first prize for the open section of 1957 of £1,000 was about half the annual salary of the Gallery's director but it involved handing over the winning painting. The highest priced picture in the exhibition of 1957 was a work by Matthew Smith priced at £525, and the cheapest only cost £15. Two works by Lowry could be bought for £250 each. In the early days the first prize was comfortably more than the price of the picture.

Faced with both an acute shortage of purchase funds and a City Council that was unsympathetic to contemporary work, Scrutton had skilfully introduced the concept of the purchase prize. With Moores's lack of interest in collecting it was highly likely that he would pass the winning paintings to the Gallery. He rarely failed to do so and work that would never have been acceptable to the City Council as purchases could enter the collection. The Council might turn down the Gallery's proposed purchase of a painting by William Scott in 1958, but the artist's *Blue Abstract*, the winner of the British painting section in the 1959 exhibition, passed to the Gallery through Moores. However, purchase prizes involving the loss of the painting to the artist reduced their value to him or her. Instead of purchase prizes the second and third exhibitions had a commitment to spend £1,000 and £750 on purchases. For the fourth, fifth and sixth exhibitions the three main prizes were purchase prizes bringing outstanding acquisitions to the permanent collection. The 1969 exhibition reverted to prizes as simple awards of money with no requirement for the winning works to pass to the organisers, thus increasing their value, and the prize money rose to £6,500. The Gallery felt that the first prize must remain a significant sum. However as the market for contemporary art grew and prices rose there was a risk that purchase prizes might give the winners less than the commercial value of their entry. The abandonment of purchase prizes seriously impaired the growth of the permanent collection and at the Gallery's request a purchase first prize set at £6,500 was reinstated in 1978 and continued until the 2002 exhibition. Sympathising with the Gallery's ambition to acquire contemporary work Moores generously found the necessary extra funds. By 1987 the first prize had risen to £11,000 and for the 1999 exhibition it was £25,000. As exhibition sales were never going to be large and certainly would never approach the level even of the last Autumn Exhibitions, the prizes were important and necessary incentives to encourage artists to submit their paintings. The lower prizes, although not of great economic consequence, were seen as an encouragement and valuable in enhancing the artist's career prospects. As the exhibition gained in prestige, just being exhibited could be a useful recommendation for a young artist and a good addition to his or her CV. Some artists won more than one prize. John Walker won third prize in 1965, second prize in 1974 and finally the first prize in 1976.

The number of entries until 2002, when slide submissions were introduced, varied between about 1,600 and 2,500. Keeping up the numbers sent in for exhibition was a major preoccupation of the exhibition secretary. The first exhibition with sculpture had 181 exhibits, the largest number so far, but well below the last Liverpool Autumn Exhibition. After 1961 the numbers exhibited dropped to below a hundred works and after 1987 to below sixty works. It was 38 for the John Moores Liverpool Exhibition, 2002 which perhaps suggests over refinement, putting too much burden on each exhibited work to be a masterpiece. For the public a larger show is more engaging. The display of the exhibition was always spacious and a clear break from the crowded Royal Academy Summer exhibitions and traditional dense hang of the Autumn Exhibitions. Artists had much less chance of exhibiting their works at the John Moores Exhibitions than at the Autumn Exhibitions, but this does not seem to have deterred them from submitting their paintings. The enthusiastic support of artists has been an important feature of the exhibition.

Moores's dealings with the Gallery were always straightforward. He was never a mere spectator nor did the Gallery think he should be. His passion was for painting and he wanted exhibitions that promoted painting and helped painters. He had a particular vision and was not too concerned if it did not always have universal critical approval or was perceived to be not entirely fashionable. He did not dislike, but had little interest in, constructions, particularly if they included electrical power and went 'whirr', as he put it. He felt understandably that there was no need to support what did not really interest him. A distinguishing feature of the 1969 exhibition was the number of constructions in perspex and other new materials together with works that involved no 'painting' in the traditional sense. The exhibition for instance included Rasheed Araeen's construction *Boo/69* which the Gallery bought. Moores was unhappy at this development and would have preferred his shows to remain more focused on pure painting. He offered to give the Gallery some money if it wanted to do a specialist construction show but this would have reduced the impact of the main exhibition. In the event the number of constructions sent in after this show diminished. The introduction for 1969 of the rule that no entry should project more than six inches from the wall had, as anticipated, little effect on the constructions submitted, but it was rather a public relations disaster. Some critics perceived it be an attempt to limit creativity rather than an effort by the Gallery to manage the handling of around 2,000 entries responsibly. Scrutton tried to shrug it off by openly stating that six inches was a pragmatic figure and saying that 'nobody can claim that this has any spiritual significance.' A depth restriction has remained. Painting, as the Gallery tried to reassure Moores, was far from dead, but it was temporarily eclipsed by other new art forms which seduced critics. Moores found it difficult to accept the Gallery's view that the wheel of fashion was always turning and that the constructions which so concerned him would soon become less prominent. This proved to be the case and over time a more balanced pluralistic approach became usual. Moores would have been delighted with Peter Doig's *Blotter*, painted in oil on canvas, which won first prize in 1993, the year of his death. From time to time the exhibition secretary learnt what it must have felt like to be the manager of an underperforming Littlewoods store, but Moores remained a loyal friend who would always help when asked. His carefully considered views of what he wanted to support and achieve earned respect.

Moores naturally left the day-to-day running of the exhibition to the Gallery. In principle he selected the jury and he had the first choice of the paintings acquired from it.[14] In practice his right to choose the jury only amounted to a veto on the selection proposed by the Gallery which he never exercised. He allowed the Gallery to retain nearly all the paintings bought from the exhibitions. He acted frequently as chairman of the jury until 1987, discharging this role in exemplary fashion, focusing on ensuring that every painting was properly assessed and not airing his personal views except when riled. He deplored 'horse-trading', that is one jury member agreeing against his better judgement to the award of a prize to one artist in return for another member consenting to give another prize to an artist admired by the first member but disliked by the second. Moores was always questioning whether his sponsorship was useful and giving value for money. The 1969 exhibition with its joint first prizes and predominance of constructions had somewhat shaken his confidence. Keeping up his enthusiasm for the series was at times challenging. The Gallery's solution was to involve him more and to have him as chairman of the jury whenever possible. This gave him the opportunity to question his fellow jurymen about the continuing relevance of a show for painting, and they appeared to enjoy each other's company. His human warmth and interpersonal skills were extraordinary. He could have a totally relaxed conversation with anyone in the lift going to his office. Equally when he came to the Gallery for the judging he would in a few seconds establish a close relationship with the team of handlers from his warehouse, talking about last night's football match or a similar topic. He also went to great trouble to establish good relations with the jury and always entertained them at his headquarters. He took a very relaxed view of the budget as most of the costs were borne directly by his company. There never was a formal budget but he always knew exactly what the exhibitions had cost him. On the first exhibition, excluding wages and salaries, the Gallery spent less than £450 which was covered by admission charges and catalogue sales. Reflecting Moores's own priorities just over £200 of this went on newspaper and bus advertising. What made the John Moores Exhibitions exceptional was

Moores's willingness to put both himself and his whole organisation behind the exhibition.

The selection of the juries as in the days of the Autumn Exhibitions was crucial to the success of the venture. A jury which could inspire confidence in both artists and critics was essential. Arguably one of the reasons why the Autumn Exhibitions had lost their credibility was the ineffectiveness of its juries and their reluctance to prune indifferent work. The Moores juries consisted of three or four independent figures with an 'in house' chairman, most usually John Moores or the director. The juries represented a mix of art critics, art dealers, gallery directors, art historians and established painters. No jury member served twice so each exhibition had its own particular view point. A quick glance over the names of those who served on the juries up to 2000 confirms that few prominent figures in the contemporary British art scene did not participate. Critics included John Russell, Norbert Lynton, Alan Bowness and Bill Feaver; among the painters were Pat Heron, Howard Hodgkin, William Scott, R. B. Kitaj and Sir William Coldstream; the dealers included Nigel Greenwood, John Kasmin and Anne Seymour. This mix was good for lively debate. Usually the painters had some link with a major London art college, which brought a special insight into what was happening in the student world. Making a jury look hard at over 2,000 paintings by the known and largely unknown as they are paraded past the jury is a challenge. Unlike the Royal Academy summer shows, which are chosen by academicians who often have some previous experience of selecting from an open submission and know each other well, the members of the Moores juries were usually fresh to the selection task. It was not unknown for the previous year's first-prize winner to be rejected, but equally many who had won minor prizes went on to improve their performance. Some jury members had preconceived notions about the type of exhibition they wanted. The American critic Clement Greenberg, the chairman of the 1965 exhibition jury, had a decided view of British painting which led to a bias towards some large abstract 'hard-edge' paintings but also many modest figurative pictures and landscapes, which he regarded as characteristically English. Some juries went for a small select exhibition while others favoured spreading the net wider. From time to time juries aimed too much perhaps for consensus and a majority view. The later ones were encouraged to retain any picture about which any one member was passionate. The Gallery felt that it was better to have every work in the show with its own enthusiastic champion than works that represented a compromise. The Gallery also learnt over the years to manage the judging more constructively, or so it liked to think. For the very early shows pictures were carried past and were declared either in the exhibition or out of it. From the late 1960s the jury was encouraged to sift the paintings into three categories: in, doubtful or out. Paintings that interested no-one were discarded in the early stages. As soon as the number provisionally accepted was low enough the paintings were all laid out so that similar paintings could be juxtaposed and a debate could take place. Some juries went on and laid out the exhibition ready for hanging. Thus Nicholas Serota, then Director of the Whitechapel Art Gallery, arranged the display of the 1985 exhibition. Some members of the juries behaved badly over awarding prizes. Their letter of appointment made it clear that they had two jobs to do, the selection of the exhibition and the awarding of prizes. However when the moment came some found it difficult to award a first, second and third prize and then a number of smaller prizes. Moores had little sympathy and took the line that they should do what they had been hired to do. He also felt reasonably enough that dividing prizes destroyed his ambition to provide a prize of sufficient value to make a real difference to the winner's life. The 1969 exhibition was famously difficult on the allocation of prizes.

The consistent support of the London art trade was an important ingredient of the success of the exhibition. Dealers such as Angela Flowers, Nigel Greenwood, Alex Gregory Hood, Godfrey Pilkington, Antony Reynolds, Edward Totah and Leslie Waddington were always supportive and encouraged their artists to participate. It was often through them that artists with established reputations sent in their paintings.

With the arrival of John Jacob as Deputy Director in 1957, the administration of the show was improved, and the Gallery had much more effective control over the movement of the paintings.[15] Artists were expected to take their entries to a major art transport firm in London or to Jackson's in Liverpool, a long established company which had handled the Autumn Exhibitions. When Jackson's felt no longer able to cope, the Gallery acted as the Liverpool collecting point and this had advantages. To encourage submissions from a wider area, collecting points were opened for later exhibitions in Birmingham, Glasgow and elsewhere. As pictures became larger and cotton duck, with its susceptibility to dents, became widely used, the challenges of handling and moving a large number of works grew. Space remained an enormous constraint on the organisation and display of the exhibition for the whole series. During the judging a large part of the permanent collection had to be taken down and galleries closed to the public. There was never enough space to display the exhibition to its best advantage in the extension galleries. Regrettably, while the exhibitions were open to the public, only a handful (and sometimes none) of the Gallery's own contemporary paintings, in particular past prize-winners, could be displayed. Visitors could not therefore see how work in the exhibition related to the immediate past. These problems were familiar from experience with the Autumn Exhibitions. Although space was always scarce the Gallery was careful not to suggest a required number for the final exhibition except on one occasion. It agreed that whatever the jury chose it would exhibit.

Moores understood the importance of marketing and public relations which in 1957 were completely unknown to the Gallery and to most local authorities. A public relations company used by him, Erwin Wasey and its later successors, were presented with the challenge of persuading as many art critics as possible to attend a press view of the exhibition and a lavish opening party. Critics, artists, artists' agents and others were corralled into reserved first-class railway carriages to bring them from London to Liverpool. After the opening evening party with a Lancashire hotpot supper provided by Moores's catering division, Erwin Wasey hosted a party for the artists and critics at the Adelphi, then the best hotel in Liverpool. Much of this activity has become the normal arrangement for an exhibition launch, but in the late 1950s it was revolutionary for a municipal gallery to cultivate the press in this manner and launch an exhibition with such lavishness. Publicity, an area of great weakness for all British art galleries before the 1980s, was essential for a new provincial exhibition of progressive contemporary paintings, a type of art then regarded with considerable suspicion outside London. Moores understood its importance far better than the Gallery did and knew how to manage it. He was quite happy to go on television to promote the show. He also provided the funds for the exhibitions to be advertised widely in the daily press and specialist art magazines. Merseyside stations displayed posters as did local buses. All this was very new for the Gallery and while it may not have generated vast numbers of visitors it certainly heightened awareness of the Gallery and of Liverpool in the wider world.

Moores appreciated the impact of consistent integrated design. At this time Gallery catalogues and publicity material were usually designed by the curatorial staff in discussion with the printer. Using a designer was exceptional and a coherent image for an exhibition completely unknown. The Littlewoods design studio was put in charge of the design and production of all printed material including writing paper, posters inviting entries, entry leaflets, invitation cards, exhibition posters and catalogues. Everything possible was done to give the exhibition its own identity, and each exhibition had its own logo which was used on every printed item. The director became the exhibition secretary and all his letters about the exhibition went out on John Moores Liverpool Exhibition headed paper. The exhibition catalogue quickly moved from a conventional exhibition square format to a tall narrow shape ideal for the pocket. Over the years the number of colour plates and illustrations steadily increased. From the 1985 exhibition the catalogue illustrated every work and included artists' biographies and statements. Facilitating the visitors' enjoyment and understanding of the exhibition was always taken extremely seriously by the Gallery. Sometimes a 'layman's guide' of a couple of pages of text was produced. The 1965 exhibition included the first full guided sound tour and commentary (with a welcome message from John Moores) for any contemporary exhibition. The later shows in the late

70s and early 80s included video films of the winners talking about their work in their studios. Moores once offered free coach transport for schools to the exhibition but the response was so disappointing that it was not repeated. Having an exhibition series enabled the Gallery to improve its skills at visitor engagement to a level not possible with other temporary exhibitions.

Newspaper editors were impressed by the idea of the exhibitions with big prizes and particularly by the fact that they were sponsored by a private individual in a municipal gallery in Liverpool, but they were rarely very enthusiastic about the content. Coverage was much more extensive than for other exhibitions mounted by the Gallery, and the publicity put the Gallery 'on the map'. Usually the more serious papers, the *Observer*, the *Sunday Times*, *The Times* and the *Daily Telegraph* could be relied on to cover them as did the local Liverpool papers. Opinion was usually mixed but the Gallery and Moores accepted that all publicity was good publicity. The critics often forgot how important it is for artists simply to have the chance to show their work publicly, and that new movements do not emerge conveniently every two years. Occasionally a picture would be targeted for ridicule in the press. It was again Bill Turnbull's serene white *Untitled No.9 1977* which caught the imagination of the *Daily Mail* reporter:

> The canvas won the Dundee artist second prize in an exhibition of modern art at Liverpool's Walker Art Gallery. The work measures 5ft by nearly 7ft and in Philistine terms Turnbull's prize works out at about £91 a square foot. Not bad for someone whose only outlay was the canvas and a few tubes of white paint and a palette knife. To be fair Turnbull does say that there is a blue ground beneath the white.[16]

Critics often focused on those artists who had not sent in paintings rather than on discussing the works on display. Sewter set this pattern and in his review of the first exhibition listed absentees, notably Ben Nicholson, John Piper and Graham Sutherland , and Bowness also talked about 'abstentions'.[17] In reality there was no practical need for economically and critically successful artists such as these to send in paintings, nor were shows principally aimed at encouraging 'contemporary artists in particular the young and progressive' going to be a natural display place for them. The early Autumn Exhibitions suffered from similar absences of many well-known artists balanced by the presence of a few famous artists such as Frederic Leighton who were keen supporters of regional galleries. The Moores exhibitions established themselves as displays to which artists submitted their paintings at a particular stage of their careers. For the most part the show did not hold painters for life. This was in the nature of the series and arguably both a great strength and a great weakness. As more public and commercial galleries engaged with contemporary art in the 1970s and 1980s the Moores had to share a field which had virtually been empty when the series was launched in 1957.

Critics also frequently complained that artists sent in works that showed them below their best. G. S. Whittet in his review of the first exhibition in 1957 noted that 'it must be admitted, however, that most of the prize-winning entries would have deserved notice, though in some cases artists have been obviously caught without works in which they have shown themselves to better advantage elsewhere.' Listing established artists showing indifferent work was frequent. Critics found it hard to accept the merits of a private sponsor focusing on a particular format which they no longer found interesting. In the 1970s painting was not seen as very fashionable. Frances Spalding criticized the 1976 exhibition noting that

> the non-appearance of conceptual art presumably means photography is excluded. As are sculpture, kinetics, watercolours and graphics...It is therefore hardly surprising that the paintings exhibited, restricted by anachronistic rules, should be in styles the majority of which are anachronistic.

Understandably even the prize winners were not immune from criticism. Myles Murphy's *Figure with a Yellow Foreground*, which won first prize in the 1974 John Moores Exhibition and was purchased by the Tate Gallery in 1994, was described by Peter Fuller as being only 'impressive in its mediocrity'.

In spite of the mixed press coverage the John Moores Exhibitions encouraged the launching of several similar exhibitions across England. Many of them involved commercial sponsorship and were often organised by local 'Arts Associations' then strongly promoted by the Arts Council. At the Whitworth Art Gallery in Manchester, an institution with which Sewter was closely associated, the Northern Young Contemporaries (later the Whitworth Young Contemporaries) was begun in 1965 with funding from the Granada Foundation and the Arts Council. It survived until 1995. A British International Print Biennale was begun at Bradford in 1959 and lasted until 1990. The Arnolfini Gallery in Bristol ran an open painting competition between 1962 and 1966. Eastern Arts launched the Tolly Cobbold Eastern Arts National Exhibitions at the Fitzwilliam Museum in Cambridge in 1978 with prizes and support from the Tolly Cobbold Brewery. None of these survived. Another imitator of the Moores exhibitions, which is still flourishing, is the well-known Turner Prize at Tate Britain. The Walker Art Gallery's serious re-engagement with contemporary art accelerated a great change in the national attitude to new art. Even the Royal Academy, long a conservative bastion, began to change. A very creditable number of current Royal Academicians, including the present president Christopher Le Brun, made an early appearance in the Moores Exhibitions. Their success in helping to reposition contemporary painting inevitably resulted in a loss of the pioneering quality of the early shows, as their engagement with the new became widely imitated.

The system of purchase prizes and heavy buying from the early exhibitions when prices were still very modest enriched the Walker's collection with many characteristic and some classic works. No gallery except perhaps the Tate has such a good overview of pop paintings with works by Anthony Donaldson, David Hockney (fig. 19), Allen Jones, Ron Kitaj and Jo Tilson, which the Gallery later expanded by acquiring work by Patrick Caulfield and Peter Phillips. The group of large abstract hard-edged and optical paintings, so characteristic of the 1960s, including work by Robyn Denny, Tess Jaray, Michael Kidner, Jeffery Steele and Michael Tyzack, can hardly be bettered elsewhere. Again the absence of Bridget Riley was made good in 1987 with the purchase of *Sea Cloud*. In retrospect the Gallery should have acquired more widely, but at the later exhibitions its resources had significantly less purchasing power than in the early 1960s as prices had risen steeply. Occasionally purchases from the exhibition were made in the 1990s including *Exposed Painting, Cadmium Orange on White* by Callum Innes bought from the 1997 exhibition.

Old age compelled Moores to withdraw from active participation in the exhibitions after 1987 and he died in 1993. However the exhibitions were continued by his family with the Gallery playing a more important role notably in contributing significantly towards the costs. For the 1989 exhibition the judging of the thousands of paintings submitted for inclusion, which had always caused considerable disruption to the display of the permanent collection, was moved to a local warehouse, and with the same motive the exhibition itself was moved to a rather smaller space at the south end of the Gallery.[18] While the reasons for the reduced space were sensible it did mean that visitors could no longer enter the exhibition on the Gallery's main axis nor enjoy the theatrical experience of passing through a gallery hung with fourteenth- and fifteenth-century Italian paintings, the earliest works in the collection, into an exhibition of the art of their own time.

If Moores's offer of sponsorship had been refused the Walker Art Gallery would have remained a well run major regional gallery, but his offer moved it into another league. Exhibitions of contemporary art selected genuinely at random rather than to a programme have an inbuilt exhilaration. They can give pleasure and outrage. Some shows were better than others but they all gave that excitement of a first encounter with the new. It is this rare opportunity that was Moores's gift to the visitors. His shows stretched very considerably the Gallery's staff and resources requiring much co-operative effort every two years.

The Moores Exhibitions have now been running for nearly as long as did the Liverpool Autumn Exhibitions and some differences and similarities between these widely respected shows can be detected. Both shared the objective of giving Merseyside the opportunity of seeing the 'best and most vital' in contemporary British art, and this objective has been seen until comparatively recently as one of the prime reasons, along with the permanent collection, for the existence of the Gallery. Both benefited from having two very powerful founders in P. H. Rathbone for the Autumn Exhibitions and Moores for his series. Neither depended significantly on public funding. The Autumn Exhibitions were funded from the income from sales and admission fees, while the Moores Exhibitions were financed almost entirely by private sponsorship until the National Museums and Galleries started contributing in 1989. The scale and ambition of the Autumn Exhibitions, which set out to embrace a far wider area of the fine and applied arts, resulting in vast numbers of exhibits, make the Moores Exhibitions, focused deliberately on much smaller exhibitions of paintings, seem very modest. The Royal Academy has played a role with both series. The Autumn Exhibitions very much depended on the Academy's Summer Exhibitions as a source for exhibits and arguably it was the decline in quality of the Academy shows in the twentieth century that undermined the Liverpool Exhibitions. The Autumn Exhibitions had in the autumn what London had had in the summer. The Moores Exhibitions did not have this recycling element, having struck a decidedly independent path. However the Royal Academy has since moved with the times and many Moores exhibitors have gone on to become Academicians. Both exhibitions have yielded significant material benefits to artists. Sales from the Autumn Exhibitions were considerable, especially in its middle years, and prize money from the Moores Exhibitions had amounted to over £313,000 by 1999.

The Gallery's representation of British art from the 1870s is firmly founded on acquisitions from these two strands of exhibitions. The Autumn Exhibitions provided about eighty important works and about twenty notable examples of popular culture for the Gallery from a total of very approximately two hundred purchases (excluding decorative art, prints, drawings and some very inexpensive, often local, paintings and sculptures). The John Moores Exhibitions up to 2000 gave to the Gallery perhaps some thirty major paintings out of a total of sixty-seven acquired. Very few indeed of the acquisitions from the Autumn Exhibitions and practically none from the Moores Exhibitions lacked merit, although some works were purchased in the early years of both series of exhibitions mainly to secure the future of the exhibitions. These figures are highly subjective and will change, and continue to change, as generally accepted standards and taste fluctuate. Whereas the extension of the permanent collection was one of the two major purposes of the Autumn Exhibitions it was not one of the two principal intentions given by Moores as his reasons for initiating his exhibitions. Moores, unlike Rathbone, was not interested in permanent collections. Six of the twenty-two main prize winners from his exhibitions up to 2000 did not enter the Gallery's collections, but he did recognise the importance of acquisitions to the Gallery and was supportive of the concept of purchase prizes.[19] Neither the Autumn nor the Moores Exhibitions could be regarded as self-sufficient sources for building up an effective permanent collection of new art. Apart from lack of funds and political opposition to purchases the Gallery was always going to be fallible in its choices and not every outstanding artist sent in works to either exhibition. There was also the absence of sculpture in nearly all the Moores Exhibitions. Judicious later acquisitions were always going to be necessary. Much earlier Lambert bought work by artists whose paintings had not been shown at or been bought from the Autumn Exhibitions.

Whereas John Moores had told Scrutton in 1955: 'I'm very interested in art, but only in a very modest way' his younger son Peter's engagement was of a different order. Sir Peter Moores discovered art and music while at school at Eton. After leaving Oxford University he worked in Vienna for about two years as an unpaid assistant opera producer and helped to give Benjamin Britten's *Rape of Lucretia* its first Austrian performance. In 1956 he returned to Liverpool to join, like his older brother John Junior, the family business. He became a director in 1965 and was chairman between 1977 and 1980. His first contact with the Gallery came in 1960 when he lent to it four old master paintings, and the art of the past has remained for him a perennial interest stimulated by working in Sotheby's Old Master Department in the 1970s.[20] In 1964 he established the Peter Moores Foundation in support of the arts and social improvement. One of its earliest and most influential ventures was the acquisition of Liverpool's spectacular classical Great George Street former Congregational church in 1967 and the launch there of the pioneering Blackie Community Arts Project under the direction of Bill and Wendy Harpe, now called the Black-E. By 2002 his Foundation had an annual income of about £10 million. He has been a trustee of the Tate Gallery (1978-1985) and a director of Scottish Opera (1988-1992) as well as Governor of the BBC (1981-83).

Unlike his father he is a dedicated art collector and the results can be seen at Compton Verney, a Warwickshire country house which his Foundation rescued from dereliction in the 1990s and opened to the public in 2002. Rather than aiming at wide coverage, the outstanding collection, owned by Compton Verney Collection Settlement, characteristically focuses almost entirely on five well defined areas: Neapolitan art, 1600-1800, Northern European art, 1450-1650, British folk art, ancient Chinese bronzes and British portraiture, categories all under-represented in British public collections.

Shortly before Scrutton left to be director of the National Galleries of Scotland Peter Moores approached the Walker Art Gallery offering to sponsor an exhibition in what he called the 'fallow year' between his father's exhibitions. Father and son share two important characteristics. They both have well-considered views about what they want to support in the arts, and both have an exceptional understanding of how to achieve it. Peter Moores arrived at the Walker with a clear concept. He wanted an exhibition made up around the work of about ten artists who would usually each be represented in depth by a handful of works so that the visitor would get a real sense of the character of each artist. Participants were to be selected across a wide age span from the artist at the threshold of his career to the grand old man. The exhibitions were not to be limited to painters but should include artists working in other ways, in particular sculptors and other media not covered in the John Moores exhibitions. Ideally he wanted the show to be focused on foreign art. It was a good formula, perfect for a Merseyside audience. His vision was to complement his father's competitive exhibitions concentrating on paintings. Reaching out to the public was a major concern and he felt that the work in the exhibition should be beautifully and elegantly presented. He disliked the 'swimming pool' character of the 1930s extension galleries with their high skirting boards and heavy classical doorways, which he rightly felt was not sympathetic to contemporary art. He regarded its fluorescent lighting of the 1950s as no longer acceptable. His knowledge of major galleries across the world and his background in retail selling gave him an insight into the importance of presentation as a means of engaging the visitor's attention. He wanted his exhibitions to be an occasion. His views on presentation are now very usual for exhibitions in London but were quite new for the time, particularly in the regions. He also had no interest in what he described as 'tomb stone catalogues' which were too long and expensive to be bought by every visitor. Later exhibitions had either a free newspaper or leaflet. As with the John Moores Exhibitions the Peter Moores Liverpool Projects charged a modest admission fee.

While his father took a relaxed view on budgets, Peter took the greatest interest in them. Although he was exceedingly generous in his sponsorship, delivering his vision always cost more than he was offering, and covering the shortfall pushed the Gallery's ingenuity to breaking point. It had for instance to become adept at selling advertising space in the catalogues and, later, newspapers. Although the Arts Council always made a grant it was never quite enough to close the gap. The Council did not share the importance that Peter correctly attached to presentation, believing that the 'swimming pool' character of the galleries was acceptable. More significantly the Council missed the opportunity to reward and encourage generous private sponsorship with a correspondingly large grant from public sources. Official funding bodies only learned this lesson in the 1980s.

The first exhibition, *New Italian Art 1953-71*, fulfilled almost completely the sponsor's expectations and gave Liverpool a stunningly beautiful exhibition.[21] It remains one of the most important post-war twentieth-century exhibitions at the Gallery for its combination of outstanding work and seductive, elegant presentation. The selector, Professor Giovanni Carandente, an art historian and museum official of very wide interests, had recently visited Liverpool as a guest of the British Council in connection with his research on Mattia Preti. Carandente persuaded the Ente Autonomo della Quadriennale di Roma and the Italian Ministries of Education and Foreign Affairs to support the exhibition financially and to cover the cost of the transport. A classic overview of Italian art of the past twenty years was presented, which has not perhaps been surpassed in Britain. The oldest of his twenty-three artists were Ettore Colle and Lucio Fontana, both born in 1899, and the youngest were Giulio Paolini and Eliseo Mattiacci, both born in 1940. Unlike the later exhibitions the recently dead were included and Merseyside had the rare opportunity to enjoy a slashed painting by Lucio Fontana and examples of his sculpture. What made the exhibition so memorable was that much of the work was completely outside the range already shown at the Gallery. Luca Patella's coppice of 1971 with perfumed and speaking trees and musical bushes was unforgettable. Arranged on a patchwork quilt was a group of real bare trees dabbed with perfume, which, when brushed against by the visitor, played music. If the visitor listened at certain points on the trees a conversation was heard between a woodworm and the tree. Cloud machines projected the illusion of a blue sky and clouds on the white muslin ceiling. Other highlights included Luciano Fabro's gilt bronze map of Italy, suspended upside down from its toe, and Michelangelo Pistoletto's series of four stainless steel panels of 1970-71, painted with a nude girl drinking tea, a wooden cage, a chair and a light bulb, which fascinated visitors as the steel acted like mirrors putting the viewer behind the painted images.

The setting for the exhibition was designed by Jim O'Donahue and Colin Wilson of Hall, O'Donahue and Wilson and constructed by Beck and Politzer. The 'swimming pool' galleries were almost totally concealed by partitions and stretched muslin ceilings creating 22 individual areas for the artists and a separate space for the sculptors. It was the first time that an exhibition at the Gallery had specially designed spot lighting and entrance. With no previous experience of exhibitions of this complexity it was remarkable that the technicians managed to install the exhibition in time. The press was positive. Eric Rowan in *The Times* wrote: 'considered from all aspects this is an important and informative exhibition', while according to Merete Bates in the *Guardian* it 'seems to have floated from silvered clouds into the rough and scrumble of Liverpool'. John Russell in *The Sunday Times* thought that 'in scale (and in installation, thanks to the ingenious devices of a Liverpool designer, Jim O'Donahue) this will put travelled visitors in mind of the Italian Pavilion at the Venice Biennale'. Carandente's exceptional success in finding substantial funds to cover transport costs was not repeated, and succeeding exhibitions focused on British art. With costs rising through inflation the Gallery was never again so completely transformed into such a sympathetic environment for enjoying art. The custom of adapting the galleries to the works on display continued, although on a diminishing scale.

All three selectors subsequently chosen, Norbert Lynton, Edward Lucie-Smith and William Feaver had served as members of the John Moores Exhibition juries and therefore knew the Gallery and its staff. All had been or were working as critics. Each exhibition had a similar spread of age within its groups of works. Some artists appeared more than once but in different contexts. Lucian Freud was chosen by all three organizers, memorably for his female nudes (by Lynton), for his Devonshire portraits (by Lucie-Smith) and for the recently finished *Large Interior W11 (After Watteau)* (by Feaver). Peter Moores discussed the selection of the artists with the organisers and occasionally put forward an artist for inclusion. Artists who had shown recently in the John Moores Exhibitions, such as Christopher Le Brun and Stephen Farthing, were included in Peter's projects, giving the visitor the opportunity to see an artist again and become more familiar with his work.

Norbert Lynton, director of exhibitions at the Arts Council with responsibility for the Hayward Gallery exhibition programme and later professor of the history of art at Sussex University, followed Carandente as selector. His authoritative shows, *Magic & Strong Medicine*, 1973 and *Body & Soul*, 1975 gave Liverpool a mixture of the familiar, the new and the overlooked.[22] Francis Bacon and Edward Burra, for instance, were amongst classic painters rarely seen in Liverpool. Lynton also introduced Merseyside to contemporary British sculpture, which had hardly appeared at the Gallery after its exclusion from the John Moores Exhibitions. One of the exhibits, Philip King's painted steel *Red Between* with its bunches of shapes, was later acquired by Liverpool University for display outside the new Sydney Jones Library. Another sculpture, John Davies's sinister group of grey-faced figures, *For the last time*, 1970-72, is now in the Museum of Modern Art in Edinburgh. Hubert Dalwood's vast evocation of ancient temple columns, dressed with strips of fabric of some ancient civilisation, was constructed by the Gallery joiners for *Magic and Strong Medicine*. Lynton also introduced Mark Boyle and his family's riveting facsimiles of the world made in resin, fibreglass and real objects. Boyle was to be commissioned to make a Liverpool Dock series. Sue Grayson Ford acting as Lynton's assistant organised a series of performance artists including a group from the Blackie and Stuart Brisley, who again had never before worked at the Gallery. Lynton's shows were well received by the press. Michael Shepherd reviewing *Body and Soul* for the *Sunday Telegraph* rightly observed that 'the ordinary visitor is offered quality, arrangement and presentation which give the maximum access and enlightenment.' Lynton's shows were remarkable for their breadth of sympathy and catholicity of taste. *Body and Soul* showed the range of his interests. It included David Hockney, Michael Craig Martin, L. S. Lowry and Norman Blamey. He favoured memorable paintings such as Hilton's *Oi Yoi Yoi December 1963* which he neatly summed up as 'a hilariously energetic nude, a great granddaughter of Dionysus.' His two catalogues, the only 'tomb stones' of the series, were crafted with great care to engage the reader.

Following Lynton's example Edward Lucie-Smith, the prolific author, poet, and critic of both old and contemporary art, also cast his net widely as selector of the next three projects, *Real Life*, 1977, *The Craft of Art*, 1979 and *Into the 80s*, 1981.[23] Lucie-Smith knew Liverpool well through his friendship with Adrian Henri and the Liverpool poets. Predictably therefore Liverpool painters, the super realists John Baum, Sam Walsh and Adrian Henri, were shown in *Real Life* alongside Michael Andrews and Frank Auerbach. Mark Boyle's *Liverpool Dock* series commissioned by Peter Moores were displayed in public for the first time. Michael Shepherd wrote enthusiastically about the show in the *Sunday Telegraph*: 'a splendid example in presenting lively art to the public...As an exercise in bringing art and public together, I can't praise this show too highly.'

Peter Moores declared in the catalogue for Lucie-Smith's second show *The Craft of Art*: 'the purpose of this exhibition is firstly to surprise, stimulate and entertain everyone who comes to it and secondly to protest against the general conservatism and reliance on fixed categories within the British art world.' Lucie-Smith blurred the boundaries of the fine arts and crafts, selecting the work of the great toy maker Sam Smith, the needlework pieces of Polly Hope and the immaculately made leather bodies of Mandy Havers alongside painters such as Bridget Riley, Howard Hodgkin and Christopher Le Brun. Characteristic of Lucie-Smith was the inclusion of Beryl Cook, with her jolly brand of lodging-house humour and pub life, very different from what visitors thought of as modern art, and a specially commissioned work from Conrad Atkinson, *For Liverpool: Outside the Golden Triangle*, a fiercely political piece attacking the European Economic Community.

Lucie-Smith's final show, *Into the 80s*, sponsored by the Nigel Moores Foundation as well as Peter's Foundation, followed the same pattern and evolved into 'a series of pairings and conjunctions'. The ceramic sculpture of Glenys Barton, who later modelled a head of Peter Moores, was related to the work of the painter Victor Newsome, and the exquisite wood carvings made by Henry Moore as a young man with those of the young sculptor Victor Newling. Typically Lucie-Smith included the work of Michael Sandle who has taken inspiration from the Edwardian bronze war memorials so despised by Moore and his generation. Liverpool also had the opportunity to see the work of Gilbert and George. Involved in the selection was James Moores, a great-nephew of Sir John Moores. All Lucie-Smith's exhibitions had a free catalogue, conceived for the first two as a free newspaper printed by the *Liverpool Daily Post* and funded almost entirely from the sale of advertising, and for the third as an edition of the *Art and Artists* magazine.

William Feaver, then art critic for the *Observer* and a man of broad tastes, selected the final two Peter Moores Liverpool Projects, *As of Now* in 1983 and *Out of Line* in 1986.[24] *As of Now* had the distinction of displaying to the public for the first time Freud's magisterial and complex *Large Interior W11 (after Watteau)*, brilliantly contrasting Watteau's world of silks and satins with Freud's messy studio. It also continued the tradition set by Norbert Lynton of a generous showing of sculpture. Liverpool was introduced to the generation of sculptors who had followed Philip King and Hubert Dalwood and had its first sight of the work of Dhruva Mistry, an Indian sculptor who had just finished his studies at the Royal College. His playful blend of traditional Indian art and legend with the western tradition was beguiling. He went on to produce for the Liverpool Garden Festival a hugely popular *Giant Sitting Bull*. Barry Flanagan was represented by his exhilarating bronzes. His hare cricketers selected by Feaver were very different from the austere, partly-stretched, bare canvas *June 6 '69* that he had shown in the John Moores Exhibition of 1969. He also was later to be in the Liverpool Garden Festival. Visitors also encountered the witty recycling of domestic and other rubbish including a Walker Art Gallery clothes locker by Bill Woodrow. Three former John Moores Exhibition prize winners, Graham Crowley, Gillian Ayres and Peter Kinley were amongst the painters selected alongside Frank Auerbach, Leon Kossoff and Michael Andrews.

Out of Line was the last Peter Moores Liverpool Project and the final show organised by Merseyside County Council before its abolition. The selection still followed the guidelines that Peter Moores had set for his first exhibition. The oldest participant was Richard Eurich, 1903-1992. His *The Ship Inn* of 1935, acquired by the Gallery from the Autumn Exhibition of that year, was shown with a group of his precisely observed and composed pictures made as a war artist and of more recent work. Typical of Feaver was the inclusion of another Second World War commentator Carl Giles, whose cartoons for the *Daily* and *Sunday Express* have been so much a part of British life. Merseyside also had the chance to see again the work of two artists familiar from the John Moores Exhibitions. Stephen Mckenna showed paintings of Ireland and of Derry, very different from the more abstract junior prize winner *Collocation* presented by John Moores from the 1963 Moores Exhibition. Bruce Maclean, who had won first prize in the 1985 Moores Exhibition, was another exhibitor.

In his foreword in the leaflet for *As of Now* Peter Moores wrote:

> I feel the art scene outside London is still meagre and that the art scene in London is introverted...Liverpool still needs to look beyond the grim realities of life. I hope I help it to do so with this exhibition...For the first Peter Moores Project I gave the brief: eight or ten artists, established and unheard of, old and young, sculptors, painters and photographers –

artists important to that year. Not a theme – the theme and title of the exhibition always emerges from the works involved. I have not changed the formula because it always seems to work.

The series certainly did work and the 'fallow' years between his father's exhibitions were very richly filled, offering Liverpool something way beyond 'the grim realities of life.'

Although following the Walker Art Gallery's transfer to the National Museums and Galleries on Merseyside in 1986 there was a marked reduction in its engagement with contemporary art, the Moores family's involvement in the arts in Liverpool has not diminished. The torch has been picked up by James Moores, a great-nephew of Sir John Moores, who is one of the founders of the Liverpool Biennial and has backed projects such as the Anthony Gormley sculptures on the beach at Crosby. Perhaps the final word, with slight amendment, should be left to Hugh Scrutton, the first exhibition secretary for the John Moores exhibitions: 'the John Moores Liverpool exhibitions [and the Peter Moores Liverpool Projects] are doing exactly what the Art Gallery is here to do in the modern field – to confront artists with their public.' That this happened was due to the insight and generosity of two remarkable men.

Chapter 9

Loan Exhibitions

Permanent collections will never attract large numbers of visitors unless they contain fashionable paintings and are situated in the centres of cities popular with tourists such as London, Oxford or Cambridge. The Gallery failed on all these counts. Its superb early Italian and Netherlandish paintings will never attract large crowds and its splendid Victorian and Edwardian paintings were widely unpopular at least until the 1980s. Tourists still do not yet come to Liverpool in large numbers. The Gallery is over half a mile from the city's shopping centre and has limited passing trade. It was surrounded until recently on its north side by council houses and flats whose residents were often regular visitors to the Gallery until the construction of new roads and flyovers in the 1970s barred their access. As in most northern industrial towns middle-class art enthusiasts had already moved out into the leafy suburbs. In 1944, responding to the considerable volume of visitors to the Gallery's temporary home in the Bluecoat Chambers, Vere Cotton proposed the building of a new municipal 'Gallery for the fine arts' incorporating the Bluecoat Chambers in the heart of Liverpool's retail area. The idea was accepted by the City Council's Post War Planning Committee, and modest but innovative exhibitions with a strong bias towards local and contemporary art have been held regularly at the Bluecoat Chambers under its own management since 1951. However Cotton's grander project, like so many schemes reflecting the social idealism of the period, had been abandoned by 1948.[1]

Until the Second World War the enormous annual Autumn Exhibitions left little time or space for loan exhibitions, although the Autumn Exhibitions themselves did include some groups of loaned paintings and some individual borrowed works within them. The situation was entirely different in Manchester and Leeds. Manchester City Art Gallery abandoned its Autumn Exhibitions and Leeds City Art Gallery terminated its Spring Exhibitions early in the twentieth century. Manchester was then able to hold about six loan exhibitions each year and Leeds became well known for its exhibitions of progressive contemporary art in the 1930s and early 1940s.[2] In Liverpool during the early Autumn Exhibitions the permanent collection was usually crowded into the ground-floor rooms, which were not ideal for showing large oil paintings. However two temporary exhibitions were on display on the ground floor at the time of the Gallery's opening in 1877, one of oriental pottery and art from the collection of Major Walter and the other, of greater interest for the future, a retrospective show of the work of the American Hudson River school artist Louis Remy Mignot (1831-1870) who had settled in Europe at the outbreak of the American Civil War. Between January and

July in the absence of the Autumn Exhibitions the permanent collection could be spread over both floors in a much more appealing display. Gradually loan exhibitions began to be held in these months. An unusual ethnographic exhibition, occupying two rooms in 1880 and containing 'objects from the primitive peoples of Africa, America and Australasia,' may have encouraged the later development of important ethnographic collections at the Liverpool Museum.[3] With the completion of the extension to the Gallery in late 1884 its rooms must have looked rather bare in the spring and summer in the absence of the Autumn Exhibitions, and in 1886 the Gallery held its first major loan exhibition during these months. This was the *Grand Loan Exhibition* with about 950 nineteenth-century paintings and watercolours from local collections.[4] This type of exhibition was held by most British provincial art galleries during their early years when their permanent collections were not large enough to fill their galleries. The *Liverpool Mercury* commented that this was 'the most attractive and important exhibition that the Corporation has yet held', which however certainly did not 'exhaust the art wealth of the neighbourhood'. It went on to claim that 'never before have the Liverpool public had the opportunity afforded them of viewing such a fine array of pictures and drawings by living and deceased painters of renown'.[5] However in this field Liverpool could not hope to compete with Manchester which, profiting from its better rail links and more central geographical position, specialized in these vast loan exhibitions with its privately promoted and hugely successful *Art Treasures Exhibition* of 1857 and its *Royal Jubilee Exhibition* of 1887. Nor rather later did the Walker Art Gallery try to imitate the large and popular loan exhibitions, each devoted to a particular artist or group of artists, which were the principal features of the early years of the Birmingham City Art Gallery between 1885 and 1903 and of the Guildhall Art Gallery in London between 1890 and 1907.[6]

The Gallery's first international 'one man show', displayed from December 1887 until February 1888 in four of its principal rooms, was devoted to a contemporary Russian artist, Vassily Verestchagin (1842-1904), an 'apostle of peace tinged with nihilism', who specialized in very appealing but rather crude and sensational religious and military paintings notable for their disturbing realism.[7] The exhibition had been shown successfully at the Grosvenor Gallery in London before moving to Liverpool.[8] There were horrific war scenes rich in carnage and sadistic executions, together with ethnologically correct scenes from the life of Christ notable for 'a literal representation of a Jewish tradesman's house.' There was praise in the local press: 'Like the late Gustave Doré the Russian artist paints on a large scale and is a lover of vast canvases and subjects and effects that astonish through their boldness and audacity'.[9] Verestchagin, who toured his paintings throughout Europe and America, held a second exhibition of his work in Liverpool in 1899.[10] In 1890 an exhibition of twelve biblical paintings by Doré himself spread over six and a half months attracted over 60,000 visitors.[11] The display, provided by the Doré Gallery in London, where most of the paintings were on permanent show, offered little novelty to wealthier Liverpool citizens familiar with London galleries. Over 3,000 visitors came during Easter week and these dramatic but distinctly unrefined paintings clearly appealed to an unsophisticated public generally starved of sacred images in English churches.[12] The exhibition, which included the *Christ Leaving the Praetorium* and the *Ecce Homo*, both huge and famous, was surprisingly well received by at least one local art critic who observed: 'on the faces of the multitude every human emotion is represented – curiosity, scorn, hatred, wonder', but he admitted that Doré was not admired in France.[13] In the following year the Walker Art Gallery, profiting perhaps from the Doré exhibition, became one of the last British public galleries to defy sabbatarian prejudice and to open on Sundays. In Liverpool the decision had to be justified on religious grounds but the liberal *Liverpool Mercury* was caustic: 'Sir W. Forwood [the chairman of the Libraries, Museums and Arts Committee] placed the influence of the pictures [by Doré] rather above the ordinary type of sermon; but there is also the other fact that no small proportion of the inhabitants of Liverpool rarely hear sermons at all.'[14] Religious art was clearly popular, and in 1900 the Gallery's display of Mihály Munkácsy's itinerant *Ecce Homo* (now Debrecen, Hungary) apparently attracted 300,000 visitors over about five months.[15] There were seventy life-size figures and about 28 square metres of canvas. Munkácsy (1844-1900) combined Courbet's realism with spectacular and theatrical crowd effects, reminiscent of Doré's work. The local advertisements claimed that 'the scene is of the most dramatic and powerful character; the varied expressions on the faces of the mob depicting terror, dismay and blind unreasoning hatred stamp this marvellous work as the Greatest Picture of the age', almost exactly repeating the comments by the Liverpool art critic on the Doré exhibition ten years earlier.[16] Lectures took place every three hours and the admission fee was only sixpence (about £1-50 today) rather than the more usual shilling (about £3 today) which had been charged for the Verestchagin and Doré exhibitions. All three exhibitions were open in the evenings. A local art critic saw the connection between Verestchagin, Doré and Munkácsy:

> On the continent several artists of note – Doré, Verestchagin and Munkácsy for instance – have treated biblical subjects with a remarkable access of dramatic, almost melodramatic effect...The direct ruthless actualism of everything on the canvas [of the *Ecce Homo*] appears to divorce it from that sublime dignity which sentiment and tradition associate with the personality of Christ. Here is a man brought by Pilate to the porch of the praetorium and presented to the most barbarous and unlovely rabble that artist ever conceived. It is the scene as it might have

appeared represented wholly in its superficial aspects.[17]

The Gallery could not attempt to compete with the more scholarly and specialised exhibitions held by the Liverpool Art Club between 1872 and 1895. These included pioneering displays of the work of David Cox in 1875, and in 1884 of the contemporary German artist Hans Thoma, who had Liverpool patrons.[18] The Gallery preferred populism and needed profitable shows. Temporary exhibitions were expected to be self-financing. This rule severely limited what the Gallery could offer. A more serious travelling exhibition of the paintings of William Holman Hunt with much religious content was displayed at four British galleries in 1906 and 1907. Each of the participating galleries could decide how many of the available works to include. There were 62 in London, 80 in Manchester, 69 in Glasgow and 125 in Liverpool.[19] The investment was shrewd. 44,516 visitors came in only four weeks and the profit was £458. In sectarian Liverpool, where church attendance figures started to decline sharply only after 1912, religious art retained its appeal.[20] There were also regular exhibitions of photographs and of watercolours, two art forms with strong amateur appeals. The International Photographic Exhibitions of 1888 and 1891, containing much foreign work, were organized by the Liverpool Amateur Photographic Association, which had been founded as early as 1853.[21] More innovative exhibitions struggled to survive. Special exhibitions concentrating on applied art, drawings, prints and photographs, all with a local emphasis, were held at the Gallery in 1889, 1893, 1894, 1895 and 1898.[22] These Spring Exhibitions reflected the influence of the Arts and Crafts Movement, and the 'Decorative and Applied Art Exhibition' of 1889 took place only a year after the first exhibition sponsored by the Arts and Crafts Exhibition Society in London. Its more immediate cause was the first conference of the National Association for the Advancement of Art and its Application to Industry, which had taken place in Liverpool late in 1888 with the participation of nearly every major figure in the late-Victorian art world. The exhibition contained over 600 objects, mostly catalogued under manufacturer rather than artist. However the craftsmen and manufacturers had to pay for the space they occupied, thus treating them as tradesmen rather than as artists.[23] A profit of £176 resulted in 1889, but the later exhibitions, although apparently reasonably high in quality, attracted few visitors and made losses. The 1893 exhibition included a selection of paintings provided by members and associates of the Liverpool Academy, an important step in the Academy's revival. The 1898 exhibition contained much Della Robbia pottery, then a new art pottery with architectural and sculptural ambitions established in Birkenhead by Harold Rathbone (1858-1929), son of Philip Rathbone. No more Spring Exhibitions were held after 1898. Dibdin's interest in prints and in continental art, clearly apparent in his policy of widening the scope of the Autumn Exhibitions after 1904, led to a remarkable exhibition at the Gallery in early 1908, organized by the great Parisian dealer Georges Petit presumably from his own stock. This was the *First Liverpool Salon of Original Etchings printed in Colours, Monochrome Etchings and Oil Paintings of the Modern and Semi-Modern French School.*[24] The exhibition was apparently an extended version of Petit's *First London Salon of Colour Printed Etchings and Engravings of the Modern French School* shown at the Doré Gallery in London in late 1907. Petit is best known for his support for impressionism but as the rather ambivalent title of his Liverpool exhibition indicates he dealt in a wide range of contemporary French art. Liverpool art dealers generally objected to the use of the Gallery by commercial art galleries, and in his speech at the opening of the exhibition Frank Leslie, chairman of the Library, Museum and Arts Committee, observed that this exhibition was 'not intended as a mercantile venture but more to introduce the art of etchings and engravings printed in colours to the dealers in this part of the country'.[25] There was no second Salon which suggests it was of limited success.

Loan exhibitions remained extremely conservative in tone. In 1911 and 1913 the very progressive Liverpool Sandon Studios Society held two exhibitions which included paintings by the French Post-Impressionist and Fauve artists and by Picasso.[26] In 1917 the much more conservative Royal Birmingham Society of Artists, whose annual exhibitions were the equivalent in the Midlands of the Liverpool Autumn Exhibitions, scandalized many of its more reactionary members by inviting Roger Fry to select for them 'an Exhibition of Works Representative of the New Movement in Art'. Brancusi, Gaudier-Brzeska, Derain, Gris, Vlaminck, Lhôte and other very modernist artists were represented.[27] Seventeen years elapsed before Lambert included the Walker Art Gallery as the initial gallery in the provincial tour of the first and only exhibition of the modernist 'Unit One' with abstract and surrealist works by Henry Moore, Paul Nash, Ben Nicholson, Barbara Hepworth and others.[28] The exhibition had first been held in the Mayor Gallery in London in April 1934 and a truncated version travelled to the municipal galleries of Liverpool, Manchester, Hanley, Derby, Swansea and Belfast.[29] In Liverpool it was reviewed reasonably sympathetically by the *Liverpool Daily Post* at a time when the popular press was still very hostile to modernism. In Paul Nash's work 'colour and composition combine to create a vital and decorative effect'. Moore and Hepworth exhibited 'unbeautiful but dramatic lumps of wood and stone'. Only Ben Nicholson's work received total condemnation.[30] The same newspaper also published between 17 May and 4 June a stream of readers' letters about the exhibition, by no means all hostile. F.W. Dwelly, Dean of Liverpool, patron of Holst and Vaughan Williams and friend of the American photographer Alvin Langdon Coburn, observed in a sermon: 'You can see how all that you have noticed in the paintings is taking shape in buildings and gardens. The rhythm is already passing into everyday activity'.[31]

With this publicity it attracted over 27,000 visitors in only a month. In 1938 Lambert organized an exhibition of modern prints and drawings for sale. About half had been assembled by the Parisian dealer Gustav Kahnweiler, brother of Daniel-Henry Kahnweiler who had been one of the most important patrons of the Cubists before 1914. Drawings and gouaches by Utrillo, Derain, Vlaminck, Maillol, Matisse, Signac, Rouault, Picasso, Braque, Léger, Klee, Dali and others could be bought for prices varying between about £20 and £60.[32] During the closure of the Gallery between 1939 and 1951 Lambert and Cotton provided a very mixed continuous programme of small loan exhibitions in the Bluecoat Chambers in central Liverpool.[33] They were often patriotic in tone and may have been suggested by the similar programme at the National Gallery in London. They concentrated on contemporary art but a few contained historic works. In 1946 there was an exhibition of works by Paul Klee, provided by the newly-formed Arts Council. The review written by George Melly (1926-2007) for the *Liverpolitan*, describing Klee's visionary world of dreams, was unusually perceptive at a time when art criticism in local newspapers and periodicals was not generally of a high standard.[34] It must have been one of the first of Melly's many contributions to the English literature of surrealism, written before he left his home in Liverpool for London.

In 1944 Lambert and Cotton decided that the Liverpool Autumn Exhibitions should not be revived but should be replaced after the war by smaller more specialized historic exhibitions.[35] In choosing as Lambert's successor Scrutton from the Whitechapel Gallery, which had no permanent collection and was solely concerned with temporary exhibitions, the City Council made it clear that they wanted the popular regular temporary exhibition programme organised by Lambert at the Bluecoat Chambers to continue and to expand. Following Scrutton's arrival in 1952 and his recruitment of a few additional curatorial and technical staff, temporary exhibitions grew in scale and number and took up a large part of the Gallery's relatively small financial and human resources, from the director down. Exhibitions were no longer expected to be self-financing with occasional modest losses made up from general resources. Now there was to be an annual exhibitions budget to distribute among all the shows of the year. New assistant keepers were often asked to originate and organise temporary exhibitions, and this experience could enable them to advance their careers.

The new effort put into building up a lively continuous temporary exhibition programme was not confined to Liverpool. The Regional Arts Officers of the Arts Council persuaded most local authority galleries, both large and small, to take their touring shows and to hold other temporary exhibitions, often with the inducement of Arts Council grants for exhibition space improvements and towards exhibition costs. Whatever reservations may be had about this energetic proselytising it breathed new life into many regional galleries. Most institutions now ran busy programmes but the Walker's was perhaps the most broad-minded, the most ambitious and the most active with usually about eight shows a year. Between 1952 and 1986 around 300 exhibitions and special displays were organised at the Walker Art Gallery and at Sudley. The Walker Art Gallery had an unrivalled advantage with its spacious extension galleries which were well suited for large exhibitions, including 'French Symbolist Painters' which came to the Gallery from the Arts Council's Hayward Gallery in 1972. However the extension's heavy use for temporary exhibitions caused part of the permanent collection, usually the most recent works, to be taken off display and this seriously impeded its proper presentation. In contrast to this vigorous regional activity between about 1950 and 1975, large-scale temporary exhibition programmes by most national institutions in London, apart from the Tate Gallery, were much rarer. When the national museums and galleries eventually adopted full exhibition programmes, further pressure was exerted on regional institutions to be even more committed to exhibitions, usually to the further detriment of the permanent collection. Inevitably the responsibility of running both a temporary exhibition programme and a permanent collection with severely limited financial resources and space led to unresolved tensions at the Gallery, as it did in many other institutions.

Temporary exhibitions at the Gallery have always been regarded as fundamental to fulfilling its mission to attract, entertain and educate visitors and essential for increasing and retaining attendance figures. They were seen as the most effective way of persuading people to make repeat visits and to bring in new visitors, particularly from outside Liverpool. Both groups coming for a temporary exhibition might also explore, it was felt, the permanent collection while there. From the Gallery's earliest days too a belief that it should keep its audience abreast of new developments in the visual arts through temporary exhibitions, in particular the Autumn Exhibitions, was deeply embedded in its consciousness, even if acquisitions for the permanent collection did not flow from most of the later exhibitions. Temporary exhibitions were also an important means of establishing the Gallery's reputation and at the same time that of Liverpool in the world outside. The exhibition programme was not unreasonably required to justify a substantial part of the cost of the Gallery to the Council. Funds for advertising and for any public relations programmes were severely limited, although Scrutton's 'And when did you last see your Walker' bus poster campaign was exceptionally inspired and successful. Word of mouth by a visitor that a show was worth visiting was the principal means of promotion.

In the Gallery's *Annual Report* for 1954-5 Scrutton had noted bitterly that whereas 166,000 visitors had come to the Gallery in 1938-9, the last year of the Autumn Exhibitions, only 105,000 had come in 1954-5, 'at a time when over the whole country public interest in the arts is rising and is unquestionably higher than before the 1939-1945 war'.[36] The building of the Gallery had been justified by the need for 'rational recreation' as a substitute for drinking in public houses. By the 1950s there were many other competing 'rational recreations', sport above all. Even in the early 1960s the Liverpool Museum, still largely closed after wartime damage and with a very small public area, attracted larger audiences than the Gallery. Other municipal art galleries in the north-west England such as Manchester City Art Gallery suffered in the same way. Until the 1960s and 1970s, when living standards rose and transport costs fell, making travel at home and abroad more affordable, the Gallery enjoyed a substantial although steadily diminishing captive local audience. For many living in Liverpool and its hinterland the Gallery was in effect the only place to enjoy and experience the visual arts and still an important place of entertainment. The decline in Liverpool's city centre population following the housing clearances, particularly behind the Gallery, further reduced the pool from which the Gallery had traditionally drawn its audience.

In putting together the exhibition programme a balance was sought between popular shows, often aimed specifically at persuading people to take that tentative first step to enter the Gallery, and more challenging ones which encouraged visitors to explore outside their comfort zones. Extremely modest funds gave opportunism an important, perhaps excessive, role in the character of the programme. Most of the exhibitions have been quite properly forgotten but a few, often ones that attracted relatively modest visitor numbers, have proved to be influential and have changed 'informed' and academic opinion, notably about Victorian art, and have contributed to the current high profile enjoyed by contemporary art. Some might question whether a local authority should have spent its scarce funds on exhibitions with limited appeal, but today Merseyside's Victorian heritage and lively contemporary cultural scene are central to its prosperity. Perhaps the Gallery's early support did have significant long-term value to Merseyside.

The Gallery also found that, as with films at the cinema, its great rival, exhibitions had to be changed frequently, ideally about once every six weeks, to keep the audience returning. Long-running shows possible at a London based national institution with its wider visitor base were not viable in Liverpool. More exhibitions usually led to more visitors. To stretch its budget for temporary exhibitions to the full, the Gallery used ready-made, free or low-cost exhibitions, from a very wide range of organisations including the Arts Council, the Victoria and Albert Museum's Department of Circulation, the National Gallery, the British Museum and the Goethe Institute. The Victoria and Albert Museum started circulating parts of its collections to provincial art galleries in 1880. This service was very popular with municipal curators who could at first make their own choices. In 1925 however their selections became confined to the collections allocated to the Museum's Circulation Department. The Museum preferred to send out works of art 'of the highest educational value' rather than 'merely attractive objects'. Some of its exhibitions were of exceptional importance, most notably the 'Italian Renaissance Bronzes' display which reached the Walker Art Gallery in 1970. However in 1978, much to the Gallery's regret, the Museum terminated its entire programme of travelling exhibitions following cuts in its central government funding imposed in 1976. [37] The National Gallery began to lend groups of its paintings to provincial art galleries in the 1880s but their loans, although often high in quality, usually lacked local impact. Until the 1980s the pictures were intended to strengthen the permanent collection display rather than to form a temporary exhibition.[38] The British Museum's exhibition of its great collection of prints by Goya, shown in Liverpool in 1983, was far more appealing. The principal national provider of exhibitions for the Gallery after 1951 was the Arts Council. In 1968 the Council began using the new Hayward Gallery on London's South Bank to display major international exhibitions and its expenditure on art exhibitions rose from about £90,000 in 1967 to £237,000 in 1972. A few of these exhibitions could tour to the larger regional galleries, and among the first was 'French Symbolist Painters' which came to the Gallery in 1972 with major paintings by Gauguin, Moreau, Puvis de Chavannes, Redon and others.[39] Like the Pre-Raphaelite exhibitions it showed an aspect of later nineteenth-century art still unfashionable in the early 1970s – and in fact strongly influenced by the Pre-Raphaelites. The catalogue entries were provided by two young innovative scholars, Geneviève Lacambre in France and Mary Anne Stevens in England. Among other important exhibitions provided by the Arts Council and by its successor, the South Bank Board, were 'British Sporting Painting' in 1975, 'La France', a large exhibition commemorating the French Revolution, in 1989, 'Georges Braque' in 1990 and 'Paintings from the Mesdag Collection' in 1994. Until the 1980s Liverpool had a full complement of consulates and many of these, notably those of Germany, Norway and France, were anxious to promote their national culture in Liverpool. The Norwegian consulate was extremely supportive. In 1972 it facilitated a highly successful exhibition, 'Edvard Munch: the Graphic Work', from the Munch Museum in Oslo, which the Gallery toured profitably around British art galleries. In 1976 it promoted a very beautiful and pioneering exhibition, 'Norwegian Romantic Landscape 1820-1920'. The Goethe Institute in Germany was a useful source of well designed exhibitions especially 'Dada 1916-66'. They were always accompanied by a memorably hospitable opening organised by the Liverpool German consulate.

Some exhibitions were exceptionally popular. To celebrate the Queen's Coronation in 1953 there was an ambitious exhibition of royal portraits appropriate enough for a city which had until then generally voted Tory.[40] It had a well-researched catalogue by David Piper and John Woodward, the two leading scholars in this field, and over four months it attracted about 50,000 visitors. In 1955 Scrutton personally negotiated a Van Gogh exhibition for that year with the artist's nephew, 'Engineer' Van Gogh, and other Dutch contacts.[41] It attracted over 41,000 paying visitors in six weeks. These figures, not far behind those for the Holman Hunt exhibition of 1907 counting on a daily basis, will almost certainly never be exceeded, although they were far behind the 100,000 visitors in three weeks claimed for the Birmingham Art Gallery's showing of their Van Gogh exhibition in 1947. Feeling no doubt that the Walker Art Gallery did not yet have the resources or the staff to cope with a major overseas exhibition, and in order to save on high insurance costs, Scrutton passed over the final arrangements and organization to the Arts Council who received the admission fees, amounting to £1,982 and in return made no charge to the Gallery for providing the exhibition. It also travelled to Manchester and Newcastle.[42] Scrutton had another popular success in 1958 with a Le Corbusier travelling exhibition which had its first British showing in Liverpool. It was seen by 17,200 visitors in six and a half weeks and occupied four large rooms.[43] At the opening Maxwell Fry, a celebrated architect and a Le Corbusier enthusiast who had been born and trained in Liverpool, observed of his native city: 'As to great parts it were better that they had never been built; they were created in a state of sin under a philosophy of materialistic self help that we think of now as we remember an old pain, a self-inflicted wound. But we are free to make a new start...We are indeed under the necessity of seeking the form for our life in a great city that is in accordance with the facts as we now see them.'[44] Scrutton observed in his *Annual Report* that it 'made a great impact on many architects and students – so much so that its influence on British architecture may prove of some importance.'[45] That of course was an under-statement and Liverpool citizens certainly could not complain that they did not know what was to hit them in the next decade. A much less popular exhibition was held in the same year, 'Painting and Sculpture in England 1700-1750'.[46] It contained only 63 exhibits including four miniatures and eight busts and was on display for less than five weeks. It was however reviewed generally sympathetically by A.C. Sewter (1926-2007) then a lecturer in art history at Manchester University,[47] and was of some importance as probably the first historic exhibition with a detailed catalogue to have been selected, organized and researched by the Gallery staff – in this case John Jacob who had joined the staff in August 1957, only about 14 months before the exhibition opened.

Although the Gallery has always intended that its temporary exhibition programme should be primarily concerned with the wider world of art outside Merseyside, it has not ignored local culture. Exhibitions of the work of local past and present artists, often accompanied by informative and well-illustrated catalogues written by Gallery staff, have always been a feature of the Gallery's programmes. As early as 1873 the Gallery's Committee had assisted with an exhibition of William Davis's work held at the Liverpool Academy's old rooms in Post Office Place in order to raise funds for his family. Davis (1812-1873) had been the most original of the Liverpool landscape painters influenced by the Pre-Raphaelites.[48] There were memorial exhibitions in the Gallery for Henry Dawson in 1883, Alfred Hunt in 1897 and John Finnie in 1907.[49] Dawson (1811-1878) achieved a national reputation as a landscape painter at Nottingham and Liverpool before moving to London. Hunt (1830-1896) was born in Liverpool where he painted some of his finest watercolours, heavily influenced by Turner and Ruskin. Finnie (1829-1907) was the greatly respected head of the Liverpool Art School from 1855 until 1896. In 1908 Dibdin's 'Historical Exhibition of Liverpool Art' made both a major contribution to the study and appreciation of local painters and established a serious concern for Liverpool culture by the Gallery. The centenary of the death of Liverpool watercolourist Samuel Austin (1796-1834) was celebrated with an exhibition in 1934.[50] Other exhibitions of this period commemorated the work of local contemporary artists, Mary McCrossan (died 1934), Robert Fowler (1853-1926), David Woodlock (1842-1929) and William Alison Martin (1878-1936).[51]

Liverpool's Festival of Britain of 1951, held to complement the more famous Festival in London, which re-invigorated the nation's self confidence after the austerity of the post-war years, was ambitious. Benjamin Britten conducted the English Opera Group in a performance of his opera *Albert Herring*, and street processions 'under the personal direction of Tyrone Guthrie' were amongst its events. The Gallery, partly as its contribution and partly to celebrate its re-opening after the war, mounted an exhibition of the work of George Stubbs, who had been born in Liverpool.[52] With over a hundred paintings and drawings this was the first exhibition of Stubbs's work organised by a public institution. It included some American loans, then very rare among British exhibitions outside London, and it contributed greatly to the re-assessment of the artist as a major figure in the creation of the British school of painting, rather than as a mere sporting artist skilful in painting horses and dogs.[53] No doubt it even impressed Sir Kenneth Clark who performed the re-opening ceremony. Although Stubbs had spent little of his professional life in the town and had very few important local patrons, Liverpool had claimed him as its own from the early nineteenth century. By 1951 Stubbs was the best represented serious eighteenth-century British artist in the collection, slightly ahead of Joseph Wright of Derby. The Gallery's catalogue of 1951 weighs less than an ounce while that for the Tate Gallery's Stubbs exhibition of 1984 hits three and a half pounds. The exhibition was 'based at least in part on the researches' of Basil Taylor, who emerged as the leading expert on Stubbs's work in the 1960s, although the catalogue itself was written by Ralph Fastnedge, the Gallery's deputy director.[54] Although the failure of the planned London showing of the exhibition at the Tate Gallery probably reduced its influence, Stubbs was to be the favourite artist of the Anglophile American collector Paul Mellon, whose enormous wealth and generosity transformed the collecting, display and study of British art over the following fifty years. By 1951 Mellon had bought only one painting by Stubbs and it is extremely unlikely that he ever saw the exhibition, but it was certainly Taylor, who later became the first director of the Paul Mellon Foundation for British Art, and Stubbs who encouraged Mellon's enthusiasm for British art.[55] The Stubbs exhibition set the pattern whereby exhibitions created in the Gallery were often aimed at increasing the visitor's understanding and enjoyment of a specific aspect of the permanent collection, normally an area then being researched by a curator. Like the later Pre-Raphaelite exhibitions, the Stubbs exhibition marked the Gallery out as an institution which had its own ideas and which did not necessarily endorse accepted national or academic critical opinion.

After the Stubbs exhibition there was another exhibition with a local theme, covering Augustus John's stay in Liverpool, which at about eighteen months, was even shorter than Stubbs's period there. Its principal attraction was John's irreverent but sensational portrait of his friend, Chaloner Dowdall, as Lord Mayor of Liverpool. John had described the Gallery as a 'stinking hole' so amends had to be made.[56] In 1958 came George W. Harris's imaginative Liverpool theatre designs.[57] In 1964 and 1967 memorial shows were devoted to two talented young artists on the threshold of their careers. Stuart Sutcliffe (1940-1962) was the bass guitar player with the Beatles who had stayed on in Hamburg where he studied at the State High School under Eduardo Paolozzi, while John Edkins (1931-1966) was a teacher at Liverpool Art School. His late hard-edged geometric abstracts promised a dazzling future.[58] A third memorial show was devoted to the Hungarian-born George Mayer-Marton (1897-1960), another teacher at the Art School who had done much to modernize it. He had worked for the Council for the Encouragement of Music and the Arts before settling in Liverpool in 1952.[59]

Generous donations or purchases on favourable terms of groups of work by artists with local connections were normally marked by an exhibition and publication aimed at keeping students and visitors informed about new acquisitions. The Gallery was anxious to obtain both works of art and historical material while they were still in the hands of the artists themselves or of their immediate families. In 1971 Geoffrey Heath Wedgwood (1900-1977), a much admired Liverpool etcher and engraver in the 1920s and 1930s, presented a group of his prints and watercolours to enlarge the Gallery's holdings of his work. In the following year, using this material, there was an exhibition of his meticulous stylised work which reflects very much the ethos of the British School in Rome, where Wedgwood studied as a winner of the Prix de Rome in engraving from the Royal College of Art in 1925.[60] Prompted by the Gallery, impressions of virtually all the etchings by James Hamilton Hay (1874-1916) not already in the collection were presented by his nephew Professor J. D. Hay in 1971. The Gallery took advantage of this donation to organise an ambitious show tracing Hay's evolution from a painter deeply under the influence of Whistler into an innovative British Post-Impressionist, using both work from the permanent collection and from loans.[61] Both exhibitions and catalogues were the work of Edward Morris. The first show by Gail Engert, a newly appointed assistant keeper of British Art, was a retrospective exhibition of the slightly younger Maxwell Gordon Lightfoot (1886-1911), who had shown with the newly founded Camden Town Group in 1911. Combining the drawings just acquired from his family, the paintings given by his brother Herbert in 1954 and other loans, her exhibition demonstrated the remarkable talent of this Liverpool artist whose suicide deprived the city of one of its most promising artists. For the first time the sunlit *Study of two sheep*, long a firm favourite with visitors, was shown in context with the artist's other work.[62] Albert Richards (1919-1945), an enthusiastic follower of surrealism, was one of the youngest official war artists in the Second World War. He was tragically killed in Holland while preparing to paint a night attack in 1945. His parents allowed the Gallery to purchase in 1974 a group of his work which on this occasion became the basis of the exhibition 'Albert Richards: The Rose of Death', organised by the Imperial War Museum and shown there and at the Gallery in 1978.[63] Roderick Bisson (1910-1987), another early Liverpool surrealist and the last serious art critic to write for the Liverpool newspapers, received a memorial exhibition in 1987.[64] In the early 1990s Alex Kidson, primarily an expert on late eighteenth-century British art, demonstrated the versatility essential in a regional curator by organizing exhibitions by contemporary artists more or less closely associated with Liverpool, Sam Walsh (1934-1989), Arturo di Stefano and Maurice Cockrill.[65] Sam Walsh, an Irishman with a wicked sense of humour, was Liverpool's leading pop artist. Arturo di Stefano was trained at Liverpool Polytechnic. Cockrill lived in Liverpool for nearly twenty years and taught at the Polytechnic before moving to London in 1982 where he gained critical success, becoming head of the Royal Academy Schools. The series continued with exhibitions of the work of Nicholas Horsfield (1917-2005) in 1997, organized by Morris, and of Adrian Henri in 2000, organized by Frank Milner.[66] Horsfield, a lecturer at the Polytechnic for over twenty years was perhaps Liverpool's most professional painter. Adrian Henri (1932-2000) had secured national fame for the Liverpool art scene of the 1960s and was the leading painter-poet of that generation. The architecture and influence in Liverpool and beyond of Sir Charles Reilly (1874-1942), Liverpool University's outstanding professor of architecture, were explored by Joseph Sharples in an exhibition of 1996 with a catalogue of exceptional importance.[67] Historic Liverpool art was not forgotten. The animal paintings of Charles Towne (1763-1840), which very plausibly imitated Dutch seventeenth-century art, were covered for good reasons in three exhibitions.[68] The furniture and sculpture of George Bullock (died 1818) provided an exhibition

9. Thomas Gainsborough (1727-1788)
Isabella, Viscountess Molyneux, later Countess of Sefton, 1769
Oil on canvas, 236 x 155 cm
Courtesy National Museums Liverpool (the Walker)
Accepted in lieu of death duties from the estate of Hugh, seventh Earl of
Sefton, by H.M. Government in 1973 and transferred to the Gallery in 1975

10. Joseph Wright of Derby (1734-1797)
The Annual Girandola, Castel Sant'Angelo, 1775-6
Oil on canvas, 138 x 173 cm
Courtesy National Museums Liverpool (the Walker)
Probably formerly owned by the artist's Liverpool friend Thomas Moss Tate;
presented by Robert Neilson in 1880

11. Louis Daguerre (1787-1851)
Ruins of Holyrood Chapel, about 1824
Oil on canvas, 211 x 256.5 cm
Courtesy National Museums Liverpool (the Walker)
Presented by Arnold Baruchson in 1864

12. John Everett Millais (1829-1896)
Isabella, 1848-1849
Oil on canvas, 103 x 142.8 cm
Courtesy National Museums Liverpool (the Walker)
Bought in 1884 for £1,050

13. William Davis (1812-1873)
At Hale, Lancashire, about 1865
Oil on canvas, 33 x 50 cm
Courtesy National Museums Liverpool (the Walker)
Bought in 1904 for £20 from John King a Liverpool picture dealer

14. Joseph Mallord William Turner (1775-1851)
Schloss Rosenau, 1840-4
Oil on canvas, 97.2 x 124.8 cm
Courtesy National Museums Liverpool (the Walker)
Part of the collection formed by George Holt; bequeathed by Emma Holt in 1944

15. Frederic, Lord Leighton (1830-1896)
Captive Andromache, about 1886-1888
Oil on canvas, 197 x 407 cm
Manchester City Galleries
Bought in 1889 for £4,000 from the artist by Manchester City Art Gallery
with the aid of private donations

16. Edgar Degas (1834-1917)
Woman Ironing, about 1885
Oil on canvas, 80 x 63.5 cm
Courtesy National Museums Liverpool (the Walker)
Bought in 1968 for £50,000 (tax remission) from the estate of Mrs A. E. Pleydell-Bouverie with the aid of the Art Fund, the Victoria and Albert Museum Grant Fund and the Special Appeal Fund

17. Harold John Gilman (1878-1919)
Mrs Mounter, about 1916
Oil on canvas 91.8 x 61.5 cm
Courtesy National Museums Liverpool (the Walker) Bought in 1943 for £550

18. William George Scott 1913-1989
Liverpool Still Life, 1957
Oil on canvas, 92 x 152.5 cm
©William Scott Foundation 2011 Musée National d'Art Moderne, Paris
Its purchase in 1958 for £247 by the Walker Art Gallery was vetoed by
the City Council's Arts Sub-Committee

19. David Hockney (born 1937)
Peter getting out of Nick's pool, 1966
Acrylic on canvas, 213.4 x 213.4 cm
©David Hockney
Courtesy National Museums Liverpool (the Walker)
Photo: Richard Schmidt
First Prize at the John Moores Liverpool Exhibition 6 1967;
presented by Sir John Moores 1968

of 1988, again accompanied by a notable and original catalogue by Lucy Wood, Timothy Stevens and others.[69] It was the most ambitious of a series of exhibitions of the 1970s and 1980s held at Sudley, where the neoclassical architecture blended superbly with Bullock's furniture.

Many of these artists were not born in Liverpool but were attracted to the city by the opportunities for employment and for working with other artists. Stubbs and Bullock spent a relatively short part of their professional lives in Liverpool before moving on to greater things. Several, notably George Bullock, Nicholas Horsfield and Adrian Henri were presidents of the Liverpool Academy and worked hard to make that body a social, educational and cultural centre for local artists and a meaningful link with general public. The exhibition catalogues, often using reminiscences of the artists and their friends, cumulatively added significantly to the documentation of Merseyside's distinctive culture and helped ensure that the Gallery continued to be an important chronicler of local art.

Local private collections have always been a useful source of exhibitions for regional museums. Inevitably new ones were rarely formed after the Second World War. In 1961 an exhibition from perhaps the best post-war collection, which had been formed by the Samuels family in Liverpool, was shown. It included work by Renoir, Pissarro, Léger and Rouault, artists then and still unrepresented in the permanent collection.[70] Links with the two important historic collections grew in this period through loan exhibitions. Before its move from Ince Blundell to Lulworth Castle in Dorset, the outstanding and then still virtually intact collection of old masters formed by Henry Blundell (1724-1810) and his son Charles (1761-1837) was displayed in 1960.[71] In spite of its many shortcomings due to pressure of time this exhibition has exerted a remarkable long-term influence over the thinking of the Gallery, and parts of the collection have since been acquired by the Gallery and returned to Merseyside. Edward Lear worked for four earls of Derby at Knowsley Hall which still has a superlative collection of his work. Colin Bailey, then assistant keeper of British art, selected a group from it for his 'Edward Lear and Knowsley' exhibition of 1975. Some of Lear's brilliant, unfaded, detailed watercolours could be seen alongside the now faded shrunk skins of the very birds painted by Lear and bequeathed by the thirteenth Earl of Derby to the Liverpool Museum.[72] The demolition of a large country house and the building of a new gallery brought two very important collections of old master paintings to the Walker Art Gallery. Both, following a period as loan exhibitions, were integrated as part of the permanent collection for a prolonged period and dramatically enriched the Gallery's display of European art. They showed what could happen if the collection was developed. Lieutenant-Colonel Heywood Lonsdale's loan from the recently demolished Shavington Hall in Shropshire, begun in 1959, brought, amongst other great paintings, a grand masterpiece by Claude, *A view of Carthage with Dido and Aeneas*, a characteristic landscape by Hobbema, a self portrait by Rembrandt and a sumptuous Genoese-period portrait by Van Dyck. These paintings were eventually sold, respectively, to the Hamburg Kunsthalle, to the Mauritshuis at The Hague and to the Norton Simon and Getty Museums in Los Angeles. These and other sales demonstrate the outstanding quality of this collection formed in the late nineteenth century on the profits of Heywood's Bank in Liverpool. The Gallery simply lacked the necessary resources to secure a single work at auction and could not persuade the family to negotiate private sales with tax advantages. It was a great opportunity missed.[73] While the Heywood Lonsdale Collection had transformed the seventeenth-century display, the loan of virtually all the pictures from Christ Church in Oxford in 1964 for two years while their new gallery was being built did the same for the early Italian and Flemish pictures.[74] For the curators it suggested it was time to re-consider the conclusion that this part of the collection was closed to new acquisitions.

Exhibitions could also be built around local institutions. In 1960 Mary Bennett and Hugh Macandrew organized an exhibition to mark the 150th anniversary of the founding of the Liverpool Academy.[75] It combined the work of current members of the Academy with paintings shown at it in the past, including Turner's *Van Tromp Going about to Please his Masters*. It also included major pictures by the Pre-Raphaelites, notably William Holman Hunt's *Valentine and Sylvia*, the winner of the Liverpool Academy's £50 prize in 1851. It had been ridiculed in the press when shown at the Royal Academy earlier that year. For the first time for many years the Liverpool followers of the Pre-Raphaelites, Davis, Campbell, D.A. Williamson and Windus, were shown alongside their source of inspiration. In 1975 works related to Ceri Richards's well-known commissions for the Liverpool Metropolitan Cathedral given by the artist's widow were exhibited with a catalogue by Colin Bailey.[76] A more ambitious exhibition was organized by Bennett to mark the centenary of Liverpool University in 1981. It surveyed the work of the artists associated with the Liverpool School of Applied Art or the 'Art Sheds', in effect an art school run by the new Liverpool University and staffed by artists of the calibre of Augustus John, Herbert MacNair and Robert Anning Bell.[77]

Liverpool's past prosperity has been so closely connected with the United States of America that the bicentenary year of American independence in 1976 had to be commemorated. Two exhibitions were mounted. In partnership with Thomas Agnew and Sons and the Hunterian Art Gallery in Glasgow 'Whistler: The Graphic Work, Amsterdam, Liverpool, London, Venice' was organised.[78] For the first time virtually all the prints connected with the city and with the Liverpool ship-owner Frederick Leyland were shown in Liverpool. Its companion show, organised by Edward Morris, was 'American Artists in Europe 1800-1900' which surveyed those American artists who had made their careers on this side of the Atlantic.[79] Both well-known painters and sculptors notably West, Cassatt, Sargent, Allston and Whistler, and the less familiar including Audubon, Bridgman, Picknell and Powers were represented. The exhibition emphasized the rich but often overlooked American holdings of the Gallery, but perhaps its outstanding discovery was George Hitchcock's symbolist *Maternité* (Aberdeen Art Gallery and Museum) full of hazy sunshine, which was cleaned at the Gallery for the show. It was perhaps a sign of the times that the catalogue contained advertisements from locally based American firms such as Otis, although commercial sponsorship for the Gallery's exhibitions had not yet been seriously considered. Advertising which had been a feature of the later Autumn Exhibition catalogues also appeared in the catalogue of the next commemorative show marking the centenary of the opening of the Gallery itself in 1977. This was an exhibition of material drawn from the Lady Lever Art Gallery, which was now to be administered by the Gallery.[80] It was a modest show in comparison to the opulence of the Lady Lever collection, and the opening was far removed from the popular processions and exclusive functions that had launched the Walker Art Gallery in 1877. At least the Temperance Movement, so outraged by the source of the funds that built the Gallery, would have noted a distinct improvement in the sobriety of the occasion. Its low cost resulted from the concentration of all available money on the care of the Lady Lever Art Gallery and from diminishing resources at the County Council. Most of these exhibitions were intended not only to provide enlightenment and pleasure but also to develop the visitors' enjoyment and understanding of the permanent collection. They were aimed at the regular gallery visitor, not the tourist making a very occasional visit to Liverpool.

The three Pre-Raphaelite shows on Ford Madox Brown in 1964, arranged with the help of the Arts Council and shown at Manchester and Birmingham, on John Everett Millais in 1967, organised with the Royal Academy, and on William Holman Hunt in 1969 organised with the assistance of the Arts Council and shown at the Victoria and Albert Museum, were all researched, selected and catalogued by Bennett. They were aimed at the visitor from beyond Merseyside and were again intended to relate temporary exhibitions to the permanent collection.[81] The curators wanted to rebuild interest in mid- and late-Victorian painting, the major constituent of the permanent collection, which they felt for too long had been dismissed as trivial. Some serious academic study on Pre-Raphaelitism was already underway particularly in America, and modest shows about the group had already been held, especially at commercial galleries. In 1948, the centenary of the foundation of the movement, Robin Ironside of the Tate Gallery and John Gere of the British Museum published an excellent picture book.[82] Scrutton himself held a notable Pre-Raphaelite exhibition at the Whitechapel Art Gallery in the same year.[83] On moving to Liverpool he began to admire aspects of Pre-

Raphaelite and Victorian art despite their moral and narrative emphasis.[84] The gradual publication of Pre-Raphaelite letters and diaries had given much popular publicity to the irregular and enticing sexual lives of the artists and their circle. The Gallery's timing was good. In Bennett it had an exceptional curator with all the necessary expertise and discrimination. There was still sufficient indifference towards Pre-Raphaelitism at the Tate Gallery for it to become a Liverpool specialism. Liverpool had some claim on the movement as the artists had all shown in the Liverpool Academy exhibitions in the 1840s and 1850s, and a few had received the £50 prizes awarded by the Academy. Many had benefited from supportive Liverpool patrons, and all were well represented in the collection. Much material was still owned by the grandchildren of the artists whose family pride and support gave the venture a personal dimension.

The challenge was to re-launch these painters as very considerable artists for a new audience. These exhibitions presented all aspects of their work for the first time since their fall from critical esteem before the First World War, and each show was accompanied by an exemplary catalogue which made use of unpublished resources and contemporary reviews. The first on Ford Madox Brown was not a large exhibition with only forty-six carefully selected oil paintings. However it did include the huge *Chaucer at the Court of Edward III* from Sydney, indispensable for any understanding of Brown's early Nazarene style which had been evolved by the artist largely for the decoration of the Palace of Westminster. Generously brought over by Ocean Transport and Trading, a very early example of commercial sponsorship of art exhibitions, this was the first time that the painting had left Australia since its arrival there in 1876. It will probably prove to have been the last time, as the ship carrying it home ran aground in the Red Sea. The Gallery had been able to place only £500 in its budget for the Ford Madox Brown show and it depended heavily on its Arts Council subsidy.[85] Critics were somewhat disappointed that no 'new' major paintings were included and they rather missed the point that for the first time Brown's evolution from an academic painter trained in Belgium into the artist of four of the most memorable Victorian paintings, *Pretty Baa Lambs, The Last of England, An English Autumn Afternoon* and *Work* could be followed. No nineteenth-century British artist could more effectively translate into paint his acute awareness of the social issues of his time. The exhibition was a landmark in the Gallery's history aiming to combine visitor appeal and serious scholarship and rediscovery. It took place in the same year as Richard Ormond's John Singer Sargent exhibition at Birmingham City Art Gallery, another pioneering regional venture in the re-appraisal of Victorian art.

The Millais exhibition of 1967 was brought forward to suit the Royal Academy, which had been compelled to abandon their planned winter exhibition for that year and needed another at very short notice. The exhibition and catalogue were the work of a very few months. However the show gained welcome publicity as the Royal Academy's replacement Winter Exhibition and it attracted around 12,000 visitors during six and a half weeks in Liverpool.[86] The very reasonable admission fee of one shilling (about 70 pence today) probably deterred some casual visitors to the Gallery, and with the benefit of hindsight the Gallery should perhaps have opted for free admission but funds were very limited. With 397 works from 94 lenders it was much the largest exhibition which the Gallery had organised since the last Autumn Exhibition in 1938, and no subsequent exhibition at the Gallery has approached its size. Having the benefit of a London audience who habitually bought exhibition catalogues a substantial publication was possible but it still had only one colour plate. With characteristic fair judgement Bennett presented a sympathetic overview of his late post-Pre-Raphaelite work, which until then had been seen as representing a disastrous decline in quality. Subsequently the late landscapes and portraits have been enthusiastically exhibited. It was the first time that a regional gallery had provided a major show for the Royal Academy and was therefore a considerable achievement for the Gallery.

Gabriel White, then director of art at the Arts Council, was, unlike some of his successors, extremely supportive financially without interfering in the content of the Gallery's exhibitions. By designating the Holman Hunt exhibition an official Arts Council show he made that exhibition possible. Their transport section took care of the collection and return of the works, their technicians helped with the hanging and a Government indemnity was available to deal with insurance. The Victoria and Albert Museum provided a London venue which was essential if a substantial catalogue was to be published and greatly enhanced the exhibition's public image. Thanks to a grant from the Paul Mellon Foundation for British Art (now the Paul Mellon Centre) over half the works in the show were reproduced in the catalogue, an unusually high proportion for exhibition catalogues in the 1960s. With more time and with the success of the Millais catalogue behind her, Bennett produced a more ambitious catalogue which was for the time highly original in its detailed use of published and unpublished sources. Knowing that Holman Hunt's religious inclination was going to be unpopular the Gallery did much to encourage local interest and arranged a lecture series, later, but not then, a usual accompaniment for an important exhibition. It included a remarkable performance by Tim Hilton, the Ruskin scholar. In comparison with exhibitions since the late 1980s these shows were puritanical in presentation with no graphic panels and very simple labels. Resources were tight and the age of low cost in-house graphics had yet to come. However in just five years the Gallery had produced three exhibitions that decisively changed the direction of popular taste and academic scholarship in British art. Pre-Raphaelitism is now a regular feature of the Tate's exhibition programme.

It has proved more difficult to re-assess the reputations of nineteenth-century British sculptors through temporary exhibitions owing to the weight and fragility of their materials. However the Gallery had their own expert in this field too, and in 1972 Stevens, together with the Leeds curator, Terry Friedman, organized an exhibition of the work of the Leeds sculptor Joseph Gott, which introduced early Victorian sculpture to a public more ignorant of it than of Pre-Raphaelite paintings. Their detailed catalogue has never been replaced by more modern research.[87]

The Gallery may have been rather self-indulgent in mounting exhibitions of the character it did. Undoubtedly they brought considerable prestige to the Gallery and to its staff in the art world outside Liverpool and did much to enhance the reputation of the city as a place of culture. The shows were not generally outstandingly successful in visitor numbers, although over the years the figures achieved an impressive improvement. The challenge though for any regional gallery dependent on local authority funding is knowing how far it can be ahead of most of its audience, while also ensuring that it does not fall behind them either, as the Gallery appears to have done in the early twentieth century.

A very different type of art was promoted by Eric Heffer (1922-1991), who joined the Libraries, Museums and Arts Committee in 1962. By profession a carpenter he was already an important political figure on the left of the Liverpool Labour Party, having been President of the Liverpool Trades Council in 1959-60.[88] In 1963 Labour retook control of the City Council and Heffer gained a seat in parliament at the 1964 general election. Like many socialists he opposed abstract art and unlike most Labour councillors he was prepared to state his views openly. Thus he formally registered his dissent to the Gallery's purchase of Fernando Zobel's largely abstract *To the Hive* in 1962.[89] His reasons may have been wrong, but his opposition was probably right. In a letter to the *Liverpool Daily Post* of 1963 he argued that 'art has largely become divorced from society. The mass of the people are little interested in it, and certain modern trends have not helped.' He went on to plead for an exhibition of artists 'who because they work in industry or have lived or live in the environment of industry clearly reflect the life around them, and in this sense marry art genuinely with society.'[90] Like many on the far left he was a man of considerable culture. He had been greatly influenced by Tolstoy's *What is Art*, demanding an unsophisticated but expressive folk art which Heffer believed could be made and understood by Merseyside industrial workers as well as by Russian peasants.[91] At his suggestion the Gallery mounted an exhibition in 1965 called 'Industry and the Artist', curated by Stevens who had only just joined the Gallery staff.[92] In his opening speech Heffer explained that its purpose was to bring artists and industrial workers closer together, emphasizing their social links rather than their cultural differences, appropriate enough at a time when Liverpool with its new car factories was becoming an industrial rather than a commercial city.[93] The exhibition was successful with the public but did not deliver quite what Heffer wanted partly because he was searching for a type of painting which hardly existed apart from amateur work and partly because no dialogue took place between Heffer and the novice curator. Heffer was the guiding force behind another exhibition of 1965, 'Apprentice Painters and Decorators: Panel Work', which showed industrial and commercial designs by apprentices studying in local art colleges, not by any means the type of exhibition then common in major British art galleries.[94] Scrutton had refused to display it in the Gallery on the grounds that it was a craft not an art exhibition, but he was over-ruled by the Arts Sub-Committee by twelve votes to four.[95] The work was technically of very high quality and the exhibition would now be praised for keeping skills alive.

Although Heffer may have regarded the Gallery as elitist it did not ignore community art. It could not resist the charismatic Reverend James Keir Murren, a member of the Pioneer Preachers from the Domestic Mission, a nineteenth-century charitable foundation established by Liverpool's great Unitarian families in a socially deprived part of south Liverpool. Murren was not 'mad about art' but he saw that making pictures gave pleasure and could bring together a disparate community. He helped to establish the 'Neighbourhood Arts Festival' in South Liverpool around 1960. Paintings, mainly by local children, were displayed in these 'Arts Festivals' as an artistic record of the life and character of particular areas. They were intended simply to promote happiness and well-being but could also act as a form of art therapy to improve social cohesion, behaviour and aspirations.[96] In 1962 Murren asked Jacob, the Gallery's deputy director, to act as the judge at the South Liverpool Festival of Art. Jacob, whose natural socialist inclinations made him a strong supporter within the Gallery for the project, secured the enthusiastic support of local schools and businesses.[97] The best of these paintings were shown at three exhibitions in the Gallery, 'Liverpool: People and Places' in 1963, 'Liverpool Today and Tomorrow' in 1966 and 'Liverpool Around and About' in 1968. The second, opened by Heffer, attracted over 15,000 visitors within a month.[98] Many were probably making their first visit to the Gallery. The third was opened by George Holt, a great supporter of the Gallery, whose ship-owning family had helped to found the Domestic Mission. John Willett, usually a dispassionate judge of amateur art, was impressed by their artistic quality. He wrote: 'As an apparently successful example of a new kind of collective (or neighbourhood) art therapy they are a most interesting precedent, suggesting that a similar but wider sense of a new artistic curiosity and vitality will be of very practical benefit to the city as a whole.'[99] Scrutton's patrician instincts were often tempered by a certain left-wing bias fashionable in artistic circles, and he later remembered these exhibitions with affection even if they did tend to reduce art to the level of a 'social cement'.[100] There was a precedent for these exhibitions in the 'exhibitions of work done at local unemployed centres' of 1935 but these were clearly a response to the economic depression of the 1930s rather than a deliberate expression of artistic policy. Keir Murren left Liverpool in 1967 and no comparable grass-roots inspirational leader emerged to take over. Heffer left the City Council in 1966 to become a major national politician, and these exhibitions were not repeated even when community art became very popular in regional galleries during the 1980s. The Gallery did not entirely desert community arts. From time to time the Great George's Community Cultural Project, 'the Blackie', organised events in the Gallery and they never failed to surprise. However, the idea did spread to other parts of Merseyside including Huyton where a show was opened by Harold Wilson, and work from Walton Jail was included in one of the Gallery's exhibitions.

'Industry and the Artist' had included a group of paintings by Lowry whose *Fever Van* of 1935 bought by the Gallery in 1943 was one of its most popular pictures, in spite of the unhappy subject. In 1973 the Liverpool Trades Council, originally a non-political body but by the 1970s closely associated with the Liverpool Labour Party, commemorated its 125th anniversary with an exhibition at the Gallery. The Council wanted paintings by Lowry whose work records with touching humanity the lives of the workers in grim northern industrial towns.[101] It was a huge popular success with an excellent and emotional opening speech about the role of art by Vic Feather. The exhibition included a small painting of a dog that Lowry had painted for Mrs Frank Lambert in response to her enthusiasm for his matchstick dogs. No one seemed to mind that Lowry's principal patrons were northern business men who made their wealth from the labours of the workers so lovingly depicted and who were to sweep away Lowry's nineteenth-century urban landscape as part of lavish redevelopment schemes. The exhibition was immensely popular. The Gallery gave the National Trades Council space later on for an exhibition of painting and craft by its members.

The obligations of the Gallery towards the provision of collective exhibitions for local living artists caused much debate. There were other attractive galleries available, often well subsidised, but artists preferred the perceived cachet of an exhibition at the Walker Art Gallery. In the early 1960s the vociferous, largely self-taught sculptor and communist Arthur Dooley (1929-1994) was not alone in believing that a local gallery's principal function was to show and buy local art, ignoring its responsibilities for keeping the public informed about the wider world of the visual arts. His own work was bought widely locally, even by the Gallery, which he held in utter contempt. Between 1948 and 1986 the Gallery supported artists living on Merseyside by providing gallery space for annual exhibitions usually organised by the Liverpool

Academy, making the occasional purchase to keep its Liverpool holdings up to date and using its influence to facilitate sales and commissions, most notably paintings and murals for the new Liverpool Royal University Hospital completed in 1978. It was a limited but positive engagement.

From 1948 to 1977 the Gallery saw the Liverpool Academy as the most effective vehicle for supporting local talent. The Academy, after achieving a national reputation in the mid-nineteenth century, had later declined into a fairly typical local art society. However after 1948 it began to hold its exhibitions under the auspices of the Gallery on a regular basis, first at the Bluecoat Gallery and then at the Walker Art Gallery itself.[102] Substantial exhibition space was made available there for the Academy's annual exhibition and for its later thematic shows. The Presidents of the Liverpool Academy (including Nicholas Horsfield, Arthur Ballard and Adrian Henri) were appointed as ex-officio advisors on the Council Committees which managed the Gallery. Thus until the Academy's collapse there was always a formal link between the Gallery and the oldest professional artists' body in Liverpool. The Committees paid considerable respect to the views of the Presidents particularly over contemporary art. From the 1950s the Academy became closely associated with the staff of the Liverpool College of Art, profiting from a new professionalism there and from expansion and improved standards at the College under William Stevenson. In 1955, partly at the Gallery's suggestion, it began to accept works by non-members at its exhibitions on a considerable scale, and during the 1960s as many as 900 works were submitted annually. These non-members did not have to rely entirely on the generosity of the Academy's own jury to gain a place in the exhibition. The abuses of this system at the Royal Academy in London were well known. Instead there was a special jury for non-members which included representatives from the Academy and the Gallery together with at least one independent expert appointed by the Gallery, usually the regional officer of the Arts Council.[103] This greatly widened the Academy's impact, and the Gallery started acquiring paintings from it on a considerable scale. Ballard, Horsfield, Henri, Walsh and Cockrill, all part of the well-publicized Liverpool artistic revival of the late 1950s and early 1960s, exhibited there and their work was purchased by the Gallery.[104] However by the late 1960s its annual exhibitions had declined in quality because members neglected to contribute and to encourage aspiring artists to submit. During Henri's energetic presidency the annual shows were replaced by a series of smaller themed exhibitions at the Gallery, sponsored by the leading and most influential local newspaper, the *Liverpool Daily Post*. These included 'Communication' in 1973 and 'The Liverpool Academy Celebrates the Walker's 100th Birthday' in 1977 which were toured to other Merseyside Galleries.[105] The *Daily Post*'s sponsorship allowed payments to be made to participating artists covering their costs and providing for a fully illustrated catalogue. The link with the local newspaper also ensured positive press coverage. As public funding for arts organisations became increasingly available in the late 1970s the Academy developed its own gallery premises and exhibition programme. However it overstretched itself financially and collapsed in 1981. There were other galleries, especially the Bluecoat Gallery, and informal exhibition spaces in coffee bars and elsewhere were developed to assist local artists, making the Academy's exhibitions much less important. However its demise left a gap in the cultural scene and the Walker Art Gallery attempted to make good the Academy's disappearance with the 'Merseyside Artists' series of exhibitions starting in 1983. The third exhibition, sponsored by London Life, toured in 1986 to Birkenhead, Chester, Prescot, St Helens and Southport and included an open submission section with guaranteed sales of £3,000.[106] This was the final overview show of local artists. After nationalisation in 1986 the Gallery reduced its commitment to the local art scene to occasional exhibitions of a single artist connected with Liverpool.

From the 1970s the Gallery's pioneering shows reassessing Victorian painters were being imitated elsewhere. The Royal Academy went on to cover Rossetti, Burne-Jones and later Lord Leighton. Newcastle mounted a show of Albert Moore while the Newlyn School found champions in Bristol and Alma-Tadema in Sheffield. The cost of mounting exhibitions of historic art rose very sharply with lenders rightly insisting that all paintings should be moved in specially designed crates using air-conditioned, vibration-free vehicles and should be accompanied by professional couriers. The Pre-Raphaelite exhibitions of 1964-1969 were probably the last to be held under the old less demanding rules. Insurance costs rose sharply alongside picture prices, and it was not until 1979 that the Gallery was able to cover loans free of charge through the government's indemnity scheme. It responded by switching to much less expensive exhibitions of living artists in mid-career, which also reflected the interests of the younger staff, growing naturally out of their involvement with contemporary art through the John Moores and Peter Moores shows.

In 1972 the Gallery recruited as an assistant keeper Richard Francis, later the first director of Tate Liverpool. This was perhaps the first appointment at the Gallery of a curator with a strong and exclusive commitment to contemporary art since Dyall chose Quigley as his assistant in 1898. Francis only stayed at the Gallery for a little over a year before joining the Arts Council, but he had time to do an elegant show of the work of Mark Lancaster, who had exhibited in the John Moores Exhibitions, as well as working on these exhibitions. However, one of his successors, Marco Livingstone, who remained at the Gallery for six years, had similar tastes and had written a thesis on Pop Art at the Courtauld Institute. Following the old principle that exhibitions should relate to the strengths of the collection and to the curator's personal interests, he embarked on a series of one-man exhibitions. The first was on Allen Jones, a cooperative venture with the Staatliche Kunsthalle Baden Baden in 1979. It was also shown at the Serpentine Gallery in London. Then he moved on to Patrick Caulfield with an exhibition organised with the Tate Gallery in 1981, and lastly to Peter Phillips in 1982. That exhibition was later shown at the Barbican Gallery in London. Each exhibition had a substantial well illustrated catalogue setting the artist and his work in context.[107] He continued the series after his move to the Museum of Modern Art Oxford with retrospectives of Stephen Buckley and Stephen Farthing, which were also shown at the Walker Art Gallery. These artists were all John Moores exhibitors, and works by them were acquired by the Gallery either from the Moores or subsequently. Even with grants from the Arts Council and from the British Council and help from Leslie Waddington of the Waddington Gallery, funding these exhibitions was always a challenge. Touring them and finding partners were a financial necessity. Few other British municipal galleries have organized such an ambitious series of exhibitions of contemporary art, and Livingstone became a leading chronicler and interpreter of artists of the 1960s.

Although artist residencies in galleries had been much promoted by the Arts Council and local Arts Associations, they had not been a feature of the Walker Art Gallery except for very brief periods of about a week, partly due to inadequate space and partly due to the lack, before Livingstone's arrival, of a curator with the necessary skills and enthusiasms. The Bridewell Studios, which had been set up by a group of artists led by Cockrill in an imposing Edwardian former police station alongside the Royal Liverpool University Hospital, persuaded the Arts Council to fund an annual year-long artist-in-residence scheme in conjunction with the Gallery, which was to exhibit the artist's work at the start of the residency and then work done in Liverpool on his or her departure. In October 1980 Ian McKeever became the first artist-in-residence. The Arts Council provided £5,870 and the Gallery contributed £1,200.[108] The living accommodation and studio conditions were fairly Spartan and the final artist involved, Adrian Wiszniewski, was provided with accommodation in a Liverpool University Hall of Residence and a studio in the Gallery, which provided much improved public access. The Gallery also undertook to buy a work from the final show and publish a catalogue for it. Managed initially by Livingstone and then by Kidson the outcome was remarkable. The final shows of Ian McKeever, Anish Kapoor, Jonathan Froud, Graham Ashton and Adrian Wiszniewski in the Prince George Gallery were spectacular, and each artist rose to the challenge of the vast space. Kapoor has gone on to be one of the most popular sculptors of his generation. His sculpture exhibition at the Royal Academy in 2009 attracted 275,000 visitors, perhaps twenty times the number of visitors to his dazzling powder pieces in his Walker Art Gallery show.

The Gallery's earliest engagement with a contemporary art competition and sponsors was a competition to provide a trophy for presentation to the owner of the winning horse in the Topham Trophy Steeplechase This was a new race first run in 1949 as the centrepiece of the opening day of the Grand National Meeting at Aintree, near Liverpool. It celebrated the acquisition of the racecourse by Messrs Tophams Ltd from Lord Sefton. Mrs Mirabel Topham, who ran the company, originated and sponsored both the competition and the making of the trophy. Initially her Liverpool collaborator was the Liverpool College of Art, but by 1952 the Gallery had taken over the competition's management. From 1961 onwards the designs were exhibited not only at the Gallery but also in Goldsmiths' Hall in London, thus giving the competition a national status. The competition began to benefit from the expertise of the Goldsmiths' Company. As well as their art director Graeme Hughes and the director of the Gallery, two outside judges, usually a sculptor and a silversmith, helped with the selection. There were no restrictions on the nature of the trophy or the material to be used except that it should measure 'at least 12 inches in one direction,' that the money for the materials and manufacture was limited and that the trophy had to be ready for presentation at next year's race. In 1951 the prize was £315 with a similar sum for manufacture and materials. By 1979 this figure had risen to £1,000. There were 250 entries for the competition from silversmiths, sculptors, painters, architects and designers by 1968. It remained predictably popular as the only competition of its type, and there were then few opportunities for innovative design particularly in the sporting field. First prize winners included Leslie Durbin and Louis Osman. The Queen Mother's horse 'Inch Arran' won her a bowl reminiscent of an ancient Chinese bronze ritual vessel designed by Ernie Blythe in 1973. Paul Mellon's 'Red Tide' brought him a sculpture designed by Sidney Harpley in 1964. The range of trophies was wide with practical pieces such as boxes, abstract and representational sculpture evocative of speed and silver 'table toys' based on the course, notably by Louis Osman.[109] Involvement brought the Gallery's chairman and his wife coveted tickets for the County Stand for the Grand National. For the Gallery it brought a loyal supporter who contributed generously and promptly to both Special Appeals for purchase funds, making it difficult for others not to follow her example on a comparable scale. The competition ceased with Mrs Topham's death in 1980.[110] In the same 'outreach' tradition the Gallery encouraged the organizers of the Liverpool International Garden Festival to include a display of contemporary sculpture and provided some assistance to Sue Grayson-Ford, who selected and organized the exhibits.[111]

Although the Gallery had first displayed photographs in 1888 and had included travelling photography exhibitions in its programmes it had acquired very few actual prints. In 1978 Kirklands, an extremely successful Liverpool bar and café, sponsored '23 Photographers 23 Directions' at the Gallery's suggestion. This exhibition, part funded by the Arts Council, was selected by

Valerie Lloyd, the curator of the Royal Photographic Society's collection. Most of the photographers were American but a few were British and European.[112] The Gallery had hoped to buy a work by each photographer to launch a permanent collection but there was insufficient money to honour this commitment or to hold the anticipated series of future exhibitions. However the Gallery did begin to buy a few prints with local connections by Henri Cartier-Bresson, Edward Chambré Hardman, Martin Parr and Tom Wood.

In 1986 national status brought sufficient new money to allow the Gallery to return to mounting ambitious loan exhibitions. The new Tate Liverpool opened in 1988, concentrating on changing shows of twentieth-century and contemporary art in Liverpool's Albert Dock. The Walker Art Gallery used its new resources to mount ambitious exhibitions of art of earlier periods on which the Tate Gallery was not concentrating. Art exhibitions were now fashionable. Nicholas Penny, a future director of the National Gallery, observed in 2000: 'Directors are judged less by purchases that they have made or gifts that they have attracted or for the skill with which they have displayed works in the permanent collection than for their success in mounting [loan] exhibitions.'[113] Julian Treuherz, the new keeper of art galleries, had a particular interest in loan exhibitions. The recruitment of a specialist registrar to deal with administration and of more conservators and picture handlers to inspect, move and pack paintings made this expansion possible. International collaborations designed to contain costs but to enhance quality and prestige were cultivated, although participation by the Gallery's own staff in organization, selection and cataloguing was encouraged. Exhibitions without a London venue were favoured in order to encourage the huge potential audience in south-east England to travel north to Liverpool. Relatively unfamiliar subjects were chosen to widen public taste. Nineteenth-century European orientalist painting was the subject of 'The East: Imagined, Experienced, Remembered' held in 1988. It was organized by the National Gallery of Ireland but was shown in Liverpool.[114] In 1994 an exhibition of self portraits organized by Xanthe Brooke was exceptionally wide ranging, including two of Rembrandt's greatest self portraits as well as many much less well-known but striking examples.[115] An ambitious exhibition devoted to Maurice Denis came to Liverpool in 1995 with other showings in Lyon, Cologne and Amsterdam. His symbolist work of the 1890s was well known in Britain, but his later more classical work was largely new to the British public.[116] In 1997 the largest exhibition of Alma-Tadema's work since the retrospective display after his death came to the Gallery after a showing in Amsterdam.[117] The great revival of interest in Victorian art had made him well known in Britain again and the exhibition attracted over 23,000 paying visitors.[118] In 1998 there was a large exhibition of Irish twentieth-century figurative painting organized by the Berkeley Art Museum in California.[119] In 2000 came an exhibition analyzing the importance of clouds and climate in Constable's work, a more specialized exhibition but arranged around the landscapes of a great and popular artist.[120] It was shared with the National Gallery of Scotland.

Lewis Biggs, curator and later director of Tate Liverpool, deplored this development towards the art of the past:

> By the end of the 1980s engagement [at the Walker Art Gallery] with contemporary art was left to less senior curators. The artists' residencies stopped and responsibility for collecting contemporary art...was not considered a priority. It is true that the opening of the Tate may have led the Walker to concentrate on the more distant past rather than the recent past or present, but the effect of this shift in policy on the broader perception of the Walker was certainly damaging. The failure of the Walker to continue to...engage with contemporary art, outside the biennial John Moores Exhibitions, ultimately meant that the remaining local and regional collectors of art became detached from it also.[121]

This seems too severe. Collective exhibitions of work by local living artists had ceased but there were five substantial exhibitions in the 1990s of work by individual contemporary artists closely associated with Merseyside. The Tate Gallery had vast resources for the display of national and international twentieth-century art, encouraging the Walker Art Gallery to concentrate on different areas.

The introduction of admission charges to the Gallery in 1997 encouraged an increased emphasis on loan exhibitions as a means of maintaining attendance figures at a reasonable level.[122] Popular appeal was therefore an essential ingredient in the selection of exhibitions and a very promising but rather specialized and unfamiliar exhibition of German symbolist art between 1870 and 1920, intended for showings in Frankfurt, Stockholm and Liverpool, was handed on to Birmingham for its British venue.[123] However, outside London admission fees never cover the costs even of successful exhibitions, and the financial stringency, which had caused both the general admission charges at the Gallery and a disastrous fall in the Gallery's purchase grant after 1997, was certainly not alleviated by an ambitious and expensive loan exhibitions programme. Indeed the Gallery's expenditure in money and in staff time on loan exhibitions between 1994 and 2003 was probably more substantial than at any other period in its post-war history. It had become the Gallery's first priority. This commitment was reflected in the updating of three large galleries into an exhibition suite equipped with new lighting and air-conditioning together with a new goods lift, an improved loading bay and ample introductory space for the sale of publications and other material. Other major regional galleries had followed a similar policy. Birmingham converted its huge 'Gas Hall', immediately below its Gallery, into a large exhibition space in 1993 and followed this with the conversion of its 'Water Hall' in 2001. Manchester Art Gallery's extension project of 1995-2002 included about 700 square metres of temporary exhibition space.[124] The refurbished space in Liverpool was opened to the public in early 2002 with Kidson's exhibition of the works of George Romney, which was also shown in the National Portrait Gallery in London and the Huntington Gallery in California. It sought to re-establish for Romney the reputation as an outstanding portraitist that he had enjoyed in the late eighteenth century.[125] A very successful exhibition devoted to Rossetti, shared with the Van Gogh Museum in Amsterdam and attracting about 54,000 visitors in Liverpool, followed in 2003.[126] Modest compensation for the absence of admission fees was provided by some sponsorship, which had proved hard to find for other exhibitions apart from those assisted by the Moores family. Manchester and Birmingham have had considerable difficulty in funding and finding major exhibitions for their new galleries, and even the Walker Art Gallery may not be entirely successful.

Chapter 10

Conservation

For many, the conservation of their collections is the most important duty of art galleries and museums. The need for action is generally recognised but there is no agreement on what course of action should be followed. Moreover there is a very human tendency to think that problems requiring a fundamental change in the use of resources and attitudes can be left to the next generation. The Walker Art Gallery's engagement with conservation well illustrates the difficulties involved. Like most municipal galleries its staff neither had the resources to provide proper care for its collections nor the authority to be able to resist the pressures for new displays, education, commercial services and loans for temporary exhibitions at other galleries, which are often inimical to a collection's wellbeing. Conservation is unglamorous and tends to be expensive. It is of very limited appeal to local authority councillors and many bodies of trustees. It does not even have universal appeal to senior art gallery professionals. However, there was at the Gallery from the early 1950s a rare effort to stop merely worrying about conservation problems and a determination to attempt to solve some of them. With the benefit of hindsight a number of the Gallery's actions have proved probably unwise or at least questionable but doing nothing was not an alternative given the dire situation. Again with hindsight it should have been more concerned with preventive conservation, to which it gave serious consideration only in the 1970s, but in these years there was at least an increasing understanding of what could and could not be achieved.

Until Frank Lambert's appointment as director paintings requiring treatment were sent to the widely used London firm, W. Holder and Sons, who also worked at the National Gallery. In 1908 Rossetti's *Dante's Dream* was sent to the National Gallery itself for treatment but this was most unusual. In the same year the Gallery accepted financial responsibility for the conservation of the old master paintings lent to the Gallery by the Royal Institution.[1] Their condition and that of the early panels bequeathed by P. H. Rathbone could present difficult problems for restorers. The transfer from panel to canvas of the large and much damaged late fifteenth-century Lucchese School *Virgin and Child with Saints* from Rathbone's collection at a cost of £100 in 1913 would have been an ambitious but a widely accepted procedure for Holder, whose methods were generally cautious and conservative.[2] In practice the painting continued to cause problems, and in the 1960s the canvas was laid down on to a board and all the nineteenth-century repainting was removed. In the late 1930s and early 1940s Lambert employed Helmut

Ruhemann to work on some of these early paintings probably on the recommendation of Kenneth Clark, the director of the National Gallery. Ruhemann, the pioneer of 'scientific restoration' in England, had been working at the National Gallery since 1934 although he refused even to speak to the more traditional Holder.[3] In 1940 he consolidated the paintwork of Simone Martini's *Christ Discovered in the Temple* (fig. 1), which was then cracking, and removed both its discoloured varnish and some old repainting on the Virgin's robe. It was claimed that after restoration the painting was 'almost in the same condition as when it left the painter's hands 600 years ago.'[4] This work was done in Avening Court in Gloucestershire, the home of Lord Lee of Fareham, chairman of the National Gallery, where Ruhemann established a studio during the Second World War. The painting remained there until the end of the war.

All the more valuable paintings were, like Simone Martini's panel, removed to safety during the war. Rossetti's *Dante's Dream* suffered some injury while being rolled ready for transport, but otherwise the only casualties were a few relatively unimportant paintings lent to the Liverpool Museum and City Library, which were both severely bombed. Lambert, whose early archaeological training may have impressed on him a sense of the fragility of even the most robust objects, was a pioneer among provincial art gallery directors in his understanding of conservation. When the Walker Art Gallery reopened in 1951 half of one of its spacious extension galleries had been converted into a restoration studio with a large new window to give excellent sidelight. Glasgow City Art Gallery had improvised a conservation studio for Ruhemann in 1941; Bristol City Art Gallery had appointed its first fine art conservator in 1949; the Shipley Art Gallery in Gateshead had opened a conservation studio in 1950. However Birmingham City Art Gallery, which still had very few art conservation facilities or staff in 1969, was probably more typical among regional art galleries with its continued reliance on leading London painting conservators.[5] From 1950 onwards about ten of the Walker Art Gallery's paintings were treated in its new studio each year. The work varied from condition checks and first-aid blister laying to more substantial work including the removal of discoloured varnish and of overpainting and repairs to split panels.

The paintings conservator, Jack Coburn Witherop (1906-1984), was not a salaried member of staff but was paid for his work on each painting which he treated. This enabled him to work on paintings not owned by the Gallery entirely at his own discretion and gave him the freedom of action which he needed. As he worked for the Lady Lever Art Gallery, for the Earls of Derby and for other notable private local collections, the Gallery staff were able to see many of the best pictures in the area under studio conditions. In practice Witherop's status made little difference to his work. Although he was not involved in the management of the collection, in framing, handling, display and storage, and although curators had to check the condition of the collection and initiate work, he always saw himself as ultimately responsible for the welfare of the whole collection and devoted most of his time to it. The curatorial staff relied on his advice particularly on the materials used in the paintings and their structures. Witherop had studied engraving at the Royal College of Art after training at the Liverpool College of Art. The Royal College was a good place to be for anyone interested in conservation as its Department of Mural and Decorative Arts taught tempera painting and Professor E.W. Tristram, the famous authority on medieval wall painting and their leading conservator, was head of the School of Design. While in Rome on a Royal College Travelling Scholarship he did some restoration work in the Vatican studios. He began his career as a painter, etcher and draughtsman spending many summers painting in Cornwall. His paintings, exhibited at the Royal Academy and elsewhere between 1933 and 1939, often influenced by surrealism, were bought both by the Gallery and by Manchester City Art Gallery. He worked in tempera in a precise, very controlled manner and this made him naturally sympathetic to early Italian and Netherlandish art. He was active as an exhibitor, member and official both at the progressive Sandon Studios Society and at the more conservative Liverpool Academy until at least the early 1960s. During the war he had worked as an experimental photographer with the Air Ministry. After demobilisation in 1946 he was asked by the Gallery to conserve some of its paintings stored in Wales which had suffered from excessive variations in relative humidity there. He started work in the Gallery itself in 1950.[6] His father, from whom he may have inherited his marvellous manual dexterity, had been a cabinet maker and he combined the careful and systematic approach of the craftsman with the more instinctive and spontaneous attitude of the artist. He also had the enquiring and sceptical mind of the scientist. He had a genius for improvising tools at a time when purpose-made conservation tools were rare and expensive. He had to use local medical facilities for X-Ray equipment, and in his early days even infra red and ultra violet lights were not easily available at the Gallery. In the early1950s he worked for a short period with Norman Brommelle, who had become a conservator at the National Gallery in 1949 after spending twelve years doing scientific research in industry. At that time however Witherop's training as an artist at the Liverpool College of Art and at the Royal College of Art, with its thorough training in techniques, together with his experience as a practising artist, would have been seen as the normal education for a restorer.

Conservation was almost universally treated as a craft not a science, and the best practitioners were often artists. Even Kenneth Clark himself was always sceptical of the new 'scientific restoration' introduced into the National Gallery by Ruhemann and by Bromelle, observing that 'personally I do not believe very much in the application of science to the problems of cleaning......but it was advisable to have in the background what purported to be scientific evidence to "prove" that every precaution had been taken.'[7] His successor as director, Philip Hendy, was much more convinced, and Witherop must have seen Hendy's 'Cleaned Pictures' exhibition of 1947 at the National Gallery with its complacent and notorious catalogue justifying the radical restoration techniques which Ruhemann had used on some eighty paintings. Hendy's tone in the catalogue, which caused considerable concern to some of his trustees, was both patronizing and contemptuous: 'Cleaning does not provoke criticism unless the public has become fond of the picture in its dirty state.'[8]

The Walker Art Gallery's immediate problem concerned the early Italian and Netherlandish panel paintings on which Ruhemann had already done some work. By 1955 it was able to mount its own 'Cleaned Pictures' exhibition consisting of forty-one paintings. Most were of this period and most had been conserved by Witherop. In the catalogue he explained modern methods of restoration and there was also extensive historical material from Fastnedge.[9] Brommelle reviewed the exhibition:

> The policy of the conservation work has been one of preservation and the complete removal of varnish and repaints, combined with the bare minimum of restoration. In most cases only the most prominent damages have been restored and occasionally even these are merely underpainted to match a lower layer of the original picture. Excluding pictures which were purposely shown with the work still incomplete the results here and there were a little disturbing to one trained in National Gallery methods, though the differences between the two galleries in this respect are in degree rather than kind. The work has, however, in every case been done with judgement and skill.[10]

No doubt Brommelle's approval of Witherop's work explained the National Gallery's willingness to allow Witherop to restore their central panel of the triptych by the Master of the Aachen Altarpiece, which was on long term loan to the Walker Art Gallery.

In assessing Witherop's work it should be understood that many of the pictures on which he worked, especially those presented by the Liverpool Royal Institution, were in poor structural condition and much damaged. Previous restorers had attempted to conceal this by excessive overpainting. Following the fashion of the time the curators in Witherop's early days wished to have all repainting removed because it was felt that it obscured the painter's original vision, and they were not enthusiastic about the reconstruction of missing areas. Witherop's removal of the careful nineteenth century-reconstruction of lost areas from the Lucchese *Virgin and Child with Saints* is perhaps the best example of this curatorial approach. The taste for infilling missing areas with neutral underpaint also owed much to curatorial preferences of the fifties. By later standards he may have done too much retouching but his general approach was commendably cautious. Although Witherop's attitude to conservation was more 'interventionist' than became fashionable in the 1980s he became much less certain that the removal of all old varnishes and restorations was either possible or desirable, and there is no evidence that he over-cleaned the Walker Art Gallery's paintings. Indeed his work on the Gallery's early panel paintings has been very generally praised. His success in repairing, adjusting, re-joining and manipulating the wooden panels on which they were painted could not be doubted. He had a deep affection for the elaborate craftsmanship of these paintings of about 1350-1550 with their successive and meticulous layers of chalk, plaster, drawing, priming, egg-tempera, under-painting, painting and glazing on carefully prepared wooden panels. His reconstruction of part of the *St Mark Enthroned* by Giovanni Mazone from bare panel to final finish is both a didactic masterpiece and an outstanding example of his technical skill. His extraordinary ability to reconstruct missing parts is best seen in the early sixteenth-century Netherlandish School *Martyrdom of St Lawrence*, where a new strip five millimetres wide was inserted down the centre of the panel from top to bottom to make a missing section.

While Witherop's first love was the early Italian and Flemish panel paintings, much of his time was spent on the British nineteenth-century paintings. By the 1950s and early 1960s many of the larger Victorian canvases were sagging and distorted with large areas of their paint beginning to lift and flake, all aggravated by poor storage and environmental conditions. The conventional solution to these problems, if sufficiently severe, was 'relining' (or more accurately 'lining'), a practice with a long history to which most pictures on canvas dating from before 1800 have been subjected. A new canvas is stuck on to the back of the original canvas and the adhesive penetrates the old canvas helping to secure the paint to it. It had however long been recognised that this technique, using an adhesive such as glue or paste and an iron to ensure that there was good adhesion between the old and new canvases, had serious drawbacks. Only the most skilful conservators could ensure that no impasto (or thick layers of paint) on the original painting were flattened and pushed into the canvas by the hot iron. The Gallery was very aware of the hazards of relining and had deliberately left some canvases, including Gainsborough's *Viscountess Folkestone*, unlined in spite of their fragility.

The development of the vacuum hot table, which eliminated the need to use the traditional iron, appeared to reduce greatly any damage to paint layers and impasto. Glue and paste were replaced as adhesives by wax and other new materials which were thought to be entirely inert and easily removed, thus apparently making relining an entirely reversible process. This new technology had been pioneered in Britain by the Shipley Art Gallery in Gateshead and by the Tate Gallery, which designed and built its own vacuum hot table in 1957. By 1964 the Tate Gallery's conservation department had wax-lined 115 paintings including 62 by Turner.[11] In principle this method could quite easily solve the most common defects in old oil paintings: decayed, torn and distorted canvases and paint lifting off the canvas. In practice it was found that the paintings often darkened, that the wax could often not be easily removed and that further restoration was sometimes difficult. The Walker Art Gallery's vacuum hot table was not installed until early in 1965, and wax lining was probably used less in Liverpool than elsewhere in Britain. Witherop had an instinctive lack of enthusiasm for the process and it was largely phased out at the Gallery after 1974. However more wax relining took place than was absolutely necessary as Scrutton wanted to continue his exceedingly generous loans policy. Many paintings, for example, were relined to enable them to be sent safely to the Royal Academy Bicentenary Exhibition in 1968.

In 1958 Witherop had been joined by a new part-time, freelance conservator from a very different background. Gigi Crompton had been trained by Sheldon Keck at the Brooklyn Museum and then worked for six months at the Fogg Art Museum, a part of Harvard University at Cambridge, Massachusetts. With her rigorous academic training, then unavailable in Britain, she was inevitably rather sceptical about some of Witherop's materials and methods. She worked separately from him on the huge collection of nineteenth-century canvases. Crompton was replaced in 1962 by Harriet Owen Hughes. She had studied art history at the Courtauld Institute and had then trained there as a conservator under Stephen Rees-Jones, who was widely respected for his scientific expertise and for his cautious approach to cleaning. She always worked closely and easily with Witherop. Both were fairly cautious but they were also generally receptive to new ideas. It was partly due to her influence that wax lining was gradually abandoned after 1974, and the consolidation of lifting paint was carried out by water-based adhesives instead of wax. Her new techniques and good relations with Witherop enabled her to make substantial progress with the later oil paintings. In 1978 she set up her own studio outside the Gallery but returned temporarily between 1987 and 1989 to do valuable work when, in the difficult period following nationalization, the Gallery had no paintings conservator at all.

Witherop retired in 1977, and Jim France was appointed to succeed him. France was the Gallery's first permanent salaried conservator. There had been some discussion in 1966 about the need for a formal conservation department at the Gallery with Witherop as the free-lance consultant, but the idea never reached the Libraries, Museums and Arts Committee for approval. Conservators were harder to recruit than curators, and there was always a shortage of qualified candidates for conservation posts owing to the lack of training opportunities and to the huge demand from the fine art trade, which made working for a local authority financially unattractive. The Courtauld Institute, the Tate Gallery and the National Gallery trained a very few students, and courses were established at Gateshead Technical College in 1968 for paintings and at Camberwell College of Arts for paper conservation.[12] In 1976 the Hamilton Kerr Institute was founded outside Cambridge for the conservation of easel paintings and for related research and training. However the badly-needed new Central Institute for the Conservation of Works of Art (or National Conservation Centre), although much discussed between 1964 and 1976, was never built despite the offer in 1972 of £150,000 from the Gulbenkian Foundation towards initial costs.[13] Just as provincial galleries were rarely able to co-operate effectively in setting up joint conservation studios within their Area Museum Councils and Services, so the great London galleries and central government failed to establish any national system for the training of conservators. France's pay was slightly above the level of the Gallery's senior curatorial staff, although it was hoped that the County Council could recover about half of it from work for outsiders – an ambition only achieved in his early years at the Gallery.[14] He had been trained over four years at the National Gallery's studios, which by then had largely lost their reputation for over-cleaning and had become highly esteemed throughout the world for their scientific rigour, experimental skill, diagnostic precision and excellent equipment. He was thus familiar with the most recent and innovative ideas and methods at a time when conservation practices were changing rapidly. To a considerable extent the physical treatment of paintings – and of works of art generally – became no longer the first option but rather one of many possible solutions. Prevention not cure became the first priority for art conservators. There was a new awareness of the irreversibility of the ageing process and the damage done by some earlier interventionist restorers in trying to reverse it. The ambition to return paintings to the state in which they left the artist's easel was largely abandoned as rarely achievable and not always desirable.[15] The assimilation of the Lady Lever Art Gallery in 1978 provided conservators with a collection of important canvases which, through the caution or inactivity of its curators, had to a considerable extent escaped excessive interventionist restoration, and both curators and conservators were determined that this happy situation should not change.

Unlike Witherop, France was expected to play a full part in the management of the collection and to supervise closely the framing, glazing and back-boarding of pictures and the packing of works going out on loan. The Gallery had been built in 1877 without any workshop for even the simplest technical procedures. It was planned for temporary exhibitions and it was thought that the paintings in them would not require any work done on them. Space was eventually found for an improvised working area.[16] Between about 1890 and 1926 a gilder was employed for work on frames and in 1909 a new workshop was set up for him.[17] In 1961 Leslie Smith was appointed as the Gallery's first craftsman. As well as framing and de-framing he made stands, pedestals, cases, shelving, crates and simple frames for display, storage and transport, work formerly contracted out to local craftsmen.[18] He then began to extend his work to some repairing and re-gilding of historic frames, to cutting mounts for prints and drawings and to some sculpture conservation.[19] He was careful not to be ambitious and was very aware that each of these types of work ideally required specialists, who were indeed, many years later, appointed to carry them out. The handing back of a large workshop under the extension galleries by Liverpool City Libraries allowed output under Roy Irlam, Smith's successor, to rise significantly in the later 1970s. Irlam soon concentrated on improving the effectiveness of framing and back-boarding. After 1990 this became his specialist responsibility, and the repair of historic frames became a major priority for the Gallery.

The Walker Art Gallery has around 5,000 works of art on paper accumulated largely by gift and bequest and by occasional bursts of systematic acquisition. While its holdings may not have the coherence of the Birmingham City Art Gallery's collection of Pre-Raphaelite drawings or the comprehensive cover of the Whitworth Art Gallery's British watercolours, it has a number of outstanding individual works notably by Fuseli, Cotman and Signorelli together with important groups by Madox Brown, Romney, Sickert, Turner and Whistler. There is also a large and important holding of old master drawings, which are rarely found in British provincial galleries. Until the late eighteenth century prints, drawings and watercolours had generally been kept in portfolios stored in cupboards or boxes. Towards the end of the century artists began producing many more drawings and watercolours which were intended, like oil paintings, for permanent display. They often placed them in specially designed mounts and frames at annual exhibitions, such as those held at the Royal Academy and at the Society of Painters in Water-Colours, in order to sell them. Their purchasers generally retained these frames on the walls of their houses. By the later nineteenth century works on paper were a major element in the Liverpool Autumn Exhibitions, and the collecting of drawings, watercolours and prints had become very fashionable. Naturally artists were concerned that their work should be framed sympathetically and sometimes designed their own frames and mounts. At the Gallery until the 1950s most of the 'exhibitable' works were kept framed and glazed on display or ready for display while the rest, often unmounted, were stored in large boxes or portfolios. Bringing this very large collection under control was the great achievement of Hugh Macandrew. As assistant keeper of British art between 1957 and 1963, he prepared a new inventory and organised a new storage system, using for the first time high quality 'solander' boxes and standard size mounts based on the system used in the British Museum and in other major print rooms.[20] His programme continued after his move to the Ashmolean Museum in Oxford, and in the early 1970s the director's office was converted into a print room lined with storage cabinets to house the growing number of conserved and remounted works. In the late 1980s a still larger print room was created in the former Lancashire County Sessions House.

The Gallery had no conservator for works of art on paper on its premises until 1981. At some time before the 1950s an important drawing by Durer had been obliterated and redrawn, and a significant drawing by Fra Bartolommeo had been seriously damaged by excessive cleaning. Much higher standards were clearly required and in 1957 John Skillen of the British Museum began systematic work on the collection on a freelance basis and continued working on the Gallery's collection after his retirement. On his death in 1975 his widow presented some important watercolours and prints from his collection to the Gallery. A series of British Museum conservation staff, notably Eric Harding and Judith Chantry (later of the Ashmolean Museum), and other freelance conservators took over from him. These conservators made serious inroads into the backlog of work but they could not devote sufficient time to complete the work within the foreseeable future.

The Gallery's watercolours, drawings and prints usually had old mounts and back-boards made of highly damaging acidic wood pulp which frequently caused them to deteriorate and discolour. Skillen and his successors therefore had to take them out of these mounts to which they were often stuck – sometimes a laborious, dangerous and difficult task. Then any necessary cleaning and conservation was done. Often they were 'inlayed' into new sheets of paper to protect their edges and to enable the entire work to be visible on exhibition. Finally they were re-mounted in thick acid-free board mounts above and below them with the upper board having a 'window' cut in it. There was much to be said for the policy. Dibdin, the Gallery's second curator, had supported it in a thoughtful article on conservation problems at the Gallery in 1912.[21] The new mounts and 'inlay' papers were of very high 'conservation quality' and could not cause any deterioration. By making the new mounts in standard sizes, completely filled boxes with tight fitting lids could be used to store the prints, drawings or watercolours, which would thus be 'cushioned' against any fluctuations in relative humidity and protected from dirt in the atmosphere. Access to them was easy and hundreds of them could be examined by conservators, curators or visitors within a single day. Their backs were visible and any watermarks in their paper or old inscriptions could be easily read. The space required for their storage was drastically reduced. They could easily be displayed as required in frames of standard sizes, matching the standard sizes used for the new mounts.

Many of the Gallery's late Victorian and Edwardian works, often acquired directly from their artists, still had their original mounts and frames, frequently specified by or even designed by their artists. With the establishment of the print room and standard size 'solander' boxes some of these frames and mounts were inevitably lost, although a few watercolours, too large to fit into the new boxes, retained their frames, and some special frames, including Birket Foster's gilt Rococo-style frames and gold mounts, were stored separately for possible future re-use. A further difficulty was the disproportion between some of the watercolours and the standard sized mounts of the new system. The storage and conservation of watercolours was not a new problem. In 1886-7 Sir James Linton and James Orrock, both professional watercolour painters and prominent in the affairs of the Royal Institute of Painters in Watercolours, conducted a very public argument on this very issue with such redoubtable opponents as Sidney Colvin of the British Museum and J.C. Robinson, Surveyor of the Queen's Pictures.[22]

In 1980 a ground-floor room and two basement rooms in the Lady Lever Art Gallery were converted into a paper conservation studio, and in the following year the Gallery appointed its first conservator for works of art on paper.[23] New courses on paper conservation at Gateshead and Camberwell had begun to provide properly trained conservators with a good understanding of both the limitations and potential of paper conservation. The new conservator, Maria Vilaincour Baker, continued the work of the freelance restorers and was also able, like France, to play a large part in the management of the collections. The curators were pleased to lose much of their responsibility for the storage, display and loans of works of art on paper. Eventually the Lady Lever Art Gallery studios closed with the provision of new much larger studios in the Maritime Museum for paper conservation for all departments of the National Museums and Galleries on Merseyside in 1990.

Very little Victorian and Edwardian sculpture, of which the Walker has a small but distinguished collection, was on display when the Gallery reopened in 1951. Even the over-life-size white marble statue of its founder, Sir Andrew Barclay Walker, had been removed from the entrance hall. The fall of nineteenth-century sculpture from popular esteem was even more dramatic than for paintings. At Leeds City Art Gallery the marbles by Joseph Gott were broken up and used as hardcore under a pavement. In Liverpool paintings had to take priority but throughout the 1960s and 1970s the task of putting the sculpture into more acceptable order and putting it back on public display began, and the founder returned to the entrance hall. As with paper conservation the Gallery was dependent on help and advice from a national museum. Some of the more complicated conservation tasks were undertaken on a freelance basis by Kenneth Hempel and John Larson of the Victoria and Albert Museum, who were at this time pioneering new methods of sculpture conservation. Some simple marble and bronze cleaning was undertaken within the Gallery following advice from the Museum.

The Gallery's stores were far too small and too badly equipped to house the reserve collections safely. Access to them for staff and visitors was difficult. The sparse hang favoured by Lambert and Scrutton reduced the number of pictures on display and worsened the storage problem. In the late 1960s Scrutton, although he never liked the idea, allowed the hang to be more dense and for some pictures to be hung very high on the walls. This became accepted practice in many parts of the Gallery. It successfully reduced pressure on the stores, and the great stacks of pictures, an outstanding feature of the Walker Art Gallery cellars, were at last reduced in size. A large proportion of the sculpture collection was put on display at Sudley Art Gallery together with, on the first floor, some furniture and paintings, again for reasons of conservation and public access rather than display. The vast Renaissance-style marble fireplace and the huge wooden buffet by Alfred Stevens from Dorchester House, which had sat in large piles in the stores since their acquisition some thirty years earlier, were finally placed on display.

Proper handling of all museum material is an essential but unappreciated part of preventive conservation. Paintings are often heavy and fragile. They must be moved, hung, stacked, stored, packed and unpacked, framed and de-framed with great care by skilled, experienced and properly trained handling teams who understand the risks involved. The packing, hanging and repacking of paintings for the large Autumn Exhibitions were done by the leading Liverpool framers and supplier of artists' materials, J. Davy and Son, who also maintained and hung pictures for local collectors, or by Jackson's, who later acted as the Liverpool agents for the John Moores Liverpool Exhibitions. The more modest day-to-day re-hanging and re-display were performed by the security attendants under the supervision of the deputy foreman when they could be spared from warding duties in the public galleries. By the late 1950s, with the dramatic increase in the number of temporary exhibitions and loans to and from the Gallery, this arrangement was no longer satisfactory, and clearly a specialist handling team was needed. Following a useful incident of poor handling in 1960 Jacob created a 'craft section' headed by Smith, the Gallery craftsman.[24] However the four object handlers under Smith's direction were seconded from the team of security attendants and were frequently needed to go back on duty as warders. It took another ten years to achieve complete separation between the two groups. There were also problems over salaries and grading for the handling team. The human resources staff at the City and County Councils were very reluctant to accept that moving, stacking and hanging paintings, together with deframing and reframing them for photography or technical examination, could properly be classified as skilled work which called for a great sense of responsibility. However in 1990 after nationalisation the new well-financed conservation division was able to establish a re-constituted specialist picture handling department with its own manager, separate from framing and craft work, and at last higher standards, monitored by the whole division, could be achieved.

Photography is of fundamental importance both to conservators and to curators. Without it the deterioration in the condition of works of art cannot be studied and their treatment cannot be recorded. Witherop was a trained photographer able to make his own excellent photographs recording his own work. Good photographs are also needed both by curators and by scholars outside the Gallery for their research on the Gallery's collections. Publishers need them to illustrate Gallery catalogues and guides, as well as for scholarly and popular books and articles on the Gallery's works of art. The Gallery's staff use them to identify objects not known to them personally. The police require them if a painting is stolen or lost. Photography is a function of conservation because conservators must train photographic teams and supervise photography sessions to ensure that lighting is appropriate and that no damage is caused to fragile works of art. With his usual foresight Lambert had asked for the creation of a new post of photographer in 1951 just as the Gallery was re-opening.[25] The photographic studio was to be adjacent to the conservation studio. His request was deferred indefinitely by the City Council's Establishment Committee, and the Gallery had to rely on contract photographers until 1986 when it was able to start using a staff photographer provided by the Liverpool Museum. In practice the Gallery was still using contract rather than staff photographers well into the 1990s owing to pressure of work. The ownership of negatives by commercial photographers led to some problems on their use. Negatives held outside the Gallery were sometimes lost or damaged and some colour transparencies did not have perfect colour rendering. However the contract photographers used by the Gallery were generally very competent, and contractors usually work more rapidly than salaried staff. By the 1970s nearly every oil painting had been photographed, and by the 1990s a black and white negative existed for most works of art except prints and some decorative art at the Lady Lever Art Gallery.

The Gallery had been built for temporary exhibitions of contemporary paintings which it did not own. Like most public galleries designed before the use of electric light huge glass roofs were provided to maximise available daylight. This led to extreme fluctuations in temperature and humidity and to high light levels. The gradual growth of the Gallery's permanent collection eventually caused concern for the welfare of the paintings inside it. Dibdin's brief article of 1912 demonstrated a concern for environmental conservation and storage unusual among curators of the period. He explained that the Gallery had been designed with a total disregard for the conservation of the paintings inside it. The heating pipes ran around the bottoms of the walls behind cast iron grills as part of the skirting boards. All the heat passed up over the paintings. The chimneys from the boilers in the basement climbed to the roof inside the walls of the Gallery. Thus, in the absence of any ventilation, the pictures were baked both from beneath and behind. Builders soon provided some crude ventilation ducts through which dirt from Liverpool's smoke-filled air flowed unchecked into the Gallery.[26] Radiators placed in the centre of each gallery eventually replaced the skirting board heating pipes. Damage resulting from atmospheric pollution and from changes in relative humidity, caused principally by central heating and the changing seasons, can be greatly reduced by the installation of air-conditioning. This filters out impurities in the air and largely eliminates those violent fluctuations in relative humidity so especially harmful to the Gallery's early panel paintings. In 1959 serious damage to five of these panel paintings was reported. Among them Ercole de' Roberti's *Pietà*, widely regarded as one of the most important paintings in the Gallery, had developed a serious warp and seemed likely to crack from top to bottom down the centre. The Gallery decided on air-conditioning after discussions with conservators at the Tate Gallery and at the British Museum.[27] Design work and installation took place between 1960 and 1962, and by 1963 the three galleries containing these early paintings were air-conditioned in order to try to keep the levels of relative humidity to a constant 58-60 per cent and temperatures to a constant 65 degrees Fahrenheit.[28]

By the early 1960s the heating pipes embedded in concrete below the cornice in the five very large extension galleries of 1931-1933 had begun to fail, and bursts of water over the walls became so common that the system had to be abandoned. The inaccessible pipes could not be repaired. The Gallery therefore prepared an ambitious scheme to extend air-conditioning to these galleries, planned for 1965-1966. The first phase involving the installation of skirting heating was carried out, but then the scheme repeatedly stalled, usually on account of central government's refusal to sanction the expenditure or the costs of the reconstruction of the Liverpool Museum and of the building of the Liverpool Central Library extension. The city architect's belief that the scheme had to be done as a whole and could not be phased caused further delays. The Gallery was left with an inadequate heating system for nearly half its display space.

In 1973 Stevens was asked by the Merseyside County Council, then about to take over the Gallery, to state his priorities. Air-conditioning stood at the top of his list.[29] Between 1972 and 1974 the 1965-1966 scheme, originally priced at £60,000, was re-costed first at £183,000 and then at £280,000. It was eventually approved in 1975 by the County Council. The city architect, who continued to run the scheme on behalf of the County Council, at last agreed that the scheme could be phased as and when funds were available. By 1984 about half of the display area in the extension galleries was air-conditioned. The further delays were partly caused by the County Council's insistence on supporting grants from outside bodies, among which the English Tourist Board with £30,000 was surprisingly generous and the North West Museums and Art Galleries Service with £7,000 rather less helpful.[30] With the nationalization of the Gallery in 1986 much more elaborate controls, essential if any air-conditioning system is to do more good than harm, were installed. Finally in 1999-2001 the last three galleries of the extension were air-conditioned as part of a scheme to provide the Gallery with greatly improved facilities for loan exhibitions. On this occasion the original architectural features within the galleries were preserved but at the cost of conditioning a much larger volume of air. Jacob was the principal architect of the schemes of the 1960s, Stevens and France controlled the work in the 1970s and 1980s while Treuherz was responsible for the loan exhibition project of 1999-2001.

Thus over half the display galleries of the Gallery were eventually air-conditioned over a period of nearly forty years. No other provincial galleries and few other national galleries made any serious attempt to air-condition existing galleries on this scale, and many now believe that the huge costs involved in such projects, together with the damage often done to the original architectural features of the galleries, suggest that money can more effectively be spent on insulation. Running costs for electricity and water are particularly high and very sensitive in an ecological age. The Gallery in the 1960s and 1970s sought to reduce these costs by the installation of false ceilings in the extension galleries, thus reducing the volume of air to be conditioned and abandoning daylight. The control of daylight was then too expensive to be contemplated but some reversible damage to the original architecture resulted. However no better evidence can be provided of the Gallery's commitment to conservation spanning many years and many staff changes.

The damaging effect of excessive daylight, particularly its ultra-violet component, on paintings and works on paper was widely understood by the 1970s. There was evidence in the Gallery itself where two narrow vertical strips on either side of Signorelli's *Virgin and Child in a Landscape* had green grass and trees, while the landscape in the central part of the painting had turned brown. The strips, but not the central area of the panel, had been protected from light by framing. Light levels were many times higher than the recommended limits in the late nineteenth-century galleries and even more so in the extension galleries of 1931-1933. Solar gain caused large fluctuations in temperature and therefore dramatic changes in the levels of relative humidity, which further damaged the paintings. Visitors suffered from exceptional heat in the summer and severe cold in the winter. A few blinds had been included in the extension galleries but their effectiveness was short lived as they were extremely difficult to maintain. Summer white-washing of the roof lights was used but cleaning the whitewash off invariably led to cracked panes and serious leaks. In the 1970s special film was applied to the roof-lights virtually eliminating the ultra-violet light and greatly reducing the ordinary daylight. More sophisticated methods of light control were eventually introduced in some galleries in the 1990s.

The Lady Lever Art Gallery initially took its environmental conditions rather more seriously than the Walker Art Gallery. Segar Owen, its architect, had included a basic humidification system. It involved blowing air through heavy damp coconut matting and then through trunking into the galleries. It was just still useable in the early 1970s. The Gallery also enjoyed, unlike the Walker Art Gallery, double glazing in its roof lights. The high cost of renewing the entire roof to make it watertight when the Gallery was transferred to the Walker Art Gallery's care reduced available funds for environmental improvement, but daylight was removed from most of the smaller galleries so that the tapestries, needlework and other light sensitive materials were protected. Light levels were reduced elsewhere by film. Fluctuations in relative humidity were generally greater than at the Walker Art Galley, but a rather ineffective heating system ensured that humidity levels were never very low and changed slowly. A new efficient heating system installed in 1987 reduced humidity levels dangerously during the winter months. Insulation, the most fashionable remedy, was tried after the cost of air-conditioning had been estimated at over £600,000.[31] Between 1994 and 1995 the Gallery was closed and new argon-filled double glazing was installed into the huge roof windows at a cost of over £300,000.[32] The problem was only partially solved, and in late 1999 the trustees were recommended to spend a further £500,000 on environmental improvements at the Gallery.[33] By then however the good years for conservators and conservation were long past.

Damage from atmospheric dirt and pollution and from casual vandalism by visitors can be greatly reduced by glazing paintings. Until 1945 most pictures in British public galleries were protected by glass. This practice was less common elsewhere probably because entrance charges reduced the number of disaffected visitors. After the second world war 'clean air' legislation, 'visitor-friendly' policies, demands for better visibility, improved warding levels and the needs of photographers and of loan exhibitions encouraged some British galleries, especially the National Gallery which had a warder in each gallery and much air-conditioning, to remove the glass from many of their paintings. The Walker Art Gallery and, very conspicuously, the Glasgow City Art Gallery under T.J. Honeyman generally resisted the trend.[34] New 'low-reflecting' German picture glass, designed to reduce reflections in glass over dark paintings became available. There was certainly less visible soot in the atmosphere but industrial and domestic pollution throughout Merseyside remained at very high levels. Glass or perspex offered some protection against accidents to paintings while they were moved, stacked, crated or loaned. Minor casual vandalism, cumulatively a serious problem, was deterred. Improved warding and security provision could not be sustained with wages rising faster than budgets. In 1960 five paintings at the Gallery were damaged by vandals. Some paint was scratched off their surfaces and small holes were made in their canvases. Similar damage on a smaller scale had occurred previously. Only about twenty paintings, mostly large, were unglazed. Scrutton was personally rather against glazing but ordered that five of these pictures should be protected by glass. Ropes were installed to prevent the public from standing too near the paintings.[35] However later in the 1960s deglazing, initiated by Scrutton, was in progress, especially on dark paintings with diminished visibility caused by reflections. The same policy was pursued at the Lady Lever Art Gallery. At Sudley, where the traditions of private collections still prevailed, some pictures had never been glazed. During the late 1970s and 1980s Irlam's framing skills enabled the Gallery to undertake a major campaign in which nearly all its paintings were glazed or re-glazed with low reflective glass to high standards. Glazing protected the fronts of paintings but their backs were also vulnerable during handling. Boards were placed over the backs giving the canvases protection from damage both through accidents and air pollution. The painted canvas or panel was thus entirely physically enclosed providing some insulation from changes in humidity and temperature.

The final main risk to the Gallery's collections came from loans outside the Gallery. In 1891 the Gallery decided that ten of its largest and most important paintings, including Rossetti's *Dante's Dream*, Millais's *Lorenzo and Isabella*, S.J. Solomon's *Samson* and Leighton's *Elijah* should never be lent again.[36] The prohibition in practice did not last for very long. It is widely believed – even in the absence of any conclusive evidence – that most fairly small well-crated oil paintings, drawings and sculptures can be lent abroad and at home with reasonable safety, provided that the artist has used traditional methods, provided that no one work of art is lent too frequently, provided that the painting is carefully examined before any loan is agreed and provided that strict controls, monitored by an accompanying courier, are in place to protect the work as it moves. The Gallery increasingly enforced these safeguards rigorously. It also gradually banned entirely the lending of its early fragile paintings on panel and severely restricted the loan of large unlined canvases, fearful that loans might accelerate the need for relining. There had in fact been considerable opposition for a long time both within the Gallery and within its governing committee to the loan of exceptional paintings on panel. In 1952 two committee members voted against the loan of Simone Martini's *Christ Discovered in the Temple* to Bordeaux and in 1958 seven members voted against sending the same painting to Brussels.[37] In 1968 Scrutton very much wanted to lend this painting to the very prestigious 'Gothic Europe' exhibition held by the Council of Europe at the Louvre. It was fortunate that the loan was not eventually approved because the organizer of the British section, Nikolaus Pevsner, found deplorable standards of care, protection, management and security for the loaned works of art in Paris.[38] Earlier in 1961 an unlikely coalition of councillors led by Eric Heffer and Vere Cotton voted to restrict the number of major paintings travelling to Hull for an exhibition of Dutch art there, but they were out-voted by seven to nine.[39] Their motives for reducing loans to exhibitions probably related not only to possible damage to the pictures but also to the inconvenience caused to visitors by the absence of paintings while away on loan. However, the councillors on the Arts Sub-Committee were greatly concerned by two serious cases of injury to important paintings in transit to loan exhibitions.

In 1957 *The Pilgrimage* by Legros arrived back in Liverpool from an exhibition in Dijon with water on its canvas. It had apparently travelled north from Newhaven on a lorry protected only by sheeting. Water had penetrated both the sheeting and the crate. The damage was irreparable and the visual appearance of the picture has not since been satisfactory. In the same year Fuseli's *Death of Oedipus* was scratched severely while on loan at Bordeaux. The Sub-Committee ruled that a curator or conservator should accompany loans in the 'most important and delicate cases' and that methods of transport should be carefully regulated by the Gallery. The Sub-Committee preferred air rather than rail, road or sea for its speed and simplicity.[40] In 1965 however this proved to be an unfortunate recommendation. In that year Holiday's *Dante and Beatrice* suffered from considerable paint loss on its way to an exhibition in Italy. The damage was caused primarily by rapid changes in relative humidity and by vibration in the aircraft. It was most severe on the left-hand side and the figures were largely unaffected. There was considerable discussion about the underlying causes of the disaster. Probably the cargo hold of the aircraft was inadequately heated with the result that relative humidity rose rapidly as the aircraft gained height and then fell sharply as it landed, causing the canvas first to expand and then to contract. This would have greatly reduced the adhesion of the paint to the canvas. Vibration would then have caused the paint to fall off the canvas. The Italian experts believed that the painting was always too unstable for loan, although Witherop and most British conservators denied this. The Italian conservators were able to recover much of the paint from the bottom of the crate and replace it on the canvas, but some repainting was also necessary. It also emerged that the Italian insurance policy taken out to cover the painting in transit excluded both damage caused by temperature or humidity and any loss caused to any painting not in a suitable condition for travel. Eventually however the claim for damage and depreciation was accepted. The painting had been insured for £2,000 and depreciation was assessed at £460. Within the Gallery Witherop became reluctant to approve proposed loans especially to overseas galleries. A less happy consequence was a decision to reline many more paintings in the belief that the damage to *Dante and Beatrice* would have been much less severe if it had been relined before departure to Italy.

Damage caused to paintings on loan to exhibitions is generally concealed both by organizers and lenders. However, as a matter of course, Scrutton made no such attempt to hide the injuries suffered by the paintings by Legros and Holiday. The unfortunate events were much discussed in the press and in conservation studios throughout Britain. The use of air travel for paintings was becoming widespread in 1965, and it now became clear that careful planning and detailed precautions were necessary for all transits. The Gallery's Arts Sub-Committee decided to ban temporarily air travel for all its pictures, to tighten restrictions on all loans and to insist on the use of reputable British insurers.[41] A special high quality crate with layers of insulation and of protective polythene would have prevented rain from reaching the canvas of Legros's *The Pilgrimage* and might have acted as a 'buffer' reducing the sudden impact of temperature and relative humidity fluctuations on Holiday's *Dante and Beatrice*. The Gallery immediately started to make its crates to the rigorous international specifications recommended by the distinguished Canadian conservator Nathan Stolow. It insisted on the use of specialist fine art carriers to move its pictures and provided its own couriers for many overseas loans. Detailed condition reports were drawn up before any loans were agreed. Most other art galleries throughout the world followed similar policies. The use of air-conditioned vans with special suspension systems reducing vibration, jolting and swaying became general. Vans travelling to continental Europe travelled straight through to their destinations using 'roll-on, roll-off' ferries. Small paintings and drawings travelling by air were placed where possible in passenger areas strapped down next to their couriers, not in cargo holds. Works of art were crated even for short journeys within Britain. Loans to travelling exhibitions were generally restricted to just one location. Important original frames were rarely lent as relatively minor but still serious damage was caused to frames by careless handling, and the Gallery did not then have the staff to repair the damage. It is difficult to compare the Gallery's policy over loans with that pursued by other comparable galleries because such policies change greatly even within a single institution. It would however be true to say that broadly the Gallery acquired a reputation for being very reluctant to lend to exhibitions at other galleries. The situation was exacerbated by a feeling at the Gallery that large metropolitan institutions tended to regard provincial collections as mere depots to hold works of art while they were not wanted for display at their own international, well-attended and even profit-making exhibitions. The element of reciprocity in these loans was not great because provincial galleries are rarely able to afford their own ambitious exhibitions in the absence of wealthy tourists and residents willing to pay substantial entrance fees. Loans to exhibitions involved curators, handling staff and above all conservators in much work which distracted them from their basic duties and primarily benefited other galleries. Policy at the Gallery, as elsewhere, could waver with staff changes and it is probably true to say that Stevens and France were the most restrictive. On their departure from the Gallery in 1987 some trustees, probably encouraged by London exhibition organisers, attempted to loosen this policy.[42] However there was still a general feeling that the demands of conservation were paramount.

In 1991 a registrar, David McNeff, was appointed for the first time to deal with fine art loans. Registrars were an American invention but had been taken up by the more progressive British galleries in order that they, working closely with conservators and handlers, should largely take over the physical care of works of art from curators. At Liverpool the registrar's most important duties lay in the control and supervision of the movement of works of art into and out of the Gallery for exhibitions held in the Gallery or outside it. This expanding work had been gradually moving away from curators and towards conservators for some years, and a professional registrar was now needed to co-ordinate conservators' requirements with the programmes and schedules of specialist carriers, of couriers and above all of the handling and packing staff within the Gallery. The registrar's expertise enabled the Gallery to increase its loans to exhibitions within Britain and abroad with reasonable safety and to expand its own exhibitions in Liverpool.

Local authorities had widely accepted the need for conservation, but rather as a joyless and expensive duty imposed on them by high-minded art gallery staff. However in 1986 the trustees of the new National Museums and Galleries on Merseyside saw conservation as a neglected responsibility in which they could demonstrate the positive benefits of their new regime as guardians of the national heritage. They also rightly believed that emphasis on conservation would attract increased funding from central government. By early 1987 both conservator posts at the Gallery were vacant and neither could be filled until the staffing and structure review throughout the whole organization was complete. The ambitious programme of conservation required for the large new sculpture gallery, opened late in 1988, had therefore to be carried out by free-lance conservators.[43] The staffing review and most of the curators advocated a single conservation department for the whole institution. However the implementation of this policy proved to be a long and contentious process, and France did not return from Cardiff to start work as the new head of conservation for both the Museums and the Gallery until early in 1989. Having worked at the Gallery between 1978 and 1987 he was able to produce within a few months a report for the trustees describing the poor state of much of the collections, the shortage of climatic controls and the absence of both staff and facilities for treatment. There was some embarrassment among senior staff but the trustees moved fast. In June the creation of a new conservation division was accepted with its head responsible to the director, and in October generous salaries were approved for the appointment of at least ten new conservators. New conservation departments were established. They did not generally correspond with existing curatorial departments. Instead each conservation department had specialist conservators responsible for objects of a particular material.[44]

The new conservators were of very considerable distinction. In 1991 John Larson, the head of the sculpture department, came from the Victoria and Albert Museum where he already had an international reputation, which was greatly enhanced by his work and research at Liverpool. Jacqueline Ridge, the head of the paintings department, went on after Liverpool to become head of paintings conservation at the Tate Gallery. Sally Ann Yates, head of paper conservation, was recruited from the British Museum where she was a senior conservator of prints and drawings. In 1998 she refused the post of head of paper conservation at the Tate Gallery, one of the summits of her profession. Nicola Christie, Jacqueline Ridge's successor, eventually left Liverpool to become the senior paintings conservator for the Royal Collections. France himself moved on from Liverpool to become director of collections and research services at the Tate Gallery. At a less senior level Anne Brodrick joined the sculpture conservation staff from the Victoria and Albert Museum and left to work at the British Museum. Others had careers of equivalent distinction. Here at last was that frequent interchange of staff between the provincial and London museums and galleries which many official reports of the previous fifty years had seen as essential for the success of the regional art galleries.

A new building for the treatment of works of art was soon supplied by the acquisition and conversion of the former Midland Railway Goods Warehouse, a monumental city-centre warehouse of the 1870s, which became the Liverpool Conservation Centre.[45] The interiors were completely rebuilt between 1992 and 1995 at a cost of about £8 million. Life-size statues and huge oil paintings could easily pass through its enormous doors and wide, high corridors. Full air-conditioning was installed. Over six thousand square metres of studio space were created, and the paintings conservation studios, covering four hundred square metres, were said to be among the largest of their type in Europe. Over £250,000 was spent on new equipment for them. There were at least three paintings conservators, five paper conservators and five sculpture conservators as well as further conservators covering other materials. In addition active placement and internship programmes for training new conservators were set up. For the first time in the Gallery's history there were far more conservators than curators. The systematic improvement to the mounting and conservation of prints, drawings and watercolours could now be carried forward more rapidly. Substantial work could be undertaken on the neglected sculpture collections.

Studios, specialist conservators and the most advanced equipment and tools were now available to restore the colossal model of Lutyens's largely unbuilt design for the Liverpool Catholic Cathedral, perhaps the most important architectural model of the twentieth century.[46]

By 1989 nobody doubted that conservators should spend as much time on the protection of their collections from damage and decay as on the repair of that damage and decay on the studio bench. In Liverpool they began a systematic inspection of paintings on display and in storage. The scope and standards of detailed reports on particular works of art were greatly improved. Conservators raised standards of picture handling and packing with training sessions for the handling team. They worked with curators in improving storage and display arrangements. There was space for research as well as treatment. Important new work was done on the development of the use of lasers in sculpture conservation by Larson and his team. A more generalist scientific officer working on the care of paintings and on environmental conservation was eventually appointed in 1999. In the past both the Walker Art Gallery and the Tate Gallery had considered the Midland Railway warehouse for use as public display galleries with its huge spaces, superb internal vistas, high ceilings, excellent metalwork and city-centre location. The enormous internal spaces and vistas together with the metalwork were irretrievably lost during the conversion, although it must be said that the final result powerfully demonstrated the primacy of conservation.

One major issue remained unresolved. Many thoughtful observers had long felt that serious art conservation outside London could only be provided in the long term by regional centres serving the needs of all local art galleries and of other institutions in the area holding significant art collections. Specialist conservators and equipment are needed for each different type of painting, drawing, watercolour, print or sculpture. Even the largest provincial gallery on its own could not provide this level of staffing, expertise, tools and machinery. The solution, outlined over many years by various consultants, conservators, trustees and by the North West Museums and Art Galleries Service, lay in the pooling of resources and in the creation of a large central multi-disciplinary conservation studio and laboratory for each area. This was the unrealised dream of the area museum councils and services created in the 1960s. The new splendid Liverpool Conservation Centre had the necessary size, staffing and equipment to fulfil this regional role. However with little or no encouragement in this direction from the trustees, the director and the finance department and even some hostility from the North West Museums and Art Galleries Service, it declined the challenge. The sculpture conservation department under Larson did substantial work for other galleries, institutions and individuals, including the conservation of some public statues, but elsewhere most conservators felt that the needs of their own collections were so great that outside work was impossible. There were of course thought to be administrative, legal and financial difficulties in working for other galleries and collections. Many conservators were hostile to the commercialism and competitive practices which they saw as inevitable once they started working for employers outside their own institution. They may not have realized that their own trustees and directors in the future might find their salaries, building and equipment unaffordable.

Chapter 11

Education

Most European museums and galleries, including the Walker Art Gallery, were established primarily for purposes of education in the widest sense of that word. The first priority was the training of the producer, the artist, but by the 1870s attention had shifted to the education of the consumer, the visitor, the spectator, the general public. Picton's vision for the museum, the public library and the art gallery was that they should provide educational opportunities but primarily for adults. In 1902 education became the most important duty of British city and county councils which naturally encouraged the art galleries in their care to participate in this commitment. By the 1960s many councillors of all political persuasions believed that local authority museums and galleries existed primarily for children rather than for adults and that this was the principal justification for local public expenditure on them. Specialist educational provision was needed for children. The educational needs of adults remained the responsibility of the curators who continued to write gallery guides, lecture on parts of the collection, and work for the Workers Education Association and Liverpool University Extramural Department. With the growth of the National Association of Decorative and Fine Art Societies and the establishment of the Friends organisation in the 1970s they became also in demand as speakers for these bodies.

The larger municipal art galleries could establish educational services more easily than national museums and galleries because they have within well-defined catchment areas a manageable number of schools and colleges, with which they can establish contacts. By the 1920s the curators at Manchester City Art Galleries were instructing selected local teachers in the educational use of their collections enabling these teachers to guide as many as 600 children around the galleries each day.[1] Leicestershire and Derbyshire had opened school museums services before the Second World War. In Leeds, where Lambert was briefly director, the Schools' Museum Scheme was extended to cover the City Art Gallery in 1931 and in that year over 800 children visited the Gallery in 22 parties. By 1937 John Rothenstein together with his assistant director at Leeds were lecturing to large groups of children aged between 11 and 14 and their teachers every Tuesday afternoon. Glasgow Art Gallery and Museum established a formal education service in 1941. It was based on American models familiar to its innovative director, T.J. Honeyman, and it resulted from unusually close co-operation between him and the Glasgow director of education. Bristol City Art Gallery followed with a schools service in 1950 and Sheffield in 1958. The Bristol venture closed in 1960. Most of the early education initiatives were more concerned with museum collections which were often seen as more engaging to children than works of art. In 1928 Miers found little educational activity in either museums or galleries. By 1938 Markham observed some enthusiasm in museums but much less in art galleries.[2]

The Walker Art Gallery had always welcomed school parties, generally escorted by their teachers. They were given free admission to the Autumn Exhibitions, and from 1871 about 8,000 children mainly from secondary schools took advantage of this concession each year.[3] The Gallery's 'Exhibition of Drawings by Children of the Liverpool Public Elementary Schools' of 1912 demonstrated its interest in the work of younger children. In the 1930s free admission to the Autumn Exhibitions was replaced by concessionary admission fees and fewer children came.[4] Once in Liverpool Lambert found that he and his assistant director (the only curatorial staff) could only allocate modest amounts of time to talking to these children owing to heavy demands from other duties.[5] However, by the mid-1950s about 6,000 children were visiting the Gallery annually in parties with large fluctuations related to the exhibitions on display each year. Some children came independently. Until the 1980s a large inner-city working-class housing estate, unnoticed by more affluent visitors, stood immediately behind the Gallery, and some of its younger residents were faithful visitors, not always appreciated by the security staff.

In 1944 the Gallery, while in temporary accommodation at the Bluecoat Chambers, was considering the payment of 'qualified and specially trained teachers' as guides and lecturers for visiting parties – an initiative already successful at Manchester City Art Gallery.[6] In 1951 Liverpool City Council's director of education had hoped that a well qualified teacher might be seconded to the Gallery as a guide lecturer.[7] However the Gallery preferred its own resources. In the same year Agnes Donaldson, who had been Lambert's secretary since 1931, started taking school parties around the Gallery. She had studied art in the 1930s and was good at languages. She gained the Museums Association Diploma in 1950, and her post was regraded in 1952 to reflect her increasing work with schools.[8] She contributed to Ralph Fastnedge's scholarly articles on the collection in the *Liverpool Bulletin*. In April 1957 she visited Glasgow Museum and Art Gallery to study the methods of their schools museums service. Later that year she was appointed as the Gallery's first schools officer.[9] By then she had a very small classroom for lectures illustrated by slides, but the emphasis was on enabling children to experience original works of art first hand. This remained the Gallery's fundamental principle, and the new service concentrated on guided tours around the galleries, not on the lecture or class room and certainly not on practical work in the studio. There was always some pressure for the teaching of painting and drawing, and in 1973 the Gallery was asked by its committee to appoint a teacher to instruct children and adults in these skills in the Gallery's education room. However, co-operation with the City's Education Committee proved difficult and the appointment was never made.[10] Copying the Gallery's pictures in front of them, however crudely, was one thing. Self-expression in a studio was quite another thing, and the Gallery lacked the space and necessary facilities to run practical classes effectively. Art films were of course shown and there were also exhibitions from the Victoria and Albert Museum and elsewhere with works of art appealing to children. In the 1950s a 'Comprehensive Scheme for a Series of Talks for both Primary and Secondary Modern and Grammar Schools' was arranged with the help of the City's education department. It involved 'Courses of Organized Talks', graded for children of different ages and comprising five visits for primary schools and seven for secondary schools. There was naturally a strong emphasis on Liverpool schools since half of the schools officer's salary was provided by the Liverpool Education Committee and the Gallery itself was funded by Liverpool City Council. There does not seem to have been a dramatic rise in the number of school parties visiting the Gallery, but clearly they had a more structured introduction to its collections.

Agnes Donaldson retired in July 1962. In March 1964 Peter Vere, a well-regarded local art teacher, was appointed at the request of the councillors on the selection panel who wanted a new schools officer with this background. In 1965 a special Sub-Committee with representatives from the Education Committee and from the Gallery's Arts Sub-Committee was set up to consider the future of the schools service. They recommended expansion.[11] A new jointly-funded post of assistant schools officer was created in 1967. The successful applicant, Halina Grubert, with a degree in history from the London School of Economics, a postgraduate diploma in education from Sussex University and an M.A. in art history from the Courtauld Institute, had exceptional academic qualifications. Her intellectual horizons were very different from the more traditional outlook of Vere with his Art Teachers Diploma. However in fact she was interested less in art history and in advanced studies but much more in younger children and in social inclusion, which did not become fashionable in art galleries for another thirty years. Through their efforts the Gallery attracted in 1968 over 15,000 children in about 670 groups. This may have been an exceptional year, but these figures were largely maintained for the rest of the century. In the 1950s and 1960s the service concentrated on primary school children probably encouraged by the widespread conviction of that period that young children developed a strong artistic sense sooner and more easily than any intellectual ability.[12] Primary schools continued to provide over half the total number of children taught by the service for the rest of the century. The emphasis shifted however from artistic creativity to the role of artists as illustrators of history and myth. The art advisors at the Liverpool Education Authority began to emphasize the need for positive instruction in crafts and techniques and to recommend less reliance on any spontaneous inspiration within the child. In the early 1960s a spacious extension gallery then used for storage replaced Miss Donaldson's tiny classroom and in 1969 the lecture theatre was allocated to the schools service. In order to make the space as flexible as possible the fixed seats and elaborate stage, which made it one of the best equipped and comfortable lecture halls in north-west England, were removed and a sink for occasional practical work installed. In an attempt to give the service a clearer identity offices were created at the rear of the former theatre. The space dramatically increased the range of activities the service could mount and it was re-named the education service to reflect greater participation from colleges of further and higher education and from adult groups generally.[13]

Guided tours and lectures for adults and students, which had previously been usually the responsibility of the curatorial staff, were organized, especially at lunchtime. The Gallery's education service began to be more concerned with older children and students. For them education staff devised more sophisticated courses exploring issues such as classicism or the rise of landscape painting. Visits were arranged for sixth formers associated with 'A' level courses, and more specialized work with 'A' level art history candidates was undertaken. As early as 1951 Liverpool's director of education had hoped for 'opportunities for groups of teachers to visit the Gallery and extend their knowledge under expert guidance'.[14] Around 1970 courses and conferences began for arts and humanities teachers to enable them to take their own students around the Gallery. Specimen teachers' notes and children's activity sheets were distributed to them. By the 1980s about 900 teachers were visiting the Gallery every year for these courses. Study days and week-ends, involving lectures, art films and guided tours were arranged for undergraduates, for sixth-form students and for adults generally, often in collaboration with Liverpool University. Numbers of participants at these events often exceeded 200.

The grants towards half the costs of the education service from the Liverpool City Council education department ceased in 1974 when the Gallery moved from the control of the City Council to that of the Merseyside County Council, which had no educational responsibilities. This enabled the Gallery's education service to widen its geographical horizons and be more selective in the types of schools and colleges it served. Co-operation with local universities, later an important concern for the Tate Gallery in Liverpool, was not however regarded as a major priority. Family holiday activities were provided during the summer months. Outreach projects involving performance art, street theatre, video and dance outside the Gallery were sponsored and organized by the service at a time when these activities were popular on Merseyside.[15] There was extensive co-operation with community arts projects, particularly the South Liverpool Arts Festivals. A mobile exhibition van service jointly organised with the Liverpool Museum took carefully selected groups of works of art to local schools until increasing costs led to cancellation in 1991. There was greater emphasis on organizing group visits related to particular exhibitions, especially the John Moores Exhibitions. Exhibitors there were asked for 'artists' statements' which were distributed to visitors and students. Tape and slide lectures on their work were organized. Filmed interviews with prize-winning artists in their studios were made and shown to students and to the general public from about 1983 onwards. These explained the various ideas and processes used by these artists in the creation of their paintings. Greater sophistication in these areas was possible with the increasing use of video cameras. The artist-in-residence schemes promoted by the Gallery and the Arts Council during the 1980s gave the education service access to the working methods and to the work in progress of distinguished young artists. In 1980 Ian McKeever, the first artist-in-residence, had for a week a temporary studio in the Gallery's education room where he worked at his paintings and talked to visitors and students. The last artist-in-residence, Adrian Wiszniewski, had his studio in the Gallery throughout his residency, offering very easy public access.

It was still true that only a small minority of Merseyside's children were visiting the Gallery and one solution was to place works of art in schools, rather than to expect the schools to come to the Gallery. It was also hoped that loaned pictures might encourage visits to the Gallery. Nationally the Art for Schools Association had been founded in 1883 with Ruskin as its President to publish and distribute appropriate prints, reproductions and photographs to schools. It remained active until 1922 and in the 1890s it was circulating over 4,000 works each year. Between about 1890 and 1900 the Fitzroy Picture Society and the Ancoats Museum of Art in Manchester were doing similar work but on a smaller scale. In 1919 the Print Society began circulating prints of a rather higher quality both to schools and to private collectors. It survived until the depression of 1929.[16] In the 1930s the Empire Marketing Board and the Post Office were distributing thousands of posters with artistic pretensions to schools for educational purposes free of charge. John Piper and Robert Wellington were trying to interest schools in their higher quality and quite expensive 'Contemporary Lithographs' but without much success. In 1946 and 1947 School Prints Ltd, managed by Brenda and Derek Rawnsley, circulated specially commissioned large colourful lithographs by leading contemporary printmakers, including John Nash and Michael Rothenstein, to schools in editions of about 5,500 for each print. They were intended to give school children 'an understanding of contemporary art', and later editions included lithographs by Picasso, Matisse and Braque. The Rawnsleys' project achieved greater success than the earlier 'Contemporary Lithographs' scheme. Advisors included Herbert Read, the great apostle of modernism, and R.R. Tomlinson, a senior inspector of art for London schools. Both men were deeply interested in child art. For them art, for which children had a natural affinity, should be the starting point for learning.[17] In 1955 the Society for Education in Art organized an exhibition at the Whitechapel Art Gallery entitled 'Pictures for Schools'. The provision of art in schools had been an essential element of the idealism of the post-war national school building programme but outside Leicestershire, Hertfordshire and a few other counties very little was achieved. Artists preferred to work for the generous commissions provided by commercial galleries rather than for the meagre wages offered by local authority education departments suffering from tight budgets.[18] In Liverpool however George Mayer-Marton at the College of Art, who had been one of the Arts Council's guide-lecturers, designed and made ambitious mosaics for some Liverpool schools, relying on their resistance to those problems of vandalism, theft and accidental damage which had resulted in the loss of many works of art on school premises.

The circulation of paintings and prints around schools from museum and art gallery collections was an alternative approach. The Liverpool Museum began circulating its specimens in boxes to schools in 1884.[19] In 1926 Charles Rutherston bequeathed his important collection of modernist British art to Manchester City Art Gallery specifying that groups of paintings from it should be circulated to art schools in the area for short periods. The more important paintings were eventually removed from the scheme but it was extended to all schools rather than just to art schools. Leicestershire and Derbyshire were sending some prints and photographs to schools along with museum specimens in the 1930s.[20] In 1948 the Society for Education in Art held an exhibition at the Tate Gallery with the help of the Arts Council entitled: 'Pictures for Schools'. In the same year London County Council began to circulate 'reproductions of good contemporary work' to London schools.[21]

The Walker Art Gallery however offered original paintings as well as prints to local schools. Security and safety for the paintings could be achieved by careful location and hanging by trained Gallery staff. At first the Gallery's schools loans service was simply an extension of the existing scheme for lending works of art from the reserve collections to municipal institutions, hospitals and other public buildings. In 1934 there were about 170 works, mainly prints, on loan to the Liverpool Art School and to a few local secondary schools.[22] This figure remained fairly constant throughout the 1930s and the works were rarely changed. In 1938 however Markham gave special mention to the Gallery's scheme in his report on provincial museums and galleries.[23] During the war about 66 paintings, 32 watercolours and 40 prints, arranged into some six groups, were circulated around the leading rural independent schools in north-west England. These included some of the most important British paintings in the Gallery by Raeburn, Devis, Madox Brown, Watts, Clausen, Sargent, Sickert, Steer, Conder, Stanley

Spencer and others. They moved to a different school at the end of each term. The motive was partly educational and partly the preservation of the paintings from German bombing raids.[24] Although this was a war-time expedient made possible by the closure of the Gallery it encouraged new developments in the 1950s.

By 1957 about 100 paintings were on loan to ten local schools and in the following year a separate school loans service was created to enable these works of art to be changed more frequently.[25] The Gallery wanted to lend to more schools on a much larger scale, but the late Victorian and Edwardian paintings available for loan were widely felt to be unattractive to children, and many were physically too large.[26] In the same year therefore ten colour lithographs by or after Picasso, Braque, Dufy, Ernst and other modern masters were bought partly to achieve some modest representation of these artists in the Gallery's collection but primarily for circulation to schools.[27] Between 1962 and 1974 about 200 prints, mainly lithographs and screenprints, together with about forty paintings and sculptures, mainly by contemporary or near-contemporary British and American artists, were bought for loan to local schools. The quality was generally high as the Gallery planned to integrate them into the permanent collection once their usefulness for schools was finished. There were British prints by Henry Moore, William Scott, Bridget Riley, Allen Jones and others. American printmakers represented included Christo, Robert Rauschenberg and Andy Warhol. There were paintings by Prunella Clough, Paul Nash and John Minton. The City Council education department provided an annual purchase grant of £500 which was matched by the Gallery. Some early twentieth-century paintings from the Gallery's historic collections were allocated to the schools service and were often given new simple wooden frames to avoid damage to their original decorated gilt frames and to make the work seem less dated.[28] In 1964 ninety paintings and sixty prints were sent to fifty-four schools. Transport difficulties that year were solved by the use of the schools meals service. Loans were generally for a period of one year. All Liverpool schools apart from infant schools could apply for these loans each year, and the selection was made by ballot, as demand always outran supply. Leaflets listing the works available for loan were sent to the schools. In 1973 346 works were allocated to 80 schools. In 1974, with the Gallery now controlled by Merseyside County Council rather than Liverpool City Council, all Merseyside schools were eligible to participate in the scheme, and 281 works were distributed to over 133 schools. In 1975 159 schools borrowed 396 prints and paintings with many schools still left dissatisfied. However with the County of Merseyside stretching north to Southport and east to St. Helens too much time was being spent by the Gallery's staff in transporting and hanging these pictures in distant schools. Essential work on the Gallery's own loan exhibitions had to take priority, and the annual schools loan service was terminated with regret in 1979 with the paintings and prints integrated into the permanent collection. However, small exhibitions involving groups of prints were still occasionally organized for individual schools and colleges which had specific teaching needs.

Scrutton had always been concerned that education and curatorial staff should work closely together. The development of the educational loans service together with work related to the artist-in-residence scheme and to the Gallery's exhibitions generally had drawn curators and education staff together. The next step in this direction was for education staff to organize exhibitions themselves. They organized the displays at the Gallery of the national children's art exhibition provided by Cadbury's, the *Daily Mirror*, the *Daily Mail* and Kellogg's. The exhibition of work by local children, 'How does your garden grow', was arranged to coincide with the Liverpool International Garden Festival of 1984. These exhibitions often encouraged children and teachers to make a first visit to the Gallery. The education department provided 'picture in focus' displays, demonstrating the artistic and social context of particular paintings and sculptures, together with more thematic exhibitions on artists' drawings and similar subjects. They contributed greatly to the arrangements for the Merseyside Artists' Exhibitions, which had replaced the Liverpool Academy exhibitions as the Gallery's showplace for local art in the early 1980s.[29] In 1986 Frank Milner, the education officer, organized an exhibition of the work of the cartoonist Bill Tidy, well known for his contributions to *Punch*, *Private Eye* and other magazines.[30] The opening of the exhibition by Richard Stilgoe was probably the wittiest event ever held at the Gallery. In 1992 Milner co-operated with Morris in an exhibition centred on W.F. Yeames's famous narrative painting of the English Civil War, *And When Did You Last See Your Father?*[31] From the curatorial angle Morris concentrated on the art history, Milner on the reception and popularization of the painting, reflecting, as with the Bill Tidy exhibition, the special interests of an education officer. Still in his quasi-curatorial role Milner published accounts of the Pre-Raphaelite paintings, of the works of George Stubbs and of the paintings by Turner in Merseyside galleries, sometimes covering collections outside those controlled by the Gallery.[32] In his educational role he offered more interpretation and ideas rather than the bare facts favoured by curators, and his books had a national circulation. In 1988 Jane Sellars, who had been lecturing on women's art at Liverpool University and elsewhere, noticed that Philip Rathbone and Lord Leverhulme had bought many paintings by female artists for the Walker and Lady Lever Art Galleries long before the artistic achievements of women had received much recognition. She gathered these paintings together for her very successful 'Women's Works' exhibition. The subject was then beginning to achieve artistic and academic respectability among progressive art historians who praised her useful exhibition catalogue.[33]

The Walker Art Gallery had education staff of exceptional ability. One has recently become director of the Walker Art Gallery. Two others moved on to direct important museums and galleries elsewhere. Another managed a national museum training centre and a fifth became a university senior lecturer in art history. Together with most other major British art galleries, the Walker Art Gallery had always recognised that the education of children and students is a small but very important part of its work. Education can sometimes be delivered more effectively by an outstanding acquisition or a good exhibition. Since its re-opening in 1964 the Liverpool Museum had pursued a very different policy recruiting a large education department and devoting extensive space and resources to it. In 1944 its director, Douglas Allan, who became a distinguished director of the National Museum of Scotland, had foreseen the re-built Museum as a 'Museum of Science and Man', concentrating on education not on collections, and these priorities greatly contributed to its rapid expansion over the rest of the century.[34]

The status of the Gallery's education department did not greatly improve after nationalisation in 1986. It gained an extra member of staff but it lost the old lecture theatre, which became a new sculpture gallery, and it had to move over Mill Lane to the County Sessions House. Largely detached from the Gallery it became a department within the administrative division of the new National Museums and Galleries on Merseyside known as central services. One explanation asserted that 'the advantage of placing the education section within Central Services was the opportunity it would give for Education Staff to co-ordinate their management and organizational approach with the other "front line" services of security, information and commercial services'.[35] Education officers at the Gallery before the merger with the Museum had sometimes complained that their status was seen as lower than that of the curators and conservators, but this new approach offered few benefits. The new trustees were primarily interested in conservation and rather less in education. Thus Milner, the Gallery's senior education officer and formerly reporting directly to the Gallery's director, found himself under a curator of education services who was responsible to the head of education and public programmes who in his turn answered to the assistant director. This imposing hierarchy however eventually unravelled, especially after the early retirement in late 1997 of the assistant director.

In 1997 the Labour party gained power nationally, loudly proclaiming its belief in education. By 1998 its demand for 'social inclusion' had been extended to art galleries and museums, although there seems to have been some official scepticism about their importance in this crusade.[36] Education therefore became essential to enable those outside the privileged and knowledgeable white middle and upper classes to understand art. The Second World War ideals of the Council for the Encouragement of Music and Art, which sent lecturers out to the provinces with its exhibitions, again became fashionable. Some argued that 'learning' should take priority over more traditional art gallery priorities, acquisition, research, conservation, display, storage and even fund-raising.[37] In practice some local, but very few national, galleries and museums changed their policies substantially, just as the leading universities successfully resisted similar initiatives in their fields. The new ideas were however expressed very clearly in yet another government report on regional museums and galleries commissioned in 2000.[38] It was perhaps one of the first official documents to abandon explicitly the so-called 'arm's length' approach to arts funding by which the state and its agencies were concerned with quality in arts institutions but did not interfere with their management or priorities. While earlier reports had emphasized the importance of independent and individual initiatives within regional galleries and the risk that these might be smothered by central government funding, the 'New Vision' outlined in this report was, so far as possible, to be imposed. It was published by the Council for Museums, Archives and Libraries (or 'Resource'), the new government body responsible for allocating government funds to regional galleries and museums, thus greatly adding to its authority. Government recommendations in the past had generally given equal weight to the usual gallery activities but this report devoted most of its space to education and very little to other traditional gallery responsibilities.[39] It also emphasized that the new government funding available to the regional galleries must be largely spent on education and related activities. It was not entirely clear whether the Walker Art Gallery, both a regional and a national institution, fell within its remit, but the frequent references within it to Merseyside indicated that it did.

The National Museums and Galleries on Merseyside had indeed already acted. In 1998 a group of trustees formed themselves into a new education committee.[40] After a detailed report by Eilean Hooper Greenhill of Leicester University that committee recommended that a separate education division should be formed under a new head of education to whom Milner, now with the same grading as the curatorial departmental heads, was directly responsible as the senior education officer within the art galleries.[41] In the new century job titles changed yet again, and the modest schools officer of 1957 became a director of learning.[42]

Abbreviations

AC: Arts Council of Great Britain, London, later Arts Council of England (ACE)
ACC: MCC, Minutes of the Arts and Culture Committee April 1974-March 1986 (NMGM, MM 30)
ACL: LCC, Minutes of the Arts, Culture and Libraries Committee, June 1972- March 1974 (LRO 352 MIN/LIB 1/42-3)
ACS: LCC, Minutes of the Arts and Culture Sub-Committee of the General Purposes Committee, January 1970- April 1972 (LRO 352 MIN/PUR 1/8-9)
ARC: LCC, Minutes of the Arts and Recreations Committee, June –December 1969 (LRO 352 MIN/LIB 1/41)
AESC: LCC, Minutes of the Arts and Exhibitions Sub-Committee of the Libraries, Museums and Arts Committee November 1888- April 1937 (LRO 352 MIN/LIB 2/1-6)
AJ: *Art Journal*
ARBWAG: Annual Report and Bulletin of the Walker Art Gallery, 1971-1976
ASC: LCC, Minutes of the Arts Sub-Committee of the Libraries Museums and Arts Committee January 1957-March 1966 (LRO 352 MIN/LIB 1/36-1/39)
BM: *Burlington Magazine*
G: *The Guardian* (or *Manchester Guardian*)
JHC: *Journal of the History of Collections*
LB: *Liverpool Bulletin* 1951-1970
LC: *Liverpool Courier*
LCC: Liverpool City Council (until 1880 Liverpool Town Council)
LDP: *Liverpool Daily Post*
LE: *Liverpool Echo*
LEE: *Liverpool Evening Express*
LLAG: Lady Lever Art Gallery. Port Sunlight
LM: *Liverpool Mercury*
LMAC: Libraries, Museums and Arts Committee of the LCC. The official title of this Committee varied slightly between 1850 and 1969
LMAC: LCC, Minutes of the Libraries Museums and Arts Committee, April 1850- April 1969 (LRO 352 MIN/LIB 1/1-40).
LR: *Liberal* (or *Liverpool*) *Review*
LRI: Liverpool Royal Institution
LRO: Liverpool Record Office
MCC: Merseyside County Council
MJ: *Museums Journal*
NMGM: National Museums and Galleries on Merseyside, later re-named National Museums Liverpool
P: *Porcupine*
SAG: Sudley Art Gallery, Liverpool or Sudley, later renamed Sudley House
T: *The Times*
THSLC: Transactions of the Historic Society of Lancashire and Cheshire
TM: Minutes of the Meetings of the Trustees of NMGM March 1986-December 2000(NMGM MM 31)
WAG: Walker Art Gallery, Liverpool

Bibliography

AC 1984: *The Glory of the Garden*, London
Ackroyd, Harold, 1987, *The Dream Palaces of Liverpool*, Birmingham
Alley, Ronald, 1961, 'The Representation of Twentieth-Century Foreign Art in British Public Collections', *MJ*, vol.61, pp.21-29
Andrews, Keith, 1956, 'Lithographic "Incunables" in the Print Collection of the Liverpool Public Libraries', *LB*, vol.6, nos.1 and 2, pp.67-72
——, 1989, Obituary by Christopher White in *BM*, 131, 1989: 706-8.
Artmonsky, Ruth, 2010, *The School Prints: A Romantic Project*, Woodbridge
Avery, Charles, 1968-70, 'Bust of a Man by Giuseppe de Levis', *LB*, vol.13, pp.20-25
Bailey, Colin, 1974-5, 'Joseph Anton Koch's *Landscape with William Tell*: An Early Watercolour Rediscovered', *ARBWAG*, vol.5: 60-71.
——, 1975-6, 'The English Poussin – An Introduction to the Life and Work of George Augustus Wallis', *ARBWAG*, vol.6, pp.34-54
Beard, Lee, 2008, 'A Very Interesting Game' in Cheltenham Art Gallery and Museum, *Surrealism Returns*, pp.2-14
Beattie, Susan, 1983, *The New Sculpture*, New Haven
Belchem, John, 2006, 'Celebrating Liverpool', in *Liverpool 800*, ed. John Belchem, Liverpool, pp.9-58
Bennett, Mary, 1958-9, 'William Windus and the Pre-Raphaelite Brotherhood in Liverpool', *LB*, vol.7, pp.18-31
——, 1963, 'A Check-List of Pre-Raphaelite Pictures Exhibited at Liverpool 1846-1867 and some of their Northern Collectors', *BM*, vol.105, pp.486-93
——, 1967, 'Footnotes to the Millais Exhibition', *LB*, vol.12, pp.32-59
——, 1968-70, 'Footnotes to the Holman Hunt Exhibition', *LB*, vol.13, pp.26-64
——, 1986, 'Waiting: An English Fireside of 1854-5, *BM*, vol.128, pp.903-4
Bethell, David et al., 2002, *Public View: A Profile of the Royal West of England Academy*, ed. John Sansom, Bristol
Biggs, Bryan and Sheldon, Julie, (ed,) 2009, *Art in a City Revisited*, Liverpool
Billcliffe, Roger, 1970-71, 'J.H. MacNair in Glasgow and Liverpool', ARBWAG, vol.1, pp.48-74
——, 1985, *The Glasgow Boys*, London
——, 1990-1993, *The Royal Glasgow Institute of the Fine Arts 1861-1989: A Dictionary of Exhibitors*, Glasgow
Bisson, R.F., 1965, *The Sandon Studios Society and the Arts*, Liverpool
Black, Graham, 2012, *Transforming Museums in the Twenty First Century*, London
Bowes, Edwin 2001, *Survey of Fine Art Collections in the Registered Museums of North West England*, Blackburn: North West Museums Service,
Brears, Peter and Davies, Stuart, 1989, *Treasures for the People: The Story of Museums and Galleries in Yorkshire and Humberside*, Yorkshire and Humberside Museums Council
Bridson, Anne, 1994, *Reports on the History of the Creation of the National Museums and Galleries on Merseyside*, unpublished typescript, 1994, NMGM MM45/VIII/27/2-4

Brighton, Andrew, 1993, 'The John Moores and its Critics' in *John Moores Liverpool Exhibition 18*, Liverpool
Brommelle, Norman, 1955, 'Cleaned Pictures at Liverpool', *BM*, vol.97, 1955, p.354
Brown, Roger, 2003, *William Stott of Oldham 1857-1900*, London and Gallery Oldham
[Bukantas, Ann], 2008, 'John Moores Exhibition Fact File' in *John Moores 25: Contemporary Painting Prize*, pp.108-139, Liverpool
Bunce, J.T., 1877, 'Art in the Community', *Fortnightly Review*, vol.22, pp.340-354
Burton, Anthony 1999, *Vision and Accident: The Story of the Victoria and Albert Museum*, London
Caine, T.H. Hall 1881, *A Disquisition on Dante Gabriel's 'Dante's Dream'* delivered at the WAG, Liverpool
Campbell, Julian, 1989, *Frank O'Meara and his Contemporaries*, Hugh Lane Municipal Gallery, Dublin
Cannon-Brookes, Peter, 1968, 'Three Centuries of Sculpture', *Apollo*, vol.87, pp.252-261
Carr, Joseph Comyns, 1883, *Art in Provincial France*, London
Cavanagh, Terry and Yarrington, Alison, 2000, *Public Sculpture of Leicestershire and Rutland*, Liverpool, 2000
Ceulemans, Charles and others, 1990, *Laat-gotische beeldsnijkunst uit Limburg en grensland*, Provinciaal Museum voor Religieuze Kunst, Sint-Truiden
Checkland, Sarah Jane, 2000, *Ben Nicholson*, London
Cheetham, Francis 1966-7, 'Towards a National Museums Service', *MJ*, vol.66, pp.167-174
——, 1968-9, 'A National Museum Service for Britain', *M J*, vol.68, pp.70-3
——, 1974-5, 'Local Government Reorganization and the Norfolk Museums Service', *MJ*, vol.74, pp.27-8
Cherry, Gordon and Penny, Leith, 1986, *Holford: A Study in Architecture, Planning and Civic Design*, London
Chun, Dongho, 2002, 'Collecting Collectors: The Liverpool Art Club and its Exhibitions', *THSLC*, vol.151, pp.127-150.
Clark, Kenneth, 1977, *The Other Half*, London
——, 1974, *Another Part of the Wood*, London
Clegg, Barbara, 1993, *The Man who made Littlewoods: The Story of John Moores*, London
Clifford, Timothy, 1982, 'The Historical Approach to the Display of Paintings', *The International Journal of Museum Management and Curatorship*, vol.1, pp.93-106
Coachworth, D.R., 1979-80, 'Purchase Grants for Public Collections', *MJ*, vol.79, pp.162-5
Compton, Michael, 1958-59, 'A Triptych by the Master of Frankfurt', *LB*, vol.7, pp.5-17
——, 1960-61, 'William Roscoe and Early Collectors of Italian Primitives', *LB*, vol.9, pp.26-51
——, 2005, British Library Sound Archive, National Life Stories, Artists' Lives, Tapes 10-25, F16699, F16700, F16721-F16723, F17626-F17630, F17632-F 17635,

F17638-F17639, recorded in 2005
Conlin, Jonathan 2006, *The Nation's Mantelpiece, A History of the National Gallery*, London
Conway, Lord, of Allington, 1932, *Episodes in a Varied Life*, London
Cooke, Anne, see Melville, Theodore
Cooper, T. Sidney, 1890, *My Life*, London
Cotton, Vere, 1948 'Municipal Art Galleries and Museums', *MJ*, vol.47, pp.177-182
——, 1951, 'Preface', *LB*, vol.1, 1951, p.1
——, 1951, *Liverpool Cathedral: The Official Handbook of the Cathedral Committee*, Liverpool
——, 1970, Obituary in the *LDP*, 20 November
——, 1970, Obituary by Hugh Scrutton in *T*, 25 November
Cox, Trenchard, 1949, 'The Provincial Museum' *MJ*, vol.49, pp.31-36
Cundall, H.M., 1895, 'Liverpool's WAG', *AJ*, 1895, pp.247-251
Curtis, Penelope, 1989, 'Liverpool Garden Festival and its Sculpture', in Curtis (ed) *Patronage and Practice: Sculpture on Merseyside*, Tate Gallery, Liverpool and NMGM, London
Darcy, C.P., 1976, *The Encouragement of the Fine Arts in Lancashire*, Manchester
Davies, Peter, 1989, *A Northern School*, Bristol
Davies, Stuart, 1985, *By the Gains of Industry: Birmingham Museums and Art Gallery 1885-1985*, Birmingham
De La Warr, Earl, 1939, 'Museums and Education', *MJ*, vol.39, pp.286-90
Dibdin, Edward Rimbault, 1888 (1), 'The Liverpool Corporation Collection: The WAG', *Magazine of Art*, pp.14-20, 50-56
——, 1888 (2) 'A Contribution towards the Art History of Liverpool', *Transactions of the National Association for the Advancement of Art and its Application to Industry*, Liverpool Meeting, London, pp.307-317
——, 1901, 'Our Rising Artists: Charles John Allen, Sculptor', *Magazine of Art*, pp.15-19
——, 1904, 'Pictures and the Public', *Pall Mall Magazine*, vol.32, pp.145-155
——, 1905, *Frank Dicksee, His Life and Work*, Art Annual, London
——, 1912, 'The Care of Paintings, Drawings, Engravings and other Art Treasures', *MJ*, vol.12, pp.101-112
——, 1918, 'Liverpool Art and Artists in the Eighteenth Century', *Walpole Society*, vol.6, pp.59-93
——, 1925, 'The Proper Function of a National Gallery', *MJ*, vol.25, pp.61-7
——, 1931 'The WAG, Liverpool, *MJ*, vol.31, pp.87-89
Documents and Papers Connected with Laying the Foundation Stone, the Opening Ceremony etc. of the WAG, Liverpool, 1877, LRO, HF708.5DOC
Dowdall, Chaloner, 1931, unpublished typescript letter of 21 May 1931 to Vere Cotton, Cotton Papers, WAG
Drew, Arthur (ed.) 1978, *Framework for a system for museums, Report by a Working Party*, Standing Commission on Museums and Galleries, HMSO, London
Drinkwater, G.N., 1969-70, 'Picture Conservation and a Training Course in Gateshead', *MJ*, vol.69, pp.15-16

Dyall, Charles 1888, 'Picture Exhibitions: Do They Promote or Impede the Progress of Art', *Transactions of the National Association for the Advancement of Art and its Application to Industry*, Liverpool Meeting, London, pp.290-295
——, 1899, 'William Roscoe and the Roscoe Collection of Pictures, *Art Journal*, pp.266-270
Ellis, Aytoun, 1960, *Heir of Adventure, The Brown Shipley Story*. London
Erffa, Helmut von, and Staley, Allen 1986, *The Paintings of Benjamin West*, New Haven
Egerton, Judy, 2007, *George Stubbs, Painter*, New Haven
Elias, Frank, 1927, *John Lea, Citizen and Art Lover*, Liverpool
Evans, Joan, 1966, *The Conways: A History of Three Generations*, London
Evans, Mark, 1981, 'A Signorelli Drawing for Liverpool', *BM*, vol.123, p.440
——, 1982, 'An Early Altar-Piece by Joos van Cleve', *BM*, vol.124, pp.623-5.
Farr, Dennis, 1984, *English Art 1870-1940*, Oxford
Fastnedge, Ralph, 1951, 'Two Cleaned Pictures from the Roscoe Collection', *LB*, vol.1, no.1, pp.14-23
——, 1953 (1), 'A Restored Work by Signorelli at Liverpool, *BM*, vol.95, pp.271-4
—— and A.F. Donaldson, 1953, 'A Note on an Early Portrait of Politian', *LB*, vol.3, nos.1 and 2, pp.4-11
——, 1953 (2), 'Two Italian Pictures Recently Restored at Liverpool', *LB*, vol.3, nos.1 and 2, pp.15-35
——, 1954 (1), 'A Note on the Roscoe Collection', *LB*, vol.4, nos.1 and 2, pp.23-47
——, 1954 (2), 'A Rediscovered Portrait by J.C. Ibbetson, *LB*, vol.4, nos1 and 2, pp.48-52
Fawcett, Trevor, 1974, *The Rise of English Provincial Art, Artists, Patrons and Institutions outside London, 1800-1830*, Oxford
Fish, Arthur, 1905, *Henrietta Rae (Mrs Ernest Normand)*, London
Ford, W.K., 1955, 'Notes on the Earlier History of the City of Liverpool Public Museums', *LB*, vol.5, nos1 and 2, pp.9-14
Forbes, Henry O. (ed), 1898-1903, *Bulletin of the Liverpool Museums*, vols 1-4, Liverpool
Forwood, William B., 1910, *Some Recollections of a Busy Life*, Liverpool
Foucart-Walter, Elisabeth, 1984, 'Paul Delaroche et le Thème du Passage du Saint-Bernard par Bonaparte', *La Revue du Louvre et des Musées de France*, nos.5-6, pp.367-84
Fox, Caroline and Greenacre, Francis, 1979, *Artists of the Newlyn School*, Newlyn Orion Galleries, Newlyn
Francis, Richard, 1971-4, 'The Red Banquet by R.B. Kitaj', *ARBWAG*, vols 2-4, pp.84-90
Frankfurt, 2000, *Kingdom of the Soul*, Schim Kunsthalle, Frankfurt-am-Main, Prins Eugens Waldemarsudde, Stockholm and Birmingham Museum and Art Gallery
Fry, Roger, 1972, *The Letters of Roger Fry*, ed. Denys Sutton, London
Fullerton, Peter, 1982, 'Patronage and Pedagogy: the British Institution in the Early Nineteenth Century', *Art History*, vol.5, pp.59-72
Gardiner, Stephen, 1993, *Epstein*, London
Gardner, Julian, 1968-70, 'A Relief in the WAG and Thirteenth-Century Italian Tomb Design', *LB*, vol.13, pp.5-19

Garrett, George, n.d., *Liverpool, 1921-1922*, Liverpool
Georgel, Chantal, 1994, 'Budget des Musées sous la Troisième République', in *La Jeunesse des Musées*, ed. Chantal Georgel, Musée d'Orsay, Paris, pp.253-258
Goldhill, Simon, 2011, *Victorian Culture and Classical Antiquity*, Princeton
Greenwood, Royston and Stewart, J.D., 1974, *Corporate Planning in English Local Government*, London
Greenwood, Thomas, 1888, *Museums and Art Galleries*, London
Grimwade, Arthur, 1974, 'The Wavertree Bequest of Racing Trophies', *Connoisseur*, vol.186, pp.239-245
Grindley, B.H., 1875, *Exhibitions of Pictures and Municipal Management*, Liverpool
Grundy, C. Reginald, 1913, 'The WAG, Liverpool', *Connoisseur*, July, pp.145-156
Gulbenkian, Calouste Foundation, 1972, *Training in the Conservation of Paintings*, London
Hackney, Stephen, 'Paintings on Canvas: Lining and Alternatives', *Tate Papers*, Autumn, 2004, www.tate.org.uk/research/tateresearch/tatepapers
Harries, Susie, 2011, *Nikolaus Pevsner: The Life*, London
Harrison, Charles, 1994, *English Art and Modernism*, New Haven
Harrison, Richard, 1971-2, 'The First Seven Years: Reflections on the Work of the Area Councils', *MJ*, vol.71, pp.20-24
Haskell, Francis, 2000, *The Ephemeral Museum*, New Haven
Hatton, Derek, 1988, *Inside Left*, London
Haward, Lawrence, 1922, 'The Problem of Provincial Galleries and Art Museums with special reference to Manchester', *Journal of the Royal Society of Arts*, vol.70, pp.631-642
Heffer, Eric, 1991, *Never a Yes Man*, London
Hill, Joseph and Midgley, William [1928], *The History of the Royal Birmingham Society of Artists*, Birmingham
Holford, William, 1949, *Proposals for the Development of a Site for the University of Liverpool*, Liverpool
Hollis, Patricia, 1998, *Jennie Lee, A Life*, Oxford
Holmes, C.J. (?), 1904, Editorial: 'No Critic Need Apply', *BM*, Vol.5, pp.334-5
——, 1906, Editorials: 'English Provincial Museums', *BM*, Vol.10, pp.3-6, 71-3, 141-3
Holroyd, Michael, 1996, *Augustus John*, London
Honeyman, T.J., 1971, *Art and Audacity*, London
Hooper-Greenhill, Eileann, 1991, *Museum and Gallery Education*, Leicester
Hopkinson, Martin, 1974-5, 'A Fra Bartolommeo Drawing once owned by William Roscoe', *ARBWAG*, vol.5, pp. 50-59
——, 2010 'Art for Schools: The Print Society', *Print Quarterly* vol.27, pp.263-278
Hornel, E.A., 1890-94, E.A. Hornel News-Cuttings Book, Hornel Trust, Kirkcudbright
Houston, John, 1968, 'The Topham Trophy', *Apollo*, vol.87, p.299
Hussey, Christopher, 1951, 'An Art Gallery Transformation', *Country Life*, 19 October, pp.1297-1299
Hutchison, S.C., 1986, *The History of the Royal Academy, 1768-1986*, London
Ironside, R. and Gere, J., 1948, *Pre-Raphaelite Painters*, London
Jacob, John, 1958-9, 'L'Italienne by André Derain', *LB*, vol.7, pp.3-4

——, 1960-61, 'The Liverpool Rubens and other Related Pictures', *LB*, vol.9, pp.4-25
——, 2001, Obituary by Timothy Stevens, *The Independent*, 10 September 2001
Jacomb-Hood, G.P., 1925, *With Brush and Pencil*, London
Jenkins, Hugh, 1979, *The Culture Gap*, London
Johnson, J. and Greutzner, A., 1976, *Dictionary of British Artists*, Woodbridge
Kelly, Thomas, 1981, *For Advancement of Learning: The University of Liverpool, 1881-1981*, Liverpool
Kennerley, Peter, 1991, *The Building of Liverpool Cathedral*, Preston
Kinchin, Juliet and Sharples, Joseph, 2006, 'Glasgow and Liverpool 1900, Commerce, Culture and Identity' in *Doves and Dreams: The Art of Frances Macdonald and J. Herbert McNair*, Hunterian Art Gallery, Glasgow and WAG, Aldershot
[Knight, Vivien] 1999, *The History of Guildhall Art Gallery*, London
Lambert, Frank, 1915, 'Recent Roman Discoveries in London, *Archaeologia*, vol.66, pp.225-274
——, 1936, 'Impressionism and the WAG', *Liverpolitan*, vol.5, no.9, September, p.11
——, 1946, 'The Drury Collection of Alfred Stevens Drawings', *BM*, vol.88, p.155
——, 1947 and 1948, 'Presidential Addresses', *MJ*, vol.47, pp.85-93 and vol.48, pp.89-96
——, 1951, 'The WAG: Growth of a Policy (1)', *LB*, vol.1, no.2, pp.33-40
——, 1952, 'The WAG: Growth of a Policy (2)', *LB*, vol.1, no.3, pp.3-17
——, 1973, Obituary by Timothy Stevens, *T*, 18 January 1973
Lea, John, 1901, unpublished and undated manuscript letter to Chaloner Dowdall, Cotton Papers, WAG
Leighton, Frederic, 1888, 'Presidential Address', *Transactions of the National Association for the Advancement of Art and its Application to Industry*, Liverpool
Le Normand-Romain, Antoinette, 2006, 'When I Consider the Honours that have been Bestowed upon me in England', in Royal Academy of Arts, *Rodin*, pp.119-131
Lewis, Geoffrey, 1989, *For Instruction and Recreation: A Centenary History of the Museums Association*, London
Liverpool Art Club, 1875, *Works of Art in illustration of Dutch, Flemish and Belgian Art*, Liverpool
——, 1881, *Loan Collection of Oil Paintings by British Artists born before 1801*, Liverpool
LDP 1951, *WAG Supplement*, 14 July
Liverpool Worthies (1), *41 Volumes of Biographical Newscuttings*, LRO Eq 330
—— (2), *20 Volumes of Biographical Newscuttings*, LRO Eq 429
LLAG, 1983, *Catalogue of Foreign Paintings, Drawings, Miniatures, Tapestries, Post-Classical Sculpture and Prints* [by Edward Morris and Mark Evans], Liverpool
——, 1986, Geoffrey Waywell, *The Lever and Hope Sculptures: Ancient Sculptures in the LLAG, Port Sunlight*, Berlin
——, 1987, Martin Robertson, *Catalogue of Greek, Etruscan and Roman Vases in the LLAG, Port Sunlight*, Liverpool
——, 1992 (1), Xanthe Brooke, *The LLAG: Catalogue of Embroideries*, Stroud
——, 1992 (2), *Art and Business in Edwardian England: The Making of the LLAG* [ed. Edward Morris, by Alex Kidson, Lucy Wood, Xanthe Brooke, Edward

Morris and others], reprinted from a special number of the *JHC*, Vol.4, No.2, Oxford
——, 1994 (1), Edward Morris, *Victorian and Edwardian Paintings in the LLAG*, London
——, 1994 (2), Lucy Wood, *LLAG: Catalogue of Commodes*, London
——, 1999 (1), Andrew Clay, Edward Morris, Sandra Penketh and Timothy Stevens, *British Sculpture in the LLAG*, Liverpool.
——, 1999 (2), Alex Kidson, *Earlier British Paintings in the LLAG*, Liverpool.
——, 2008, Lucy Wood, *Upholstered Furniture in the LLAG*, New Haven
LMAC, 1852-1962, *Annual Reports*, Liverpool
——, 1951-1956, *LB*, vols.1- 6, Liverpool
Longmore, Jane, 2006 'Civic Liverpool' in *Liverpool 800*, ed. John Belchem, Liverpool, pp.113-170
LRI 1819, *Catalogue of a Series of Pictures Illustrating the Rise and Early Progress of the Art of Painting......Collected by William Roscoe and now Deposited in the LRI* [by William Roscoe] Liverpool
——, 1836, *Catalogue of the Pictures, Casts from the Antique etc in the LRI* [by Thomas Winstanley], Liverpool
——, 1843, *Catalogue of the Paintings, Drawings and Casts in the Permanent Gallery of Art, Royal Institution, opened in January 1843*, Liverpool
——, 1851, *Catalogue of the Paintings, Drawings and Casts in the Permanent Gallery of Art, Royal Institution*, Liverpool
——, 1859, *Descriptive and Historical Catalogue of the Pictures, Drawings and Casts in the Gallery of Art of the Royal Institution* [by Theodore Rathbone], Liverpool
Lynton, Norbert, 2007, *William Scott*, London
Macandrew, Hugh, 1959-60, 'Henry Fuseli and William Roscoe', *LB*, vol.8, pp.4-52
——, 1963, 'Selected Letters from the Correspondence of Henry Fuseli and William Roscoe of Liverpool', *Gazette des Beaux-Arts*, vol. 62
——, 1994, Obituary by Duncan Bull in *BM*, vol.136, pp.553-4
MacColl, D.S., 1892, 'Art: Manchester, Liverpool, Glasgow', *The Spectator* 22 October, pp.497-8
MacCunn, W.S., 1956, *Bluecoat Chambers*, Liverpool
Macdonald Stuart, 1970, *The History and Philosophy of Art Education*, London
——, 1985, 'The Royal Manchester Institution' in *Art and Architecture in Victorian Manchester*, ed. J.H.G. Archer, Manchester
McKinsey and Co., 1969, *A New Management System for Liverpool Corporation*, unpublished typescript, Liverpool University Library, JS3487, M47
Macleod, D.S., 1989, 'Private and Public Patronage in Victorian Newcastle', *Journal of the Warburg and Courtauld Institutes*, vol.52, pp.189-208
MacLeod, Suzanne, 2007, 'Occupying the Architecture of the Gallery: Spatial, Social and Professional Change at the WAG, Liverpool, 1877-1933', in *Museum Revolutions* ed. S.J. Knell, Suzanne MacLeod and Sheila Watson, London, pp.72-86
——, 2006 'Civil Disobedience and Political Agitation: the Art Museum as a Site of Protest in the Early Twentieth Century', *Museum and Society*, Vol.5, No.1, pp.44-57

——, forthcoming, *Museum Architecture: A New Biography*
Markham, S.F., 1938, *The Museums and Art Galleries of the British Isles (other than the National Museums)*, Carnegie United Kingdom Trustees, Dunfermline
Marillier, H.C., 1904, *The Liverpool School of Painters* London: John Murray
Mellon, Paul, 1992, *Reflections in a Silver Spoon*, London
Melville, Theodore and Cooke, Anne, 1962, 'Some Recent Acquisitions', *LB*, vol.10, pp.4-13
Miers, Henry, 1928, *A Report on the Public Museums of the British Isles (other than the National Museums)*. Edinburgh: Carnegie United Kingdom Trustees
Millard, John, 2010, *Liverpool's Museum: the first 150 Years*, NMGM, www.liverpoolmuseums.org.uk/wm/history
Milne, G.J., 2006 'Maritime Liverpool' in *Liverpool 800*, ed. John Belchem, Liverpool, pp.257-310
Montagu, Jennifer 1967, 'Atalanta and Meleager: A Newly Identified Painting by Le Brun', *LB*, vol.12, pp.17-27
Moore, George, 1892 (1), 'Rival Cities', *The Speaker* 15 October, pp.466-7
——, 1892 (2), 'The Alderman in Art', *The Speaker* 22 October, pp.497-8 reprinted in an abbreviated form in 'The Alderman in Art' in George Moore, *Modern Painting*, London, 1897, pp.160-174
——, 1892 (3) 'On the Necessity for a Director of Fine Arts', *The Speaker*, 29 October, pp.528-9
Moore, James, 2004, 'The Art of Philanthropy? The Formation and Development of the WAG in Liverpool', *Museum and Society*, vol.2, No.2, pp.68-83
Morris, Colin, 1985, *History of the Liverpool Regional College of Art*, Unpublished Liverpool Polytechnic M.Phil. Thesis (now Liverpool John Moores University Library)
Morris Edward, 1970-71, 'Alfred Stevens's Bible Illustrations', *ARBWAG*, vol.1, pp.38-47
——, 1971-4, 'Napoleon Crossing the Alps by Paul Delaroche, *ARBWAG*, vols. 2-4, pp.65-83
——, 1974-5, 'John Naylor and other Collectors of Modern Paintings in Nineteenth-Century Britain', *ARBWAG*, vol.5, pp.72-119
——, 1975-6, 'Philip Henry Rathbone and the Purchase of Contemporary Foreign Paintings for the WAG, Liverpool, 1871-1914', *ARBWAG*, vol.6, pp.58-81
——, 1989, 'James Smith of Liverpool and Auguste Rodin' in Curtis (ed.) *Patronage and Practice: Sculpture on Merseyside*, Tate Gallery, Liverpool and NMGM, London
——, 1990, 'Lutyens's Roman Catholic Cathedral in Liverpool: The Restoration of a Great Model', *Apollo*, vol.132, 1990, pp.414-5
——. 1992, 'The Formation of the Gallery of Art in the Liverpool Royal Institution, 1816-1819', *THSLC*, vol.142, pp.87-98
——, 1997, 'Provincial Internationalism: Contemporary Foreign Art in Nineteenth-Century Liverpool and Manchester', *THSLC*, vol.147, pp.81-113
——, 2001, *Public Art Collections in North-West England*, Liverpool
——, 2005(1), 'James Orrock, dentist, artist, patron, collector, dealer, curator, connoisseur, forger, propagandist', *Visual Culture in Britain*, vol.6, no.2, pp.85-98

——, 2005(2), *French Art in Nineteenth-Century Britain*, New Haven
——, n.d., 'Andrew Barclay Walker, John Warrington Wood, Philip Henry Rathbone and the Making of the Statue of Liverpool for the WAG 1875-1877', in NMGM, *Liverpool Renewed* [ed. Edward Morris] Liverpool, pp.6-12
—— and Fifield, Christopher, 1995, 'A.G. Kurtz: A Patron of Classical Art and Music in Victorian Liverpool', *JHC*, vol.7, pp.103-114
—— and Roberts, Emma 1998, *The Liverpool Academy and Other Exhibitions of Contemporary Art in Liverpool 1774-1867*, Liverpool
Morrison, John, 1996, 'Victorian Municipal Patronage', *JHC*, vol.8, No.1, pp.93-102
Murden, Jon, 2006, 'Liverpool: "City of Change and Challenge": Liverpool since 1945' in *Liverpool 800*, ed. John Belchem, Liverpool, pp.393-485
Muspratt, E.K., 1917, *My Life and Work*, London
Muther, Richard, 1907, *The History of Modern Painting*, London
Myerscough, John, 1988, *The Economic Importance of the Arts in Merseyside*, London
National Gallery, London, 1947, *Cleaned Pictures*
Newman, Andrew, 2005, '"Social Exclusion Zone" and "The Feelgood Factor"' in *Heritage, Museums and Galleries*, ed Gerard Corsane, London
Newton, John, 1907, *W.S. Caine, M.P.*, London
[Nicolson, Benedict] 1953, 'Editorial: the WAG, Liverpool', *BM*, vol.95, pp.259-60
—— 1955, 'Editorial: Recent Acquisitions by Museums and Galleries', *BM*, vol.97, p.131
Nicolson, Benedict, 1979, *The International Caravaggesque Movement: Lists of pictures by Caravaggio and his followers throughout Europe from 1590-1650*, Oxford
NMGM 1986-9, 1989-1992, 1992-1995, 1995-1998, 1998-2001, *Reviews*, Liverpool
Nottingham, Lucie 1992, *Rathbone Brothers: From Merchant to Banker, 1742-1992*, London: Rathbone Brothers plc
ODNB, 2004, H.C.G. Matthew and Brian Harrison (ed.), *Oxford Dictionary of National Biography*
Oratory, The, 1991, *The Oratory: St James's Cemetery, Liverpool*, [by Joseph Sharples] Liverpool
Ormerod, Henry, 1953, *The Liverpool Royal Institution*, Liverpool
Ormond, Richard and Leonée, 1975, *Lord Leighton*, New Haven
Orchard, B.G., 1893, *Liverpool's Legion of Honour*, Birkenhead
Panayatova, Stella, 2008, *I turned it into a Palace: Sydney Cockerell and the Fitzwilliam Museum*, Cambridge
Paris, John H. 1945, *English Watercolour Painters*, London
Parkinson, Michael, 1985, *Liverpool on the Brink*, Hermitage
Pearson, N.M., 1982, *The State and the Visual Arts*, London
Pedersen, Susan, 2004, *Eleanor Rathbone and the Politics of Conscience*, New Haven
Picton, J. Allanson, 1891, *Sir James A. Picton: A Biography*, London
Picton, J.A., 1903, *Memorials of Liverpool*, Liverpool
Pope-Hennessy, John, 1991, *Learning to Look: An Autobiography*, London
Pomian, Krzysztof, 1994, 'Musées français, musées européens' in *La jeunesse des*

musées, ed. Chantal Georgel, Musée d'Orsay, Paris
Powers, Alan 1996 'Liverpool and Architectural Education' in WAG 1996 (1)
——, 2002, 'The Reluctant Romantics: *Axis Magazine* 1935-1937', in *The Geographies of Englishness, Studies in British Art*, vol.10, ed. D.P. Corbett and others, New Haven
Prettejohn, Elizabeth, 1994, 'Checklist of Samuel Courtauld's Acquisitions of Modern French Paintings' in Courtauld Institute Galleries, *Impressionism for England*, London, pp.221-4
Rathbone, Eleanor F., 1905, *William Rathbone, A Memoir*, London
Rathbone, Hugh. R., 1924, *Letter to Councillor H.A. Cole, Chairman of the Libraries, Museums and Arts Committee, 11 January 1924*, LRO H 708.5 RAT
Rathbone, Philip, 1875, *The Political Value of Art to the Municipal Life of a Nation: A Lecture at the Liverpool Free Library*, Liverpool
——.1879, The Mission of the Undraped Figure in Art: A Defense of the 'Sculptor's Model', *Transactions of the National Association for the Promotion of Social Science*; Cheltenham Meeting, London, pp.715-2, also published as a pamphlet in Liverpool
——, 1883, *The English School of Impressionists as Illustrated in the Liverpool Autumn Exhibition*, Liverpool
——, 1886, 'The Autumn Exhibition of Pictures', *University College Magazine*, Liverpool, vol.1, pp.286-292
——, 1888, 'Lessons from France as to Imperial and Municipal Encouragement of National Art' in *Transactions of the National Association for the Advancement of Art and its Application to Industry*, London
——, 1892, 'Corporate Management of Art Galleries', *The Speaker* 5 November, p.563
——, 1893-4 'The Liverpool Autumn Exhibition', *The Sphinx*, Liverpool, pp.66-67
——, 1895-6, 'The Whistler Room', *The Sphinx*, Liverpool, pp.33-4
Read, Donald, 1964, *The English Provinces*, London
Reade, A.L., 1929-32, *Audley Pedigrees*, London: Lund Humphries
Redcliffe-Maud, Lord, (ed.) 1969: *Report of the Royal Commission on Local Government in England*, HMSO
——, 1976, *Support for the Arts in England and Wales*, London: Calouste Gulbenkian Foundation
Reilly, C.H., 1921, *Some Liverpool Streets and Buildings in 1921*, Liverpool
——, 1938, *Scaffolding in the Sky*, London
Remy, Michel, 1999, *Surrealism in Britain*, Aldershot
Resource (The Council for Museums, Archives and Libraries), 2001, *Renaissance in the Regions: A New Vision for England's Museums*, London
Reynolds, Simon, 1995, *William Blake Richmond: An Artist's Life*, Norwich
Roberts, Keith, 1970, 'Current and forthcoming exhibitions', *BM*, vol.112, p.553
Rosse, Earl of (ed.), 1963, *Survey of Provincial Museums and Galleries*, Standing Commission on Museums and Galleries, London
Rothenstein, John, 1937, 'The Relation between Schools and Art Galleries and Museums', *MJ*, vol.37, pp.328-335
——, 1946, *Augustus John*, Oxford

—––, 1965, *Summer's Lease: Autobiography, 1901-1938*, London
Rothenstein, William, 1939, *Since Fifty: Men and Memories 1922-38*, London
Rowe, Robert, 1994, *Artefacts and Figures: A History of my Administration of Leeds City Art Galleries*, unpublished typescript in Leeds University Library, Special Collections, MS 1607
Rowley, Charles, [1911] *Fifty Years of Work without Wages*, London
Royal Academy of Arts, 1954, *Works by Augustus John*, London
—––, 1980, *Lord Leverhulme*, [ed. Edward Morris] and organized by the WAG, London
Russell-Cotes, Merton, 1921, *Home and Abroad*, Bournemouth
Rutter, Frank, 1927, *Since I was Twenty-Five*, London
—––, 1933, *Art in my Time*, London
—––, n.d, *Modern Masterpieces*, London
Ryder, C.F., 1992, 'Two Sculpture Displays: The Designer's View', *Museum Management and Curatorship*, vol.11, No.3, September 1992, pp.235-256
SAG 1971, *The Emma Holt Bequest, Liverpool, SAG* [by Mary Bennett and Edward Morris], Liverpool
—–– 1988, *George Bullock, Cabinet Maker*, [by Lucy Wood, Clive Wainwright, Timothy Stevens and Martin Levy] with H. Blairman and Sons Ltd., London
—––, 1992, *SAG, The Emma Holt Bequest* [by Alex Kidson] Liverpool
Saint, A., 1987, *Towards a Social Architecture: the Role of School Building in Post-War England*, New Haven
Sandell, Richard (ed.), 2002, *Museums, Society, Inequality*, London
—––, 2003, 'Social Inclusion, the Museum and the Dynamics of Sectoral Change', *Museum and Society*, Vol.1, No.1, pp.45
Sandilands, G.S., 1960 'London County Council as Patron of Art' I, *Studio*, vol.159, pp.6-9
Savage, Nicholas, 1998, 'The Royal Academy and Regional Museums 1870-1900', in Royal Academy, *The Art Treasures of England: The Regional Collections*, London
Scrutton, Hugh, 1963-1966, 'An early Cézanne, "The Murder" and its Context', *LB*, vol.11, pp.23-27
—––, 1967, 'Some Sculpture at the WAG', *LB*, vol.12, pp.4-15
—––, 1968, 'Estate Duty Purchase and the Auction Room: the Technique under the Finance Act 1930', *MJ*, vol.68, pp.112-115
—––, 1971-2, 'Presidential Address', *MJ*, vol.71, pp.92-7
—––, 1991, obituaries in *The Independent*, 11 September, *G*, 13 September.
Sharpe, Charles W. (ed.) 1909: *The Sport of Civic Life or Art and the Municipality*, Liverpool
Sharples, Joseph, 2007, 'Harry Bates's Mors Janua Vitae, *BM*, vol.149, pp.836-843
—––, see also Kinchin
Sheffield City Council, 1958, Town Clerk's Office, *The Nation's Art Treasures: Record of Proceedings*, Sheffield
Sheppard, David, 2003, *Steps along Hope Street*, London
Simey, Margaret, 1996, *The Disinherited Society*, Liverpool
Slabczynski, Stefan, 1960, 'The Large Vacuum Hot-Table for Wax Relining of Paint-

ings in the Conservation Department of the Tate Gallery', *Studies in Conservation*, vol.5, no.1, 1960, pp.1ff.
Smith, Alison, 1996, *The Victorian Nude*, Manchester
Smith, Bill, 1997, *Hornel*, Edinburgh, 1997
Smith, Charles Saumarez, 1997, 'National Consciousness, National Heritage and the Idea of Englishness' in *A Grand Design: The Art of the Victoria and Albert Museum*, Baltimore Museum and elsewhere, pp.275-283
[Smith, James] n.d., *In Memoriam: D. A. Williamson and W.L. Windus*, Liverpool
Smith, Samuel, 1903, *My Life-Work*, London
Spalding, Frances, 1980, *Roger Fry*, London
——, 1998, *The Tate: A History*, London
——, 2009, *John Piper, Myfanwy Piper*, Oxford
Spielmann, M.H., 1888, 'Current Art: The Royal Academy Exhibition', *Magazine of Art*, p.236
Stephenson, Gordon, 1992, *On a Human Scale*, Freemantle
Stevens, Timothy, 1971, 'Roman Heyday of an English Sculptor', *Apollo*, vol.94, pp.226-31
Stevenson, Moira, 2005, 'From cultural institution to cultural consumer experience: the Manchester Art Gallery Expansion Project', in Suzanne Macleod (ed), *Reshaping Museum Space: Architecture, Design, Exhibitions*, London, pp.65-77
Strathie, Anne and Wilson, Sophia, 2009, *Hugh Willoughby, the Man who Loved Picassos*, Cheltenham Art Gallery and Museum
Strickland-Constable, Miranda, 1974, *City Art Gallery, Leeds: Early Days*, Leeds
Strong, Roy, 1997, *The Roy Strong Diaries*, London
Stross, Barnett, 1947, 'The Museums Service and Government Aid', *MJ*, vol.47, p.159
Summerfield, Angela, 1991 'Hanging Matters: The Revolution in the Display of National Collections', *Apollo*, vol. 134, pp.387-93
Sutton, Denys, 1968, 'Editorial: Change or Decay', *Apollo*, vol.87, pp.238-40
Swanson, Vern, 1990, *The Biography and Catalogue Raisonné of the Paintings of Sir Lawrence Alma-Tadema*, London
Taylor, Basil, 1975, obituary *T*, 12 July 1975
Temple, A.G., 1918, *Guildhall Memories*, London
Thornton, Alfred, 1938, *The Diary of an Art Student of the Nineties*, London
Tietze, Anna, 2011, 'Artistically or Historically Important?', *JHC*, vol.23, pp.165-177
Tiffen, H.J., 1935, *History of the Liverpool Institute Schools*, Liverpool
Toronto 1938, Canadian National Exhibition, *British Painting and Sculpture, Canadian Painting and Sculpture, Surrealist Art etc*, Toronto
Towndrow, K.R., 1942, 'An Alfred Stevens Collection for Liverpool', *BM*, vol.81, p.229
Trevelyan, Vanessa, 1985, 'The V&A grant fund', *M J*, vol. 85, pp.217-224
Verdi, Richard and others, 2003, *Saved! 100 Years of the National Art-Collections Fund*, Hayward Gallery, London
Von Holst, Christian, 1970-1971, 'Three Panels of a Renaissance Room Decoration at Liverpool and a New Work by Granacci', *ARBWAG*, vol.1, pp.32-37
WAG Newscuttings: Five Volumes of Newscuttings on the History of the WAG, LRO

Hq 708.5 WAL
——, 1871-1938, *Liverpool Autumn Exhibition*, Liverpool (held annually except in 1917, 1918, 1931 and 1932, the first six exhibitions held in the Liverpool Museum)
——, 1880, *The Loan Collection of Prehistoric Antiquities and Ethnography*, Liverpool
——, 1883 (1), *Works of Henry Dawson*, Liverpool
——, 1883 (2), *Descriptive Catalogue of the Permanent Collection of Pictures* [by Charles Dyall], Liverpool
——, 1886, *Grand Loan Exhibition of Pictures from the Principal Lancashire Collections*, Liverpool
——, 1887, *Catalogue of the Museum of Casts, Architectural and Sculptural*, Liverpool
——, 1887-8, *Works of Vassili Verestchagin: Illustrated Descriptive Catalogue*, Liverpool
——, 1888 (1), *First Decade: A Report on its Operations from 1877 to 1887* [by Charles Dyall], Liverpool
——, 1888 (2), *International Photographic Exhibition*, (organized by the Liverpool Amateur Photographic Association), Liverpool
——, 1889, *Decorative and Applied Art Exhibition with Essays on the Decorative Arts*, Liverpool
——, 1890, *Winter Exhibition of a Collection of Pictures by M. Gustave Doré*, (organized by the Doré Gallery Limited), Liverpool
——, 1891, *International Photographic Exhibition* (organized by the Liverpool Amateur Photographic Association), Liverpool
——, 1893 (1), *Catalogue of the Roscoe Collection ... condensed from the Catalogue Raisonné, compiled by the late Theodore W. Rathbone with abridged opinions of the critics and experts*, Liverpool
——, 1893 (2), *Spring Exhibition: The Roscoe Collection and Pictures in Oil and Watercolour*, Liverpool
——, 1894, *Spring Exhibition: Pictures in oil and watercolours by local artists, Decorative and Applied Art, Photographic Art*, Liverpool
——, 1895, *Spring Exhibition: Works in Black and White, watercolours, architecture, applied art etc.*, Liverpool
——, 1897, *Alfred W. Hunt: Memorial Exhibition* [by Cosmo Monkhouse], Liverpool
——, 1898, *Spring Exhibition: Arts and Crafts, Indian Art (lent by the Department of Science and Art, London), Architectural Drawings, Photographs*, Liverpool
——, 1902, *Descriptive Catalogue of the Permanent Collection of Pictures* [by Charles Dyall], Liverpool
——, 1907 (1), *Catalogue of the Historical Exhibition of Liverpool Antiquities held...in connection with the celebration of the seven hundredth anniversary of the foundation of Liverpool*, Liverpool
——, 1907 (2), *Memorial Exhibition of the Art of John Finnie*, Liverpool
——, 1907 (3), *Collective Exhibition of the Art of W. Holman Hunt* [ed E. Rimbault Dibdin], Liverpool
——, 1907 (4), *Northern Photographic Exhibition*, Liverpool
——, 1908 (1), *Catalogue of the Historical Exhibition of Liverpool Art* [ed E. Rimbault

Dibdin], Liverpool

——, 1908 (2), *First Liverpool Salon of Original Etchings Printed in Colours, Monochrome Etchings, and Oil Paintings of the Modern and Semi-Modern French School* (organized by the Galerie Georges Petit, Paris), Liverpool

——, 1912, *Curator's Report in response to Councillor H.R. Rathbone's and Councillor P.C. Kelly's motion at the Arts and Exhibitions Sub-Committee meeting of 29 January 1912 asking for a report on the system for buying pictures*, Liverpool, 1912 (WAG files and LRO 352 MIN/LIB 2/2)

——, 1924 (1),*Curator's Report on a Letter from Councillor H.R. Rathbone of 11 January 1924 addressed to Councillor Henry A. Cole*, Liverpool, AESC 13 June and 18 July 1924 (WAG files and LRO 352 MIN/LIB 2/4)

——, 1924 (2), *Report by Curator on Purchases of Works of Art*, Liverpool, AESC 19 November 1924 (WAG files)

——, 1926, *The Gaskell Collection*, Liverpool

——, 1927(1), *Illustrated Catalogue of the Permanent Collection*, Liverpool

——, 1927(2), *Robert Fowler Memorial Exhibition*, Liverpool

——, 1927(3), *Albert Goodwin Exhibition*, Liverpool

——, 1929, *David Woodlock Memorial Exhibition*, Liverpool

——, 1928, Maurice Brockwell, *Catalogue of the Roscoe Collection and other Paintings, Drawings and Engravings deposited by the........Liverpool Royal Institution in the WAG*, Liverpool

——, 1932 (1), *Report of the Director on the General Condition and Quality of the Works of Art in the Gallery*, Liverpool, January 1932 (LRO 352 MIN/LIB 2/6)

——, 1932 (2), *Lancashire and Cheshire Artists Exhibition*

——, 1934 (1), *Director's Report on Future Policy of the Gallery*, Liverpool, AESC 19 January 1934 (WAG files and LRO 352 MIN/LIB 2/6)

——, 1934 (2), *Unit One*, Liverpool

——, 1934 (3), *Samuel Austin Centenary Exhibition*, Liverpool

——, 1934 (4), *Mary McCrossan Memorial Exhibition*, Liverpool

——, 1937, *Joseph Andrews and W. Alison Martin*, Liverpool

——, 1938, *Modern Prints and Drawings*, Liverpool

——, 1945, *Some Acquisitions of the WAG, 1935-1945* (at the National Gallery, London), Liverpool

——, 1949, LMAC, *Report by a Deputation which visited Sweden, Denmark and Holland etc*, Liverpool (LRO 352 MIN/LIB 1/33)

——, 1951(1), *George Stubbs*, Liverpool

——, 1951 (2), *Annual Exhibition of Paintings, Engravings and Sculptures by Members, Associates, and Young Contemporaries* (organized by the Liverpool Academy of Arts), Liverpool

——, 1951 (3), *Alfred Stevens: WAG Monograph Number One* [by K.R. Towndrow], Liverpool

——, 1951 (4), *Guide to the Paintings* [by Frank Lambert], Liverpool

——, 1953 (1), *Kings and Queens of England* [by David Piper and John Woodward], Liverpool

——, 1953 (2), *Liverpool Amateur Photographic Association: Centenary Exhibition*,

Liverpool
——, 1954, *Augustus John in Liverpool*, Liverpool
——, 1955 (1), *Cleaned Pictures* [by Jack Witherop and Ralph Fastnedge], Liverpool
——, 1955 (2), *Vincent van Gogh* with the AC, London
——, 1955 (3), *Selected Acquisitions of the WAG 1945-1955*, Liverpool (also Agnew's London)
——, 1955-1975, *Liverpool Academy Open Exhibition*, Liverpool (held annually)
——, 1956, *Children Painted by Dutch Artists 1550-1820*, with the Cultural Department of the Royal Netherlands Embassy in London, Liverpool
——, 1957(1), Sheila Somers, *WAG Guide*, first edition, Liverpool
——, 1957 (2), *Works by Uli Nimptsch* [by Hugh Scrutton], Liverpool
——, 1957-the present, *John Moores Liverpool Exhibition*, Liverpool (held biennially)
——, 1958 (1), *George W. Harris: Theatre Designs*, [by Hugh Macandrew], Liverpool
——, 1958 (2), *Painting and Sculpture in England 1700-1750* [by John Jacob], Liverpool
——, 1958 (3), *Alan Davie in Retrospect*, Liverpool
——, 1958-9, *Le Corbusier* [by Theo Crosby and others], Liverpool
——, 1958-1970, *LB, WAG Numbers*, vols. 7-13
——, 1959 (1), *The Heywood-Lonsdale Loan* [by Michael Compton], Liverpool
——, 1959 (2), *John Napper Retrospective Exhibition* [by Hugh Scrutton], Liverpool
——, 1960 (1), *Pictures from Ince Blundell Hall* [by John Jacob], Liverpool
——, 1960 (2), *Liverpool Academy of Arts: 150th Anniversary Exhibitions* [by Mary Bennett and Hugh Macandrew], Liverpool
——, 1961 (1), *George Mayer-Marton: Memorial Exhibition*, Liverpool
——, 1961 (2), *French Paintings from the Samuels Collection*, Liverpool
——, 1961 (3), *Personal Choice: Paintings and Sculpture from Local Private Collections*, Liverpool
——, 1962-1970, *Annual Reports*, Liverpool
——, 1963, *Foreign Schools Catalogue: Text* [by Michael Compton], and *Plates* [ed. Anna Goode], 1966
——, 1964 (1), *Ford Madox Brown* [by Mary Bennett], Liverpool
——, 1964 (2), *Masterpieces from Christ Church: The Paintings and the Drawings*, two volumes, [by James Byam Shaw], Liverpool
——, 1964 (3), *Stuart Sutcliffe* [by John Willett], Liverpool
——, 1965, *Industry and the Artist* [by Timothy Stevens], Liverpool
——, 1966, *Victorian Watercolours and Drawings* [by Andrew Wilton], Liverpool
——, 1967 (1), *Old Master Drawings and Prints in the WAG* [by Timothy Stevens and Edward Morris], Liverpool
——, 1967 (2), *Millais* [by Mary Bennett], with the Royal Academy of Arts, London
——, 1967 (3), *John Edkins 1931-1966*, Liverpool
——, 1967 (4), *Life of Christ as seen in the Prints of the 15th, 16th and 17th Centuries* [by Timothy Stevens and Edward Morris], Liverpool
——, 1968 (1), *Twentieth-Century British Drawings and Watercolours* [by Roger Billcliffe], Liverpool
——, 1968 (2), *Early English Drawings and Watercolours in the WAG* [by Edward Morris and Timothy Stevens], Liverpool

——, 1969, *William Holman Hunt* [by Mary Bennett], with the Victoria and Albert Museum, London and the AC, Liverpool
——, 1970 (1), *Taste of Yesterday* [by Mary Bennett, Timothy Stevens and Edward Morris], Liverpool
——, 1970 (2), *English Watercolours in the Collection of C.F.J. Beausire* [by Edward Morris], Liverpool
——, 1970-1976, *ARBWAG*, vols.1- 6, Liverpool
——, 1971 (1), *Charles Towne of Liverpool* [by Mary Bennett], Liverpool
——, 1971 (2), *Peter Moores Liverpool Project: New Italian Art 1953-1971* [by Giovanni Carandente], Liverpool
——, 1972 (1), *Geoffrey Heath Wedgwood* [by Edward Morris], Liverpool
——, 1972 (2), *Maxwell Gordon Lightfoot* [by Gail Engert] Liverpool
——, 1972 (3), *Joseph Gott Sculptor* [by Terry Friedman and Timothy Stevens], with Temple Newsam House, Leeds, London
——, 1972 (4), *French Symbolist Painters* [by Geneviève Lacambre, Mary Anne Stevens, Alan Bowness and Philippe Julian] organized by the AC with the Hayward Gallery, London
——, 1973 (1), *James Hamilton Hay* [by Edward Morris], Liverpool
——, 1973 (2), *Peter Moores Liverpool Project: Magic and Strong Medicine* [by Norbert Lynton], Liverpool
——, 1973 (3), *L.S. Lowry*, Liverpool
——, 1973 (4), *Mark Lancaster: Paintings, Cambridge/New York* [by Richard Francis], Liverpool
——, 1973 (5), *Communication: 18 Works by Members of the Liverpool Academy*, Liverpool
——, 1974, *Victorian Watercolours from the Collection of the WAG* [by Edward Morris], Liverpool
——, 1975 (1), *Ceri Richards and the Metropolitan Cathedral of Christ the King* [by Colin Bailey], Liverpool
——, 1975 (2), *Edward Lear and Knowsley* [by Colin Bailey], Liverpool
——, 1975 (3), *Peter Moores Liverpool Project: Body and Soul* [by Norbert Lynton], Liverpool
——, 1975 (4), *A Selection of Massive Victorians*, Liverpool
——, 1976 (1), *Whistler, The Graphic Work* [by Margaret MacDonald], with Thomas Agnew and Son, London and Glasgow Art Gallery and Museum, London
——, 1976 (2), *The Face of Merseyside*, Liverpool
——, 1976-7, *American Artists in Europe 1800-1900* [by Edward Morris], Liverpool
——, 1977 (1), *Foreign Catalogue, Text* and *Plates* [by Edward Morris and Martin Hopkinson], Liverpool
——, 1977 (2), *The Danson Collection of Paintings by Charles Towne* [by Mary Bennett], Liverpool
——, 1977 (3), *Peter Moores Liverpool Project: Real Life* [by Edward Lucie-Smith], Liverpool
——, 1977 (4), *The Liverpool Academy Celebrates the Walker's 100th Birthday*, Liverpool
——, 1977 (5), *Colin Hitchmough, Six Works* [by Marco Livingstone], Liverpool

——, 1977 (6), *Treasures from the LLAG*, Liverpool
——, 1978 (1), *Merseyside: Painters, People and Places, Text* and *Plates* [by Mary Bennett], Liverpool
——, 1978 (2), *The Rose of Death: Paintings and Drawings by Captain Albert Richards* [by Joseph Darracott], organized by the Imperial War Museum
——, 1978 (3), *23 Photographers, 23 Directions* [by Valerie Lloyd], Liverpool
——, 1979 (1), *Allen Jones 1957-1978* [by Marco Livingstone], with the Staatliche Kunsthalle Baden-Baden and two other galleries, Liverpool
——, 1979 (2), *Peter Moores Liverpool Project: The Craft of Art* [by Edward Lucie-Smith], Liverpool
——, 1980 (1), *Charles Towne* [by Mary Bennett], Liverpool
——, 1980 (2), *Pictures in the WAG, Liverpool*, Liverpool
——, 1981 (1), *Patrick Caulfield: Paintings 1963-1981* [by Marco Livingstone], with the Tate Gallery, Liverpool
——, 1981 (2), *The Art Sheds 1894-1905* [by Mary Bennett], Liverpool
——, 1981 (3), *Islands and Night Flak: Ian McKeever: One Year's Work, 1980-1981* [by Marco Livingstone], Liverpool
——, 1981 (4), *Peter Moores Liverpool Project: Art into the 80s* [by Edward Lucie-Smith], special number of *Art and Artists*
——, 1982, *Retrovision: Peter Phillips Paintings, 1960-1982* [by Marco Livingstone], Liverpool
——, 1983 (1), *Anish Kapoor: Feeling into Form* [by Marco Livingstone], with Le Nouveau Musée, Lyon, Lyon
——, 1983 (2), *Peter Moores Liverpool Project: As of Now* [by William Feaver], Liverpool
——, 1983-4, *Merseyside Artists 1* [ed. Jane Sellars], Liverpool
——, 1984 (1), *Supplementary Foreign Catalogue* [by Edward Morris and Mark Evans], Liverpool
——, 1984 (2), *Dumb Reminders: Graham Ashton* [by Alex Kidson], Liverpool
——, 1985 (1), Frank Milner, *The Pre-Raphaelites: Paintings and Drawings in Merseyside Collections*, Liverpool
——, 1985 (2), *Jonathan Froud: Made up about it* [by Alex Kidson], Liverpool
——, 1985 (3), *Merseyside Artists 2* [ed. Frank Milner and Xanthe Brooke], Liverpool
——, 1986 (1), *Bill Tidy Drawings 1957-1986* [by Frank Milner], Liverpool
——, 1986 (2), *Peter Moores Liverpool Project: Out of Line* [by William Feaver], Liverpool
——, 1986 (3), *Merseyside Artists 3* [ed. Xanthe Brooke], Liverpool
——, 1987 (1) Frank Milner, *George Stubbs: Paintings, Ceramics, Prints and Documents in Merseyside Collections*, Liverpool
——, 1987 (2), *Roderick Bisson: A Survey of his Work* [by Nicholas Horsfield], Liverpool
——, 1987 (3), *Adrian Wiszniewski* [by Alex Kidson], Liverpool
——, 1988 (1), *The East Imagined, Experienced, Remembered* [by James Thompson and David Scott], organized by the National Gallery of Ireland, Dublin
——, 1988 (2), *Women's Works* [by Jane Sellars], Liverpool
——, 1988 (3), Mary Bennett, *Artists of the Pre-Raphaelite Circle: Catalogue of Works in the WAG, LLAG and SAG*, London

——, 1988(4), *European Sculpture 1750-1920 from the Permanent Collection* [by Martin Greenwood], Liverpool
——, 1989, *George Mayer-Marton*, Liverpool
——, 1990 (1), Frank Milner, *J.M.W. Turner: Paintings in Merseyside Collections*, Liverpool
——, 1990 (2), *The Artist at War* [by Angela Summerfield], Liverpool
——, 1990 (3), *Murillo in Focus* [by Xanthe Brooke], Liverpool
——, 1991, *Sam Walsh* [by Alex Kidson and Adrian Henri], Liverpool
——, 1992 (1), *And When Did You Last See Your Father?* [by Edward Morris and Frank Milner] Liverpool
——, 1992 (2), *Why Artists Draw: Old Master Drawings from the WAG* [by Xanthe Brooke], Liverpool
——, 1993 (1), *Arturo di Stefano* [by Alex Kidson], Liverpool
——, 1993 (2), *Derek Wardale* [by Alex Kidson], Liverpool
——, 1994 (1), *Face to Face: Three Centuries of Artists' Self-Portraiture* [by Xanthe Brooke], Liverpool
——, 1994 (2), *Maurice Denis* [by Guy Cogeval, Claire Denis, Thérèse Barruel and others], organized by the Musée des Beaux Arts, Lyon with two other galleries
——, 1994 (3), *The WAG* [by Edward Morris, Xanthe Brooke, Alex Kidson and others] London
——, 1995(1), *Maurice Cockrill; Paintings and Drawings, 1974-1994* [by Alex Kidson and Nicholas Alfrey], with the Djanogly Art Gallery, University of Nottingham, Liverpool
——, 1995 (2), *Concise Illustrated Catalogue of British Paintings in the WAG and at SAG*, [ed. Sandra Penketh] Liverpool
——, 1996 (1), *Charles Reilly and the Liverpool School of Architecture* [by Joseph Sharples, Alan Powers and Michael Shippobottom], Liverpool
——, 1996 (2), *Sir Lawrence Alma Tadema* [by Edwin Becker, Elizabeth Prettejohn, Julian Treuherz, Edward Morris and others], with the Van Gogh Museum, Amsterdam, Zwolle
——, 1996 (3), Edward Morris, *Victorian and Edwardian Paintings in the WAG and at SAG*, London
——, 1997, *Nicholas Horsfield* [by Nicholas Horsfield and John Willett, ed. Edward Morris], Liverpool
——, 1998 (1), Xanthe Brooke, *Mantegna to Rubens: The Weld-Blundell Drawings Collection*, London
——, 1998 (2), *When Time began to Rant and Rage* [ed. James C. Steward], organized by the Berkeley Art Museum, University of California with other galleries, London
——, 1999, *The Black Presence: The Representation of Black People in the Paintings of the National Museums and Galleries on Merseyside* [by Miranda Stacey], Liverpool
——, 2000 (1), *Adrian Henri* [by Frank Milner], Liverpool
——, 2000 (2), *Constable's Clouds* [by Anne Lyles, Timothy Wilcox, John Gage, and John Thornes, ed. Edward Morris], with the National Galleries of Scotland, Edinburgh

——, 2002, *George Romney* [by Alex Kidson], with the National Portrait Gallery, London
——, 2003, *Dante Gabriel Rossetti* [by Julian Treuherz, Edwin Becker and Elizabeth Prettejohn], with the Van Gogh Museum, Amsterdam, Zwolle
——, 2006, Xanthe Brooke, *Catalogue of Foreign Art Acquisitions 1984-2006*, available on-line at www.liverpoolmuseums.org.uk
——, 2012, Alex Kidson, *Earlier British Paintings in the WAG and SAG*, Liverpool
Walden, Sarah, 1985, *The Ravished Image*, London
Waller, P.J., 1981, *Democracy and Sectarianism: A Political and Social History of Liverpool 1868-1939*, Liverpool
Wallis, Whitworth, 1888, 'The City of Birmingham Museum and Art Gallery: Its Development, Its Work and Its Sunday Opening', *Transactions of the National Association for the Advancement of Art and its Application to Industry*, London, pp.297-301
——, 1904, 'Minutes of Evidence', in *Report from the Select Committee of the House of Lords on the Chantrey Trust*, London
Walton, Karin, 1980, *Bristol City Art Gallery: 1905-1980*, Bristol
Waterfield, Giles, 2005, 'A Culture of Exhibitions', *Bulletin of the John Rylands University Library of Manchester*, vol.87. no.2, pp. 21-36
——, forthcoming, *The People's Galleries: Art Museums in Britain, 1800-1914*
Whistler, James McNeill, 1994, *Whistler on Art*, ed. Nigel Thorp, Manchester
White, B.D., 1951, *A History of the Corporation of Liverpool 1835-1914*, Liverpool
White, Adam, 1988, 'Old Masters: Curators and Directors at the Art Gallery through the past hundred years', *Leeds Art Calendar*, No.102, pp.3-7
Whitechapel Art Gallery, 1948, *The Pre-Raphaelites*, London
Whitworth Art Gallery, 1988, *The First Hundred Years*, Manchester
Wilding, Richard, 2006, *Civil Servant: A Memoir*, Stanhope
Willett, John, 1967, *Art in a City*, London
Williamson, Paul, 1990, 'Late Gothic Sculpture from Limburg', *BM*, vol.132, pp.893-4
Witts, Richard, 1998, *Artist Unknown: An Alternative History of the Arts Council*, London
Woodson-Boulton, Amy, 2003, *Temples of Art in Cities of Industry: Municipal Art Museums in Birmingham, Liverpool and Manchester, 1870-1914*, unpublished Ph.D. thesis, University of California, Los Angeles
——, 2012, *Transformative Beauty: Art Museums in Industrial Britain*, Stanford
Woodward, John, 1954, 'Four Royal Portraits at the WAG' *LB*, vol.4, nos.1 and 2, pp.3-22
Wright, C.W. (ed.), 1973, *Provincial Museums and Galleries: A Report of a Committee appointed by the Paymaster General*, Department of Education and Science, HMSO, London
Young, Andrew McLaren and others, 1980, *The Paintings of James McNeill Whistler*, New Haven
Zimmern, Helen, 1885, 'An Eastern Painter', *Art Journal*, pp.9-12, 38-42

Notes

Chapter 1

1 This title will be used throughout the book for this committee although its official title varied over the period 1850 to 1969
2 Ormerod 1953, pp.32-53; Morris 1992 (2), pp.87-98; Picton 1891, pp.197-208
3 This institution has been known by a bewildering variety of names: the Free Public Library and Museum, the Derby Museum, the Derby and Mayer Museum, the Liverpool City Museums, the Merseyside County Museums, the Liverpool Museum and the World Museum, Liverpool. For convenience throughout this book it will be referred to as the Liverpool Museum
4 Millard 2010, pp.1-25; Ellis 1960
5 Picton 1891; Woodson-Boulton 2012, pp.34-8
6 See Morris 1975-6, pp.58-81; WAG 1996 (3) pp.8-15; Woodson-Boulton 2012, p.36
7 Waller 1981 p.68
8 LR 9 September 1893, pp.3-4
9 Rathbone 1875, p.44
10 Rathbone 1905, pp.460-1
11 Beattie 1983 pp.44-5; P 3 July 1875 pp.216-7; LR 8 January 1876 p.9; Reynolds 1995, p.106
12 LR 10 and 24 January 1880, pp.3 and 9
13 Morris 1975-6, pp.58-81
14 LMAC Annual Report 1895-6, p.4
15 WAG 1886
16 LC 21 December 1896; Orchard 1893, pp.619-20
17 Rathbone 1905, pp.460-1; Muspratt 1917, p.252
18 Orchard 1893, p.449
19 *Sunday School Chronicle* 26 January 1905 pp.82-3 included in *Liverpool Worthies* (2) vol.8, pp.197-8
20 P 30 August 1913
21 Elias 1927, pp.25-42
22 LC 10 May 1904
23 Dibdin 1931, pp.87-9
24 Dibdin 1931, p.89
25 LDP 15 June 1939
26 Longmore 2006, p.169
27 LMAC 29 January, 21 May and 31 December 1868
28 White 1951, pp.79-81
29 LR 9 and 16 August 1873; LC 7 and 29 August 1873
30 P 6 September 1873; see Woodson-Boulton, pp.38-9
31 Morrison 1996, pp.93-4
32 Morris 1975-6, p.66; LDP 4 September 1873
33 LR 25 October 1873
34 LDP 11 November 1873
35 Moore 2004, p.73
36 Quoted in Waller 1981, p.515
37 Quoted in Waller 1981, p.98
38 LR 6 December 1873, 26 September 1874, 8 September 1877; Smith 1903, p.126
39 Moore 2004, p.74; MacLeod forthcoming; a copy of the cartoon is in Documents 1877
40 Wallis 1888, p.297
41 LDP 2 April 1874
42 P 21July 1877, p.249; Picton vol. 2, p.496; MacLeod 2007, pp.77-79
43 LR 11 November 1876, p.9
44 Academy 9 October 1875, p.390
45 *British Architect* 6 July 1877; Morris n.d. pp.6-12
46 Reilly 1921, p.70
47 *Builder* 11 April 1874, p.303,13 June 1874, pp.500 and 502, 13 October 1877, p.1022
48 Russell-Cotes 1921, pp.686-695
49 See WAG 1888 (1), 7-9
50 See WAG 1996 (3), pp.1-17 and Grindley 1875
51 LMAC 14 December 1870
52 LM 6 April 1871; LMAC 6 April 1871
53 Morris and Roberts 1998
54 Grindley 1875
55 See Morris and Roberts 1998
56 Cooper 1890, vol.2, p.323
57 LM 15 September 1854
58 Rathbone in LDP 30 October 1888; Forwood 1910, pp.74-79
59 P 5 September 1874, p.36
60 AESC 21 May 1889

NOTES

61 AESC 5 September 1913, 20 May and 23 September 1914
62 AESC 13 June 1924
63 The ownership of these paintings is not very clear
64 AESC 7 April 1916; AESC 20 July 1923; LEE 20 September 1935
65 Elias 1927, p.34-42
66 Jacomb-Hood 1925, p.37
67 Sharpe 1909, pp.20-2
68 Newton 1907, pp.35-45; LMAC 19 April, 26 April and 10 May 1877; LM 7 June 1877
69 Rathbone 1879, pp.715-21; LM 17, 18 and 31 October 1878
70 LR 19 October 1878, p.6; LM 31 October 1878; Morris 1975-6, pp.62-3
71 WAG 1912
72 LM 3 October 1871, 4 December 1873
73 LMAC 29 August 1872
74 LAMC 6 February 1873
75 P 2 and 9 September, 7 October 1871, pp.361, 378 and 438
76 P 7 September and 30 November 1872, pp.364 and 549
77 Morris and Fifield 1995, pp.105-6
78 Ormond 1975, pp.108, 119, 160-161; Morris and Roberts 1998, p.385; WAG 1996 (3), pp.265-6, 371-2; Grindley 1875
79 P 12 September 1874, p.377
80 LR 9 September 1876 p.9
81 LR 14 September 1878, p.9
82 *Leeds Mercury* 18 May 1878
83 LM 7 October 1878
84 Morris 1975-6, pp.62-3; Smith 1996, pp.202-9; Swanson 1990, pp.52, 196; Woodson-Boulton 2003, p.261 and 2012, pp.98-100; WAG Press Cuttings Books; Rathbone 1879, pp.715-21
85 LM 29 August 1891
86 Whistler 1994, p.125
87 See Johnson and Greutzner 1976
88 Campbell 1989, p.29; Brown 2003, p.127
89 Fry 1972, vol.1, p.159; Autumn Exhibition, cat. no. 20
90 Elias 1927, p.49; Gardiner 1993, p.266; LDP 20 September 1926
91 LM 4 September 1886

92 'Autumn Exhibitions', AJ 1886, p.317; see also LR 18 September 1886, p.14
93 Rathbone 1883, pp.1-8
94 Rathbone 1886, pp.290-1
95 Rathbone 1893-4, p.66
96 Rathbone 1895-6, pp.33-4
97 Smith 1997, pp.72-4
98 LE 5 September 1892, quoted in Smith 1997, p.73
99 LM 6 September 1877
100 LMAC Annual Report 1914-15, p.85
101 LMAC Annual Report 1929-30, p.64; AESC 13 June 1919
102 AESC 18 November 1932
103 LMAC Annual Report, 1913-14, p.80
104 See Ackroyd 1987
105 AESC 16 February 1934
106 AESC 15 February 1935; LMAC 28 January 1938; Lambert 1952, pp.3-6; LMAC Annual Report 1914-15, p.85 and 1929-30, p.64
107 LDP 12 May 1934 and 2 March 1936
108 *Axis*, No.5, Spring, 1936, pp.2-19 with many reproductions; Farr 1984, pp.275-7, 287-8; Remy 1999, pp.147-52; Harrison 1994, pp.275-9, 319-21; *ODNB* 2004, vol.23, pp.445-7; Powers 2002, pp.249-74; Spalding 2009, pp.86-89
109 Stephenson 1992, pp.26-30, 44; WAG 1996(1) p.17
110 Cherry and Penny 1986, pp.17-62; Joseph Sharples kindly drew our attention to Stephenson and Holford
111 Toronto 1938, cat. nos. 223-286, pp.49-61
112 AESC 22 July and 16 September 1938; *London Bulletin* 4-5 July 1938, p.40; Beard 2008, pp.2-14; Thornton 1938, pp.95-102; Strathie and Wilson 2009, pp.2-40
113 Remy 1999, pp.147-52
114 LMAC Annual Report 1938-9 pp.53-4
115 LDP 12 October 1938
116 WAG 1978, p.178; Davies 1992, p.150; LDP 30 October 2002
117 Milne 2006, p.286
118 P, 6 September 1873, p.363
119 LMAC Annual Report 1929-30, p.64
120 Hutchison 1986, p.112

121 See *The Year's Art*, ed. A.C.R. Carter, London, 1903
122 AESC 7 April 1891
123 LMAC Annual Report 1902, p.68
124 P 15 December 1877, pp.582-3
125 'Provincial Art Exhibitions', AJ 1880, p.338
126 Quoted in Woodson-Boulton 2012, pp.50-51
127 Macdonald 1985, pp.38-45
128 LM, 31 August 1891
129 Waterfield 2005, p.27
130 'Autumn Exhibitions', AJ, 1884, pp.317
131 Macleod 1989, p.203
132 Moore 1892 (2), p.498
133 Morris 2001, pp.24, 131, 168-9
134 Hill and Midgley 1928, pp.52-53; Bethell et al. 2002, pp.50-56
135 WAG 1967(2) pp.49-50 P 16 April and 29 October1870, pp.14, 322-3; 7 October 1871, p.411, 31 August and 21 September 1872, pp.348, 394, 29 August 1874, p.342
136 P 6 September 1873, p.363
137 LM 10 and 28 November 1890
138 LDP 3 March 1916
139 Willett 1967, p.121
140 Bisson 1965, pp.145, 161, 167, 208
141 Johnson and Greutzner 1976
142 Bisson 1965, pp.153, 157
143 Billcliffe 1990-1993; Macdonald 1985; Hill and Midgley 1928; Johnson and Greutzner 1976
144 Sharpe 1909, pp.20-22
145 AESC 1 April 1890
146 Moore 1892 (2), pp.497-8
147 'Autumn Exhibitions', AJ 1887, pp.349-50
148 Lambert 1952, pp.3-6

Chapter 2

1 WAG 1888 (1), p.5.
2 Morris 2001
3 Dyall 1888, pp.290-295
4 White 1951, pp.15, 79-81
5 See Moore 2004, p.78 for some technicalities.
6 Woodson-Boulton 2003, p.261
7 LMAC Annual Report 1914-1915, p.85,
1929-30, p.64; *LR* 6 April 1878, pp.9-10 and 19 October 1878, p.6; *LM* 31 October 1878; Morris 1975-6, p.62
8 *LM* 5 February 1890
9 AESC 15 October 1889, 15 July 1890, 5 October 1891
10 Rathbone in *LDP* 30 October 1888
11 WAG 1996 (3) p.315; Elias 1927, p.36; AESC 2 September, 26 November and 2 December 1890.
12 AESC 10 January 1913
13 AESC 18 December 1912
14 AESC 18 January 1924
15 Woodson-Boulton 2003, p.261; WAG 1912
16 *LM* 31 October 1878
17 Fullerton 1982, pp.59ff
18 For French provincial museum purchase funds in the 1880s see Georgel1994 pp.253-258
19 See Ormond 1975, p.119
20 *LM* 7 June 1877
21 *LM* 30 October 1877 and 7 July 1881
22 *LM* 21 June, 26 June and 5 July 1877, *P* 7 July 1877, p.216, LMAC 25 June 1877
23 Copies in the LRO
24 *LM* 3 June 1897; Spalding 1998, p.23
25 Moore 1892 (2); WAG 1996 (3), pp.13-15
26 Rathbone 1892, p.563
27 Knight 1999, p.12
28 *LDP* 27 May and 7 July 1904; Holmes 1904, pp.334-5; Ford 1955, pp.9-14
29 Haward 1922, pp.631-5
30 Reilly 1938, pp.124-5; WAG 1996 (3), p.16; Dowdall 1931; Morris 1985, pp.110-111
31 Willett 1967, pp.60-1
32 Dibdin 1905, p.31
33 Dibdin 1888 (1) and 1904
34 Dibdin 1888 (2) pp.307-317; Dibdin 1918, pp.59-93
35 Dibdin 1901, pp.15-19
36 Willett 1967, p.61; *T* 13 July 1925; Dibdin 1925, pp.61-7
37 *LDP* 30 October 1941
38 LMAC 26 July 1912
39 Wallis 1904, pp.149-153
40 *LDP* 7 July 1904
41 Rutter 1927, pp.200-210
42 *LDP* 28 March 1931 and 18 December

1945
43 Woodson-Boulton 2003, p.261
44 WAG 1988 (2)
45 *LM* 31 October 1878
46 *LM* 8 September 1881
47 WAG 1988 (3), pp.176-7; Morris 1975-6, p.63
48 Caine 1881
49 *Athenaeum* 13 September 1884, p.344
50 *LM* 15 October 1891 (letter from Dyall)
51 Spielmann 1888, p.236
52 Erffa, von and Staley 1986, p.347
53 AESC 27 November 1888; LMAC 13 December 1888; *LM* 13 December 1888
54 Conway 1932, pp.85-6
55 Picton 1891, p.381; Leighton 1888, pp.16-35
56 *LM* and *LC* 3 January 1889
57 Forwood 1910, p.76
58 *LR* 5 January 1889, p.5
59 LMAC 3 and 10 January and 13 February 1889
60 *Manchester T* 9 March 1889
61 WAG 1988 (3), pp.91-94
62 Young 1980, pp.105-6
63 Undated MSS letters from Whistler to his wife and from Stevenson to Whistler at Glasgow University Library (MS Whistler W591 and R241, www.whistler.arts.gla.ac.uk)
64 WAG 1996 (3), pp.11-12, 54-5, 144-5, 185-8, 463-4
65 *LE* 5 September 1892, quoted in Smith 1997, p.73
66 *LM* 6 and 27 October 1892
67 WAG 1996 (3), pp.11-13; Billcliffe 1985, pp.252-4; Smith 1997, pp.71-7; Brown 2003, pp.104-5; *P* 10 and 17 September and 8 October 1892; *LDP* 13 and 14 October 1892; Hornel 1890-1894; Moore 1892 (2) pp.497-8
68 *LC* 14 September 1892 quoted in Smith 1997, p.73
69 *LM* and *LC* 23 November 1895
70 Rathbone 1905, pp.460-1
71 WAG 1992
72 WAG 1888 (1), p.5
73 Sharples 2007, pp.836-43

74 Morris 1975-6, pp. 59-67; Morris 2005(2), p.143; Alley 1961
75 WAG 1886
76 Morris 2001, p.168
77 *LM* 8 May 1886
78 Morris 1974-5 pp.72-119
79 Chun 2002; Liverpool Art Club 1881
80 Marillier, 1904, pp.41-2
81 Kelly 1981, p.139
82 Cotton 1951, p.56
83 *LDP* 17 and 19 April 1923; Orchard 1893, p.638; Tiffen, 1935, p.777
84 Morris 1989, pp.67-73
85 Le Normand-Romain 2006, pp.119-131
86 Reade 1929-32, pp.307-11
87 Morris 2001, pp.38, 172
88 Morris 1992, pp.87-98
89 Evans 1966, p.113
90 Dyall 1899, p.268
91 *LM* 19 December 1892 and 5 January 1893. Ormerod 1953, pp.33-5, 59-62. WAG 1893(1) and (2); Dyall 1899, p.267
92 WAG 1928
93 *P* 26 September 1874, p.409
94 Marillier 1904, p.40
95 WAG 1908 (1)
96 Especially Dibdin 1888 (2)
97 *LC* 2 January 1917: *LDP* 4 January 1917
98 [Smith] n.d p.22
99 Holmes 1906, pp.3-6, 71-3, 141-3
100 Martin Hopkinson, e-mail 19 March 2010
101 Grundy 1913, pp.145-156
102 Cundall 1895, pp.247-251
103 Moore 1892 (1) pp.466-7; Moore 1892 (2), pp.497-8; Moore 1892 (3), pp.528-9; MacColl 1892 pp.497-8
104 *LC* 13 June 1901
105 Lea 1901
106 Dowdall 1931
107 Sharpe 1909, p.12; Bisson 1965, pp.47-9
108 Rutter 1927, p.201 and 1933, p.86
109 Rothenstein 1965, p.176
110 Marillier 1904 pp.25, 113
111 Rowley 1911, p.79
112 AESC 29 January 1912, 13 June and 18 July 1924; WAG 1912; WAG 1924 (1); Rathbone 1924

113 WAG 1912
114 AESC 13 June 1924
115 AESC 19 November and 5 December 1924
116 Woodeson-Boulton 2003, p.261
117 Rathbone 1886, p.288
118 'The Royal Academy', *Spectator*, 29 May 1886, p.719
119 'Art Notes', *AJ*, 1886, p.320
120 WAG 1996 (3), pp.188-9
121 See particularly Fox and Greenacre 1979, pp.173-185
122 Sharpe 1909, p.10
123 Macleod 1989, pp.189-208; Brears and Davies 1989, pp.54-7
124 *LDP* 4 November 1912; *LC* 5 November 1912
125 MacLeod 2007, pp.74-84

Chapter 3

1 See Waller 1981, pp.274-280
2 Pedersen 2004, pp.56-58
3 Nottingham 1992, pp.72-90
4 Kelly 1981, pp.292-305, 519-20; Cotton 1970 (Liverpool); Cotton 1970; Cotton 1951 p.127
5 *LDP* 2 April 1931; LDP 1951, p.1
6 Panayotova 2008; Davies 1985, pp26-57
7 *LDP* 25 April 1931
8 Lambert 1952, p.9
9 *LDP* 19 December 1931
10 WAG 1932 (1)
11 Dibdin 1931, pp.87-8
12 Rothenstein 1965, p.213
13 Davies 1985, p.18; see also Woodeson-Boulton 2012, p.169
14 Smith 1997, pp.275-283
15 WAG1927(1), p.ix
16 WAG 2012, pp.xvi-xxi, 312
17 Rothenstein 1965, pp.192, 199
18 *LDP* 10 June 1931;*LEE* 2 October 1931.
19 Rothenstein 1965 pp.176-7; LMAC 2 October 1931
20 Information kindly supplied by John Clark of the Museum of London; see particularly Lambert 1915, pp.225-274
21 Dibdin 1925, pp.61-7

22 Rothenstein 1965, p.194; Compton 2005 and e-mail 24 May 2011; White 1988, pp.5-6
23 Rothenstein 1965 pp.191-6
24 White 1988, p.5
25 Cotton 1948, p.178
26 Lambert 1947 pp. 85-93 and 1948 pp.89-96
27 Lambert 1952, p.9
28 Cotton 1970
29 Woodson-Boulton 2012, p.168
30 Lambert 1952, p.16
31 AESC 7 February 1913.
32 Dibdin 1925, pp.61-67
33 Lambert 1936, p.11
34 Cotton 1948, pp.177-182; LDP 1951, p.1
35 LDP 1951, p.1
36 WAG 1934(1)
37 Prettejohn 1994 pp.221-4; Lambert 1936, p.11; Lambert 1947 pp.85-93
38 LMAC 14 November 1947; *LE* 28 November 1947
39 Lambert 1952, p.16
40 Rothenstein 1946, pl.39
41 Holroyd 1996, pp.287-93
42 WAG 1945, pp.1-3
43 Royal Academy 1954, No.337; WAG 1954
44 Nicolson 1979, p.46
45 Lambert 1952, p.10
46 LMAC 14 September 1951
47 *Ibid.*
48 Lambert 1946, p.155; Towndrow 1942, p.229; Morris 1970-71, pp.38-47
49 WAG 1951(3), p.5
50 LMAC 26 January 1945
51 Nottingham 1992 pp.66-7
52 Morris 1974-5, pp.77-101
53 SAG 1971; *LC* and *LDP* 4 April 1896
54 LMAC 14 March 1947
55 *LE* 18 July 1947
56 WAG 1945
57 LMAC 17 June 1949; *LDP* 27 May 1949
58 LMAC 14 June 1946; *LDP*, 12 October 1946
59 WAG 1949
60 Belchem 2006 p.46
61 *LDP* 4 May 1950
62 Macleod 2006, pp.44-57; Garrett, n.d., pp.11-22

63 LMAC 15 September 1950 and 19 January 1951
64 LMAC 16 December 1949
65 LDP 1951, p.1; Hussey 1951, pp.1297-1299
66 Spalding 1980, p.258
67 *Courtauld Association News* March 1994
68 Libraries Museums and Arts Committee, Annual Report, 1951-2, p.3
69 *LDP*, 18 September 1951
70 Nicholson 1953, pp.259-60
71 LMAC 13 February 1953
72 AESC 28 January 1938
73 *T* 4 December 1986
74 Tietze 2011, pp.170-1
75 Rowe 1994, p.70; Compton 2005 and e-mail 24 May 2011
76 Dr Peter Kidson, verbally 22 January 2010
77 Rowe 1994, p.532
78 WAG 1955; Fastnedge, 1953 (1), pp.271-4
79 Fastnedge 1951, pp.14-23; Fastnedge 1953 (2), pp.15-35; Fastnedge and Davidson 1953, pp.4-11; Fastnedge 1954 (1), pp.23-47; Fastnedge 1954 (2), pp.48-52
80 LMAC 1951-1956, WAG 1958-1970
81 Millard 2010, p.36; Forbes 1898-1903; Ford 1955, pp.13-14
82 Honeyman 1971, pp.115-119; White 1988, p.7
83 Cotton 1951, p.1
84 Woodward 1954; Bennett 1958-9, pp.18-31; Macandrew 1959-60, pp.4-52; Compton 1960-61, pp.26-51; Bennett 1967, pp.32-59; Bennett 1968-70, pp.26-74
85 Billcliffe 1970-1, pp.48-74; Morris 1971-4, pp.65-83; Francis 1971-4, pp.84-90; Bailey 1974-5, pp.60-71; Bailey 1975-6, pp.34-54
86 WAG 1951(3)
87 TM 6 December 1988
88 White 1988, pp.3-7; Davies 1985, p.73; Rothenstein 1965, pp.191-230; Rutter 1927, pp.200-210

Chapter 4

1 Burton 1999, p.89
2 Bunce 1877, p.343; Read 1964, p.266
3 *T* 16 August, 30 August and 8 September, 1880
4 *Builder*, 4 December 1880, pp.669-70
5 House of Commons Debates, 8 August 1881 and 3 April 1882, *Hansard*, vol.264, 1236-1265, vol. 268, 576-98
6 *LM* 9 March 1882
7 Carr 1883, pp.9-10; Pomian 1994, p.355
8 Greenwood 1888, pp.10, 20-25
9 Coachworth 1979-80, pp.162-5; Trevelyan 1985, pp. 217-224
10 Rathbone 1888, p.396; Janet Davies kindly provided the figures
11 Read 1964, pp.224-267
12 Markham 1938, p.171; Rosse 1963, p.5; Miers 1928, pp. 72 and 81; Lewis 1989, pp.56-7; De La Warr 1939, pp.286-90
13 'Museums and Art Galleries: A National Service', *MJ*, vol.45, 1945, pp.33-45
14 For example: House of Commons Debates, 13 February 1951, 15 February 1951, 26 June 1956, *Hansard*, vol.484, 199 and 591, vol.555, 35-36W
15 Stross 1947, p.159; 'Editorial', *MJ*, vol.48, 1948, p.65; Lambert 1948, pp.89-96
16 Holford 1949
17 Cotton 1948, p.180
18 Unidentified press-cutting in WAG *Newscuttings*
19 *T* 31 October 1955
20 'The Philistines', *MJ*, vol.56, 1956, pp.207-8
21 *T* 11 July 1958.
22 House of Commons 25 January 1944, *Hansard*, vol.396, 538-9
23 Rosse 1963, pp.7, 55,78-9
24 AC Annual Report 1954-5, pp.27-8
25 Clark 1977, p.136
26 See for example AC Annual Report 1983-4, pp.45-6, 1984-5, pp.45-6.
27 Pearson 1982, pp.65-6; Witts 1998, pp.384-5
28 Rowe 1994, pp.620-664; AC Annual Report, 1976-7, p.119, 1977-8, p.120, 1978-9, p.125, 1979-80, pp.82, 129,1980-

81, pp.74, 121, 1981-2, p.43, 1982-3, p.51
29 AC 1984, pp.13-14
30 AC Annual Report, 1985-6, pp.15, 52
31 Witts 1998, pp.389-90
32 AC Annual Report 1985-6, pp.52-3, 1987-8, p.73
33 Resource 2001, p.88
34 See Jenkins 1979
35 Wright 1973, pp.2, 16-17, 48-51
36 ACC 13 December 1973
37 WAG, *Annual Report and Bulletin*, Vols.2-4, 1971-4, pp.62-4
38 Redcliffe-Maud, 1976
39 Jenkins 1979, p.107
40 House of Lords 31 October 1979, *Hansard*, vol.402, 435-77
41 Drew 1978
42 Rosse 1963, p.67
43 Walton 1980, pp.31-2
44 Wright 1973, pp.29-52
45 Harrison 1971-2, pp.20-24
46 'The Annual Conference in Dundee', *MJ*, vol.73, 1973, pp.120-122; Resource 2001, p.102
47 Morris 2001 and Bowes 2001, pp.52-3
48 ASC 1 February 1962; LMAC 13 April 1962
49 Willett 1967, p.81
50 Hugh Scrutton's record of his meeting with Robert Rowe, 23 May 1966
51 ASC 12 July 1963; LMAC, 13 September 1963
52 Drew 1978 p.78
53 *T* 7 February 1958
54 Sheffield 1958
55 ASC 13 September 1957, 15 November 1957, 17 January 1958
56 'The Annual Conference in Sheffield', *MJ*, vol.66, 1966, pp.92-127; Hollis 1998, pp.246-296; 'The Annual Conference in Durham' *MJ*, vol.75, 1975, pp.ix-xi
57 WAG, *Annual Report*, 1965-6, p.4
58 Cheetham 1966-7, pp.167-174 and 1968-9, pp.70-3
59 Sutton 1968, pp.238-40
60 Strong 1998, p.23; Pope-Hennessy 1991, p.163
61 Hugh Scrutton's record of his meeting with Michael Walker, 27 August 1968
62 Lewis 1989
63 *T* 6 June 1973

Chapter 5

1 LMAC 14 December 1951
2 *LE* 11 February 1952
3 *T* 15 January 1975
4 Sandilands 1960, p.8
5 ASC 10 June 1960
6 Clark 1977, p.3
7 Scrutton 1971-2, pp.92-7
8 WAG 1959 (2); *LE* 5.7 and 11 May 1953; *LDP* 5 May 1953
9 *LE* 8 January 1955
10 *LE* 26 February 1954
11 Hugh Scrutton to Alderman Sir Alfred Shennan 24 August 1953
12 LMAC 2 February 1967.
13 Christie's Sale, London, 14 March 1947
14 LMAC 16 June 1950
15 LMAC 18 December 1953
16 LMAC 18 September 1953
17 Nicolson 1955, p.131
18 LMAC 13 November 1964
19 'The Annual Conference in Sheffield', *MJ*, vol.66, 1966, p.127
20 Davies 1985, p.74
21 *LDP* 21 November 1956.
22 LMAC 7 March 1955
23 Compton 2005
24 ASC 28 July 1960
25 ACC 3 September 1981
26 Wright 1973, pp.80-90
27 Hugh Scrutton to Alderman Harold Hughes 1 November 1967
28 ASC 12 February 1960
29 ASC 10 April 1964
30 Libraries, Museums and Arts Committee, *Annual Report* 1956-7, pp.53-4
31 LRI 1819, 1836, 1843, 1851, 1859, WAG 1928
32 Montagu 1967, pp.17-27
33 AESC 4 February and 10 March 1916, 16 November 1917; LMAC 21 December 1917
34 Picton 1891, pp.225-6

35 LMAC 9 April 1954; LMAC (Libraries Sub-Committee) 15 October 1954
36 Andrews 1989
37 Spalding 1998, pp.167-8
38 Andrews 1956, pp.67-72
39 Rowe 1994, p.170
40 ASC 15 July 1957
41 WAG 1963
42 Compton 2005; his e-mail of 19 April 2005
43 WAG 1967 (1) and 1968 (2)
44 WAG 1977 (1) and 1984 (1)
45 WAG 1978 (1)
46 LLAG 1983, 1986, 1987, 1992(1), 1994(1), 1994(2), 1999(1), 1999(2) and WAG 1988(3)
47 ASC 11 July 1958
48 Rowe 1994 pp.470-3
49 *LDP* 16 March 1957
50 ASC 8 September 1958
51 *LDP*, 10 November 1954
52 ASC 19 December 1958
53 *LDP* 25 and 29 January 1968
54 AC Annual Report, 1955-6, pp.27-8
55 *T* 31 December 1959 and 7 January 1960
56 Jacob 1960-1961, pp.4-25
57 Jacob 1958-9, pp.3-4
58 *LDP* 14 February and 13 June 1959
59 *LDP* 1951, p.1
60 Libraries Museums and Arts Committee Annual Report 1960-61, p.50
61 Michael Compton e-mail 19 April 2011
62 See Waller 1981, pp.274-80
63 WAG 1961(3)WAG *Annual Report* 1969-70, p.7; Willett 1967, pp.71-3
64 Melville and Cooke 1962, pp.4-9
65 Scrutton 1963-66, p.25
66 Verdi and others 2003, p.176
67 Scrutton 1968, pp.112-5
68 ASC 12 October 1962
69 Hugh Scrutton to Alderman Reginald Bailey 11 October 1962 and to Ben Shaw 3 June 1964
70 Libraries, Museums and Arts Committee Annual Report 1953-4, p.45
71 Melville and Cooke 1962, pp.9-10
72 WAG 1970 (2)
73 LMAC 19 December 1968; TM 27 June 1995
74 NMGM *Review* 1995-1998, p.12
75 WAG *Annual Report* 1963-4 p.6
76 ASC 10 June 1960
77 ASC 10 September 1965; *LDP* 11 September 1965
78 Panayatova 2008, pp.73-5
79 White 1988, p.4
80 WAG 1912; AESC 10 March 1916
81 WAG 1924
82 Honeyman 1971, pp.113-119
83 Walton 1980, p.35
84 Spalding 1998, pp.134-6, 150-1
85 ACL 13 June 1972 and 9 January 1973
86 Cannon-Brookes 1968, pp.252-261
87 Scrutton 1967, pp.4-15
88 LMAC 15 September 1966; Scrutton to Councillor Thomas Greenwood 20 September 1966
89 Melville and Cooke 1962, p.10; WAG 1977(1) p.335
90 Jacob 2001
91 WAG 1977(1) pp.312-3; Ceulemans and others 1990; Williamson 1990, pp.893-4
92 AESC 17 January and 13 March 1936; LMAC 18 March 1960
93 WAG 1977(1) pp.310,327
94 Scrutton 1967, pp.4-15; Gardner 1968-70, pp.5-19; Avery 1968-70, pp.20-25; WAG 1977(1) pp.289, 323, 327, 286
95 Hopkinson 1974-5, pp.50-59
96 WAG 1998 (1)
97 Bennett 1958-9, pp.19-31
98 Stevens 1971, pp.226-31
99 Morris 1971-4, pp.65-83; Morris 1974-5, pp.72-101; Foucart-Walter 1984, pp.367-84
100 See Von Holst 1970-1971, pp.32-37
101 WAG 1970 (1)
102 Roberts 1970, p.553
103 ASC 17 January and 21 February 1958; *LDP* 22 February 1958; Willett 1967, p.115
104 Lynton 2007, p.206; Inv. No. AM3713P at the Musée Nationale; Lucy Inglis e-mail 17 May 2011
105 Checkland 2000, p.274
106 *LDP* 14 November 1963
107 ARC 23 October 1969
108 *LDP* 15 December 1970
109 Waller 1981, p.350

110 Greenwood and Stewart 1974, pp.115-125, 225-233, 515-525 with many extracts from McKinsey's Liverpool documents
111 Rowe 1994, p.461
112 House of Lords 31 October 1979, *Hansard* vol.402, 435-77
113 Simey 1996, pp.122-123
114 McKinsey and Co., 1969, 3, 2.1,5
115 Spalding 1998, pp.142-3

Chapter 6

1 Rosse 1963, p.162
2 Spalding 1998, pp.93, 144, 192, 204
3 Conlin 2006, p.425
4 *G* 13 September 2001
5 Liverpool City Council, Policy and Finance Committee 28 July 1971 (Liverpool Record Office 352 MIN/FIN II / 131)
6 Redcliffe-Maud 1969
7 Wright 1973, pp.51-2
8 Their circular 17/23
9 'The Annual Conference in Dundee', *MJ*, vol.73,1973, pp.120-122
10 Whitworth Art Gallery 1988, p.14
11 *T* 15 January 1975 and 15 January 1976
12 Cheetham 1974-5 pp.27-28
13 Rowe, p.611
14 John Millard e-mail July 2009
15 Witts 1998, p.316
16 ACC 19 September 1974
17 ACC 18 July 1975
18 *T* 31 December 1975 and 4 February 1976
19 ACC 11 February 1974
20 ACC 27 June 1974
21 *T* 9 December 1977, letter from John Last
22 Bailey 1974-5, p.61
23 Christie's Sale 19 September 1973
24 ACC 19 September 1974
25 Oratory 1991, pp.1-13
26 Walton 1980, pp.14-15
27 ACC 10 March 1977
28 ACC 2 March 1978
29 ACC 16 November 1978 and 30 April 1979
30 Royal Academy 1980
31 TM 3 November 1987, 16 February 1988
32 LLAG 1992 (2)
33 LLAG 1983, LLAG 1986, LLAG 1987, LLAG 1992 (1), LLAG 1994 (2), LLAG 1994 (1), LLAG 1999 (1), LLAG 1999 (1), LLAG 2008
34 WAG 1988 (3)
35 TM 15 April 1986
36 ACC 15 January 1976
37 Evans 1981, p.440
38 Evans 1982, pp.623-5
39 Bennett 1986, pp.903-4
40 See Billcliffe 1970-71
41 Bailey 1975-6, pp.34-5
42 Davies 1985 p.105; Rowe 1994, pp.3-40
43 Walton 1980 p.35
44 Black 2012, p.205
45 Resource 2001

Chapter 7

1 See particularly Bridson 1994 for details of the nationalisation process.
2 Spalding 1998, p.225
3 Hatton 1988, pp.56-110; Parkinson 1985
4 Belchem 2006, p.461
5 Wilding 2006, p.103
6 *T* 11 April 1984
7 See for example Sheppard 2003, p.229
8 *LE* 5 March 1985
9 TM 18 September 1990 and 27 June 1995
10 TM 3 March 1986
11 TM 3 March 1986
12 Rosse 1963, pp.82-230
13 Rowe 1994, pp.467-8
14 Honeyman 1971, p.240-2
15 Lewis Biggs, 'Individuals and Institutions in Dialogue' in Biggs and Sheldon 2009, p.38
16 Myerscough 1988; Sara Selwood, 'Liverpool, Art City?' in Biggs and Sheldon 2009, pp.74-5
17 TM 5 January 1988
18 Summerfield 1991, pp.387-393; Clifford 1982, pp.93-106
19 Morris, n.d.
20 TM 6 December 1988, 6 December 1994; LLAG 1992 (1) and WAG 1998 (1); LLAG 1999 (1); LLAG 1992 (2), 1994 (1), WAG 1996 (3)
21 TM 9 May 2000

22 ASC 12 November 1965; *Liverpool Daily Post* 11 October 1965
23 WAG 1970 (1), p.1
24 ASC 21 December 1965
25 LMAC 29 December 1966
26 LMAC 13 April 1967; Scrutton to Councillor Thomas Greenwood 31 March 1967
27 ACC 19 September 1974
28 Ryder 1992; WAG 1988 (4); *T* 23 December 1988
29 TM 18 May and 5 October 1988, 24 November 1992, 25 June and 3 December 1996
30 ACL 9 October 1973
31 ACC 30 August 1984
32 ACC 1 September 1983
33 ACC 17 January, 14 March, 8 May, 1 August and 29 August 1985
34 TM 3 March 1986
35 TM 16 February 1988
36 TM 2 September and 4 November 1986, 17 September 1991; Millard 2010, p.90
37 TM: Building and Design Committee 16 September 1997
38 TM 14 December 1993, 15 January 1997
39 Amy de Joia, e-mail 7 December 2009
40 TM: Building and Design Committee 4 February 1997
41 TM 18 February 1997
42 TM 1 October 1998, 6 July 1999
43 Millard 2010, p.104
44 TM 16 September 1997
45 TM 18 February 1997; *T* 3 July and 15 October 1997
46 NMGM *Review* 1989-1992, p.18; TM 24 November 1992
47 TM 16 April 1991
48 TM 11 April and 27 June 1995
49 Evans 1981, p.440
50 WAG 1998 (1)
51 TM 17 February 1998; Millard 2010, pp.110-111

Chapter 8

1 Clegg 1993, 64, 148-9, 169-77, 226-7
2 *T* 27 September 1993

3 Davies 1989, p.59; WAG 1997, p.29
4 LMAC 16 December 1955
5 LMAC 16 March 1956
6 LMAC 16 November 1956 and 18 January 1957
7 Hugh Scrutton to Alderman James Johnstone 10 October 1956
8 *Sunday Times* 7 August 1957
9 *T* 11 July 1959 for Moores's letter with the same wording
10 *Observer* 19 November 1957
11 *G* 11 November 1957
12 ASC 21 February 1958
13 *Art and Artists*, Vol.13, February 1979, pp.18-21
14 ASC 18 December 1959, 15 July and 9 September1960, 7 December 1962
15 Jacob 2001
16 *Daily Mail* 30 November 1978
17 *G* 11 November 1957, *Observer* 19 November 1957
18 TM 5 January 1988
19 Bukantas 2008, pp.108-139
20 ASC 7 October 1960
21 WAG 1971 (2)
22 WAG 1973 (2); WAG 1975 (3)
23 WAG 1977 (3); WAG 1979 (2); WAG 1981 (4)
24 WAG 1983 (2); WAG 1986 (2)

Chapter 9

1 MacCunn 1956 pp.45-54
2 Haward 1922, pp.631-5; Strickland-Constable 1974, pp.1-2
3 WAG 1880; *LM* 11 and 26 May 1880
4 WAG 1886
5 *LM* 8 and 31 May 1886
6 Temple 1918, pp.85-329; Davies 1985, pp.38-40; Knight 1999, pp.17-22
7 WAG 1887-1888; Muther 1907, vol.4, pp.261-266
8 See *Athenaeum* 15 October 1887, p.510
9 *LM* 19 December 1887
10 See Zimmern 1885, pp.9-12 and 38-42
11 WAG 1890
12 *LM* 15 April 1890, 1 January 1891
13 *LM* 18 January 1890

14 *LM* 3 December 1891
15 *LM*, 28 June 1900
16 *LM* 13 February 1900
17 *LM* 7 February 1900
18 See Chun 2002
19 WAG 1907(3)
20 Waller 1981, p.286
21 WAG 1888 (2) and 1891; LM 6 March 1891
22 WAG 1889, 1893(2), 1894, 1895, 1898; *LM* 11 March 1893
23 LMAC 14 February 1889; AESC 12 February and 3 September 1889
24 WAG 1908 (2)
25 *LDP* 13 March 1908
26 Bisson 1965, pp.62, 88
27 Fry 1972, vol.2, pp.413-4
28 WAG 1934(2)
29 Harrison 1994, p.250
30 *LDP* 12 May 1934
31 *LDP* 4 June 1934 quoted in Harrison 1994, p.250
32 WAG 1938; there is a catalogue marked with prices in the WAG
33 See *LDP* 26 October and 6 November 1939 for these exhibitions
34 'The Works of Paul Klee', *The Liverpolitan*, vol.11, October 1946, p.15
35 *LDP* 12 April 1944
36 LMAC *Annual Report*, 1954-5, p.43
37 Burton 1999, pp.104, 142, 150, 172, 228-9
38 Conlin 2006, p.144
39 WAG 1972 (4)
40 WAG 1953 (1)
41 WAG 1955 (2)
42 Cox 1949, p.33; AC Annual Report, 1955-6, p.34; *LE* 12 December 1955; LMAC 17 June 1955 and 20 April 1956
43 WAG 1958-9; Willett 1967, p.75
44 *LDP* 4 December 1958
45 LMAC, *Annual Report*, 1958-9, p.55
46 WAG 1958
47 *G* 15 October 1958
48 LMAC 15 May 1873; *P* 2 and 9 August 1873, pp.281 and 300
49 WAG 1883 (1): WAG 1897; WAG 1907 (2)
50 WAG 1934 (3)
51 WAG 1927 (2), 1929, 1934 (4) and 1937

52 WAG 1951(1)
53 Egerton 2007, p.97
54 Taylor 1975
55 Nicholson 1953, p.259; Mellon 1992, pp.276-296, 333-337
56 Holroyd 1996, p.97
57 WAG 1958 (1)
58 WAG 1964 (3) and WAG 1967 (3)
59 WAG 1961 (1) and 1989
60 WAG 1972 (1)
61 WAG 1973 (1)
62 WAG 1972 (2)
63 WAG 1978 (2)
64 WAG 1987 (2)
65 WAG 1991, 1993 (1) and 1995 (1)
66 WAG 1997 and 2000 (1)
67 WAG 1996 (1)
68 WAG 1971(1), 1977 (2), 1980 (1)
69 SAG 1988
70 WAG 1961 (2)
71 WAG 1960 (1)
72 WAG 1975 (2)
73 WAG 1959 (1)
74 WAG 1964 (2)
75 WAG 1960 (2)
76 WAG 1975 (1)
77 WAG 1981 (2)
78 WAG 1976 (1)
79 WAG 1976-77
80 WAG 1977 (6)
81 WAG 1964 (1), WAG 1967 (2), WAG 1969
82 Ironside and Gere 1948
83 Whitechapel Art Gallery 1948
84 Scrutton 1971-2, pp.92-7
85 ASC 12 June 1964
86 LMAC 1 June 1967
87 WAG 1972 (3)
88 Waller 1981 p.493
89 ASC 8 June 1962
90 *LDP* 2 July 1963; Willett, p.87
91 Heffer 1991 pp.102-3
92 WAG 1965; ASC 12 July 1965
93 *LE* 1 March 1965, *LDP* 2 March 1965
94 *LE* 19 March 1966
95 ASC 8 January 1965
96 Willett 1967, p.128
97 ASC 8 June 1962; Jacob 2001
98 *LDP* 23 April 1965 and 26 November 1966

99 Willett 1967, pp.128-9
100 *LDP* 15 December 1970
101 WAG 1973 (3)
102 WAG 1951 (2)
103 LMAC 18 March 1955
104 See Davies 1989 pp.45-64
105 WAG 1973 (5) and 1977 (4)
106 WAG 1983-1984, 1985 (3) and 1986 (3)
107 WAG 1979 (1), 1981 (1) and 1982
108 ACC 9 July 1981; AC Annual Report, 1980-81, p.66
109 Houston 1968, p.299
110 *T* 6 June 1990, letter from Timothy Stevens
111 Curtis 1989, p.112
112 WAG 1978 (3)
113 Haskell 2000, p.146
114 WAG 1988 (1)
115 WAG 1994 (1)
116 WAG 1994 (2)
117 WAG 1996 (2)
118 TM Building and Design Committee 10 June 1997
119 WAG 1998 (2)
120 WAG 2000 (2)
121 Lewis Biggs, 'Individuals and Institutions in Dialogue' in Biggs and Sheldon 2009, p.41
122 NMGM *Review 1995-8*, 1998, p.25
123 Frankfurt 2000
124 Stevenson 2005, p.70
125 WAG 2002
126 WAG 2003; *LDP* 19 February 2004

Chapter 10

1 Ormerod 1953, p.62
2 AESC 4 July 1913
3 Clark 1977 pp.2-3, 77
4 LMAC 15 December 1939; *LDP*, 6 February and 11 December 1940
5 Honeyman 1971, p.100; Walton 1980, p.31; Drinkwater 1969-70, p.15;Davies 1985, p.101
6 *LDP*, 14 September 1972
7 Clark 1977, p.77
8 National Gallery 1947, p.xvi; Conlin 2006 pp.179-81
9 WAG 1955 (1)
10 Brommelle 1955, p.354
11 Drinkwater 1969-70, p.15; Spalding 1998, pp.131-2
12 Drinkwater 1969-70, p.15
13 Spalding 1998, pp.168-9; Gulbenkian 1972
14 ACC 25 November 1976, 12 January 1978
15 See Walden 1985
16 Dibdin 1912, pp.101-112
17 AESC 18 March 1890, 7 February 1913, 12 February 1926.
18 ASC 10 March and 6 April 1961
19 ASC 11 February 1966
20 ASC 13 September 1963
21 Dibdin 1912, pp.101-112
22 Morris 2005(1), p.91
23 ACC 16 October 1980
24 ASC 10 March and 6 April 1961; Jacob 2001
25 LMAC 16 March and 15 June 1951
26 Dibdin 1912, pp.101-112
27 ASC 16 October 1959
28 ASC 9 September 1960
29 ACC 13 December 1973
30 ACC 13 December 1973; *LDP* 9 October 1974, and 9 September 1975, *LE* 8 September 1975; ACC 9 October 1975, 28 April 1982
31 TM: Estates Committee 10 March 1992
32 TM 28 June 1994; TM: Building and Design Committee 18 May 1994
33 TM 7 December 1999
34 Honeyman 1971, p.99
35 ASC 9 September 1960; *LE* 10 September 1960
36 AESC 19 January 1891
37 LMAC 14 March 1952 and ASC 13 June 1958
38 Harries 2011, p.681
39 ASC 10 March 1961
40 ASC 13 December 1957; LE 13 September, 13 December 1957
41 ASC 11 February and 2 June1966; LDP 13 November 1965, LE 6 June 1966; Scrutton to Vere Cotton 15 November 1965 and to Councillor Thomas Greenwood 14 July 1966
42 TM 18 May 1988 and 7 February 1989

43 WAG 1988 (4) and Ryder 1992, pp.235-255
44 TM 27 June and 30 October 1989
45 TM 17 September 1991
46 Morris 1990, pp.414-5

Chapter 11
1 Haward 1922, pp.631-5
2 Rothenstein 1937, pp.328-335; Rosse 1963, pp.287-296; Honeyman 1971, pp.94-98; Walton 1980, p.22; Miers 1928, p.31; Markham 1938, pp.90, 115-6; Hooper-Greenhill 1991, pp.32-55
3 LMAC 24 October 1872
4 AESC 12 February 1937
5 AESC 12 February 1937
6 *LDP* 12 April 1944
7 *Liverpool Daily Post* 1951, p.1
8 AESC 15 September 1933; LMAC 17 November 1950 and 17 October 1952
9 LMAC 15 March 1957 and *LDP* 1 August 1957
10 ACL 9 January 1973
11 ASC 12 March 1965
12 See Macdonald 1970, pp.320-354
13 LMAC 30 May 1968
14 *Liverpool Daily Post* 1951, p.1
15 See Cathy Butterworth, 'Dissenters of the Creative Universe' in Biggs and Sheldon 2009, p.191
16 Hopkinson 2010, pp.263-277
17 Artmonsky 2010, pp.29-40; Macdonald 1970, p.352
18 Saint 1987, pp.118-23; Cavanagh and Yarrington, 2000, pp.xvi-xix
19 Hooper-Greenhill 1991, pp.29-30; Millard 2010, pp.29 and 44
20 Rothenstein 1939, pp.148-52; Rowe 1994, p.99; Markham 1938, pp.124-8
21 Sandilands 1960, p.8
22 'Works out on loan from the Permanent Collection, 8 May 1934' (typescript list)
23 Markham 1938, p.126
24 *LDP* 19 November 1940, 26 November 1945, *T* 23 November 1940
25 ASC 8 September 1958
26 LMAC 15 March 1957
27 LMAC 18 January 1957
28 ASC 15 September 1961
29 WAG 1983-4, 1985 (3) and 1986 (3)
30 WAG 1986 (1)
31 WAG 1992(1)
32 WAG 1985 (1), 1987 (1) and 1990 (1)
33 WAG 1988 (2)
34 Millard 2010, p.62
35 'Report on Structural Review of Department of Education and Public Programmes': Discussion Document 29/91, March 1991, TM 16 April 1991
36 See Newman 2005, pp.325-332
37 See Sandell 2003 and some of the essays in Sandell 2002
38 Resource 2001
39 Black 2012, p.205
40 TM 28 April 1998
41 TM Education Committee 19 January and 22 September 1999
42 Julie Sheldon, 'Learning and Interpretation' in Biggs and Sheldon 2009, p.166

Index

Aachen Altarpiece, Master of the: triptych, 227
Abbey, Edwin Austin: *O Mistress Mine*, 60
Abbeystead (estate), Lancashire, 138
Aberdeen Art Gallery: purchase grant, 109
'Abstract and Concrete' exhibition (1936), 29
Adams, Hugh, 179
Aestheticism, 145
Agnew, Thomas and Son, 33, 34, 78, 107, 147, 210
'Albert Richards: The Rose of Death' exhibition (1978), 208
Allan, Douglas, 254
Allen, Charles John, 43
    Love and the Mermaid (sculpture), 51
Allied Artists' Association, 86
Allston, Washington, 211
Alma-Tadema, Sir Lawrence, 27, 218
    exhibition (1997), 221
    Sculptor's Model, 20, 23
Aman-Jean, Edmond, 19
'American Artists in Europe 1800-1900' exhibition (1976), 210
Ancoats Museum of Art, Manchester, 250
Anderson, Sophie: *Elaine*, 44
Andrews, Keith (born Kurt Aufrichtig), 112-13
Andrews, Michael, 193-4
Ansdell, Richard, 138
    The Earl of Sefton and Party Retuning from Grouse Shooting with a View of Glen Lyon, Perthshire, 137
    The Waterloo Cup, 137
'Apprentice Painters and Decorators: Panel Work' exhibition (1965), 215
Araeen, Rasheed: *Boo/69*, 180
Area Museums Councils and Services, 98-9
Armitage, Edward
    Julian the Apostate Presiding at a Conference of Sectaries, 23
    Serf Emancipation, 22
Arnolfini Gallery, Bristol, 94, 186
Art and Artists (magazine), 178, 193
Art Journal, 25, 32
Art Treasures Exhibition (Manchester, 1857), 197
Art Union: established (1911), 27-8
art works: accepted in lieu of tax, 100-1
Arts Council (*earlier* Council for the Encouragement of Music and the Arts), 7, 91-2, 94-6, 190, 201, 203-4, 211, 213, 219, 254
Arts and Crafts Movement, 27, 58, 199
As of Now exhibition (1983), 194
Ashburnham, Henrietta Maria, Lady, 120
Ashby Potters Guild, 57
Ashmolean Museum, Oxford, 93
Ashton, Graham, exhibition (1984), 219
Askham, Colin, 171
Aspertini, Amico: *Virgin and Child with Saints*, 160
Athenaeum (periodical), 45
Atkinson Art Gallery, Southport, 32-3, 55, 134, 136
Atkinson, Conrad: *For Liverpool: Outside the Golden Triangle.*, 193
Audley, George, 54-5, 63, 74
Audubon, John James, 211

Auerbach, Frank, 106, 193-4
Austin, Samuel, 206
Avening Court, Gloucestershire, 79, 225
Axis (magazine), 29
Ayres, Gillian, 194

Baden Baden, Staatliche Kunsthalle, 219
Bacon, Francis, 34, 177, 192
Bailey, Colin, 210
Baker, Maria Vilaincour, 233
Ball, G.H., 38
Ballard, Arthur, 217
Barbican Gallery, London, 219
Barrow, Sarah, 55
Barry, Sir Charles, 15
Bartlett, Thomas, 63, 174
Bartolommeo, Fra, 123, 232
Barye, Antoine Louis, 54
Bastien-Lepage, Jules, 24-5
Bates, Harry: *Mars Janua Vitae*, 51
Bates, Merete, 191
Baum, John, 193
Baxandall, David, 86, 105-6, 129
Beatles, the, 207
Beausire, C.F.J., 120
Bebington Corporation, 149
Beck and Politzer (company), 191
Belfast: Ulster Museum, 156
Bell, Robert Anning, 58, 77, 149, 210
Bellori, Giovanni Pietro: *Le Vite de'Pittori* (book), 113
Bennett, Mary, 57, 85, 110-12, 114-15, 210-12
Bennett, William, 23
Berkeley Art Museum, California, 221
Bernard, Paul Albert, 19
Bertieri, Pilade: *Lady in Black Furs*, 52
Bertos, Francesco: *Homage to Sculpture*, 123
Betjeman, Sir John, 125
Bevan, Robert: *Under the Hammer*, 71
Biggs, Lewis, 161, 222
Birkenhead: annual exhibitions, 33
Birmingham: municipal improvement, 88
Birmingham Museum and Art Gallery, 14, 40, 66-7, 102, 107-9, 114, 122, 149, 159,197, 205, 212, 222, 225, 231
Birmingham School (of painters), 48
Bishop, William James, 16, 19
Bisson, Roderick, 208
Black-E (*earlier* Blackie Community Arts Project), 189, 216
Blamey, Norman, 192-3
Blanche, Jacques Émile, 19
Bluecoat Chambers, 196, 201, 247
Bluecoat Gallery, 162, 217-18
Blundell family, 147-8
    exhibition (1960), 209
Blundell, Charles, 120, 123, 169
Blundell, Henry, 169
Blunt, Anthony, 83-4
Blythe, Ernie, 220
Body & Soul exhibition (1975), 192
Bomberg, David, 34

289

Bond, William Joseph J.C., 53
Bone, Sir Muirhead, 61
Bonington, Richard, 78
Bor, Paulus, 107
　The Magdalen, 108
Boughton, George Henry: *Road to Camelot*, 60
Bowness, Alan, 176, 182, 185
Bowring Bequest Fund, 166
Bowring, Frederick, 11, 34, 63, 115, 174
Boyle, Mark, 192
　Liverpool Dock (series), 193
Braddock, Bessie, 80, 171
Braddock, John (Jack), 80, 131, 171, 175
Brancusi, Constantine, 200
Brangwyn, Frank, 24
Braque, Georges, 201, 204, 250, 252
Brett, John: *Stonebreaker*, 55
Breughel, Jan the elder, 123
Bridewell Studios, Liverpool, 219
Bridgman, Frederick Arthur, 52, 117, 211
Brisley, Stuart, 192
Bristol City Art Gallery, 98, 122, 150, 225, 246
British Institution, London, 40, 46
British International Print Biennale, Bradford, 186
British Museum, London
　loans to Walker Gallery, 203-4
　Turner watercolours, 89
British School: *Portrait of George Delves and a female companion*, 76
'British Sporting Painting' exhibition (1975), 204
British Surrealist Group, 29
Britten, Benjamin: *Albert Herring* (opera), 206
Brocklebank, Ralph, 52
Brockwell, Maurice, 111
Brodrick, Anne, 243
Brommelle, Norman, 226-7
Brooke, Xanthe, 169, 221
Brown, Ford Madox, 24, 231, 251
　exhibition (1964), 211-212
　Chaucer at the Court of Edward III, 212
　Coat of Many Colours, 55
　An English Autumn Afternoon, 212
　The Last of England, 212
　Pretty Baa Lambs, 212
　Waiting: An English Fireside, 148
　Work, 67, 212
Brown, Fred, 37
　Hard Times, 48-9
Brown, Mather, 76
Brown, Shipley & Co. (bank), 9
Brown, Sir William, 9
Browne, Henriette: *Alsace, 1870*, 18
Buckley, Stephen, 219
Builder, The (magazine), 15, 88-9
Bullock, George, exhibition (1988), 208-9
Bunce, J.T., 87-8
Burlington Magazine, 42, 57, 84, 102, 108, 125
Burne-Jones, Sir Edward, 44, 218
　Briar Rose paintings, 34
　Sponsa de Libano, 60
Burra, Edward, 192
Butler, Josephine, 149

Cadbury's (company), 253
Caddick, Richard, 149
Caddick, William, 149
Caine, Sir Thomas Henry Hall, 45
Caine, William Sproston, 13, 20, 89
Calcott, Augustus Wall, 78
Calderon, Philip Hermogenes: *Ruth and Naomi*, 61-2
Camberwell College of Art, 230, 233
Cambio, Arnoldo di, 123
Camden Town Group (artists), 24, 28, 71, 208
Cameron, David, 24
Campbell, James, 210
Cannon-Brookes, Peter, 122
Carandente, Giovanni, 191-2
Carr, Henry, 20
Carr, John Comyns, 89-90
Carrington, Peter, 6th Baron, 155
Carter, Charles, 83
Cartier-Bresson, Henri, 149, 221
Cartwright Hall Art Gallery, Bradford, 32
Cassatt, Mary, 118, 211
Caton, Richard, 42
Caulfield, Patrick, 187
　exhibition (1981), 219
ceramics *see* pottery
Cézanne, Paul, 19, 106, 172
　The Murder, 118-19
Chamberlain, Joseph, 67, 72, 88
Chandler, George, 112
Chantrey Bequest, 40, 48
Chantrey, Francis, 140
Chantry, Judith, 232
Chapman, Alfred, 22
Charles, James: *In the Garden*, 138
Chatsworth House, Derbyshire, 100-1
Cheetham, Francis, 102
Chirico, Giorgio de, 30
Christ Church, Oxford, exhibition (1964-6), 210
Christie, Nicola, 243
Christie's auction house, 147
Christo, 252
Ciechanowiecki, Andrew, 122
Clark, Sir Kenneth (*later* Baron), 82, 94, 106, 206, 225-6
Claude Lorraine, 123
　A View of Carthage with Dido and Aeneas, 209-10
Clausen family, 124
Clausen, George, 24, 55, 251
Clayton, Sir Robert, 76
'Cleaned Pictures' exhibition (National Gallery, 1947), 227
'Cleaned Pictures' exhibition (Walker Gallery, 1955), 227
Cleve, Joos van: *The Virgin and Child with Angels*, 119, 147; fig. 2
Clifford, Timothy, 150, 163
Clough, Prunella, 105, 252
Cockerell, Charles Robert, 165
Cockerell, Sydney, 66
Cockrill, Maurice, 217, 219
　exhibition (1995), 208
Coldstream, Sir William, 182

Cole, Henry, 12, 66, 87
Colle, Ettore, 191
Collings, Jesse, 88-90
Collins, William, 55, 68-1
Collinson family, 71
Colnaghi (dealer), 107, 124
Coltart, Mrs William, 55
Colvin, Sidney, 233
Commercial Cable Company, 171
'Communication' exhibition (1973), 217
Compton, Michael
    joins staff, 110-11, 113-14
    leaves, 113
    writes on Roscoe, 85
    New *Foreign Schools Catalogue*, 84
Compton Verney, Warwickshire, 189
Conder, Charles, 66, 251
    Newquay, 71
Conran, George Loraine, 83
Conservation
    official attitude to, 242, 244-5
    principles, 224-7
    techniques, 228-9
    training, 230
    and travel damage, 240-1
Conservative Party, 131
Constable, John, 68
    exhibition (2000), 221-2
    Seashore with fisherman near a boat, 76
constructions, 180-1
'Contemporary Lithographs' scheme, 250
Conway, Martin, 56
Cook, Beryl, 193
Cookson, Ernest, 83
Cooper, Thomas Sidney, 17
Copenhagen Royal Porcelain Manufactury, 57
Corbould, Edward Henry, 42
Cormack, Malcolm, 114
Cornbury Park, 125
Correggio, Antonio Allegri da, 169
Cotman, Frederick George, 231
    One of the Family, 50
Cottet, Charles, 19
Cotton, Elfreda (*née* Moore), 65
Cotton, Vere
    advocates staff professionalism, 84-5, 105
    attends conference on regional galleries, 100
    death, 119
    Dowdall discusses reforms with, 59
    favours concentrating on British art, 107, 109, 118
    fund-raising skills, 117, 131
    on Gallery as national institution, 7
    joins Arts Council, 94
    knowledge of art history, 131-2, 248
    loan restrictions, 240
    as policy-maker, 65-8, 70-7, 79-80, 82, 86, 170
    proposes building new gallery, 196
    proposes re-using space, 164
    replaces Autumn Exhibitions with smaller shows, 201
    seeks government grants, 92-3, 103
    and sporting pictures, 138

succeeded by Ben Shaw, 120-1
    and taxation in-lieu concessions, 101
    and university funding, 92
Council for Museums, Archives and Libraries ('Resource'), London, 255
Courbet, Gustave, 118
Courtauld Institute of Art, London, 83-4
Courtauld, Samuel, 73
Cowie, James: *Intermission*, 72-3
Cox, David, 53, 120, 199
Cox, Sir George Trenchard, 86, 150
Craft of Art, The exhibition (1979), 193
Crane, Walter, 24, 77
Crome, John, 86
Crompton, Gigi, 229
Cross, James, 75
Crowley, Graham, 194
Croxteth Hall, Liverpool, 136-9, 143, 147, 152, 154
Cundall, H.M., 59

Daguerre, Louis Jacques Mande, 37
    Ruins of Holyrood Chapel, 15, 111; fig.11
Dahl, Michael, 120
Daily Mail, 253
Daily Mirror, 253
Dali, Salvador, 201
Dalou, Jules, 59
Dalwood, Hubert, 192, 194
Danson, F.C. & Co., 138
Danson, Lieut. Col. John Raymond, exhibition (1977), 138
Danzig, c.1700, cabinet, 169
Daumier, Honoré, 113
Davies, John: *For the last time* (sculpture), 192
Davis, William, 53, 57, 210
    At Hale, Lancashire, fig. 13
    exhibition (1873), 205
Davison, Sydney, 68
Davy, J. and Sons, 234
Dawson, Henry, exhibition (1883) 206
'Decorative and Applied Art Exhibition' (1889), 199
Degas, Edgar, 19
    Woman Ironing, 118, 147; fig. 16
Delacroix, Fernand Victor Eugène, 113
Delamere, Ron, 143
Delaroche, Paul, 85
    Napoleon crossing the Alps, 124
De La Warr, Herbrand Brassey Sackville, 9th Earl, 91
Della Robbia, Luca, 199
De Morgan, Evelyn: *Life and Thought*, 60
Denis, Maurice, exhibition (1995), 221
Denny, Robyn, 187
Derain, André, 117, 200-1
    L'Italienne, 76
Derby, Edward Henry Stanley, 15th Earl of, 14
Derby, Edward John Stanley, 18th Earl of, 148
Derby, Edward Smith Stanley, 13th Earl of, 9, 15, 209
Designation Challenge Fund, 104
Designation Scheme, 104
Devis, Arthur, 251
    Mr and Mrs William Atherton, 75
Devonshire, Andrew Cavendish, 11th Duke of, 116

Deysbrook House, Liverpool, 77
Dibdin, Edward Rimbault
  appointed curator, 42-4
  on Caddicks, 149
  and changing taste, 67
  on conservation problems, 232
  differences with Lambert, 69
  on Hornel's style, 50
  on Lea, 11
  proposes Friends organisation, 122
  purchases prints, 58, 199
  research on Liverpool art, 57
  on space limits, 63
Dicksee, Frank, 43
Dobson, William: *The Executioner with the Head of John the Baptist* (after Matias Stom), 75
Dodgson, Campbell, 83
Domenichino, Domenico Zampieri, 169
Domestic Mission, Liverpool, 215
Donaldson, Agnes, 247-9
Donaldson, Anthony, 187
  Three Portraits of You, 172
Dooley, Arthur, 216
Dorchester House, London, 776
Doré Gallery, London, 198, 200
Doré, Gustave,
  exhibition (1890), 197-8
  Christ Leaving the Praetorium, 198
  Ecce Homo, 198
Doulton and Company, 57, 99
Dow, Millie: *Eve*, 60
Dowdall, Harold Chaloner, 42, 59, 74, 207
Dresser, Christopher, 57
Drew, Sir Arthur: Committee report (1982), 97-8, 128
Dublin City Gallery, 156
Dufy, Raoul, 252
Dughet, Gaspard, 107
Durbin, Leslie, 220
Durer, Albrecht, 232
Dwelly, Frederick William, 200
Dyall, Charles, 31, 37, 41-3, 50, 56, 218
Dyce, William, 78
Dyck, Sir Anthony van, 210

Eames, Penelope, 143
East, Alfred, 24
'East, The: Imagined, Experienced, Remembered' exhibition (1988), 221
Eastern Arts, 186
Eccles, David, 1st Viscount, 96
Edinburgh: National Gallery, 156-7
Edinburgh, Prince Alfred Ernest Albert, Duke of, 14
Edkins, John, exhibition (1967), 207
'Edvard Munch: the Graphic Work' exhibition (1972), 204
Egg, Augustus, 55
Elias, Frank, 11
Elizabeth II, Queen, 106
  Coronation (1953), 204
Elliot, John, 57
Elmes, Harvey Lonsdale, 165
Elsheimer, Adam: *Apollo and Coronis*, 148

Elsloo, Master of: *A Warrior Saint*, 123
Elton, Oliver, 42
Empire Marketing Board, 250
Engert, Gail, 208
England, Major Philip, 120
  English Conversation Pieces exhibition (1930), 75
English Tourist Board, 237
Ente Autonomo della Quadriennale di Roma, 191
Epstein, Sir Jacob, 24-5, 66
  Genesis, 70
  Madonna and Child, 28
  Man of Aran, 120
  Sonia, 73
Ernst, Max, 30, 252
Etty, William, 37, 145
Eurich, Richard: *The Ship Inn*, 72, 194
European 'Objective One' Funding, 162
European Regional Development Fund, 162, 167
Evans, Mark, 160
Everyman Theatre, Liverpool, 122
'Exhibition of Drawings by Children of the Liverpool Public Elementary Schools' (1912), 247
Expressionists (German), 119

Fabro, Luciano, 191
Faed, Thomas, 53
Fantin-Latour, Henri: *Portrait of Mr and Mrs Edwin Edwards*, 22
Farquharson, Joseph, 24
Farthing, Stephen, 192, 219
Fastnedge, Ralph, 83-4, 105, 109, 112-14, 206, 247
Faulds, Andrew, 103
Fauve artists, 200
Feather, Vic, 216
Feaver, William, 192, 194
Ferens Art Gallery, Hull, 62, 113
Ferneley, John, 139
Ferri, Ciro, 107
Festival of Britain (1951), 80, 82, 206
Fielding, Copley, 120
Fildes, Luke
  portrait of George V, 106
  portraits of 1st Viscount and Lady Leverhulme, 145
  Applicants for Admission to a Casual Ward, 22
  The Widower, 22
Finance Acts (1930 and 1956), 471
Fine Art Society, 51
Finnie, John, 12, 16, 19
  exhibition (1907), 206
  First Liverpool Salon of Original Etchings... of the Modern and Semi-Modern French School (1908), 200
Fisher, Mark: *Harlow Mill*, 71
Fitzroy Picture Society, 250
Fitzwilliam Museum, Cambridge, 55, 66, 67, 93, 121, 186
Flanagan, Barry, 194
  June 6 '69, 194
Fleetwood-Walker, Bernard: *Amity*, 72-3
Flint, William Russell, 58
Flowers, Angela, 183

Fontana, Lucio, 191
Forbes, Stanhope, 24, 37
   A Street in Brittany, 48
Ford, Edward Onslow: *Peace* (sculpture), 51
Ford, Ford Madox, 57
Foreign Schools Catalogue (1963), 130
Forty, Gerald, 95
Forwood, Arthur, 40-1
Forwood, Sir William, 59
Foster, John, the younger, 139
Foster, Myles Birket, 233
Foster, Richard, 154, 158-60, 166
Foundation for Art and Creative Technology, Liverpool, 162
Fowler, Robert, exhibition (1927), 206
frames *see* picture frames
Frampton, Edward Reginald: *Our Lady of Snows*, 58
Frampton, George: *Mysteriarch*, 60
France: provincial galleries, 88-90
France, James (Jim), 229-30, 233, 237, 242
'France, La' exhibition (1989), 204
Francis, Richard, 162, 218
Franklin, Maud, 48
French, Annie: *The Sleepless Daisy*, 58
'French Symbolist Painters' exhibition (1972), 202, 204
Freud, Lucian, 177, 192
   Large Interior W11 (After Watteau), 192, 194
Frick Gallery, New York, 146
Friedman, Terry, 214
Friends of the Liverpool Museums and of the Walker Art Gallery, 121-2, 147, 246
Fripp, Alfred Downing, 20
Frith, William Powell, 33, 105
Froud, Jonathan, exhibition (1985), 219
Fry, Maxwell, 205
Fry, Roger, 33, 55, 67, 81, 106, 200
   Portrait of Edward Carpenter, 24
Fuller, Peter, 186
Fuseli, Henry, 37, 75, 85, 231
   Death of Oedipus, 240
   Milton when a Boy Instructed by his Mother, 55
   Return of Milton's Wife, 55

Gabo, Naum, 29
Gainsborough, Thomas, 76, 78
   Isabella, Viscountess Molyneux, later Countess of Sefton, 137; fig.9
   Viscountess Folkestone, 228
Galltfaenan, Denbighshire, 79
Garrido, Leandro Ramon: *His First Offence*, 52
Gateshead Technical College, 230, 233
Gaudier-Brzeska, Henri, 200
Gauguin, Paul, 204
   Harvest: Le Pouldu, 101
Geets, William: *Awaiting an Audience*, 52
Gentileschi, Orazio: *Rest on the Flight into Egypt*, 107
Georges Braque exhibition (1990), 204
Gere, Charles: *Finding of the Infant St George*, 48-9
Gere, John, 211
German symbolist art, 222
Germany: provincial galleries, 88

Gérôme, Jean Leon, 118
Gertler, Mark, 24, 105
Gervex, Henri, 19
Giacometti, Alberto, 30
Gibson, John, 37, 124, 140
Gilbert and George, 193
Giles, Carl (cartoonist), 194
Giles, William, 58
Gill, Chapple, 148
Gilman, Harold, 118
   Interior with Flowers, 71, 73
   Mrs Mounter, 71-2; fig. 17
Ginner, Charles, *Le Quai ensoleillé, Dieppe*, 72
Giordano, Luca, 168
Gladstone, William Ewart, 89, 93
Glasgow Art Gallery and Museums, 54, 93, 109, 122, 161, 225, 238, 246
Glasgow City Council, 12-13
Glasgow School (of painters), 26-7, 48-50
glazing (of pictures), 239
Goethe Institute, 203-4
Gogh,'Engineer' van, 205
Gogh, Vincent van, 19
   exhibition (1955), 204-5
   The Blue Cart, 172
Goldsmiths' Company, 220
Goodall, Frederick: *New Light in the Hareem*, 50
Goodall, Thomas F.: *The Bow Net*, 48
Gore, Spencer, 118
   The Garden, Garth House, 71
Gormley, Anthony, 195
Gotch, Thomas Cooper, 24
   A Pageant of Childhood, 62
'Gothic Europe' exhibition (1968), 239
Gott, Joseph, 140, 233
   exhibition (1972), 214
Gowrie, Alexander Patrick Greysteil-Ruthven, 2nd Earl of, 153-5
Goya, Francisco de, exhibition (1983), 204
Granacci, Francesco, 125
Granada Foundation, 186
Grand Loan Exhibition (1886), 52, 197
Grant, Duncan, 24, 66, 105
   Farm in Sussex, 72
Gray, Nicolete, 29
Grayson-Ford, Sue, 192, 220
Great George Street Congregational Church, Liverpool, 189
Great George's Cultural Community Project, 216
Greenberg, Clement, 182
Greenhill, Eilean Hooper, 255
Greenwood, Nigel, 182-3
Greenwood, Thomas, 102
Grindley, Edward (*later* Grindley and Palmer), 34
Gris, Juan, 200
Grossmann, Fritz, 150
Grosvenor Gallery, London, 26
Grubert, Halina, 248
Grundy, Robert, 58
Guardi, Gian Antonio, 125
Guercino, 123, 168
Guildhall Art Gallery, London, 197

Gulbenkian Foundation, 230
Gussow, Carl: *Old Man's Treasure*, 52
Guthrie, Sir Tyrone, 206

Hafodunos Hall, Denbighshire, 124
Hague, Denys, 19
Hallé Orchestra, Manchester, 103
Halliday, Edward, 107
Halswelle, Keeley, 33
Hamilton, Gawen, 76
Hamilton Kerr Institute, near Cambridge, 230
Harding, Eric, 232
Hardman, Edward Chambré, 221
 The Ark Royal (photograph), 149
Harpe, Bill and Wendy, 189
Harpley, Sidney, 220
Harris, George W., exhibition (1958), 207
Harrison, Richard, 98
Hartley, Sir William, 55
Havers, Mandy, 193
Haward, Lawrence, 42
Hay, James Hamilton, exhibition (1973), 207-8
Hay, John Duncan, 207
Hayward Gallery, London, 202, 204
Heap, Richard, 55
Heath, Sir Edward, 167
Heesom, Patrick Glynn, 172
Heffer, Eric, 214-16, 240
Hélion, Jean, 29
Hempel, Kenneth, 233
Hemy, Charles Napier: *A Nautical Argument*, 49
Hendy, Sir Philip, 73, 86, 227
Henri, Adrian, 193, 208-9, 217
Hepworth, Dame Barbara, 29, 73, 200
 Mother and Child, 28
Heritage Lottery Fund, 162-3, 167, 170
Herkomer, Hubert, 37
 Eventide, 44
Heron, Patrick, 182
Heseltine, Michael, 155
Hesketh, Fleetwood, 168-9
Heywood's Bank, Liverpool, 210
Highmore, Joseph, 119
Hilliard, Nicholas: *Queen Elizabeth: the Pelican Portrait*, 74
Hilton, Tim, 213
Hilton, Roger: *Oi Yoi Yoi December 1963*, 193
'Historical Exhibition of Liverpool Art' (1908), 206
Hitchcock, George: *Maternité*, 211
Hitchens, Ivon, 24
Hobbema, Meindert, 210
Hockney, David, 187, 192
 Peter getting out of Nick's pool, fig. 19
Hodgkin, Howard, 182, 193
Hogarth, William, 125
 David Garrick as Richard III, 28, 76, 109; fig. 6
 Portrait of a Lady, 76
 Card Party (attrib.), 76
Holbein, Hans, the younger, 74
Holbrook, Gaskell II, 75
Holder, W. and Sons, 224-5
Holford, William, 29, 92

Holiday, Henry: *Dante and Beatrice*, 50, 240-1
Holme, F. and G., 165
Holmes, Sir Stanley, 127, 135
Holt family, 58, 79
Holt, Anne, 79
Holt, Eliza, Lady, 76
Holt, Emma, 78
Holt, George, 22-3, 53, 78-9, 148, 153, 158, 174, 215
Holt, Robert Durning, 446
Honeyman, Tom John, 161, 238, 246
Hood, Alex Gregory, 183
Hook, James Clarke, 55
Hope, Polly, 193
Hoppner, John, 76
Hornby Library (Liverpool), 113
Hornel, Edward Atkinson, 24, 59
 Summer, 48-50
Horsfield, Nicholas, 217
 exhibition (1997), 208-9
Hosmer, Harriet: *Puck* (marble), 149
'How does your garden grow' exhibition (1984), 253
Howard, George, 89
Hoyland, John: *18.1.69*, 127
Huggins, William, 57
 Portrait of a Man, 77
Hughes, Graeme, 220
Hughes, Harriet Owen, 229
Humphris, Cyril, 122
Humphry, Ozias, 57
Hunt, Alfred William, 57
 exhibition (1997), 206
Hunt, Andrew, 57
Hunt, Violet, 57
Hunt, William Holman, 124, 205
 exhibitions (1907 and 1969), 199, 211-213
 Triumph of the Innocents, 47
 Valentine and Sylvia, 210
Hunterian Art Gallery, Glasgow, 210

Ibbetson, Julius Caesar, 77
Ikon Gallery, Birmingham, 94
Imperial War Museum, London, 208
Impressionists, English, 25
Impressionists, French, 61, 118-19, 146
Ince Blundell Hall, Lancashire, 147
'Industry and the Artist' exhibition (1965), 214, 216
Innes, Callum: *Exposed Painting, Cadmium Orange on White*, 187
International Photographic Exhibitions, 199
International Surrealist Exhibition (London, 1936), 29
Into the 80s exhibition (1981), 193
Ionides, Constantine Alexander, 45
Irlam, Roy, 231, 239
Ironside, Robin, 211
Isabella Stuart Gardner Museum, Boston, 86
Ismay, Thomas Henry, 53
Italian art, 55-6, 84, 169
Italian Bronze Statuettes (Arts Council exhibition, 1961), 123

Jackson's (art transport company), 183, 234
Jacob, John, 113, 123, 183, 205, 215, 237

INDEX

Jaffé, Michael, 82
James, Edward, 30
Jaray, Tess, 187
Jardine, George, 30
Jawlensky, Alexei von, 172
Jenkins, Hugh, 97
JM Centre, Liverpool, 172
John, Augustus, 24, 28-9, 66, 74, 145, 210
 exhibition (1954), 207
 Scottish Canadian Soldier, 72
 Two Jamaican Girls, 72
John Moores Exhibitions (biennial)
 juries, 182
 organised and presented, 127, 164, 172-4, 177-82, 185-9, 218, 250
 prizes, 178-9, 181, 183
 promotion, 184
Johnson, Cornelius: *Portrait of a Lady*, 76
Jones, Allen, 187, 252
 exhibition (1979), 219
Jones, E. Peter, 74

Kahnweiler, Daniel-Henry, 201
Kahnweiler, Gustav, exhibition (1938), 201
Kandinsky, Vasily, 29
Kant, Immanuel, 161
Kapoor, Anish, exhibition (1983), 219
Kasmin, John, 182
Kauffmann, Angelica, 137
Keck, Sheldon, 229
Kellogg's (company), 253
Kelly, Sir Gerald, 106
Kendal Museum, 149
Kennerley, George, 172
 Irises (Homage to Van Gogh), 172
Kerry, William Lewis, 16, 20
Kettle's Yard, Cambridge, 94
Kidner, Michael, 187
Kidson, Alex, 208, 223
King, Philip, 194
 Red Between (sculpture), 192
Koninck, Philips: *Landscape*, 148
Kinley, Peter, 194
Kirklands (bar and café), Liverpool, 220
Kitaj, Ronald Brooks, 85, 182, 187
Kitson, Michael, 82
Klee, Paul, 30
 exhibition (1946), 201
Kneller, Godfrey, 68
 Charles II, 75
 Lady and Child (attrib.), 68
Knight, John Baverstock, 58
Knight, Joseph
 Showery Weather, 48
 A Tidal River, 48
Knight, Dame Laura, 24, 27
 Spring in St John's Wood, 72
Knowsley Hall, Prescot, Lancashire, 79, 148, 209
Koch, Joseph Anton, 85, 137
Kokoschka, Oskar, 178
Kossoff, Leon, 106, 194
Kurtz, Andrew G., 13, 22, 52-3

Labia sale (Sotheby's, 1970), 125
Labour Party, 103-4, 109, 120, 153, 156, 166, 254
Lacambre, Geneviève, 204
Lady Lever Art Gallery, Port Sunlight
 catalogues, 144-5
 character and collections, 63, 68, 70, 144-5
 deglazing of pictures, 239
 environmental conditions, 238
 Fastnedge appointed director, 84
 government funding, 154
 importance, 8
 new picture racking, 99
 paper conservation studio, 233
 proposed change of responsibility, 152
 structural repairs and gallery rearrangement, 143-4, 150
 Walker Art Gallery takes over (1978), 85, 115, 130, 140-3
Laing, Alexander, 15, 62
Laing Art Gallery, Newcastle, 61, 134
Lamb, Henry, 66
Lambert, Frank
 applies to appoint photographer, 235
 and conservation, 224
 develops 18th-century British art collection, 109
 as director and policy-maker, 65, 68-77, 79-84
 doubts on Autumn Exhibitions, 36, 173, 201
 educational functions, 24
 on expense of Impressionist paintings, 119
 on financial failures, 26, 28
 hanging policy, 234
 and modernists, 29
 popular exhibitions at Bluecoat Chambers, 201
 retires, 105, 107
 Rothenstein succeeds at Leeds, 86
 seeks government money, 91-2
 selection policy, 189
 and 'Unit One' exhibition, 200
 visits Sweden, 79-80
Lambert, Mrs Frank, 216
Lancashire County Sessions House
 see Sessions House
Lancaster, Mark, exhibition (1973), 218
Landseer, Sir Edwin, 68
Langley, Walter, 24
Langton, Charles, 52-3
Larson, John, 233, 243-4
Last, John, 131, 136, 142, 154, 158-9, 166
La Thangue, Henry Herbert, 24
Lavery, Sir John, 24, 27
Lawrence, Sir Thomas, 37, 76, 107
 Thomas William Coke of Holkham, 77
Lawrenson, Edward Louis, 58
Lea, John, 11-12, 19, 25, 58-9, 61
Leader, Benjamin William, 33
Leahy, Sir Terry, 131
Lear, Edward, 120,
 exhibition (1975), 209
Le Brun, Charles: *Atalanta and Meleager*, 111-12
Le Brun, Christopher, 186, 192-3
Le Corbusier (Charles-Édouard Jeanneret-Gris), 29

exhibition (1958), 205
Lee of Fareham, Arthur Hamilton Lee, Viscount, 225
Lee, Jennie, 101, 103
Lee, John J.: *Sweethearts and Wives*, 149
Lee, Sydney, 58
Lee, Thomas Stirling: *The Progress of Justice* (relief), 10
Leeds: Schools' Museum Scheme, 246
Leeds Art Calendar, 84
Leeds Art-Collections Fund, 121
Leeds City Art Gallery, 32, 40, 44, 69-70, 73, 95, 99, 109, 116, 150, 196, 233, 246
Léger, Fernand, 106, 201, 209
Legros, Alphonse, 37, 118
   The Pilgrimage, 22, 240-1
Le Hongre, Étienne (attrib.): *Cupid holding Laurel Wreaths*, 123
Leighton, Frederic, Baron, 24, 37, 47, 55, 62, 218
   Antique Juggling Girl, 22
   Captive Andromache, 45-8, 54; fig. 15
   Clytemnestra on the Battlements of Argos, 18, 22
   Crossbow Man, 55
   Eastern Slinger Scaring Birds, 22
   Elijah in the Wilderness, 22, 53, 124, 239
   Hercules Wrestling with Death for the Body of Alcestis, 21
   Perseus and Andromeda, 48, 55
   Weaving the Wreath, 22
Le Sidaner, Henri, 19
   St Paul's from the River, 52
Leslie, Frank, 200
Leverhulme, Philip William Bryce Lever, 3rd Viscount, 141, 145, 153
Leverhulme, William Hesketh Lever, 1st Viscount, 42-3, 63, 68, 70, 141-4, 253
   portraits, 145
Levey, Michael, 102
Levis, Giuseppe de, 123
Lewis, John Frederick, 120
Lewis, Samuel, 22
Lewis's Ltd, 75, 78
Leyland, Frederick Richard, 21-2, 52, 54, 210
Lhermite, Léon, 19
Lhôte, André, 200
Liberal Party, 132, 135, 153
Liberal Review, 12, 14, 22
Lightfoot, Herbert, 208
Lightfoot, Maxwell Gordon, exhibition (1972), 208
Linton, Sir James, 233
Lister, Samuel Cunliffe, 15
Littlewoods (companies), 131, 171-2
'Liverpool: People and Places' exhibition (1963), 215
Liverpool
   capital projects expenditure on arts, 161
   commercial art dealers, 33-4
   lacks tourists, 196
   population decline, 161
Liverpool Academy, 16-17, 21, 34-5, 149, 172, 199
   exhibitions (1948-1977), 210, 217-8
'Liverpool Academy Celebrates the Walker's 100th Birthday, The' exhibition (1977), 217
Liverpool Amateur Photographic Association, 199
'Liverpool Around and About' exhibition (1968), 215

Liverpool Art Club, 53, 199
Liverpool Bulletin, 84-5, 113
Liverpool Cathedral (Anglican), 53, 65
Liverpool Catholic Cathedral, 244
Liverpool City Council
   Arts and Recreations Committee, 127-8
   committees restructured, 127-9
   Labour regain control (1983), 153
   Libraries, Museums and Arts Committee, 7, 9, 37-9, 116
   and Merseyside County Council, 133
Liverpool City Library, 112-13, 132, 164-5
Liverpool College of Art, 217, 220
Liverpool Conservation Centre, 243-4
Liverpool Courier, 50
Liverpool Daily Post, 29, 30, 66, 76, 78, 200, 217
Liverpool Echo, 26, 78
Liverpool Institute Schools, 54
Liverpool International Garden Festival, 194, 220, 253
Liverpool Library and Museum Act (1852), 9
Liverpool and London Chambers, 33
Liverpool Mercury, 25, 52, 197-8
Liverpool Museum (*earlier* William Brown Library and Museum, *later* Merseyside County Museums)
   annual expenditure, 136
   archaeological conservation, 98
   bombed and reopened, 83, 124
   collection, 58, 88
   completed (1860), 9, 12, 16, 53
   education department, 254
   ethnographic collection, 197
   funding, 152, 163
   publishes bulletin, 84
   purchase grant, 109
   renamed, 152, 162
   staff recruitment, 160
   visitor numbers, 203
Liverpool Review, The, 47
Liverpool Royal Institution, 9, 55-6, 79, 111, 227
Liverpool School of Applied Arts ('Art Sheds'), 210
Liverpool School of Painters, 53, 57
'Liverpool Today and Tomorrow' exhibition (1966), 215
Liverpool Trades Council, 216
Liverpool University, 53-4, 56
   Extramural Department, 246
   School of Architecture, 29, 34
Livingstone, Mark, 218-19
Lloyd, Valerie, 221
Lloyd George, David, 1st Earl, 157
local government: administrative changes, 133-5
London: galleries and museums, 87-8
London Gallery, Cork Street, 29
London Group (of artists), 24
London Life (company), 218
London, Museum of, 69
Lonsdale, Lieut.-Col. Heywood, exhibition (1959-), 209
Loutherbourg, Philippe Jacques, 120
Lowry, Laurence Stephen, 179, 192, 216
   Fever Van, 71-2, 216
Lucchese School, *Virgin and Child with Saints*,

224, 227
Lucie-Smith, Edward, 192, 193
Lutyens, Sir Edwin, 244
Lynton, Norbert, 182, 192-4

Macandrew, Hugh, 85, 111, 113, 123, 210, 231
MacColl, Dugald Sutherland, 33, 42-3, 59
McCrossan, Mary, exhibition (1934), 206
Macdonald, John, 143
McKeever, Ian, 250
   exhibition (1981), 219
Mckenna, Stephen: *Collocation*, 194
Mackie, Charles, 58
McKinsey and Company (management consultants), 127-8, 135
Mackintosh, James Rennie, 148
Maclean, Bruce, 194
McLellan, Archibald, 12-13
MacNair, James Herbert, 85, 148, 210
McNeff, David, 242
Magazine of Art, 43
Magic & Strong Medicine exhibition (1973), 192
Magritte, René, 30
Mahon, Sir Denis, 168
Maillol, Aristide, 201
Manchester City Art Gallery, 15, 35, 40, 67, 73, 98, 109, 133-4, 196, 203, 223, 246, 247, 251
Manchester School (of artists), 48
Mantegna, Andrea, 169
Mappin, John Newton, 15
Maria, Giacomo di: *Death of Virginia* (sculpture), 124
Marillier, Henry Currie, 53, 56, 60
Maritime Museum, Liverpool, 139-40, 152, 154, 160, 233
Markham, Sydney Frank, 93, 247, 251
   Report (1938), 91, 100
Marquet, Albert, 172
Marshall, Ben, 138
Martin Brothers (potters), 57
Martin, Carew, 42
Martin, Henri, 19
Martin, John, 42
   The Last Man, 55
Martin, Michael Craig, 192
Martin, William Alison, exhibition (1937), 206
Martini, Simone: *Christ Discovered in the Temple*, 56, 225, 239; fig. 1
Martin's Bank Ltd, 107
Martyrdom of St Lawrence (Netherlandish School), 228
Mason, George H., 78
Matisse, Henri, 19, 172, 201, 250
Mattiacci, Eliseo, 191
Mayer, Joseph, 9, 15, 53, 57, 149
Mayer-Marton, George, 251
   exhibition (1961), 207
Mayor, Frederick: bequest, 123, 130, 146
Mayor Gallery, London, 200
Mazone, Giovanni: *St Mark Enthroned*, 228
Meleager (ivory), 122
Mellon, Paul, 76, 137, 206-7, 220
Melly, George, 201

Mengs, Anton Raphael: *Self-portrait*, 107-8
Merseyside: economic decline, 119, 131, 162, 175
'Merseyside Artists' series (exhibitions, 1983-6), 218, 253
Merseyside Arts Association, 124
Merseyside County Council
   established, 131-2, 134-6, 152
   resists central government plans, 153, 155
Merseyside Development Corporation, 155, 164
Merton, Sir Thomas and Lady, 147
Mesdag Collection, exhibition (1994), 204
Methuen, Paul Ayshford Methuen, 4th Baron, 148
Metropolitan Museum, New York, 125
Midland Railway Goods Warehouse, Liverpool, 243-4
Miers Report (1928), 91, 247
Mignot, Louis Remy, exhibition (1877), 196
Miles, Jeremiah, 46
Militant (Labour party faction), 153, 156
Millais, Sir John Everett, 24, 37,
   exhibition (1967), 211-13
   Apple Blossoms (or *Spring*), 145
   Chill October, 33
   Cymon and Iphigenia, 145
   Flowing to the River, 22
   Isabella, 45, 67, 239; fig. 12
Miller, John, 148
Milner, Frank, 208, 253-4
Minton, John, 252
Miró, Joán, 29-30
Mistry, Dhruva: *Giant Sitting Bull* (sculpture), 194
Moholy-Nagy, László, 29
Mola, Pier Francesco, 168
Mond, Ludwig, 147
Monet, Claude, 19, 25, 73, 118
   Seine at Bennecourt, 119
Montagna, Bartolomeo: *Virgin and Child with John the Baptist*, 147
Montagu of Beaulieu, Edward Douglas-Scott-Montagu, 3rd Baron, 128
Moore, Albert, 24, 55, 218
   Shells, 55
   Summer Night, 38-9
   A Venus, 21
Moore, George, 32, 35, 41-2, 59
Moore, Henry, 73, 193, 252
   Falling Warrior (bronze), 120
Moores, James, 193, 195
Moores, Sir John, 127, 171-6, 178-82, 184-5, 187-8
   see also John Moores Exhibitions
Moores, John, Jr, 189
Moores, Sir Peter, 171, 175, 189-90, 192-4
   see also Peter Moores Foundation; Peter Moores Liverpool Projects
Morandi, Giorgio: *Still Life*, 172
Moreau, Gustave, 204
Morgan, John: *Don't 'ee Tipty Toe*, 50
Morris, Edward, 208, 210, 253
Moss, Gilbert, 52
Mostyn, Tom, 27
Muller, William James: *Arab Shepherd*, 67
Mulligan, Hugh, 77

Mulready, William, 78
Munch, Edvard, exhibition (1972), 204
Mundella, Anthony John, 89-90
Munich Glaspalast, 26
Municipal Franchise Act (1869), 38
Munkácsy, Mihály
　exhibition (1900), 198
　Ecce Homo, 198
Munnings, Sir Alfred, 24
　The Start of the St Buryan Races, Cornwall, 71
Munro, Alexander, 149
Murillo, Bartolomé Esteban: *Virgin and Child*, 107-8
Murphy, Myles: *Figure with a Yellow Foreground*, 86
Murray, David, 24
Murray, Peter and Linda, 82
Murren, Revd James Keir, 215-16
Museum of Labour History (*later* Museum of Liverpool Life), 166
Museum of Liverpool, 162
Museum of Modern Art, Oxford, 94
Museum Service for the Nation, A (1970), 103
Museums and Art Galleries: A National Service: A Post-War Policy, 91
Museums Association, 69-70, 91-3, 101, 109, 133
Museums and Galleries Commission, 98, 150, 166
Museums and Galleries Grants Board, 91
Museums Journal, 92, 102
Musgrave, Ernest, 69

Nairne, Sandy, 96
Napper, John, 106
Nash, John, 24, 250
Nash, Paul, 24, 28, 66, 106, 200, 252
　Landscape of the Moon's Last Phase, 72
Nasmyth, Patrick, 78
National Art-Collections Fund (now Art Fund), 58, 72, 90, 107-8, 117-18, 119, 146, 169-70
National Association for the Advancement of Art, 46, 199
National Association of Decorative and Fine Art Societies, 246
National Galleries Loan Act (1883), 89
National Galleries of Scotland, Edinburgh, 85, 109, 129
National Gallery of Ireland, Dublin, 221
National Gallery, London
　lends to Walker Art Gallery, 37, 89, 203-4
　purchase grant, 116
　staff, 131
National Gallery of Victoria, Melbourne, 74
National Heritage Memorial Fund, 146, 147-8, 169-70
National Maritime Museum, Greenwich, 167
National Museum of Wales, Cardiff, 156-8, 160
National Museums Capital Fund, 103
National Museums and Galleries on Merseyside, 85, 158, 165, 188, 195, 242, 254-5
National Museums Liverpool Conservation Centre, 155, 161, 164
National Portrait Gallery, London, 162
National Trust, 90, 138-9, 154
National Unemployed Workers' Committee, 80
Naylor, John, 53, 78, 124

'Neighbourhood Arts Festival', South Liverpool, 215
Neilson, Robert, 55
Nelson-Atkins Museum of Art, Kansas City, 116
Netherlandish art, 55-6, 84, 169
Netherlandish School: *Rest on the Flight into Egypt*, 108
Nettlefold, Frederick John, 76
New English Art Club, 25-6, 30, 43, 48-9, 60, 67, 69, 71-2
New Italian Art 1953-71 exhibition, 190-1
New Sculpture movement, 51, 54
New Shakespeare Theatre Club, 34
Newcastle Arts Association, 32
Newcastle upon Tyne: administrative changes, 134
Newling, Victor, 193
Newlyn artists, 60, 62, 218
Newsome, Victor, 193
Newton, Algernon: *Townscape*, 72-3
Newton, John, 53
Nicholson, Ben, 28, 73, 106, 168, 185, 200
　Still Life 1950, 127
Nigel Moores Foundation, 193
North Italian School, *Virgin and Child* (terracotta), 123
North West Development Agency, 162
North West Museums and Art Galleries Service (*later* North West Museums, Libraries and Archives Council), Blackburn, 98-100, 237, 244
Northern Young Contemporaries (*later* Whitworth Young Contemporaries), 186
Northwick Park, Gloucestershire, 125
'Norwegian Romantic Landscape 1820-1920' exhibition (1976), 204

O'Brien, Ray, 159
Ocean Steamship Company, 107
O'Donahue, Jim, 191
Office of Arts and Libaries, 153-4, 156, 158
Oldham Gallery: annual exhibitions, 32
Oliphant, Morton, 118
O'Meara, Frank, 24
Opie, John, 78
Oratory, The, Liverpool 154, 164
Orchardson, William Quiller: *St Mark's Venice*, 21
orchestras: funding, 94-5
Ormond, Richard, 212
Orpen, Sir William, 24
　Lottie and the Baby, 148
Orrock, James, 233
Osman, Louis, 220
Oulton, Therese, 172
Owen, Owen, 78
Owen, Segar, 238

'Painting and Sculpture in England 1700-1750' exhibition (1958), 205
'Paintings from the Mesdag Collection' exhibition (1994), 204
Pall Mall Gazette, 62
Pall Mall Magazine, 43
Paolini, Giulio, 191
Paolozzi, Sir Eduardo, 207

INDEX

Paris, John, 83
Parmigianino, 169
Parr, Martin, 221
Pasmore, Victor, 178
Patella, Luca, 191
Paterson, James, 26
Patrick, McIntosh: *Springtime in Eskdale*, 30, 72-3
Paul Mellon Foundation for British Art (now Paul Mellon Centre), 207, 213
Pearson, N.M., 95
Peel, David, 122-3
Penny, Nicholas, 221
Penrose, Roland, 30
Perolo, Antonio (attrib.): *Education of Christ*, 123
Peter Moores Foundation, 189, 193
Peter Moores Liverpool Projects, 189-95, 218
Petit, Georges, 200
Pettie, John, 55
    Love Song, 21
Pevsner, Sir Nikolaus, 240
P.H. Holt Trust, 78, 107, 114
Phillips, Peter, 187
    exhibition (1982), 219
Phillips, Thomas, 107
photography: in recording and conservation, 235
Picasso, Pablo, 30, 73, 106, 200-1, 250, 252
Pickering, Henry, 107
Pickersgill, Frederick Richard, 55
Picknell, William Lamb, 52, 211
Picton, James, 9, 11-14, 40-1, 45-7, 56, 89, 112, 246
picture frames, 107-8, 231
'Pictures for Schools' exhibition (1948), 251
'Pictures for Schools' exhibition (1955), 251
Pilkington, Godfrey, 183
Pilkington's Tile and Pottery Company, 57
Piper, David, 106, 204
Piper, John, 29, 185, 250
Pissarro, Camille, 118, 209
    Red Roofs, 61
Pissarro, Lucien: *Cerisiers en Fleur*, 72-3
Pistolotto, Michelangelo, 191
Pittoni, Giovanni Battista, 107
Pleydell-Bouverie, Mrs A.E., 119
Ponter, Christopher, 147
Pop Art, 187, 218
Pope-Hennessy, Sir John, 103, 123
Popham, Arthur Ewart, 106
Porcupine (journal), 11-12, 21, 31, 41
Port Sunlight Village, 144
Post Office: posters, 250
Post-Impressionists, 118, 172, 200
Pottery, 57-8
Poussin, Nicolas, 56
    Landscape with the Ashes of Phocion, 119, 138, 146, 148; fig. 5
Powers, Hiram, 211
Poynter, Edward John, 24, 55
    Faithful unto Death, 53
Practical Arts Policy, A (Labour Party paper), 103
Pre-Raphaelites, 15, 16, 23, 67, 83, 105, 112, 115, 124, 145, 178
    exhibitions, 130, 211-13, 218

Preti, Mattia, 191
Primaticcio, Francesco: *Ulysses winning the archery contest in the presence of Penelope's suitors*, 169; fig. 3
Primitivism, 56
Prinsep, Val: *Leonora di Mantua*, 22
Print Society, 250
Prints, 57, 58
Prizes, 178-9
Property Services Agency, 163
provincial galleries and museums
    government support for, 87-104, 116
    national status, 102
Pugin, August Welby Northmore, 123
Pullé, E.E., 30
Puvis de Chavannes, Pierre, 204

Quigley, Arthur, 19, 43-4, 60-1, 63, 66, 73, 122, 218

Rae, George, 52, 55, 124
Raeburn, Sir Henry, 68, 78, 251
    Mrs Anne Graham, 28, 75
    Portrait of a Lady (attrib.), 68
Ramsay, Allan, 76
Rankin, James and Robert, 75
Rate Support Grant, 97
Rathbone Brothers (company), 65
Rathbone, Bertram (or Larry), 65
Rathbone, Eleanor, 10-12, 50
Rathbone, Harold, 199
Rathbone, Herbert, 60
Rathbone, Hugh, 65
Rathbone, Philip
    acquisition policy, 48-50, 61
    Autumn Exhibitions selection, 20-3, 35-6, 52
    bequeaths panels, 125, 224
    and competition from German galleries, 31
    death, 41-2, 59, 62, 78
    on importance of permanent collection, 44, 188
    and Leighton's works, 46, 48
    marble bust of, 51
    offends Rossetti, 45
    and profits from exhibitions, 40
    and sculpture, 51
    serves on Libraries, Museums and Arts Committee, 10-14
    as sponsor, 174
    wins support from London artists, 16
    The English School of Impressionists as Illustrated in the Liverpool Autumn Exhibition (pamphlet), 25
Rauschenberg, Robert, 252
Rawnsley, Brenda and Derek, 250
Read, Sir Herbert, 33, 250
Real Life exhibition (1977), 193
'Realism and Surrealism' exhibition (1938), 29, 253
Redcliffe-Maud, John, Baron, 97, 133
Redon, Odilon, 204
Rees-Jones, Stephen, 229
Reid, Sir Norman, 101, 129
Reilly, Sir Charles H., 14, 29
    exhibition (1996), 208

Rembrandt van Rijn, 107, 210, 221
  Belshazzar's Feast, 148
  Betrothal, The (follower), 107
  Coat of Many Colours (follower), 169
Renoir, Pierre Auguste, 19, 73, 209
Reynolds, Antony, 183
Reynolds, Sir Joshua, 76, 78
  Miss Elizabeth Ingram, 76
Richards, Albert, 30
  exhibition (1978), 208
Richards, Ceri, 168
  exhibition (1975), 210
Richmond, William Blake
  Triumph of Commerce over the Elements of Barbarism, 10
  Venus and Anchises, 49-50
Rickards, Charles Hilditch, 54
Ridge, Jacqueline, 243
Riley, Bridget, 127, 193, 252
  Sea Cloud, 187
Riley, James, 156
Riley, John, 120
Ritchie, John, 140, 143
Riviere, Briton, 323
  Daniel in the Lion's Den, 53
Roberti, Ercole de': *Pietà*, 56, 236
Roberts, David, 37, 53, 120
Roberts, Henry Benjamin, 16, 20
Robinson, John Charles, 87, 233
Rodin, Auguste, 51, 54, 118
  The Death of Athens (sculpture), 54
Romney, George, 71, 78, 231
  exhibition (2002), 223
Rooker, Michael Angelo, 149
Roscoe, Sir Henry, 55
Roscoe, William, 9, 55-6, 77, 79, 85, 111, 123, 148, 160, 169
Roscoe, Mrs William, 77
Rosse Report (1963), 96
Rossetti, Dante Gabriel, 37, 218
  Dante's Dream, 23, 44-5, 47, 224-5, 239
  exhibition (2003), 223
Rothenstein, Sir John, 60, 69-70, 82, 86, 246
Rothenstein, Michael, 250
Rouault, Georges, 34, 201, 209
Rowan, Eric, 34, 191
Rowe, Robert, 99, 150
Rowley, Charles, 60
Royal Academy, Burlington House, London
  Bicentenary Exhibition (1968), 229
  conservatism, 60
  contemporary art at, 186
  drawings and water colours, 231
  exhibitions, 18, 23, 211, 217
  Millais exhibition (1967), 212
  sales, 31
  staircase, 15
  Summer Exhbitions, 178, 180, 182, 188
  Victorian artists at, 218
Royal Birmingham Society of Artists, 35, 200
Royal College of Art, London, 226
Royal Glasgow Institute of the Fine Arts, 35

Royal Institution for the Encouragement of the Fine Arts in Scotland, 40
Royal Institution, London, 224
Royal Insurance Company, 78
Royal Jubilee Exhibition (Manchester, 1887), 197
Royal Liverpool Philharmonic Orchestra, 122, 135
Royal Manchester Institution (City Art Gallery), 27, 31-2, 35, 40
Royal Staffordshire Pottery, 57
Royden, Sir Ernest, 119
Rubens, Peter Paul, 169
  Virgin and Child with St Elizabeth and the Child Baptist, 76, 116-17, 125, 130; fig. 4
Ruhemann, Helmut, 224-7
Ruskin, John, 9, 23, 120, 250
Russell, John, 182, 191
Russell-Cotes, Merton, 15, 39
Rutherston, Charles, 251
Rutter, Frank, 44, 59-60, 86, 121
Ruysdael, Salomon: *River Scene*, 107
Ryder, Charles, 165

Sadler, Michael, 121
St George's Hall, Liverpool, 165
St James's Cemetery, Liverpool, 139
St John's Wood School (of painters), 61
Salmon, Robert
  Liverpool Town Hall in 1806, 77
  A Sailing Ship in the Mersey, 77
Salvidge, Archibald, 11
Samuels family, exhibition (1961), 209
Samuels, Mr and Mrs S., 120
Samuelson, Sir Bernhard, 21
Samuelson, Edward, 10-12, 16, 20, 23, 41, 44-6, 49-51, 53, 59, 62
Sandbach family, 124
Sandle, Michael, 193
Sandon, Dudley Francis Stuart Ryder, Viscount, 13
Sandon Studios Society, 34-5, 59, 61, 148, 200
Sangster, Vernon, 172
Sargent, John Singer, 24, 55, 211, 212, 251
Sassoon, Sir Philip, 75
Scarisbrick Hall, Lancashire, 123
Scheffer, Ary: *Temptation of Christ*, 124
Schloesser, Carl: *Village Lawyer*, 52
Schongauer, Martin, 113
School Prints Ltd, 250
Science Museum, London: outstations, 162
Scott, Charles Prestwich, 32
Scott, William, 172, 182, 252
  Blue Abstract, 27, 179
  Liverpool Still Life, 126-7; fig. 18
Scottish Art Review, 84
Scottish Masters (series), 85
Scrutton, Hugh
  acquisitions and selection, 123-6, 146-7
  administrative control, 127
  appointed director, 106-8
  attends Sheffield conference on regional galleries, 100
  buys Impressionists and Post-Impressionists, 76
  and constructions, 180

INDEX

on Cotton's reforms, 70
doubts over Moores exhibitions, 175
education functions, 253
encourages scholarship, 112
hanging policy, 234
and John Moores' interest in art, 189
loans policy, 229, 239, 241
modernises appearance of Gallery, 108
on national support for provincial galleries, 102
opposes glazing of pictures, 239
on pressures of space, 164
purchase grant, 108
on purpose of Moores' exhibitions, 195
refuses apprentice crafts display, 215
resists reviving Autumn Exhibitions, 173
and sale of pictures, 116
sculpture purchases, 122-3
short-listed for Tate Gallery post and moves to Scotland, 229
staffing, 110, 201
on structure of N.W. Museums and Arts Galleries Service, 99
tours US galleries, 121
twentieth-century purchases, 117-18
on visitor numbers, 204
on visitors from outside area, 177
Whitechapel Pre-Raphaelite exhibition (1948), 211
Sculpture, 51, 123, 177, 192, 214, 233
   conservation, 244
Sefton family, 137
Sefton, Isabella, Countess of: portrait, 137; fig. 9
Sefton, Josephine, Countess of: bequest, 137-8
Sefton Metropolitan Borough Council, 134
Sefton, William (*later* Baron), 131, 135, 140-2, 156, 220
Segantini, Giovanni, 118
   Punishment of Luxury (or Lust), 50-1
Sellars, Jane, 253
Serota, Sir Nicholas, 183
Serpentine Gallery, London, 219
Sessions House, Liverpool, 115, 150, 160, 164-7, 232, 254
Seurat, Georges Pierre, 118
Sewter, Albert Charles, 176, 185-6, 205
Seymour, Anne, 182
Shannon, Charles, 24, 59
Sharples, Joseph, 208
Shavington Hall, Shropshire, 209
Shaw, Ben
   and acquisition of Lady Lever Gallery, 141-2
   chairs City Council committee, 120-1, 127
   chairs County Council committee, 135
   forms Friends organisation, 122
   and Gallery's national status, 153, 158-9
   qualities, 131
   stands down, 165
   and Ulster Museum, 103
Sheffield conferences on regional galleries (1958 and 1966), 100-2
Sheffield City Art Galleries, 109
Shepherd, Michael, 192-3

Sherlock, Cornelius, 13-15
Shipley Art Gallery, Gateshead, 225, 229
Sickert, Walter, 24, 28, 118, 231, 251
   Bathers, Dieppe, 71-2
   Mamma mia Poveretta, 72
   Old Bedford, 71-3
   The Pork Pie Hat, 72
   Summer Lightning, 72
   Theatre of the Young Artists, Dieppe, 72
Sielle, Robert, 107-8
Signac, Paul, 201
Signorelli, Luca, 147, 231
   Virgin and Child in a Landscape, 237
Simey, Margaret, 129
Simon, Lucien, 19
Sims, Charles, 24
Sisley, Alfred, 19, 118
   Landscape with an abandoned cottage, 61
Skeaping, John: *So Clever*, 138
Skillen, John, 232
Slade School, London 43
Slagg, John, 89
Smith Art Gallery, Brighouse, 149
Smith, Chris, 168
Smith, Frank Hindley, 55
Smith, George Grainger: *The Enemy Raid, May 3rd 1941*, 77
Smith, James, 54-5, 57-8, 174
Smith, Leslie, 231, 234
Smith, Sir Matthew, 24, 106, 179
   Black Hat, 108
Smith, Sam, 193
Smith, Solomon Kaines, 86
Society for Education in Art, 251
Society of Graver-Painters in Colour, 27, 58
Society of Painters in Water Colours, 231
Solimena, Francesco: *Birth of the Baptist*, 107
   Diana and Endymion 125
Solomon, Solomon Joseph: *Samson*, 239
Somers, Sheila, 82, 84, 109, 112-14
South Liverpool Arts Festivals, 249
Soutine, Chaim, 172
Speaker, The (journal), 59
Spectator, The (journal), 59, 62
Speke Hall, Liverpool, 136, 138-9, 143, 152, 154
Spence, Benjamin E., 124
Spencer Churchill, Captain, 125
Spencer, John Poyntz, 5th Earl, 89
Spencer, Stanley, 24, 66, 251-2
   Villas at Cookham, 72
Spielmann, Marion Harry, 45
Sprat, Thomas, Bishop of Rochester, 119
Stael, Nicolas de, 172
Standing Commission on Museums and Galleries, 93
Starkie, Le Gendre, 124
Starr, Louise: *Sintram*, 44
Steele, Jeffery, 187
Steer, Philip Wilson, 28, 66, 251
   Corfe Castle and the Isle of Purbeck, 71
   The Wye at Chepstow, 71-2
Stefano, Arturo di, exhibition (1993), 208
Stephenson, Gordon, 29

Stevens, Alfred, 77, 81-2, 85, 99, 234
Stevens, Mary Anne, 204
Stevens, Timothy, 8, 129, 141, 154, 158-62, 209, 214, 236, 242
Stevenson, Robert Alan Mowbray, 48
Stevenson, William, 172, 217
Stilgoe, Richard, 253
Stocks, Alfred, 129, 134-5
Stoke City Art Gallery, 95
Stokes, Adrian, 24
Stolow, Nathan, 241
Stom, Mattias, 75
Stone, Mary, 138
Stone, Walter, 82, 138
Stott, Edward, 24
Stott, William, 24, 59
   Alps by Night, 49-50
Streamlining the Cities (White Paper, 1983), 152
Strong, Sir Roy, 103
Stross, Barnett, 91-2
Strudwick, John Melhuish, 78
Stubbs, George, 75, 209, 253
   exhibition (1951), 206-7
   Gnawpost and two other colts, 75
   Haymakers, 75
   Horse frightened by a Lion, 57
   Molly Longlegs with her jockey, 75; fig. 7
   A Monkey, 75
   Reapers, 75
Sudley Art Gallery and house, Liverpool, 8, 78-9, 115, 145, 154, 164, 209, 234, 239
Surrealism, 29-30, 201
Sutcliffe, Stuart, exhibition (1964), 207
Sutherland, Graham, 73, 106, 185
Sweden: Lambert and Cotton visit, 79-80
Symons, Antony, 113

Tacconi, Innocenzo, 107
Taste of Yesterday, The exhibition (1969), 125-6
Tate Gallery, London
   buys Stubbs pictures, 75
   Chantrey Bequest purchases, 40
   conservation techniques, 229
   declines responsibility for Walker Gallery, 152, 154
   Dibdin denounces, 69
   director's salary, 105
   expenditure on art works, 109
   Friends, 122
   and Pre-Raphaelitism, 212-13
   purchase grant, 116
   selection policy, 52
   specialises in British art, 68, 77
   temporary exhibitions, 202
Tate Liverpool, 161-2, 221
taxes: remissions on works of art and 'in lieu' payments, 147
Taylor, Basil, 206-7
Thatcher, Margaret, Baroness, 150, 155
Thoma, Hans, 53, 199
Thompson, John, 134
Thompson, Sir Kenneth, 140, 142, 156

Thornely, Sir Arnold, 63
Thornycroft, Hamo: *The Mower* (sculpture), 51
Thornton, Alfred, 30
Thyssen, August, 54
Tidy, Bill, 253
Tillotson, Geoffrey, 119
Tilson, Jo, 187
Times, The, 87, 92, 100, 155
Tintoretto, 169
Tissot, James, 148
Tolly Cobbold Eastern Arts National Exhibitions, 186
Tolstoy, Count Leo: *What is Art*, 214
Tomlinson, Reginald Robert, 250
Tonge, Robert, 53
Tonks, Henry, 24, 66
Topham, Mirabel, 220
Topham Trophy Steeplechase, 220
Tophams Ltd, Messrs, 220
Totah, Edward, 183
Towndrow, Kenneth Romney, 77
Towne, Charles, 138
   exhibitions (1971, 1977, 1980), 208
Towneley Hall Art Gallery, Burnley, 124, 139
Toxteth riots (1981), 162
Treuherz, Julian, 161, 163, 221, 237
Tristram, E.W., 226
Tuke, Henry Scott: *The Promise*, 55
Turnbull, William: *Untitled No 9 1977*, 178, 185
Turner, Joseph Mallord William, 37, 89, 120, 231, 253
   Fall of the Clyde, Lanarkshire Noon, 58
   Landscape, 76
   Linlithgow Palace, 76
   Schloss Rosenau, 78; fig. 14
   Van Tromp Going About to Please his Masters, 210
   The Wreck Buoy, 78
Turner Prize, 186
'23 Photographers 23 Directions' exhibition (1978), 220
Tyzack, Michael, 187

Ulster Museum, 103
Unit One, 30, 200
United States of America: independence celebrated (1976), 210
University Grants Committee, 91-2
Utrillo, Maurice, 201

Vale H.H. (architect), 14
Value Added Tax reclaim, 167-8
Van Gogh Museum, Amsterdam, 223
Verestchagin, Vassily, exhibition (1887-8) 197-8
Vernet, Claude Joseph
   Bathers, 169
   Moonlight, 169
Vernons Pools, 172
Victoria and Albert Museum (*earlier* South Kensington Museum), London
   British art at, 68
   collects Alfred Stevens, 77
   Department of Circulation, 203

INDEX

Grant Fund, 100, 118, 146
loans to other galleries, 89-90, 95
seeks government grant for provincial galleries, 87
Victoria University Gallery and Museum, Liverpool, 162
Vlaminck, Maurice de, 117, 200-1

Waddington, Leslie, 183, 219
Wadsworth, Edward, 21, 73, 149
Walker, Sr Andrew Barclay
   founds and pays for gallery, 7, 13-14, 47, 146, 174
   marble statue, 233
Walker Art Gallery
   abandons plan to sell paintings to Council's Superannuation Fund, 156
   acquisitions policy, 40, 45-6, 48, 50-2, 57-61
   admission charges, 38, 167-8, 222
   air conditioning, 130, 163-4, 236-7
   appeals for support from local industrial and commercial concerns, 117
   applies to become government assisted provincial centre of excellence (1973), 97
   appointment of curators, 40-3
   artists-in-residence, 219, 250
   attempts to establish paper conservation studio, 99-100
   attendance figures, 37, 130, 168
   Autumn Exhibitions, 16-36, 37-40, 44-5, 49, 56, 60-1, 63, 67, 71, 105, 173, 187-9, 196, 231
   British collection, 66-78, 109, 146, 188
   budget (1974), 136
   building developments and improvements (1974-2002), 164-5, 167
   built and opened, 12-14
   café, 115
   catalogues, 111-15, 130, 164
   as centre of scholarship, 84, 112
   chronological hanging, 71
   colour scheme and hangings, 108, 126
   commercial sponsorship, 211
   commission on picture sales, 38
   conservation, 224-5, 230-3, 243
   design, 15
   director's title and status changed, 135
   drawings, water colours and prints, 123-4, 231-2
   education department, 254
   entrance hall and galleries re-decorated, 163
   environmental and heating conditions, 235-8
   exhibition costs, 218
   exhibition of Liverpool art (1908), 56, 57
   exhibitions suite formed from three galleries, 222
   expenditure, 10
   first extension (1884), 41, 45, 63
   Friends organisation, 121-2, 147, 246
   funding for purchases, 37-9
   gifts and bequests, 53-5, 63, 78-9, 119-20, 123, 137-8
   government grants, 90, 130-1, 150-1, 154-5, 160
   government proposals for (1983), 152-4
   hanging policy, 234
   income from sales and reproductions, 115
   invaded by National Unemployed Workers' Committee (1921), 80-1
   inventory compiled, 110-11
   lectures and guided tours, 81-2, 249
   library, 113
   loan exhibitions, 196-223
   loan restrictions, 239, 241
   loans to schools, 252
   local political control, 131-2
   Merseyside artists' collection, 114-15, 149, 216
   national status (1986), 96, 103-4, 110, 152, 154-7
   occupied by Ministry of Food, 1939-50, 79-80
   opening days, 37
   photographic studio, 235
   photographs, 149, 199, 220
   pop art, 187
   post-Second World War structural repairs, 81
   power of purchase, 31-2
   Prince George Gallery, 63, 125, 163-4
   publications, 84-6
   purchase grant, 71, 108, 146, 161, 168-70, 222
   re-opened with new extension (1933), 28, 71
   reopening (1951), 92
   reserve collection and loans, 115-16, 234
   running costs, 83
   salary scales, 105, 109-10, 130
   sale of catalogues, 38
   school parties and children's activities, 247-50
   sculpture, 233
   security, 239
   selection procedure and juries, 19-21, 24
   space problems, 146, 164, 167
   Special Appeal Fund, 130, 146
   Spring Exhibitions, 27, 199
   staff appointments, 83-4, 86
   staff numbers, 110, 130-1
   Sunday opening, 198
   takes over Lady Lever Gallery, 130, 140-3
   total expenditure figures, 110
   trustees and chairman, 157-9
   under administration of Merseyside County Council, 135
   visitors analysed, 177
   watercolours, 58, 120
   women curators, 84
   works on paper, 231-2
Walker Art Gallery Picture Books, 81
Walker, Ethel: *Spanish Gesture*, 72
Walker, John, 180
Walker, Michael, 103
Wallis, George Augustus, 85
   Landscape near Rome, 149
Wallis, George Harry, 41-2
Wallis, G.P. Dudley, 68
Wallis, Whitworth, 41, 43, 66, 150
Walsh, Sam, 193, 217
   exhibition (1991), 208
Walter, Major, 196
Wanamaker, Sam, 34

Warhol, Andy, 252
Warren, Edward Perry, 74
Wasey, Erwin, 184
Waterhouse, Ellis, 24, 114
Waterlow, Ernest Albert, 24
   A Summer Shower, 48
Watney, Oliver Vernon, 125
Watt, Miss Adelaide (of Speke Hall), 138
Watts, George Frederick, 24, 54, 59, 251
   Prodigal Son, 22
   Riders, 54
Wavertree, William Walker, 1st Baron, 24, 63, 71, 73, 74, 76, 108, 138, 174
Wedgwood, Geoffrey Heath, exhibition (1971), 207
Wedgwood, Josiah and Sons, 57
Wellington, Robert, 250
West, Benjamin, 37, 211
   Christ Healing the Sick, 46
Wheeler, Sir Mortimer, 93
Whinney, Margaret, 82
'Whistler: The Graphic Work, Amsterdam, Liverpool, London, Venice' exhibition (1976), 210
Whistler, James Abbot McNeill, 24-5, 54, 113, 149, 231
   Arrangement in Black and Brown: The Fur Jacket, 24, 48, 54
   Arrangement in Grey and Black: Portrait of the Artist's Mother, 22
White, Gabriel, 213
White, John, 82
White, Thomas, 112
Whitechapel Art Gallery, London, 94, 105, 201, 211, 251
Whittet, G.S., 186
Whitworth Art Gallery, Manchester, 99-100, 133, 186, 231
Whitworth, Sir Joseph, 15
Wildenstein's (dealers), 119
Wilding, Richard, 153, 159
Wilkie, Sir David: *Bathsheba at the Bath*, 55
Willett, John, 99, 215
Williams, Frank, 141
Williamson Art Gallery, Birkenhead, 134, 136
Williamson, Daniel Alexander, 53-4, 57, 210
Williamson, Paul, 123
Willoughby, Hugh, 30
Wills, Sir William, 15
Wilson, Colin, 191
Wilson, Harold (*later* Baron), 167, 216
Wilson, Richard, 68
   Landscape with Phaeton's petition to Apollo, 169
   Snowdon from Llyn Nantlle, 75; fig. 8
   Valley of the Mawddach and Cader Idris, 75
Windus, William Lindsay, 53-4, 57, 85, 210
   Burd Helen, 124
Wirral Metropolitan Borough Council, 134, 136, 142
Wiszniewski, Adrian, 250
   exhibition (1987), 219
Witherop, Jack Coburn, 225-9, 235, 240
Wood, Christopher, 73
Wood, John Warrington, 14
Wood, Lucy, 109, 144
Wood, Tom, 221

Wood, Warrington, 164
Woodall, Mary, 105-7, 150
Woodlock, David, exhibition (1929), 206
Woodrow, Bill, 194
Woods, Henry: *The Admonition*, 62
Woodward, John, 85, 114, 204
Woolton, Frederick James Marquis, 1st Earl of, 75
Works, Ministry of, 90
Worthington, Thomas, 32
Wright of Derby, Joseph, 37, 75, 86, 168, 206
   The Annual Girandola at the Castel Sant-Angelo, Rome, 55; fig. 10
Wright, William: Report on provincial art galleries (1973), 96-8, 133
Wyllie, William Lionel: *Blessing the sea*, 55

Yates, Sally Ann, 243
Yeames, William Frederick: *And When Did You Last See Your Father?*, 50, 253
Young, Sir Leslie, 159

Zobel, Fernando: *To the Hive*, 214
Zoffany, Johan: *Family of Sir William Young*, 75